THE JOURNAL JURISPRUDENCE

VOLUME SEVEN

"THE CANENGUSIAN CONNECTION"

Contributors

Allan C Hutchinson
Osgoode Hall University

T.T. Arvind
University of York

Derek Morgan
The University of Sheffield

Richard Mullender
Newcastle University

Patrick O'Callaghan
Newcastle University

Man Chun Siu
Newcastle Law School

Ole Pedersen
Newcastle University

Emilia Mickiewicz
Newcastle Law School

Gemma Turton
University of Leicester

Thomas Bennett
BPP Law School, London

David Campbell
University of Durham

Guest Editor Richard Mullender
Newcastle University

Editor Aron Ping D'Souza
The Journal Jurisprudence

SUMMER TERM
SEPTEMBER 2010

Elias Clark

PUBLISHED BY THE ELIAS CLARK GROUP
DISTRIBUTED IN CONNECTION WITH THE GALE GROUP,
A PART OF CENGAGE LEARNING

(2010) J. JURIS 261

The Elias Clark Group
www.elias-clark.com

GPO Box 5001, Melbourne, Victoria 3001, Australia.

First Published 2010.

Cataloguing-in-Publication entry

Editors: D'Souza, Aron Ping.
Mullender, Richard.

Authors: D'Souza, Aron Ping.
Mullender, Richard.
O'Callaghan, Patrick.
Pedersen, Ole.
Turton, Gemma.
Campbell, David.
Arvind, T.T.
Siu, Man Chun.
Mickiewicz, Emilia.
Bennett, Thomas.
Hutchinson, Allan C.
Morgan, Derek.

Title: The Journal Jurisprudence, Volume Seven, "The Canengusian Connection."

ISBN: 978-0-9807318-5-9 (pbk.)
ISSN: 1836-0955

Subjects: Law – jurisprudence.
Philosophy –general.

This edition may be cited as

(2010) J. Juris.

followed by the page number

About the Typeface

The Journal Jurisprudence is typeset in Garamond 12 and the footnotes are set in Garamond 10. The typeface was named for Claude Garamond (c. 1480 - 1561) and are based on the work of Jean Jannon. By 1540, Garamond became a popular choice in the books of the French imperial court, particularly under King Francis I. Garamond was said to be based on the handwriting of Angelo Vergecio, a librarian to the King. The italics of Garamond are credited to Robert Grandjon, an assistant to Claude Garamond. The font was re-popularised in the art deco era and became a mainstay on twentieth-century publication. In the 1970s, the font was redesigned by the International Typeface Corporation, which forms the basis of the variant of Garamond used in this Journal.

TABLE OF CONTENTS

CALL FOR PAPERS

The field of jurisprudence lies at the nexus of law and politics, the practical and the philosophical. By understanding the theoretical foundations of law, jurisprudence can inform us of the place of legal structures within larger philosophical frameworks. In its inaugural edition, *The Journal Jurisprudence* received many creative and telling answers to the question, "What is Law?" For the second edition, the editors challenged the scholarly and lay communities to inquire into intersection between jurisprudence and economics.

With the backing of our diverse and disparate community, *The Journal Jurisprudence* has now evolved into a more diverse form. We will no longer be setting a question for each issue, but instead designing issues around the articles we received. Therefore, we invite scholars, lawyers, judges, philosophers and lay people tackle the any and all of the great questions of law. Knowing that ideas come in all forms, papers can be of any length, although emphasis is placed on readability by lay audiences.

Papers may engage with case studies, philosophical arguments or any other method that answers philosophical question applicable to the law. Importantly, articles will be selected based upon quality and the readability of works by non-specialists. The intent of the Journal is to involve non-scholars in the important debates of legal philosophy.

The Journal also welcomes and encourages submissions of articles typically not found in law journals, including opinionated or personalised insights into the philosophy of law and its applications to practical situations.

Jurisprudence is published four times per year, to coincide with the four terms of the legal year, in an attractive paperback and electronic edition.

All authors who submit to this edition will be provided with a complementary copy of the journal.

Length:	Any length is acceptable, although readability to non-specialist is key.
Presentation Style:	Papers must comply with the Australian Guide to Legal Citations, Second Edition published by the Melbourne University Law Review. An electronic edition is available at, http://mulr.law.unimelb.edu.au/PDFs/aglc_dl.pdf
Submission:	You must submit electronically in Microsoft Word format to editor@jurisprudence.com.au. Extraneous formatting is discouraged.

Correspondence can also be sent to this address. If you are considering submitting an article, you are invited to contact the editor to discuss ideas before authoring a work.

SUBSCRIPTION INFORMATION

The Journal is published four times per year in an attractive softcover book. Subscription to the Journal can be achieved by two methods:

1) Single issues can be purchased on amazon.com. Our publishers, the Elias Clark Group, set a retail price for each edition, typically AU$40. However, due to their agreement with amazon.com, the price may vary for retail customers.

2) A subscription to the Journal can be purchased for AU$150 per year, or AU$280 for two years. This price includes postage throughout the world. Payment can be made by international bank cheque, but not a personal cheque, to:

    The Journal Jurisprudence,
    C/o The Elias Clark Group
    GPO Box 5001
    Melbourne, Victoria, Australia.

Alternatively, the Journal is available online at www.jurisprudence.com.au and can be read there free of charge.

INTRODUCTION

Summer brings with it relief from classes and students, it is the breathing time of academia. I have no doubt that summers away from our respective campuses provides a welcome respite and the opportunity for quiet contemplation.

Jason A. Beckett, who wrote in these pages in the inaugural issue of *Jurisprudence*, introduced me to Richard Mullender of the University of Newcastle's School of Law, who is the guest editor of this edition. It is through Richard's vision that Allan C. Hutchinson's and Derek Morgan's landmark article 'The Canengusian Connection' been subjected to close analysis in the essays contained in this edition. Not only has our distinguished guest editor brought together many notable scholars in the field of tort to analyze the Hutchinson and Morgan article, but this issue also contextualises the impact of the article in contemporary legal practice.

In some ways a compilation of this importance, scope and magnitude could have only emerged in the summer. Richard Mullender sowed the seeds of this special edition late last year, and through tireless work the fruits emerged early this summer. Yet, I must applaud Richard's dedication, for he is a man not satisfied by mere fruits, but aspires to the highest degrees of quality. He relentlessly polished and improved each article, and it is through his vision that this collection, I am sure, will have a long term impact on the study of tort.

Richard's passion for the study of tort is evidenced by this issue. He is a leader in the field; the diversity and stature of the contributors to this issue is a testament to the high esteem in which he is held in England and abroad. It is truly an honour for the Journal to have been blessed with his guest editorship of this issue.

A very pleasing aspect of this project has been the opportunity to include essays by two students, Man Chun Siu and Emilia Mickiewicz. Among the aims of the Journal Jurisprudence is to create opportunities for legal scholars, at an early point in their careers, to refine their analyses and arguments under the guidance of those with more experience. It is also pleasing to have been able to assist a group of scholars who have been - to use Andrew Halpin's apt phrase - pursuing an 'exploratory project.' As this project has unfolded, it has become clear that those involved have been able to make a great deal of progress while raking over their ideas together. This is as much a good use of the space created by *The Journal Jurisprudence* as it is of the opportunities opened up for reflection over the summer.

Aron Ping D'Souza
Editor
Berlin, Germany

(2010) J. Juris 272

EDITORIAL: A DANCE TO THE MUSIC OF TORT

Richard Mullender*

'The Canengusian Connection: The Kaleidoscope of Tort Theory' captures a body of law in flux and a moment in time. The body of law on which Allan Hutchinson and Derek Morgan focus their attention is broad. It encompasses negligence, tort more generally, and other branches of law concerned with accident compensation (*e.g.*, New Zealand's comprehensive no-fault compensation scheme). We find Hutchinson and Morgan exploring these areas of legal activity at a time when Margaret Thatcher's Conservative government was attacking an assumption with which they had each grown up. This is the assumption that government should (through, *inter alia*, the instrumentality of law) fashion a set of socially just practical arrangements (*e.g.*, an egalitarian society offering all its members a high level of security from cradle to grave). Margaret Thatcher and her colleagues were prepared to consign this assumption (at least in a form strongly inflected by the ideal of distributive justice) to the dustbin of history.[1] Hutchinson and Morgan, by contrast, indicate (in the second half of their essay) that social justice is a matter that government, the judiciary, and academic commentators should take seriously.

Two-and-a-half decades on from its appearance in the *Osgoode Hall Law Journal*, this is only one of many ways in which 'The Canengusian Connection' retains legal and political significance. For it offers five responses to the problem of accidents that still constitute moves in various of the language games that have grown up around this issue. For this reason, the essay is a help to those who seek to get to grips with tort and alternative means of accident compensation.[2] This is not simply because Hutchinson

---

* Reader in Law and Legal Theory, Newcastle Law School. I owe thanks to John Alder, David Campbell, Patrick O'Callaghan, Ole Pedersen, David Raw, Ian Ward and Ashley Wilton for comments on earlier drafts of this Introduction.

[1] D. Marquand, *The Unprincipled Society: New Demands and Old Politics* (London: Fontana Press, 1988), ch 3; A.W. Turner, *Rejoice! Rejoice! Britain in the 1980s* (Aurum: London, 2010), ch 1. *Cf* R. Vinen, *Thatcher's Britain: The Politics and Social Upheaval of the 1980s* (London: Simon & Schuster, 2009), 292-295 (arguing that 'we should hesitate before labelling Thatcher as the destroyer of the post-war consensus').

[2] See C. Douzinas, S. McVeigh, and R. Warrington, 'Thrashing in the Dwelling House' (1989) 52 *Modern LR* 261, 263 (describing the reworked version of 'The Canengusian

and Morgan offer an accessible taxonomy of responses to the problem of accident compensation. The essay also models a style of open-minded engagement with a matter of practical concern that will be of benefit to those who acquire it. While Hutchinson and Morgan alert their readers to five ways in which they might respond to accidents, they do not identify any one of them as (in some sense) 'the best'. This is an approach that bespeaks a commitment to what John Keats called 'negative capability'. This is the capacity to be in 'doubts' and 'uncertainties' without hastily deciding to identify any particular view as capturing the truth of the situation we are contemplating.[3]

To the extent that a commitment to 'negative capability' informs 'The Canengusian Connection', it speaks well of its authors. But we might also see this virtue as having something to do with the character of British higher education at the time Hutchinson and Morgan put pen to paper. They began composing the essay in Newcastle University's Faculty of Law in 1983. To think of this place at that time is contemplate a social milieu that no longer exists. While British universities had been subject to 'cutbacks' in the early 1980s, they still offered those working within them a high-trust environment – free from the pressures of teaching- and research-related processes of audit.[4] This was a context in which academics were largely free to pursue their research-related inclinations.[5] In 'The Canengusian Connection', Hutchinson and Morgan made use of this freedom to work up an account of accident compensation law informed by the agenda of Critical Legal Studies (a self-consciously radical body of thought that had its origins in the USA).

Connection' that appeared in A.C. Hutchinson, *Dwelling on the Threshold: Critical Essays on Modern Legal Thought* (London: Sweet & Maxwell, 1988) as yielding 'excellent tutorial material').

3 J.A. Cuddon, *A Dictionary of Literary Terms* (Penguin Books, Harmondsworth, 1979, rev edn), 418. See also M. Heidegger, *What Is Called Thinking* (New York: Harper & Row, 1968, J. Glenn Gray, trans), 48 (arguing that '[w]e must stay with the question' and 'guard against the blind urge to snatch at a quick answer').

4 See R. Stevens, *From University To Uni: The Politics of Higher Education in England Since 1944* (London: Politico's, 2004), 45-47 (on university-related 'cuts'), and R. Mullender, 'The Virtues of Silliness', *Times Higher Education Supplement*, 15th September 1995, 13 (describing the impact of audit culture on British universities).

5 For a fictive (but informed) account of the high-trust academic environment referred to in the text, see M. Bradbury, *The History Man* (London: Arrow Books, 1975), 49 (where the novel's central character, Professor Howard Kirk, declares that '[c]rtical consciousness reigns').

This approach to law itself became the subject of debate in Newcastle Law Faculty at the time Hutchinson and Morgan were writing the essay. So too did the 'black-letter' view with which Hutchinson and Morgan contrasted it. They dwelt on these debates when they returned to Newcastle in July of 2009 to lead a symposium on 'The Canengusian Connection'. For those of us who were not in Newcastle in the early 1980s, some of the exchanges between Hutchinson and Morgan and former colleagues had the ring of reminiscences shared by combatants in a war long since over. Former 'Crits' and 'black-letter lawyers' recognized that they were guilty of caricaturing one another. All concerned spoke with mixed feelings about the benefits of growing older and wiser (and, as a consequence, more tolerant).

These preliminaries over, discussion of the essay began. Patrick O'Callaghan and Gemma Turton pointed up its virtues as an aid to those delivering undergraduate tort courses. Jenny Steele identified herself as highly sympathetic to the agenda of social justice that finds expression in the second half of the essay, while Richard Mullender argued that Hutchinson and Morgan had presented negligence law in an uncharitable light. Hutchinson and Morgan professed themselves disappointed that accident compensation law remains far from perfect and surprised that their assessment of it continues to have great relevance. They also dwelt on the increased prominence that the ideal of corrective justice and the associated principle of personal responsibility now enjoy among commentators on tort law.[6]

This was a development about which Hutchinson and Morgan had misgivings. The theme that accident compensation law had lost its way was evident in their respective contributions to discussion. This theme gave expression to assumptions that may have their roots in the writings of E.H. Carr – a historian who exerted a considerable influence over the young Hutchinson. According to Carr, progress depends on our ability to 'master, transform, and utilize [our] environment'.[7] In the context of accident compensation law, these assets include (as Hutchinson and Morgan made plain in the symposium) institutions that place emphasis on social rather than personal responsibility. But it would be wrong to see Hutchinson and

[6] See G. Edward White, *Tort Law in America: An Intellectual History* (New York: Oxford University Press, 2003, expanded edition), ch 8 (on the increased emphasis placed on corrective justice (and personal responsibility) in tort since 1980).

[7] E.H. Carr, *What is History?* (London: Penguin Books, 1990, 2nd edn), 127. See also 119 (where Carr states that '[b]elief in progress means belief not in any automatic or inevitable process, but in the progressive development of human potentialities').

Morgan as proponents of a suffocating collectivism rather than individualism. Derek Morgan drove this point home when he identified Arthur Leff's views as having exerted an influence over the composition of 'The Canegusian Connection'. For Leff tells us that 'What we want is simultaneously to be perfectly ruled and perfectly free'.[8]

In the fifteen months since the symposium took place, the essays that now appear in *The Journal Jurisprudence* have taken shape. While each of these essays offers a distinct response to 'The Canengusian Connection', common concerns and/or features unite subsets of the collection. While recognizing that Hutchinson and Morgan offer a wide-ranging account of accident compensation law, Turton and Siu stake out positions that Hutchinson and Morgan do not consider in 'The Canengusian Connection'. Arvind, Bennett, Campbell, O'Callaghan, and Siu each dwell on the relationship between private and public impulses in tort law (see Appendix 1). Pedersen, Mickiewicz, O'Callaghan, and Mullender advance arguments that share concerns that we might categorise as anthropological.[9] For they dwell (while pursuing complementary themes) on the nature of those who fashion and reflect upon the operations of negligence law, tort more generally, and other institutions concerned with accident compensation (see Appendix 2).

Pedersen identifies the positions on accident compensation law explored by Hutchinson and Morgan as throwing light on environmental law. He also argues that 'The Canengusian Connection' provides a basis on which to explain a common reaction to controversy on practical questions. A wide variety of responses to such questions, may, on Pedersen's account, induce in those who contemplate them a sense of cognitive dissonance. This unpleasant feeling arises in circumstances where people find themselves considering contradictory ideas simultaneously. Pedersen argues that those who experience this feeling may respond to it by engaging in denial. To this end, they may fasten on one response to the question they are contemplating and identify it as 'the answer'. This leads Pedersen to pursue the theme that those who make responses of this sort would do better to engage in a form of rational reflection that he explains and defends by reference to the writings of, *inter alios*, Karl Popper and John Dewey.

---

[8] A.A. Leff, 'Unspeakable Ethics, Unnatural Law' (1979) 6 *Duke LJ* 1229, 1229.

[9] The adjective 'anthropological' is apt since the relevant papers exhibit an interest in the behaviour and thought processes of a particular group of people (those concerned with accident compensation) and their relations with the social context in which they have acquired this interest.

Mickiewicz's essay complements that of Pedersen. For she argues that we should seek to pursue coherence in negligence law (and in tort more generally) by drawing on the account of 'aspect perception' elaborated in the later philosophy of Ludwig Wittgenstein and in the writings of Martin Heidegger. Aspect perception is a theory according to which interpreters are apt to pick out some items (while excluding others) in the fields that they are scrutinising. Mickiewicz argues that, by sensitizing ourselves to this problem, we will be better placed to pursue coherence in areas of activity such as negligence law (where we are called upon to contemplate a wide range of practical impulses). On her account, we can, by applying this approach to negligence law, bring, among other things, the ideals of corrective and distributive justice into a mutually supporting relationship. While unfolding this analysis, Mickiewicz also offers a critique of Ernest Weinrib's corrective justice-based account of tort. She recognises that Weinrib's thinking has a clear-cut, hard-edged quality. However, she criticises the theoretical framework that he has worked up on the ground that it is one into which actually-existing tort law never quite manages to fit.

While Mickiewicz's essay (like that of Pedersen) identifies open-mindedness as a capacity we can cultivate, O'Callaghan and Mullender pursue themes that tend in a contrary direction. Drawing on the account of judicial behaviour in 'The Canengusian Connection', O'Callaghan scrutinizes an area of private and public law that has grown dramatically in the years since Hutchinson and Morgan wrote their essay. This is the body of English law concerned with protecting the human right to privacy (while, at the same time, adequately accommodating the equally fundamental right to free expression). O'Callaghan identifies some of those who have sought to fashion new private law protections (grounded on Article 8 of the European Convention on Human Rights) as having fallen victim to 'monologue creep'. By this he means a process that issues in those who embrace a particular practical agenda becoming less and less sensitive to arguments that challenge the assumptions on which they act. In support of his argument, O'Callaghan draws on the literary theory of Mikhail Bakhtin and the philosophical writings of Martin Buber. Moreover, he applies his account of monologue creep to a group of commentators and judges – the 'Strasbourg enthusiasts' - who have been in the van of the process of doctrinal development he describes. There is much in this essay that merits further exploration – not least the relationship between the process of monologue creep and the notion of 'enthusiasm'. For 'enthusiasts' do not (on an account written in circumstances far different from our own) 'become narrow-mindedly obsessed with something'.[10] Rather, they 'take[ ] to the air, ignor[ing] the actual state of things on the ground and allow[ ] [their] enthusiasm to soar upwards to take residence in castles in the sky'.[11] However, movement – even creeping movement – in the direction of monologue does suggest something of a descent into obsession.

While 'monologue creep' suggests a slow retreat from open-mindedness, Mullender finds in the work of the eighteenth century novelist, Laurence Sterne, grounds for thinking that few people may ever be open-minded. For Sterne argued in *Tristram Shandy* that people regularly respond to practical questions by riding hobby-horses. Mullender argues that 'The Canengusian Connection' lends support to Sterne's view. For a number of the positions on accident compensation law described by Hutchinson and Morgan exhibit what Sterne would call a 'hobby-horsical' character. Having forged this connection between *Tristram Shandy* and Hutchinson and Morgan, Mullender argues that we are confronted both in 'The Canengusian Connection' and in tort law by (to draw on Sterne once more) a 'scampering' discourse. This arises in circumstances where contributors to debate, rather than being attentive to the views of others, simply jump on their respective hobby-horses and ride off in the direction that they find most appealing.

But often, in the sphere of accident compensation law, the reasons for embracing a particular view or agenda are very attractive. This is a point to which Gemma Turton's essay lends force. She identifies Hutchinson and Morgan as having written an essay that is enormously useful to undergraduates studying tort law. For it presents them with a range of perspectives on this body of law that will encourage them to think critically about its operations – and about alternative compensation schemes. As well as pointing up the usefulness of 'The Canegusian Connection' to those who study and teach tort, she argues that Hutchinson and Morgan fail to offer a suitably strong defence of negligence law. To make good this defect in their exposition, she identifies negligence law as a means by which to do corrective justice and to promote, *inter alia*, the principle of personal responsibility. Moreover, she notes that, in the years since the essay's appearance, this view has gained increasing currency – finding expression in, for example, the writings of Allan Beever and Ernest Weinrib. Turton makes these points while offering an account of the ways in which she has used

10 V. Klemperer, *LTI – Lingua Tertii Imperii: A Philologist's Notebook* (London: Continuum, 2006, M. Brady, trans), 54.
11 *Ibid.*

'The Canengusian Connection' in her own classes. Among other things, she identifies Hutchinson and Morgan as having written an essay that is a means to the end of 'enculturation'. For it helps students to become better attuned to the disciplinary community that they are joining.[12]

While Turton's essay is much concerned with corrective justice, Siu's response to 'The Canengusian Connection' makes plain the relevance of distributive justice to accident compensation law. Following the lead of, *inter alios*, Calabresi, he recognises that many accidents are the inevitable by-product of socially valuable activity. This being so, accident compensation on the model of New Zealand's no-fault scheme has much to recommend it. Moreover, Siu defends this position in terms that differ from those that appear in 'The Canengusian Connection'. For he is a proponent of qualified consequentialist moral philosophy. This is the view that a society committed to distributive justice should pursue socially valuable outcomes while protecting interests that its members regard as intrinsically valuable.

Siu's emphasis on social (or distributive) justice reveals a focus on matters of public concern that he shares with Arvind and Campbell. Arvind identifies 'The Canengusian Connection' as shedding considerable light on the question as to whether we should regard tort law's essential nature as purely private or straightforwardly public. Before staking out a position of his own, Arvind examines the analysis of those who argue for each of these views (including, *inter alios*, Weinrib and Beever (the private account) and Posner (the public view)). He also examines the arguments for a 'middle way' between the public and private accounts (as set out by, for example, Gordley). Having mapped the terrain on which this debate has long been unfolding, Arvind makes a highly distinctive contribution of his own that draws on Christian theology.

Like Arvind, Campbell dwells on the presence in tort law of private and public concerns. Unlike the other contributors to this collection, he does not, however, offer a direct response to 'The Canengusian Connection'. Rather, he focuses his critical attention on an assumption that finds expression in a number of the positions on accident compensation law presented by Hutchinson and Morgan. This is the assumption (associated with functionalist or green light conceptions of public law) that we can rely on government to treat justly all those affected by its activities. Campbell

[12] On 'enculturation', see J. Seeley Brown and P. Duguid, 'Space for the Chattering Classes', *Times Higher Education Supplement*, 10th May 1996 (Multimedia Feature, iv, iv-vi).

notes that this assumption has long informed commentary on a prominent nineteenth century English tort case, *Bradford v Pickles*. He finds it in, for example, Brian Simpson's account of this case. Drawing on, and developing, a later analysis of *Bradford* (offered by Michael Taggart), Campbell calls into question the plausibility of the assumption that we can rely on government to advance the cause of justice.[13]

Bennett focuses, in his essay, on an area of the law where he sees government (in the form of Tony Blair's New Labour administration) as having advanced the cause of justice. On Bennett's analysis, the judiciary has responded to the Human Rights Act 1998 by establishing a new and highly distinctive cause of action for 'misuse of private information'. Moreover, he finds in this development support for the conclusion that the human right to privacy is (after much procrastination) receiving the attention it deserves. He also argues that a commitment to corrective justice informs the new cause of action on which he dwells. This leads him to argue that Wright J's judgment in 'The Canengusian Connection' is a useful source of guidance to the judges (*e.g.*, Eady J) concerned with fashioning privacy-related protections. Bennett notes that, while Wright J attaches importance to the ideal of corrective justice, he does not lose sight of the fact that law is an artefact. Hence, those concerned with its development must pay close attention to detailed questions of institutional design (*e.g.*, whether liability should be fault-based or strict).

The contribution to this collection made by Hutchinson and Morgan suggests that they are more positively disposed towards the common law then they were in 1984. Through the medium of their fictive judge, Derall Lefft, they describe the common law 'as always moving but never arriving' and as 'always [being] on the road to somewhere, but never getting anywhere in particular'. These observations sound a note reminiscent of Michael Oakeshott, a thinker of a decidedly conservative disposition – and someone we might expect to have little in common with Lefft J.[14] But Oakeshott

[13] This theme in Campbell's essay is neatly summed up by a character in A. Powell, *A Dance To The Music Of Time*, Vol III, *Autumn* (London: Arrow Books, 2002), 573 (on 'the great illusion that government is carried on by an infallible … machine'). This observation has particular relevance to a solicitor who played a prominent role in *Bradford v Pickles*: Bradford Council's long-serving, highly respected and (to use Campbell's word) 'intransigent' Town Clerk, Mr W.T. McGowen.

[14] M. Loughlin, *Public Law and Political Theory* (Oxford: Clarendon Press, 1992), 70 (noting that Oakeshott described those who engage in 'political activity' as 'sail[ing] a boundless and bottomless sea' where there is 'neither starting-point nor appointed destination').

argued that the common law is a form of 'civil association'. By this he meant a modest politico-legal framework that, while providing stability for those who live within it, does not retain precisely the same shape over time. This is because those who bear responsibility for elaborating it constantly pursue intimations within the form of life that it sustains.[15]

While an echo of Oakeshott is something new in the Hutchinson and Morgan *oeuvre*, their contribution points up a feature of their approach to the law that has held constant over time. In their examination of recent Australian case law on wrongful life, a commitment to close reading is, as it was in 1984, on display. This attention to the detail of the law serves to explain, just as much as their commitment to Critical Legal scholarship, the power of 'The Canengusian Connection' as a contribution to debate. The lemon-squeezing approach to legal texts adopted by Hutchinson and Morgan is not at all surprising. For they bear the 'blind impress' of a culture that finds expression in the common law and that has adopted this approach to interpretative questions and the practical matters they concern for many centuries.[16] This influence has surely shaped their thinking more profoundly than the American politico-legal materials that figure prominently in 'The Canegusian Connection'.

The fact that two students studying in Newcastle Law School, Emilia Mickiewicz and Man Chun Siu, have responded to 'The Canengusian Connection' by contributing essays to this collection is particularly pleasing. The importance of energizing law students is a theme in the body of Critical Legal thought that informs 'The Canengusian Connection'. In the case of Mickeiwicz and Siu, Hutchinson and Morgan have certainly prompted energetic and ambitious responses. However, neither of these contributors to this collection has acted on the Critical Legal impulse to trash the existing legal (and social) script.[17] In embracing the Wittgensteinian practice of paying close attention to an existing form of life, Mickiewicz's essay is

---

[15] *Ibid*, 64-83.

[16] See R. Rorty, *Contingency, Irony and Solidarity* (Cambridge: Cambridge University Press, 1989), 23 (quoting Philip Larkin on 'the blind impress' that '[a]ll our behaving bear'). On close reading as a 'lemon-squeezing style of analysis', see T. Eagleton, *Literary Theory* (Oxford: Blackwell, 1983), 44 and 51.

[17] See R. M. Unger, *False Necessity: Anti-Necessitarian Social Theory in the Service of Radical Democracy* (Cambridge: Cambridge University Press, 1987), 319-320 (on 'trashing the script', 'resistance to determination by our contexts, and 'our capacity to overcome the contexts', and 'redirect the forces that seem[ ] to hold us in thrall'). See also A.C. Hutchinson and P.J. Monahan, 'The "Rights" Stuff: Roberto Unger and Beyond' (1984) 62 *Texas LR* 1477.

somewhat conservative in orientation. Siu, by contrast, seeks to synthesise consequentialist and deontological positions on negligence law and emerges from the process not as a radical but as a reformer. In each case, they present us with the fruit of independent thinking. That is surely as much as Crits can hope to inspire in their readers.

As well as preparing their respective papers, the contributors to this collection have participated in a dialogue that has unfolded for over a year – embracing the symposium in 2009, a number of later presentations, and numerous e-mail exchanges. This has enabled them to identify, among other things, the common themes mentioned earlier. Among the highlights in this dialogue was a presentation by David Campbell in Newcastle Law School in June 2010. As well as raking over *Bradford v Pickles* and the extensive commentary it has inspired, he offered an analysis of the relationship between tort and the welfare state that challenges many of the optimistic assumptions that have informed its development. David followed this up by travelling to Newcastle a month later to discuss with other contributors to the collection the relationship between the public and private impulses at work in tort.

Along with these meetings, a more open-ended exchange took place between Bennett and O'Callaghan. It concerned the relationship between the European Convention on Human Rights (ECHR), the Human Rights Act (HRA), and the bodies of private law developed by the judiciary with the aim of protecting privacy-related interests. While this exchange has been centrally concerned with a cause of action that did not exist when Hutchinson and Morgan wrote their essay (the misuse of private information), it nonetheless provided evidence of its continuing usefulness as an aid to understanding. Like the judges in 'The Canengusian Connection', Bennett and O'Callaghan would, in short order, move from matters of legal detail to relevant political philosophy. At the level of detail, Bennett took the view that we can grasp the character of the changes wrought in this rapidly developing area by reference to a notion of 'direct horizontality'. The gist of Bennett's argument is that the shaping force of higher-order public law best explains, *inter alia*, the House of Lords' decision to recognize a cause of action for 'misuse of personal information'. O'Callaghan rejects this claim on the ground that private law has been the medium through which the sources of legal protection fashioned by their Lordships and other judges have arisen. This leads him to conclude that we should not talk of 'direct' but, rather of 'indirect horizontality'. As these exchanges unfolded, Bennett and O'Callaghan placed increasing emphasis on relevant political philosophy. Bennett defended his public law-based analysis on rationalist grounds. On his view the ECHR and HRA state (at a high level of generality) morally attractive and adequate grounds for legal development. By contrast, O'Callaghan finds in relevant private law intimations of the 'slow-growing wisdom' that, on some analyses, is a feature of common law culture.[18] While he baulks at efforts to pigeonhole him, we might see him as a proponent of historical reason.[19]

The exchange between Bennett and O'Callaghan, like that between the judges in 'The Canengusian Connection' calls attention, among other things, to the 'space' within which legal disputes unfold.[20] In each of these instances, the space in question is not a legal field shaped by clearly specified purposes that all participants share. Rather, it is a field within which a range of legal institutions are situated: public and private law in the case of Bennett and O'Callaghan; fault-based and strict liability, along with alternative compensation schemes, in that of the Canengusian judges. Fields of this sort endure over time. But they do not retain a settled shape. Judges reconfigure doctrine. Legislators usher new compensation schemes into existence. Commentators respond to linguistic uncertainties by stipulating new definitions. Ideals of justice gain adherents or lose currency. To seek to grasp, much less to control, these developments is to come face-to-face with the fact that few in the fields contemplated by Hutchinson and Morgan and Bennett and O'Callaghan are agents in any very strong sense. They are, in truth, rather like the characters that Anthony Powell describes in *A Dance To*

---

[18] K.N. Llewellyn, *The Bramble Bush* (New York: Oceana, 1930), 43.

[19] See, G.J. Postema, *Bentham and the Common Law Tradition* (Oxford: Clarendon Press, 1986), 37 (on the common law as 'a historically embodied tradition', prominent within which is the assumption that 'reason' is 'immanent' within the developing body of judge-made norms and the social practices that they seek to track). For more general discussion of 'historical reason', see D. Boucher, *Political Theories and International Relations* (Oxford: Oxford University Press, 1998), 37-40 and 317-319.

[20] 'Space' predicates extension. But when we remember that we are using this word to describe a collection of abstractions (legal norms) we grasp that it is metaphoric. This encourages the thought that 'space' is imprecise. However, this may not be the case. Karl Popper's account of 'world 3' provides support for this view. Popper identifies abstract artefacts that have objective contents as falling within world 3. Legal norms are obvious candidates for inclusion in this category. So too are the relations in which they stand relative to one another. For these relations yield a system: *e.g.*, a body of higher-order and lower-order norms of the sort described by Kelsen in his account of a *Stufenbau*. On 'world 3', see K. Popper, 'Knowledge: Subjective Versus Objective', ch 4 in D. Miller, ed, *A Pocket Popper* (Glasgow: Fontana Press, 1983). See also H. Kelsen, *Introduction to the Problems of Legal Theory* (Oxford: Clarendon Press, 1992), 64, 75, and 77-78.

The Music Of Time – 'unable to control the melody, perhaps, to control the steps of the dance'.[21]

But we can, at least, seek to make sense, in an exploratory spirit, of the field that features in 'The Canengusian Connection' and others like it. And this is what each of the contributors to this collection has aimed to do. In each case, they have sought to stake out a position that, while tentative, makes a plausible claim to advance understanding.[22] The exploratory character of these contributions to debate is a feature that they have in common with 'The Canengusian Connection'. For Hutchinson and Morgan identify accident compensation law as, among other things, a battlefield – but they do not seek to offer the final word on the nature of this site of conflict.[23] Exploratory research is an activity that calls on those who engage in it to run risks.[24] This is not something that a low-trust higher education sector reshaped by processes of audit is as well equipped to do as it was twenty-five years ago.[25] But, if this collection has value, it is (in significant part) as a demonstration of the fact that this sort of thing is still possible.

---

21 A. Powell, *A Dance To The Music Of Time*, Vol 1, *Spring* (London: Arrow Books, 2000), 2.

22 The idea of an 'exploratory' contribution to debate owes much to a paper given by Andrew Halpin in Newcastle in May 2010. While contributing to a symposium on 'Law Beyond the Nation State', Halpin distinguished between two types of philosophy – the 'elevated' and the 'exploratory'. Elevated philosophy claims to offer a secure basis on which to capture the reality to which it applies (and so has about it the character of a 'final vocabulary' as described in R. Rorty, n 16, above, 122). Exploratory philosophy, by contrast, is more tentative *vis-à-vis* the nature of the field it surveys and the language it uses to advance claims that are nonetheless oriented towards the pursuit of truth. For a tentative claim as to how things stand in such-and-such a field nonetheless exhibits what John Searle has called a 'mind-to-world direction of fit'. See J.R. Searle, *Making the Social World: The Structure of Human Civilization* (Oxford: Oxford University Press, 2010), 28. Halpin also insists that both the explorer and that which he or she explores undergo change as the process of exploration unfolds. See A. Halpin & V. Roeben (eds), *Theorising the Global Legal Order* (Oxford: Hart Publishing, 2009), 2.

23 *Cf* A.C. Hutchinson, *Waiting for Coraf: A Critique of Law and Rights* (Toronto: University of Toronto Press, 1995), 88 (describing law as a bottomless pit on the ground that '[i]t is capable of accommodating all manner of philosophical insight, ideological choice, and hermeneutical possibility').

24 For a brief but powerful statement on the relationship between 'thoughtful' (or exploratory) legal research and risk-taking, see J. Waldron, 'Dignity and Defamation: The Visibility of Hate' (2010) 123 *Harvard LR* 1596, 1615..

25 See A. Giddens, *Modernity and Self-Identity: Self and Society in the Late-Modern Age* (Cambridge: Polity Press, 1992), 41 (on the relationship between creativity ('which means the capability to act or think innovatively in relationship to pre-established modes of activity') and high levels of trust).

Acknowledgements

Thanks are due to Ashley Wilton who, as Head of Newcastle Law School, made it possible for me, at very short notice, to host the symposium out of which this collection has grown. Thanks are also due to the North East Regional Obligations Group for the support it gave the series. Aron Ping D'Souza, the Editor of *The Journal Jurisprudence* has helped each of the contributors to sharpen his or her essay. Carol Forrest, Patrick O'Callaghan, and Ole Pedersen have each helped me to edit the collection, and David Kairys and Chris Riley have assisted me with particular points. I must also place on record my thanks to Professor Jo Shaw (Edinburgh Law School) who (when based in Exeter) very decently ordered a copy of 'The Canengusian Connection' for me to read (as I prepared an undergraduate dissertation on accident compensation law). The collection has also been enhanced by the decision of Professor Benjamin Richardson, Editor of the *Osgoode Hall Law Journal*, to allow 'The Canegusian Connection' to be reproduced alongside the essays that appear below.

APPENDIX 1

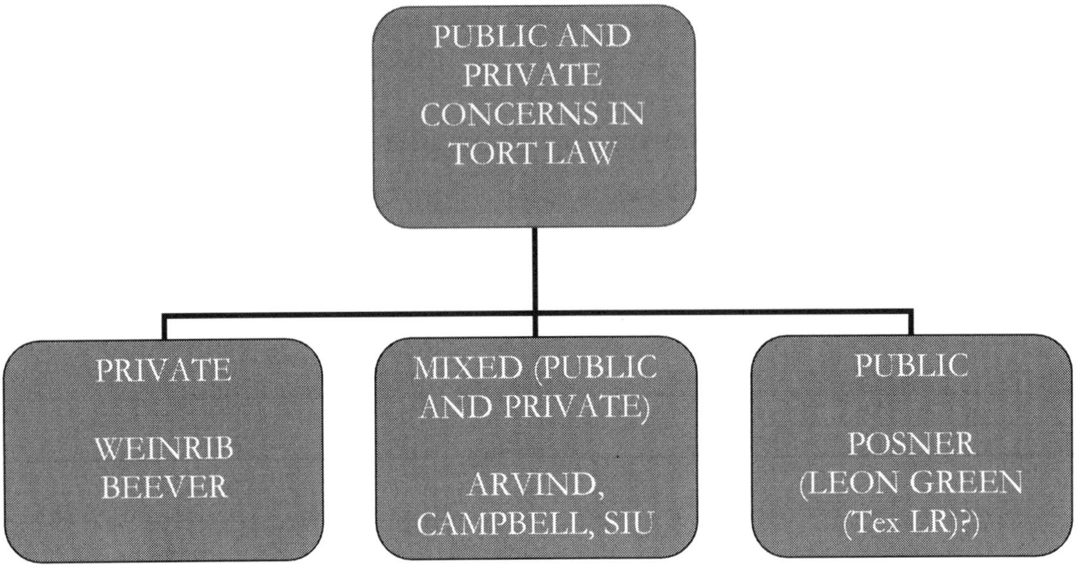
PUBLIC AND PRIVATE CONCERNS IN TORT LAW
PRIVATE
WEINRIB
BEEVER
MIXED (PUBLIC AND PRIVATE)
ARVIND, CAMPBELL, SIU
PUBLIC
POSNER
(LEON GREEN (Tex LR)?)

APPENDIX 2

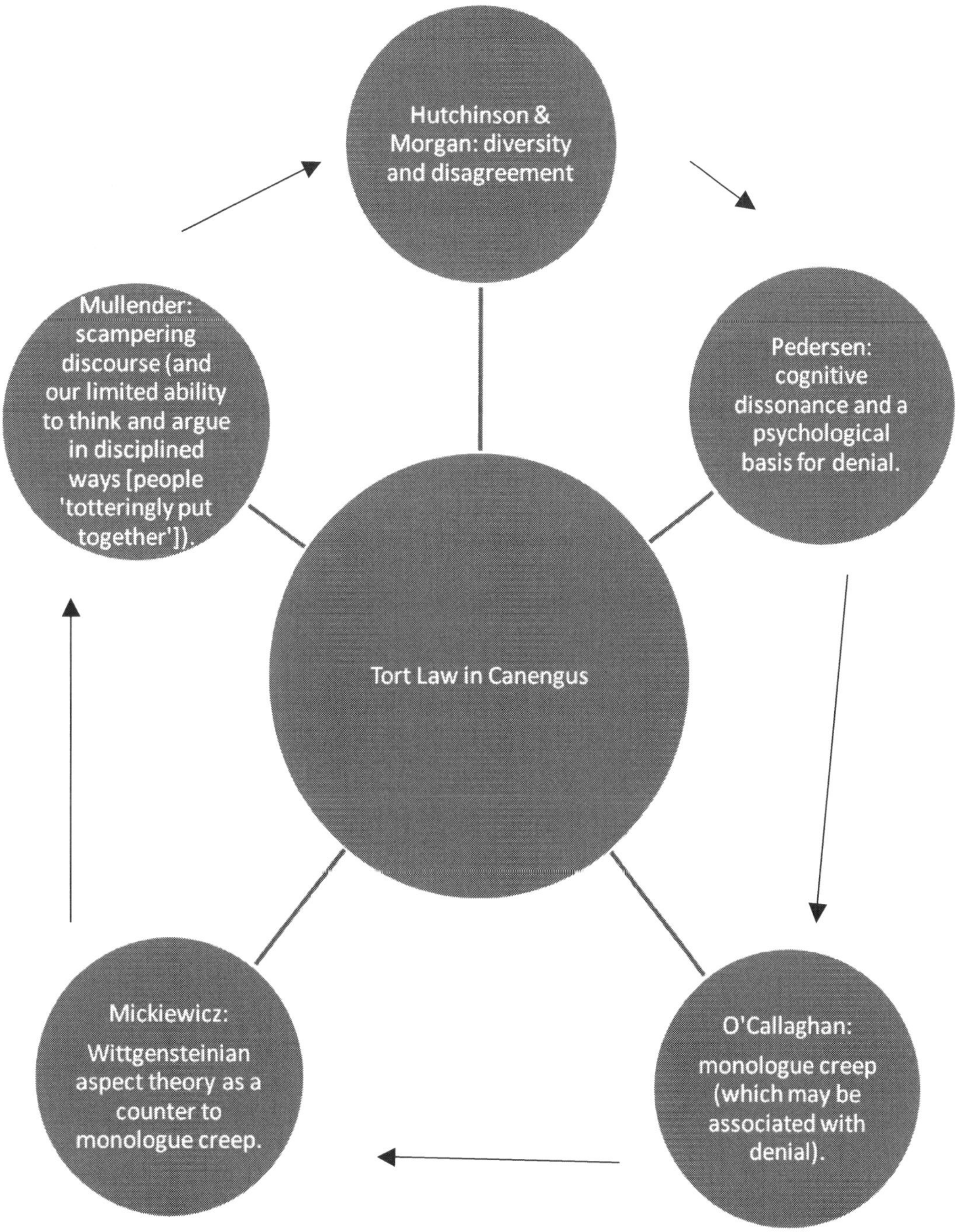
Hutchinson & Morgan: diversity and disagreement
Pedersen: cognitive dissonance and a psychological basis for denial.
Tort Law in Canengus
O'Callaghan:
monologue creep (which may be associated with denial).
Mickiewicz:
Wittgensteinian aspect theory as a counter to monologue creep.
Mullender: scampering discourse (and our limited ability to think and argue in disciplined ways [people 'totteringly put together']).

THE CANENGUSIAN CONNECTION: THE KALEIDOSCOPE OF TORT THEORY

BY ALLAN C. HUTCHINSON* AND DEREK MORGAN**

In the course of our teaching and research, we uncovered a recent decision of the Supreme Court of Canengus.[1] *The judgment in* Allan v. Derek *was handed down on 1st April, 1984. We reproduce it here in the hope that it will be of some interest to tort lawyers and legal scholars generally.*

DOCTRIN C.J.: This appeal arises from a road traffic accident near Ottlonwash on 18 May, 1980 in the late evening. The accident has given rise to several causes of action that have been consolidated for the purposes of this appeal. There are four central issues to be decided: whether Derek can recover damages from Allan for Allan's negligence; whether Derek was contributorily negligent; whether Martin was responsible in damages for his failure to rescue Derek; and whether Charles can recover damages for emotional distress and, if so, against whom.

The facts of the case are relatively clear and are not in dispute. Derek was driving home along a quiet, narrow and winding country road that was unpaved, unmarked and unlit. As he rounded a sweeping bend, he saw a single headlight approaching close to the other side of the road; he assumed this to be a motorcyclist. Unfortunately, it transpired that this light was that of a sports car driven by Allan, whose off-side headlight was not working. At the last minute, Derek realized his mistake and applied his brakes. Regrettably, his braking system did not function properly. The car swerved, left the road, and ended in a shallow ditch at the side of the road. Allan, who had also taken avoidance action, was unaware that a serious accident had occurred and continued on his journey home.

This accident occurred near the isolated farm of Martin. At the

---

* Associate Professor of Law, Osgoode Hall Law School, York University, Toronto.

** Visiting Professor of Law, Osgoode Hall Law School, York University, Toronto. We are indebted to many friends and colleagues for their help and advice in writing this paper. We are also happy to record our thanks to Oonaugh Fitzgerald, Michael Gottheil, Catherine Smee and Kevin Whitaker for their generous research and assistance.

[1]Canengus is a small, little-known island in the mid-Atlantic. Something of a geographical enigma, its capital, Ottlonwash, is equidistant from Ottawa, London and Washington. Coincidentally, it is a common law jurisdiction and its law is a unique blend of Canadian, English and American sources.

time of the accident, he was standing on his front porch, calling in his dog for the night. Although he saw and heard the accident, he did nothing to ascertain whether anyone was injured or in need of help. For reasons best known to himself, he closed the door and retired to bed. Derek was trapped in his car. His right leg, stuck under the dashboard, was broken in two places. Reliable medical evidence has indicated that if Derek had then received immediate assistance, for example, by having the pressure on his leg relieved, the further complications which arose could have been averted. Sadly, he remained trapped for over half an hour and the blood flow to his leg was irreversibly impaired. As a result, his leg has been amputated.

Approximately thirty-five minutes after the accident, Jane came upon the scene. She was driving from Ottlonwash to her home in the village of Tormanyork. She immediately went to Derek's aid, dragging him from the wreckage after levering away the dashboard. She administered artificial respiration, which probably saved his life. Jane then ran to Martin's farm and persuaded Martin to telephone for an ambulance. Derek was rushed to hospital where an emergency operation was carried out. His life was in the balance. A telephone call was made by the police to Charles, who lived with and apparently enjoyed a homosexual relationship with Derek. Charles' answering service advised them that Charles was away on business. The police succeeded in locating Charles and left a message for him. Charles telephoned the hospital and was told by the staff that it would be some time before there would be any definite news, but that Derek was presently in the intensive care unit. Fortunately, through the skill of the hospital staff, Derek's life was saved. But this experience has left its tragic mark on Charles. The psychiatric evidence establishes that Charles has suffered severe shock, organic depression and a change of personality as a direct result of the injury suffered by his friend. Also, the relationship between Charles and Derek has ended. After spending three months in hospital, Derek moved back to his parents' home. He is confined to a wheelchair.

The trial judge held that, as Derek was fifty percent to blame, his damages should be reduced accordingly. In the third party proceedings brought by Allan against Martin, the action was dismissed. The judge concluded that there was no duty to rescue. Charles' claim against Allan for compensation for his emotional distress was allowed. Allan's application to the Court of Appeal was dismissed and Derek's cross-appeal on the question of duty to rescue was also dismissed. Allan now appeals to this court and Derek cross-appeals.

The case appears to raise a number of moral issues. However, I should make it clear from the outset that my concern is with the legal aspects of this case alone. Of course, the law, as a social force, overlaps with religion and morality, but it is incumbent upon me to resolve the issues presented in accordance with the law as it is, and not as some think it ought to be. Like Sir George Baker, "my task is to apply the law free of emotion and predilection"; see *Paton* v. *Trustees of British Pregnancy Advisory Services*, [1978] 2 All E.R. 987 at 989. In blunt terms, "with purely moral obligation the law does not deal"; see *Buch* v. *Amory Manufacturing Co.*, 69 N.H. 257 (1897).

Furthermore, as has been constantly emphasized, the desirability and continued existence of any particular law is for the legislature and not for the judiciary to decide. There is a clear separation of governmental powers in Canengus. The legislature has the constitutional responsibility to enact laws designed to achieve substantively just results; the judiciary has the task of interpreting, applying and dispensing this received wisdom. In this way, the fundamental democratic demands of consensus, as sought in the political process, and rationality, as embodied in the legal process, are met. Within this constitutional arrangement, arguments of law and morality are rendered mutually exclusive. The formal and neutral application of the rules infuses the law with a central integrity. The law is insulated from political controversy; see *Duport Steel Ltd.* v. *Sirs*, [1980] All E.R. 529 at 551.

Was Allan Negligent?

The issue of negligence can be dealt with expeditiously. The task for the Court is to determine whether Allan owed Derek a duty of care, whether that duty was breached and whether the breach has led to cognizable damages; see *Donoghue* v. *Stevenson*, [1932] A.C. 526. There is, of course, no general duty of care. In order to be successful, a plaintiff must show that he was a foreseeable plaintiff. The defendant must owe him a duty of care; see *Palsgraf* v. *Long Island Railroad Co.*, 162 N.E. 99 (1928). The court must be persuaded that there are no reasons or considerations of policy which dictate that this *prima facie* duty of care be circumscribed so as to deny the liability of the defendant; see *Anns* v. *Merton London Borough Council*, [1978] A.C. 728 at 751-52. The essence of the law has been succinctly captured by Macdonald J. in *Nova Mink* v. *Trans Canada Airlines* (1951), 2 D.L.R. 241:

> The common law yields the conclusion that there is a duty only where the circumstances of time, place and person would create in the mind of a reasonable man in those circumstances such a probability of harm resulting to other persons as to require him to take care to avert the probable result.

That a road user owes a duty of care to other road users is without question. The issue is whether Allan, in failing to have his car in proper working order, breached the standard of care to which a reasonable man would adhere.

It is well established that a breach of a statutory duty, while not conclusive evidence of liability, raises a *prima facie* case that the standard has been breached; see, for example, *Queen* v. *Saskatchewan Wheat Pool* (1983), 143 D.L.R. (3d) 9 and *Clinkscales* v. *Carver* 22 Cal. 2d 72 (1943). It was argued by counsel for the respondent that the *Highway Traffic Act*, R.S.C.E.S., c. 198, being a regulatory statute and carrying its own penalties for violations, was not designed to determine the standard of care in civil suits. It seems to me that if the legislature, in its wisdom, has seen fit to enact legislation to ensure safety on our nation's highways, this Court ought not treat such a pronouncement lightly. The legislature is in the best position to decide what the appropriate standards should be. Though let it be clear that, by accepting such a definition, this Court is in no way fettering its judicial discretion.

In *Sterling Trusts Corp.* v. *Postma*, [1965] S.C.R. 324, Cartwright J. considered the effect of a statutory duty in the context of a civil action for negligence. He settled on the following rule (at 329):

> I think it is plain that once it has been found (i) that the respondents committed a breach of the statutory duty. . . and, (ii) that the breach was an effective cause of the appellants' injuries, the respondents were prima facie liable for the damages suffered by the appellants.

In the present case, the evidence satisfies this two-fold test. A defendant can rebut the *prima facie* case by showing that the statutory breach occurred without any negligence on his part. I agree with the trial judge that the malfunctioning headlights could reasonably have been discovered. Accordingly, negligence on Allan's part has been established.

Was Derek Contributorily Negligent?

The more contentious question is whether Derek was also negligent and, if so, to what extent his negligence reduces Allan's liability. When two people are on the highway and their movement is such as to involve a risk of a collision, each owes to the other a duty to move with due care. Although Allan's negligence may have increased the likelihood of an accident, the realization of that risk was in large part the responsiblity of Derek who was also in breach of the relevant statutory provisions. The duty on Derek is aptly summed up by Lord Justice Buckley in *Lee* v. *Lever*, [1974] R.T.R. 35 at 39:

> It is not the law that a driver is entitled to assume that all other users of the road

> will in all respects and at all other times obey the Highway Code or otherwise drive with all due care and circumspection or use the road in every way in which it should be used. It is incumbent upon any driver to be prepared for foreseeable hazards, including hazards resulting from the foreseeable bad driving of other drivers or a foreseeable breach. . . .[I]t is incumbent upon every user of such a roadway to drive in a way which enables him to meet an emergency or a hazard presented [by other drivers].

The failure of Derek to ensure that his car was maintained in a roadworthy condition, such that it would be able to negotiate the normal hazards of night driving in the country, is strong evidence of his contributory negligence; see *Parish* v. *Judd*, [1960] 3 All E.R. 33. Accordingly, the Court of Appeal was quite correct in refusing to disturb the trial judge's reduction of the $1 million in damages by fifty percent under the *Negligence Act*, R.S.C.E.S., c. 315, ss. 2 and 5.

Did Martin Have a Legal Duty to Rescue?

The issue of whether there is a legal duty to rescue Derek raises what counsel has told us is one of the most sensitive and heated academic debates in tort law. Indeed, counsel for the appellant presented a most able and humanistic argument to suggest that this Court should give legal effect to what all agree is a clear moral obligation to one's fellow man. Appellant's counsel went on to argue that the law of tort itself was based on society's conception of right and wrong. In fact, the "neighbour principle" itself was said to stem from the biblical duty to love one's neighbour; see Luke, ch. 10, v. 29.

I am not persuaded, however, that we should vest this moral duty with legal sanction. The opinion of the court in *Union Pacific R. Co.* v. *Cappier* 72 P. 282 at 282-83 (1903), is as relevant today as it was at the turn of the century:

> With the humane side of the question courts are not concerned. It is the omission or negligent discharge of legal duties only which come within the sphere of judicial cognizance. For withholding relief from the suffering, for failure to respond to the calls of worthy charity, or for faltering in the bestowment of brotherly love on the unfortunate, penalties are found not in the laws of men, but in that higher law, the violation of which is condemned by the voice of conscience, whose sentence of punishment for the recreant act is swift and sure.

A survey of early cases reveals no legal duty to rescue, even where the litigants had a particular relationship such as a business association or the like; *Osterlind* v. *Hill* 160 N.E. 301 (1920) and *Yania* v. *Bigan* 155 A. 2d 343 (1959). In *Yania*, the plaintiff was the widow of a business visitor, who had jumped into the water to aid the defendant. The plaintiff's husband subsequently drowned when the defendant refused to come to his aid. The court held that there was no legal duty unless the defendant places the plaintiff in peril. Likewise, in *Osterlind*, the defendant rented a canoe to the plaintiff which, in full view of the defendant, capsized and the plaintiff drowned. Once again, the court held no legal duty to effect a rescue.

Appellant's counsel pointed to a recent decision which held that a ship's captain has a duty to rescue a passenger who falls overboard; see *Horsley* v. *Maclaren*, [1969] 2 O.R. 137. Counsel argued that the courts are expanding the duty to rescue and urged this court to do so in this case. It is true that there are now several specific relationships that will give rise to a duty to rescue. However, most of these are founded upon statutory duties, such as the obligations of parent to child, or upon some implicit agreement, as between members of a social outing; see *Farwell* v. *Keaton* 396 Mich. 281 (1976). This court is bound by a long line of eminent authority. Until the legislature deems it appropriate to substitute a general duty to rescue for these cases where special relationships exist, we ought not to upset the delicate balance the common law has developed. Also, aside from the moral dimension, there exist very real technical and administrative difficulties associated with the introduction of such a general duty. What would be the extent of Martin's liability? And to whom would he be liable? Would Allan benefit from Martin's misfeasance? Both these administrative and moral problems combine to support the existing rules. Consequently, Martin cannot be found legally liable for his failure to rescue Derek.

Can Charles Recover for Emotional Distress?

Recovery for nervous shock caused by negligence is a relatively recent arrival on the tort scene. Prior to 1925 and the decision of *Hambrook* v. *Stokes Bros.*, [1925] 1 K.B. 141, courts were quite markedly reluctant to allow plaintiffs to recover for nervous shock without any bodily injury to themselves. This reluctance was founded upon the view that such awards were difficult, if not impossible, to determine, and that nervous disorder and emotional upset was easy to feign. The remarks of Mitchell C.J. in *Huston* v. *Borough of Fremansburg* 61 A. 1022 at 1023 (1905), are pertinent:

> It requires but brief judicial experience to be convinced of the large proportion of exaggeration and even of actual fraud in the ordinary action for physical injuries from negligence; and if we opened the door to this new invention the result would be great danger, if not disaster to the cause of practical justice.

Since the turn of this century, the marvels and advances of medical science have come upon us with great speed. The field of psychiatry has grown to a point where diseases of the mind can be diagnosed and treated with a confidence that approaches certainty. And it is with matters of certainty that the courts of justice deal. As a result, courts have now begun to award redress to plaintiffs who have suffered recognizable psychiatric illness as a result of defendants' negligence; see *Hinz* v. *Berry*, [1970] 2 Q.B. 40. Initially, it was only admitted in cases where the plaintiff personally was in peril of physical harm, *Dulieu* v. *White & Sons*, [1901] 2 K.B. 669, but the *Hambrook* case (*supra*) recognized that in certain specific relationships, such as between a mother and child, serious injury to another could be the basis for recovery; see *King* v. *Phillips*, [1953] 1 Q.B. 429.

There has been a gradual widening of the liability. The general trend has been to allow recovery where the plaintiff has come upon the immediate aftermath of an accident; see *Marshall* v. *Lionel Enterprises*, [1972] 2 O.R. 177. Perhaps the best test is the one laid down by Torbriner J. of the California Supreme Court in *Dillon* v. *Legg* 29 A.L.R. 3d 1316 at 1326-27 (1968):

> In determining, in such a case, whether defendant should reasonably foresee the injury to plaintiff, or, in other terminology, whether defendant owes plaintiff a duty of due care, the courts will take into account such factors as the following. (1) Whether plaintiff was located near the scene of the accident as contrasted with one who was a distance away from it. (2) Whether the shock resulted from a direct emotional impact upon plaintiff from the sensory and contemporaneous observance of the accident, as contrasted with learning of the accident from them after the occurrence. (3) Whether plaintiff and the victim were closely related, as contrasted with an absence of any relationship or the presence of only a distant relationship. The evaluation of these factors will indicate the degree of the defendant's foreseeability.

In the present case, Charles was nowhere near the scene of the accident and did not even come upon the aftermath. He was some 250 miles from the scene. Secondly, while he may well have experienced a true emotional disturbance rather than mere grief (which is not recoverable; see *Duwyn* v. *Kaprielian* (1978), 2 O.R.(2d) 736), it was not from the "sensory and contemporaneous observance of the accident" as is required; see, for example, *Hathaway* v. *Supreme Court* 112 Cal. App. 3d 728 (1980). Furthermore, I am not persuaded that there existed the necessary relationship between Derek and Charles to warrant an extension of the rule. In *McLoughlin* v. *O'Brian*, [1982] 2 W.L.R. 982, where a mother was two miles away from the accident and only heard of it two hours later, the lack of immediate physical proximity was counterbalanced by the fundamental nature of their relationship as mother and family and her arrival at what amounted to the "immediate aftermath" of the accident. Notwithstanding this, it was argued that the facts of the present case were sufficiently analogous to existing doctrine to warrant recovery. Although it is true that the law must develop from case to case, we must also strive to maintain certainty and generality so as to avoid a doctrinal wilderness of single instances.

The limits of liability must be drawn where the "good sense of the judges decides"; see *Bourhill* v. *Young*, [1943] A.C. 92 at 110 per Lord Wright. The words of Allan J. in *Spade* v. *Lynn & B.R. Co.* 47 N.E. 497 (1897), offer an appropriate warning:

> The law must be administered in the courts according to general rules. Courts will aim to make these rules as just as possible, bearing in mind that they are to be of general application. But as the law is a practical science, having to do with the affairs of life, any rule is unwise if, in its general application, it will not, as a usual result, serve the purposes of justice. A new rule cannot be made for each case. . . . One may be held bound to anticipate and guard against the probable consequences to ordinary people, but to carry the rule of damages further imposes an undue measure of responsiblity upon those who are guilty only of unintentional negligence.

In conclusion, therefore, I hold that, although Derek is entitled to recover from Allan, his damages will be reduced by fifty percent as a result of his own contributory negligence. Further, Charles has no claim against Allan or Martin for his emotional distress and Martin, while worthy of our moral opprobrium, is not liable to anyone for his failure to rescue Derek.

* * *

MILL J.: This appeal requires this Court to decide the proper basis of liablity for physical harm, whether the law of civil wrongs should be extended to impose legal liability for nonfeasance (the so-called "duty to rescue") and, finally, the extent of liability for negligently inflicted emotional distress.

Reading the judgment of Doctrin C.J., it readily becomes apparent that her conception of the judicial role is confused, schizophrenic, and altogether too restricted. It also involves an ineffectual sleight of hand which a moment's mature reflection reveals as self-contradictory. I say this more by way of clarification and introduction to my own judgment than as vindictive criticism of much of the doctrinal substance of her view of the common law. Indeed, I hope that it will become clear that I am in broad agreement with some of her conclusions. My concern here, however, is to clear away the rhetoric behind which her cloak-and-dagger approach to public policy lurks.

As with all law and life, two guiding principles dominate the law of tort: risk and uncertainty. It is the task of courts, as agents of the law, to select doctrines that minimize both. By creating the law through decisions operating as precedents in subsequent cases, the courts promote efficient resource allocation by optimizing these two related concepts. In tort law, concepts such as duty, reasonable foreseeability and causation are veiled terms through which the courts formally express the choices they have made. They operate as a convenient and accommodating screen behind which the real social drama is played out. As Lord Denning bluntly noted, "common law adjudication is . . . at bottom a matter of public policy which we, as judges, must resolve"; *Home Office* v. *Dorset Yacht Co. Ltd.*, [1969] 2 Q.B. 412 at 426. This sentiment gained the express approval of Lords Dilhorne and Diplock; see [1970] A.C. 1004 at 1051 and 1058 respectively. The accuracy of this admission is richly illustrated in English cases that have established the advocate's immunity from negligence liability; see *Rondel* v. *Worsley*, [1969] 1 A.C. 191 and *Saif Ali* v. *Sidney Mitchell & Co.*, [1980] A.C. 198. The common law is a vast and intricate doctrinal edifice, but its chief architect has been policy and not logic.

Formerly, this allusion to policy considerations was exemplified by cases which mooted a novel claim. In practice, judges have shown reluctance to expand the ambit of liability other than by way of rationalizing or arguing by analogy; see *McLoughlin* v. *O'Brian*, [1982] 2 W.L.R. 982 at 988-89. Whenever a court decides that compensation is payable only for loss that was "reasonably foreseeable," it *reaffirms* a policy decision taken years or decades ago. The appeal to "policy" is unavoidable. That being the case, the judges ought now, openly and legitimately, to abandon their public naiveté to take stock of the law of torts. There is obviously potential danger in this course of action. What strikes one judge as a suitable "policy risk" may appear to another to be the height of folly. But such idiosyncratic appeals may be properly guided by a systematic theory of civil liability.

For too long we have lacked a theory to explain adequately the social function of negligence liability and of the fault system of liability that is built upon it. The true test of any theory, of course, is its ability to predict or explain the full diversity and complexity of life. Without the capacity to formulate some general hypothesis we can have no system of law that is properly understood. And, without that facility, we cannot have the system of law which we understand to be one in which people can properly and confidently place their expectations and plan their behaviour. To reply with Aristotle, as my colleague Justice Wright is wont to do, that the real purpose and only proper effect of tortious liability is to restore to a person what has been wrongfully appropriated in some way — the concept of "corrective justice" — would offer no insights into the source of the norms by which the conduct was judged wrongful. Thus, the experiential basis of my proposed theory confounds any critics who would suggest that the theory rests on unrealistic behavioural assumptions. My theoretical model is concerned with the proper rules of tort law. It is open to criticism only insofar as the postulates seek to explain not simply nor exclusively individual conditions, but the totality of those conditions. The behavioural consequences of the rules which this theory produces are beyond the scope of this Court to examine, beyond even the bounds of the theory to predict, *in the individual case.*

My model is premised on the fact that the world is finite, an aggregate of scarce resources. Choices must be made, for example, as to the use, conservation and distribution of fossil fuel. So too must difficult choices be countenanced everywhere in our society. In torts, we must recognize the continuing force of Lord Atkin's dictum that "acts or omissions which any moral code would censure cannot, in a practical world, be treated so as to give a right to every person injured by them to demand relief"; *Donoghue* v. *Stevenson,* [1932] A.C. 562 at 580. Ours is a practical world. We judges are practical men and women of that world. It is for this reason that I find Justice Lefft's abdication of the judicial task so distasteful and unjustified.

It is this concentration on the life of the practical world, with its scarce resources, which further leads me to reject the constitutional separation of powers doctrine so rigidly adhered to by Chief Justice Doctrin. We would close our eyes to the distributive effects of our decisions in this Court if we were to accept wholeheartedly her inflexible and formal distinction of law-making roles. To believe that the legislature, with its tightly constrained timetable of political, social, moral and economic issues, can necessarily accommodate law reform at the drop of this Court's hat is to live in some other world. Political indifference and its legislative ally, inertia, are facts of life. Unless we properly appreciate the effects of these forces, we will relentlessly pursue the "principled" decision-making of Chief Justice Doctrin to the ultimate swamping of our tort system. Irrespective of the inefficiencies which this approach would sanction, we would fail in our political and social duty to ensure that the law meets the demands of *contemporary* society or, as with our present system of *ad hoc* decision-making, the demands of society for some years past. The true measure of common law adjudication is the extent to which it can resolve today's problems in a fashion that will allow for the dual considerations of the predictive certainty of the law to meet the expectation of society and the optimalization of accident costs and resources.

How, then, can theory construct an adequate response to these conditions? It is not without interest that the response to uncertainty has occupied the forefront of human endeavour. Many of the distinctive institutions of primitive society, such as polygamy and extended family groups, can be understood as such a response. Further, with the recognition of the institution of private property comes the related doctrine of contract, for the purpose of all contracting is risk-shifting; see *Photoproductions Ltd.* v. *Securicor*, [1980] 1 All E.R. 556 and *Globe Refining Co.* v. *Landa Cotton Oil Co.*, 190 U.S. 540 (1903). As a society develops, its wealth increases. Moreover, as the opportunity for interaction expands, there will be a corresponding rise in the probability of interfering with or harming others' interests. More state-imposed control and protection is demanded. But, unless we are particularly watchful, this increased control and protection could interfere with the perfect market in which voluntary exchanges result in resources gravitating toward their most valuable uses. The goals of private and social allocative efficiency may be lost. Information becomes more difficult to obtain. The transaction costs between individuals will become prohibitively high, particularly in modern accident claims which typically arise from random and chance occurrences. Resources will be wasted.

If there were no barriers to effective bargaining, the assignment of legal rights would not affect the social efficiency of the final outcome. For example, Dexter lives next to a cricket ground, owned by Cowdrey, and is frequently assailed by hard-hit balls. Dexter could take adequate precautions at $500, but it would cost Cowdrey $1,000. If Cowdrey was legally liable, he would bargain to pay Dexter $500 to take the necessary precautions. If Cowdrey was not legally liable, Dexter would have to spend $500 on precautions. Either way, the *socially* efficient level of precautions would be taken. But bargaining is a costly business and becomes prohibitively so between strangers. We must strive to mimic a market in which these very real costs are accounted for and in which our goal, in tort law, is to reduce the sum of the costs of accidents and the cost of avoiding accidents. As such, tort seeks to regulate the relations between strangers on the basis of the implied terms of some hypothetical contract.

Undoubtedly, the desirability of social efficiency as a goal requires a value judgment as to the justness of the underlying distribution of income and property rights. The model is limited to the extent that it seeks to optimize the use and exchange of whatever rights people start out with. But this bespeaks not so much a limitation of the theory itself, as a limitation and appreciation of the proper bounds of political and judicial action. The dominant contemporary theory of the state is no longer one of general optimism concerning governmental intervention in the economic system, it is now a theory of redistribution. Tort law, dealing as it does mainly with accidents, does not lend itself well to a redistributive theory that emphasizes the intervention of the state to redistribute wealth from the powerless to the powerful. It is not plausible to think that interest groups will overly concern themselves with redistribution through the tort system or will place accident compensation reform on their agenda for legislative action anyway. This point is perhaps not fully grasped by Justice Lefft, whose well intentioned, but misguided energies may now become a real cost in the world of imperfect information. My theory attempts to come to terms with this precise problem.

Rules of tort law must be designed and implemented so as to facilitate and simulate the operation of a free and competitive market. In a world of transaction costs, the initial assignment of rights is of crucial importance and has a fundamental impact on the allocative efficiency of societal resources. The practical implementation of my thesis must, and does, take account of this factor. The rule of liability is relevant and will determine whether resources are used in an economically efficient manner. In most accident situations, private bargaining is not feasible; bargaining costs may be prohibitively high. The necessary information may be unavailable, imperfect or too expensive, there may be too many parties to the potential transaction or there may be the problem of excluding free riders — those who do not pay for the benefits they receive — from the bargain. This, of course, is the case with Allan and Derek. Consequently, the rules of liability must as closely as possible approximate the apportionment of risk that would have been arrived at by the litigants *if they had been able to bargain.* Any dispute which reaches a court is, after all, only a case in which the bargaining process — settlement out of court — has broken down. Where this result is impractical or impossible, the law should seek to simulate an outcome that would be produced by market forces in a world which generates no transaction costs.

The economic logic of the competitive market must become the unifying force of the common law. The market and the legal system are similar operational institutions. Like the market, the legal system could be a competitive process in which the pursuit of self-interest serves to promote an efficient allocation of resources. If the invisible hand of the market is replicated by the pen of the detached and impartial judge inefficient rules will be litigated out of the system. The adversary system could be a substitute for marketing strategies and consequently oblige the judge to act as a consumer in choosing between two fiercely promoted products. Legal rules could be cast as economic incentives to encourage individuals to maximize efficiency. Like the economic actor, the legal actor could be presented with the costs of any course of action in order to decide whether to incur those costs. The common law of tort, therefore, should be assiduous in its allocation of responsibilities between people engaged in interacting activities, so that the joint value of those activities is maximized and the joint cost of those activities is minimized. More particularly, the law must seek to encourage individuals to achieve a level of safety at which the value of the risks involved in an activity is equal to the cost of the precautions necessary to maintain that degree of safety. In short, individuals must be persuaded to "internalize" the costs of accidents.

Accordingly, the notion of "economic efficiency" is a broad one. It explains how scarce resources are allocated among competing and alternative choices. Alternatively, it is not simply confined to the minimization of administrative cost or the maximization of technical output, but also deals with the welfare of society, whether the actual allocation fits with and responds to what people want or can afford. The failure to appreciate that "efficiency" is a relative term has led to much confusion. An efficient allocation of resources exists where there is no other pattern of allocation that would improve any one person's welfare without making any other person worse off, or when those who do benefit from a reallocation of resources can compensate those who do not and still themselves point up an improvement in their own welfare. In this context, the central task for tort law is to design rules of liability which will provide a sufficient incentive to achieve an efficient level of safety by deterring carelessness and rewarding care. As the Court summarized in *Losee* v. *Buchanan* 51 N.Y. 476 at 484 (1873):

> By becoming a member of civilized society, I am compelled to give up many of my natural rights, but I receive more than a compensation from the surrender by every other man of the same rights, and the security, advantage and protection which the laws give me. . . .We must have factories, machinery, dams, canals and railroads. They are demanded by the manifold wants of mankind, and lay at the basis of all our civilization. If I have any of these upon my lands. . . . I am not responsible for any damage they accidentally and unavoidably do to my neighbor. He receives his compensation for such damage by the general good in which he shares and the right which he has to place the same things upon his lands. I hold my property subject to the risk that it may be unavoidably or accidentally injured by those who live near me; and as I move about upon the public highways and in all places where other persons may lawfully be, I take the risk of being accidentally injured in my person by them without fault on their part. Most of the rights of property, as well as of person, in the social state, are not absolute but relative, and they must be so arranged and modified, not unnecessarily infringing upon natural rights, as upon the whole to promote the general welfare.

Some will enthusiastically accept this theory, while others will vehemently reject it. However, all might reasonably inquire as to its relevance and applicability to legal disputes. As Doctrin C.J. correctly, if with some exaggeration, points out, the judicial task is to apply the law and not to legislate one's preferences or prejudices. I fully agree. But the court can and must go beyond a blind and mechanistic application of formal rules. In order to keep the law in step with the march of modern society, judges must look beyond the letter of the law to its motive force and spirit. It is my honest and firm conviction that the notion of "allocative efficiency" is the golden thread which weaves together into a fine garment the seemingly disparate strands of the common law. Hitherto, this has only been vaguely glimpsed and partially grasped. Accordingly, although the theory of tort law suggested here has a clear political dimension, it does not represent a naked and personal political choice on my part. Indeed, a judge who follows and substantiates the logic of "allocative efficiency" more closely satisfies the democratic ideal of adjudication than the unthinking formalist.

The centrepiece of negligence law is the seminal judgment of Judge Learned Hand in *U.S.* v. *Carroll Towing* 159 F. 2d 169 (1947). The test for liability developed by him has a long and impeccable pedigree; see, for example, *Mackintosh* v. *Mackintosh* 36 Jur. 678 (1864), *Chicago, Burlington & Quincy Rly. Co.* v. *Krayenbuhl* 65 Neb. 889 (1902) and *Conway* v. *O'Brien* 111 F. 2d 611 (1940). The beauty of this test is its simplicity and comprehensiveness. With subtle adjustments that remain loyal to Learned Hand's ambition, it can be made to resolve all the problems of accident liability. It is an algorithm for all negligence law. When viewed and applied correctly, the problems of causation, contributory negligence and rescue that so vex Doctrin C.J. and others like her dissolve.

In *U.S.* v. *Carroll Towing, supra*, an unattended barge had slipped its moorings and collided with another ship. In holding the barge owners liable, Judge Learned Hand stated that:

> [T]here is no general rule to determine when the absence of a bargee or other attendant will make the owner of the barge liable for injuries to other vessels if she breaks away from her moorings. . . . It becomes apparent why there can be no such general rule, when we consider the grounds for such a liability. Since there are occasions when every vessel will break from her moorings, and since, if she does, she becomes a menace to those about her, the owner's duty, as in other similar situations, to provide against resulting injuries is a function of three variables: (1) The probability that she will break away; (2) The gravity of the resulting injury, if she does; (3) The burden of adequate precautions. Possibly it serves to bring this notion into relief to state it in algebraic terms: if the probability be called P; the injury, L; and the burden, B; liability depends upon whether B is less than L multiplied by P: i.e., whether $B < PL$. . . . In the case at bar the bargee left at five o'clock in the afternoon of January 3rd, and the flotilla broke away at about two o'clock in the afternoon of the following day, twenty-one hours afterwards. The bargee had been away all the time. . . . At the locus *in quo*,. . . barges were being constantly "drilled" in and out. Certainly it was not beyond reasonable expectation that, with the inevitable haste and bustle, the work might not be done with adequate care. In such circumstances, we hold —

> and it is all that we do hold — that it was a fair requirement that the [barge owners] should have a bargee aboard (unless he had some excuse for his absence), during the working hours of daylight.

Following from this, a basic presumption operates that losses will lie where they fall unless there are compelling economic reasons for their reallocation, such as a reduction in total accident costs and avoidance costs. This will only occur if it would have been cheaper for the defendant to have avoided the accident than to make good the expected losses. The accident cost is the magnitude of the loss if an accident occurs multiplied by the probability of the accident occurring. If the defendant were to compensate the plaintiff under any other circumstances, it would lead to an economically inefficient result. It would be a waste of societal resources to require the defendant to spend a greater sum to avoid one accident which results in losses of a lesser amount. The Learned Hand test encourages cost-rational actors to modify their behaviour by taking cost-justified precautions to avoid liability; see *Watt* v. *Hertfordshire C.C.*, [1954] 1 W.L.R. 535. As such, carelessness *per se* does not result in actionable negligence and "it is only the requirement that the care be commensurate with the risk and danger"; see *Nussbum* v. *Lacapo*, 27 N.Y. 2d 311 at 319 (1970).

Two examples will suffice to illustrate the efficacy and desirability of this approach. In *Hendricks* v. *Peabody Coal Co.* 115 Ill. App. 2d 35 (1969), a child was gravely injured in an accident at the defendant's waterhole. The alleged negligence comprised the failure to prevent the use of the inherently dangerous waterhole by children known to play there. Damages to the child were assessed at $200,000, but the cost of fencing off the water hole would have been between $12,000 and $14,000. The defendant was found liable as the prevention "cost was slight compared to the risk to the children involved"; *id.* at 45. Also, in *Bolton* v. *Stone*, [1951] A.C. 850, plaintiff was struck by a ball hit out of the defendants' neighbouring cricket ground. There was a twelve foot perimeter fence and a ball had only been hit out of the ground six times in about thirty years. The House of Lords held that no liability had been incurred. The risk of injury was negligible and the cost of further precautions immense. As Lord Reid said:

> In the crowded conditions of modern life even the most careful person cannot avoid creating some risks and accepting others. What a man must not do, and what I think a careful man tries not to do is to create a risk which is substantial. . . . In my judgment, the test to be applied here is whether the risk of damage to a person on the road was so small that a reasonable man in the position of the appellants, considering the matter from the point of view of safety, would have thought it right to refrain from taking steps to prevent the danger.

An application of the Learned Hand test to the facts of the case at bar is instructive. Interestingly, Doctrin C.J. failed to mention some of the more pertinent facts. As we know, the loss to Derek was estimated at $1 million, but we also know from the evidence that Allan could have repaired his headlight for $250 and that there was a relatively significant possibility that an accident would have occurred, say .001 or a one in a thousand chance. Translating these into "economic" terms it means that, as the accident cost is $1,000 (.001 x $1 m.) and the avoidance costs were $250, Allan ought to be held liable. It would have been more efficient for Allan to take precautions than to have allowed the accident to occur. It is an economically efficient use of society's resources to require an expenditure of $250 to save a loss of $1,000. However, this finding does not conclusively dispose of Allan's liability. As the objective of the law is to maximize overall social welfare, it is important to consider the economic position of Derek.

In crude and general terms, where the cost to the plaintiff of avoiding the accident is less than the cost to the defendant, the impetus for shifting the loss disappears. Indeed, it would be inefficient to do so. Consequently, the loss should lie where expected accident cost *and* the defendant's avoidance costs are less than the plaintiff's. Under such a straightforward regime, optimal safety would be achieved as each party would have a powerful incentive to minimize accident costs and maximize avoidance costs. In the present case, as Derek could have repaired his faulty brakes for $200 ($50 less than Allan's avoidance costs), the loss will remain with Derek and Allan will not be liable. Derek should have invested in the marginal safety costs as they were less than the marginal accident costs.

To interpret the *Negligence Act* as requiring a distribution of loss based on the proportionate fault of the parties, as Doctrin C.J. does, undermines the clarity and deterrent effect of that law. Moreover, such an apportionment of liability would have inefficient consequences; the parties would be obliged to spend, jointly, more than an efficient amount on accident prevention. If Allan were fully liable for the accident, he would spend $250 to prevent it and Derek nothing. If Derek were completely debarred from recovery, he would spend $200 to prevent it and Allan nothing. Where each party is liable for fifty percent of the loss, that is $500 each in this case, Allan would have an incentive to spend $250 to avoid the accident and Derek would have an incentive to spend $200. This means that either a total of $450 will be invested in accident avoidance (an increase of $250 over the *cheaper* avoidance cost) or nothing will be invested, on the basis that, knowing the other to have an incentive to prevent the accident, each might make no investment at all. This would result in an avoidable cost of $800;

that is, the loss less the cheaper avoidance cost. The attempt to achieve an efficient level of accidents and safety can only be undermined by liability rules which enjoin the judge to assess the individual and relative culpability of the parties' conduct in each case.

Finally, at least as regards the claim of Derek against Allan, a word ought to be said about causation. This issue has created considerable consternation for Doctrin C.J., if not in this particular case, certainly in other cases. Also, Justice Wright, by making causation the fulcrum of liability, has had to grapple continually and inconclusively with this traditionally perplexing problem. All of this is unnecessary. Once the Learned Hand test is accepted as the basis for liability, the puzzles of causation can be solved with confidence. As Lord Reid observed, causation exists when the defendant's act increases the risk of injury to the plaintiff; see *McGhee* v. *N.C.B.*, [1971] 1 W.L.R. 1. In that case, the fact that an employer's failure to provide showers added to the risk that the plaintiff's dermatitis might develop was held to be a sufficient ground for liability. In strict terms, therefore, the probability of harm in the Hand formula is the difference between the probability that the accident will occur if the defendant is negligent and if the defendant is careful. For instance, in *Berry* v. *Sugar Notch Borough* 191 Pa. 345 (1899), the fact that the plaintiff was speeding when his car was hit by a fallen tree during a violent windstorm was not a cause of the accident as the probability of the accident occurring was the same whether he drove slowly or speedily. In the present case, Allan's failure to repair his headlight undoubtedly increased the chance of an accident by at least .001, as did Derek's failure to fix his brakes. This latter fact seems to elude Wright J. and undermine his whole fragile "background theory of rights."

Another dilemma for my judicial colleagues has been the duty to rescue. The "efficiency" account of the law offers a convincing and moral response. As the courts are slowly beginning to accept, there is no significant or meaningful difference between misfeasance and nonfeasance; see *Rowland* v. *Christian* 69 Cal. 2d 108 (1968) and *Spreacher* v. *Adamson Companies* 30 Cal. 3d 358 (1981). Furthermore, the courts and legislatures seem to be committed to extending the liability of potential rescuers; see *Farwell* v. *Keaton* 396 Mich. 281 (1976) and Utah Code Ann. § 41-29 to 31 (1953). The natural and obvious next stop is to establish a general duty to rescue. This advance will reflect and respect the moral and economic underpinnings of the common law. It is both inefficient and immoral for a good swimmer to be free to ignore cries of a drowning person; see *Gautret* v. *Egerton* (1867), L.R. 2 C.P. 371. In such circumstances, the costs to the swimmer are slight compared to the tragic and high costs of the drowning person. Nevertheless, it would be counter-productive to impose an obligation to rescue in all circumstances. It might, for instance, discourage people from becoming good swimmers or visiting the beach. Also, the incidence of rescue might decrease as such acts would no longer be seen as motivated by heroic altruism, but by fear of legal liability. However, as Martin could have at least telephoned for an ambulance at little or no cost and certainly at less cost than Allan, Derek or Charles, he must assume liability.

Doctrin C.J.'s refusal to establish such a duty of "easy rescue" is indicative of her pusillanimous approach to the judicial task. Further, she fails to appreciate the workings of the legislature. Legislative inaction does not necessarily mean a desire to retain the *status quo*, but can be interpreted as an indication that the legislature feels it is more appropriate for the courts to change the law; see *Alvis* v. *Ribar* 85 Ill. 2d 1 (1981). As regards the administrative problems, while they do present difficulties, they are of no greater magnitude than the initial question of liability under Doctrin C.J.'s approach. The most sensible distribution of losses is to have the original tortfeasor pay for the damages *as if* an early rescue had been effected and the "rescuer" pay for the remainder. In the present case, therefore, Martin would be responsible for the payment of a large portion of Derek's and Charles' damages.

Finally, Charles' claim for emotional distress can be easily and expeditiously disposed of. It is not so much a matter of liability as of proof; see *Molien* v. *Kaiser Foundation Hospitals* 27 Cal. 3d 916 (1980). Clearly it is difficult to imagine what cost-effective steps he could have taken to avoid injury. We can safely assume that they would outweigh the accident and avoidance costs of Allan, Derek or Martin. Liability, therefore, seems established. However, I do agree with Doctrin C.J. that we must be careful not to encourage or facilitate bogus claims. It is desirable that the law should march with medicine, "but in the rear and limping a little"; see *Mount Isa Mines* v. *Pusey* (1970), 125 C.L.R. 383 at 395. Nonetheless, in line with increasing medical sophistication, the courts have recently begun to recognize and accept broader recovery for nervous shock; see *McLoughlin* v. *O'Brian*, [1982] 2 W.L.R. 982 and *Sinn* v. *Burd* 486 Pa. 146 (1979). Accordingly, as cogent medical evidence was led, Charles ought to recover for his emotional distress.

In conclusion, therefore, I hold that Derek cannot recover against Allan, but that he ought to receive a significant amount of damages from Martin. Also Charles would be eligible for recovery of damages from Martin and Allan.

* * *

WRIGHT J.: As is often the case, I have the dubious distinction of following Justice Mill. It will come as little surprise to those who follow the proceedings of this Court that Justice Mill and I do not see eye to eye on the proper basis for compensation for injuries. The central thrust of my rejection of his scheme of compensation is that such matters are intrinsically questions of the moral entitlement of individuals in particular circumstances and not impersonal measurements of social utility. As Cicero said, "the study of law must be derived from the depths of philosophy"; see *De Legibus* i, 5. The resort to economic calculations does not take individuals seriously. Emphasis should be on individual liberty and not social welfare. When one person harms another, the injured has a moral right to demand and the injurer a moral duty to pay compensation.

The utilitarian ethic, espoused by Mill J., is incapable of furnishing sufficiently compelling reasons to deserve the allegiance and support of actual human beings. It demands that individuals' wants, desires and projects be submerged or discarded in the interest of utility maximization; they are to be treated as mere entries on the debit side of a society's moral accounts. Yet such tastes and preferences constitute an individual's moral integrity. Without these, individuals would cease to exist morally. Under a utilitarian regime, individual projects are simply resources for use in the general welfare and are liable to be acquired by others. Utilitarianism seeks to maximize benefits, regardless of their distribution throughout society. Individuals are robbed of any intrinsic merit or importance. Indeed, the sacrifice of individuals is not only permissible, but is often demanded and sanctioned.

The recent tragedy of some Pinto owners provides a topical and revealing illustration of the callousness of life under such an "efficient" regime; see *Grimshaw* v. *Ford Motor Co.* 174 Cal. Rptr. 348 (1981). A number of tort actions for death or injury had been commenced as a result of the explosion of Pinto fuel tanks in rear-end, low-velocity collisions. Ford carried out a cost-benefit analysis of whether to recall and reinforce the cars:

Benefit

> **Savings — 180 burn deaths, 180 serious burn injuries, 2,100 burned vehicles.**
> **Unit Cost — $200,000 per death, $67,000 per injury, $700 per vehicle.**
> **Total Benefit — 180 X ($200,000)   180 X ($67,000)   2100 X ($700) = $49.5 million.**

Costs

Sales — 11 million cars, 1.5 million light trucks.
Unit Cost — $11 per car, $11 per truck.
Total Cost — 11,000,000 X ($11) 15,000,000 X ($11) = $137 million.

If I understand Mill J.'s theory of liability, Ford not only made a good commercial decision, but adopted a commendable course of action. To have recalled the cars would have been to squander social resources. That corporations rest their accident prevention and compensation business strategies on cost-benefit analysis is deplorable. For the courts to sanction and clothe such operations with moral legitimacy is intolerable.

Fortunately, the courts are not so irresponsible as Mill J. would have them. In *Grimshaw*, the plaintiff received a total of $74 million in damages. The courts openly condemned such reprehensible conduct. Importantly, the court applied the principles of strict liability rather than the negligence standard. This points up a fatal flaw in Mill J.'s arguments. Not only does his liability scheme lead to a perverse decision, but it confounds his central claim that "economic efficiency" is the structural framework of the common law. On the contrary, it can be exposed as his own personal political preference and an unjust one at that.

Clearly, information costs undermine and reduce the potential internalization of accident costs. How are Derek and Allan to discover the avoidance costs of the other? His whole scheme assumes that everyone has information about everyone else's costs. Indeed, even Learned Hand J. conceded that "care is the only one ever susceptible of quantitative estimate, and often that is not"; see *Moisan* v. *Loftus* 178 F. 2d 148 at 149 (1949). At best, all risk quantifications are more impressionistic than precise. Moreover, at least in a theoretical sense, all risk is necessarily foreseeable and, therefore, one can place no limits on liability. No greater a supporter of utilitarian arguments than Posner J. has opined, while speaking of assessment of damages, that "the exactness which economic analysis rigorously pursued appears to offer is, at least in the litigation setting, somewhat delusive"; see *O'Shea* v. *Riverway Towing Co.*, 677 F. 2d 1194 at 1201 (1982). Indeed, the whole operation is artificial and counter-factual. The retrospective evaluation of the probability of something happening which has already happened is fanciful. The problem of applying the pseudo-scientific standard of "efficiency" to real-life problems is amply revealed in *Union Oil Co.* v. *Oppen*, 501 F. 2d 558 (1974). Furthermore, economic welfare is so protean a concept as to be able to justify as "efficient" a regime which determined beforehand the most likely cheapest cost-avoider in particular activities and held them strictly liable whatever the actual costs.

Also, although attitudes to risk in our society are not uniform, Mill J. seems to assume widespread risk-neutrality. But there exists an asymmetrical distribution of risk-aversion and risk-preference. For instance, large-scale manufacturers can afford to be relatively indifferent to risk as they can effectively spread and pass on anticipated losses. On the other hand, individuals tend to be risk-averse and are less able to plan for and off-set future losses. Mill J. seems to overlook entirely the maldistribution of both attitudes and exposure to risk. At the very least, the Learned Hand test would need substantial adaptation to affect these realities. Moreover, the very act of allocating and settling risk favours the risk averse. For instance, he offers no account of why we ought not to have a reverse Learned Hand test in which loss would be carried by the person who caused it unless there were sufficient reasons to shift it. As the Pinto fiasco demonstrates, this would effect a complete change in patterns of compensation. Furthermore, according to Mill J. the law provides incentives to individuals to organize their behaviour in accordance with the dictates of economic efficiency; they will be rational maximizers of their resources. In order to do this, of course, a major piece of information will be knowledge of what that law is. There is nothing to suggest that people do take the law into account in actually planning their daily lives, and what information does exist suggests that individuals do not consult legal materials before planning their activities.

A case that Mill J. relies on to support and substantiate his analysis, when read properly, exposes the disingenuousness of his approach. In *Bolton* v. *Stone*, [1951] A.C. 850, the plaintiff failed to recover after being hit by a cricket ball from the defendant's ground because the risk of such an accident was not sufficiently substantial. However, as the later case of *Miller* v. *Jackson*, [1977] Q.B. 966, makes clear, there is a hidden ordering of the social utility of the respective activities. Cricket occupies a special place in the hearts of Englishmen. It is not so clear that the courts would have reacted similarly if the cricket ground had been a water sports centre; see *Kennaway* v. *Thompson*, [1981] Q.B. 88. Under Mill J.'s scheme, all activities are accorded equal significance; the playing of cricket is considered at least as important as the right of individuals not to be injured.

There arises from these difficulties a conclusion that strikes at the root of any utilitarian argument. Although its rationale is to enhance and promote individual freedom, its operation reduces and neglects that liberty, forcing individuals to concern themselves with the projects and plans of others. Individuals deserve and merit respect simply as individuals. They are autonomous: they possess certain rights that cannot be overridden by appeals to general utility. Rights are trumps over social welfare. Individuals are not to be conceived of as a means by which to maximize social utility, but instead are to be treated as ends in themselves. What is needed is not a maximizing and collective principle, but a distributive and individualizing principle. The law must control the market, not be controlled by it. Individuals count. For Mill J., individuals only provide the raw materials for measuring the general welfare. Although rather overstatedly, Lord Scarman in *McLoughlin* v. *O'Brian*, [1982] 2 W.L.R. 982 at 987, emphasizes the priority of principle over policy:

> The distinguishing feature of the common law is this judicial development and formation of principle. Policy considerations will have to be weighed: but the objective of the judges is the formulation of principle. And, if principle inexorably requires a decision which entails a degree of policy risk, the court's function is to adjudicate according to principle, leaving policy curtailment to the judgment of Parliament. Here lies the true role of the two law-making institutions in our constitution. By concentrating on principle the judges can keep the common law alive, flexible and consistent; and can keep the legal system clear of policy problems which neither they, nor the forensic process which it is their duty to operate, are equipped to resolve. If principle leads to results which are thought to be socially unacceptable, Parliament can legislate to draw a line or map out a new path.

The imposition of legal liability ought to depend on moral entitlements as determined by causal enquiries. "Efficiency" is to be deplored for its casual nihilism. A deep sense of morality and rights pervades the common law. The Learned Hand test is, at best, a crude and misguided device to compromise and concretize individual rights. People are completely free to act, except when they cause harm to others. This moral principle is the driving force behind the common law and any system of tort must respect and implement such a moral notion. As Lord Dunedin said, liability is "to be determined by common-sense principles. What is the cause of the loss?"; *Leyland Shipping Co.* v. *Norwich Universal Fire Insurance Co.*, [1918] A.C. 350.

It would, of course, be ridiculous to pretend that negligence did not once form the backbone of accident liability. Yet, over recent decades, there has been a gradual movement from negligence to strict liability. The negligence principle was firmly established in *MacPherson* v. *Buick Motor Co.*, 217 N.Y. 330 (1918), notwithstanding decisions like *Rylands* v. *Fletcher* (1868), L.R. 3 H.L. 330. Strict liability began to reassert itself in *Escola* v. *Coca Cola Bottling Co.*, 150 P. 2d 436 (1944). On holding that a soda bottle manufacturer was absolutely liable for injury caused by a defective product, Traynor J., *id.* at 440 - 41, articulated the rationale for strict liability:

> Even if there is no negligence, however, public policy demands that responsibility be fixed wherever it will most effectively reduce the hazards to life and health inherent in defective products that reach the market. It is evident that the manufacturer can anticipate some hazards and guard against the recurrence of others as the public cannot. Those who suffer injury from defective products are unprepared to meet its consequences. The cost of an injury and the loss of time or health may be an overwhelming misfortune to the person injured, and a needless one, for the risk can be insured by the manufacturer and distributed among the public as a cost of doing business. . . .Against such a risk [of injury from defective products whether negligently manufactured or not] there should be general and constant protection and the manufacturer is best situated to afford such protection.

Since that seminal judgment, strict liability has begun to colonize and control accident liability; see *Greenman* v. *Yuba Power Products*, 377 P. 2d 897 (1963), and *Shaffer* v. *Victoria Station Inc.*, 588 P. 2d 233 (1978). Those cases which speak in the rhetoric of negligence achieve results more consistent with the dictates of strict liability. For instance, in *Hughes* v. *Lord Advocate*, [1963] A.C. 837, the defendants were liable for injuries caused by an explosion which the court accepted to be "so unlikely as not to be foreseeable." Also, in the Australian case of *Cuckow* v. *Polyester Products* (1970), 19 F.L.R. 122, the defendants could not escape liability for the death of the plaintiff by smoke-inhalation as a result of "fire-resistant" insulation material erupting in tremendous smoke when it "set alight." Throughout the law of tort, there has been a subtle, but profound shift in the structural foundations of the law. To recognize that change is to take a step much smaller and less controversial than that in *MacPherson supra*, or *Donoghue* v. *Stevenson*, [1932] A.C. 562.

The political morality that explains and shows the doctrinal materials in their best light is one centred upon the right of individuals to be secure against non-consensual invasions of their personal integrity. Fault amounts to an interference *per se*. The focus is rightly placed upon the activity rather than the defendant's conduct: the *what* happened is more important than the *how* or *why*. Within such a regime, causation becomes not *a* basis for liability but *the* basis. It is the fulcrum of liability. Not only does that make strong ethical sense, but accords with common sense and intuitive notions of fairness. While this might give rise to the occasional penumbral puzzle, it is clear that Allan was the cause of the accident in the present case. But for Allan's failure to repair his headlight, the accident would not have occurred.

No doubt, Doctrin C.J. and Mill J. will complain strenuously that this ignores Derek's contribution to his own misfortune. Yet it is surely an incontrovertible rule of the common law that the defendants take their victims as they find them; see *Smith* v. *Leech Brain &Co.*, [1962] 2 Q.B. 405 and *Watts* v. *Rake* (1960), 108 C.L.R. 158. While the condition of Derek's car may well have extended the causal chain, it does not alter the primary fact that Allan was responsible for setting the chain in motion. Such a determination is as simple as it is fair. Further, it avoids another doctrinal swamp into which Doctrin C.J. and Mill J. have allowed themselves to be lured; see *Daly* v. *General Motors Corp.*, 20 Cal. 3d 725 (1978) and *Overseas Tankship (U.K.) Ltd.* v. *Morts Dock and Eng. Co. (The Wagon Mound)*, [1961] A.C. 388. Also, the acceptance of a defence of contributory negligence would admit through the back door the very same utilitarian constraints on individual rights that were refused entry at the front. To use Derek's conduct to off-set Allan's liability is to set in motion a process that would ultimately lead to an erosion of Derek's rights. Although a sleeping passenger is more susceptible to serious injury than an alert one, it seems ludicrous to reduce the defendant's liability on this account; see *Sloan* v. *Flack* 150 So. 2d 640 (1963).

Both Derek's and Charles' injuries were caused by Allan's activities; if he had not acted as he did, there would have been no harm. The fact that Charles' injuries are emotional rather than physical is irrelevant. Once the court is satisfied, as Burke J. in *Battalla* v. *State of New York*, 10 N.Y. 2d 237 (1960), put it, of "the quality and genuineness of proof," there need be no further argument. It is illogical and unfair to hinge liability, as Doctrin C.J. seems to do, on whether the damage suffered is physical or emotional.

The refusal of the common law to recognize a general duty to rescue supports many of the arguments used to justify a regime of strict liability. Moreover, it offers further illustration of the perversity and uncertainty of Mill J.'s "efficiency thesis." As Jessup J. succinctly expressed it, "no principle is more deeply rooted in the common law than that there is no duty to take positive action in aid of another no matter how helpless or perilous his position is"; see *Horsley* v. *MacLaren*, [1970] O.R. 487. The imposition of a duty of care has depended upon the existence of some special relationship or the creation of risk; see *Racine* v. *C.N.R.*, [1923] 1 D.L.R. 924 and *South* v. *National Railroad Passenger Corp.*, 290 N.W. 2d 819 (1980). In other circumstances, there is no promise or commitment to act and, therefore, no expectation of rescue. To require gratuitous acts of rescue seriously infringes individual freedom. A similar principle animates other areas of the law. In contract, there is no general duty to co-operate, unless it is necessary in order to effectuate the exchange; see *Seaman's Direct Buying Service*

v. *Standard Oil*, 181 Cal. Rptr. 126 (1981). In a very real sense, the "rescuer" ought not to be liable as she did not *cause* the plaintiff's dilemma or damages.

A glance at the solution offered by Mill J. betrays the muddled and dangerous nature of his thinking. In general, the imposition of a duty to rescue underlines the fact that a person's own welfare is of no special interest; it must be discarded for the social good. The pauper might have to sacrifice his life to rescue the president. However, in the converse situation, the president might be acting irresponsibly to attempt a rescue of the pauper. Apart from its obvious iniquity, such a rule is unworkable as the rescuer must first ascertain the "worth" of the plaintiff before being able to ascertain whether there is a social obligation to perform or refrain from a rescue. Further, a rescue rule is a form of conscription into social service; the rescuer becomes an insurer for the fool-hardy, risk-preferring or powerful. An obliged rescue is tantamount to a forced exchange exacted by government. It operates as a tax and unjustly curtails individual liberty. Whereas a rescue rule leads to unjust results and renders it uncertain where liberty ends and obligation begins, a no-rescue rule is consistent with both moral *and* economic principle. In the present case, Martin would be free to engage in any rescue attempt he chose, but he would not be obliged to attempt any rescue. At least in my conclusion, I fully agree with Doctrin C.J. on this issue. However, I disassociate myself entirely from Mill J.'s decision. He has sown the wind and reaped the whirlwind. He has managed to contrive a decision that places almost exclusive responsibility upon Martin for the losses to Derek and Charles. The logic or fairness of such a distribution of liability completely eludes and defeats me.

However, I would like to conclude my judgment with some general remarks on why strict liability is to be preferred to the introduction of some no-fault compensation scheme, so ably and fondly espoused by Mr. Justice Prudential. I believe that strict liability comes out on top in any comparison based on the two major objectives of any scheme of compensation, its effectiveness in reducing accidents and its administrative costs.

As Mill J. states, any system of accident liability must create incentives that minimize accident costs and avoidance costs. In general, as everyone is a potential plaintiff or defendant, a move from one scheme to another will tend to shuffle incentives around rather than reduce the overall level of accidents. What a no-fault system loses in incentives can be made up for by the rigorous enforcement of a robust criminal law. But the ideal world is not the practical world. Unless a change is made in the criminal law and its enforcement, the introduction of a no-fault system will actually reduce the incentives. Although other legal systems, such as Sweden's, may manage to enforce vigorously and effectively the criminal law, Canengus has neither the appropriate substantive criminal law nor, it seems, the will to enforce it fully. Accordingly, a de-centralized system of private actions, based on strict liability, provides the most self-contained and realistic method to maintain and enforce the norms of optimal behaviour.

Prudential J. astutely notes that the costs of administering any tort system are considerable. Certainly under a negligence regime as proposed by Doctrin C.J. and Mill J., the uncertainty of the standard generates immense costs; see, for example, *Hammontree* v. *Jenner*, 97 Cal. Rptr. 739 (1971). A scheme of strict liability is not so vulnerable. Its focus of inquiry is narrow and clear; therefore, the frequency of litigation and its cost will be reduced. Moreover, if the present litigation process is streamlined, much of the cost of the reduced litigation can be pared down. Finally, under any scheme, the cost of hiring a physician to determine the actual damages in each individual case remains high.

In conclusion, therefore, I hold that Allan is responsible to Derek and Charles for the full extent of their damages. Martin is relieved of any liability.

* * *

PRUDENTIAL J.: The late F.R. Leavis wrote in his *New Bearings in English Poetry* (1932) at 17, that:

> [P]oetry can communicate the actual quality of experience with a sublety and precision unapproachable by any other means. But if the poetry and the intelligence of the Age lose touch with each other, poetry will cease to matter much and the age will be lacking in finer awareness.

I have read in draft the opinions delivered by my colleagues. Whereas Mill J., Doctrin C.J. and Wright J. allow intellect to operate unmitigated by poetry, Lefft J. indulges in a poetry that drifts free from intellect. My own solution to this appeal lies in forging a rapprochement between the actual quality of experience (partially, but cynically demonstrated by Justice Lefft) and the intellectual fervour of Justice Wright. It will become clear that I reject the sentiments espoused by Doctrin C.J. whose moral inquiry into the conduct of the parties distorts the real task with which this Court should be concerned. It is the plight of the injured plaintiff and not the conduct of the defendants that deserves our attention. The pseudo-intellectual rigour of Mill J. and his indifference to the fate of individuals in the march to improved social welfare fills me with despondency and horror.

On its face, the judgment of Wright J. has intuitive appeal; it seems ethical, practical and efficient. Yet, his central allocative device of causation is thoroughly unequal to the massive task he sets it. In practice, it amounts to a crude and cumbersome process of accident compensation. Justice Wright still lives in the Platonic realm of abstract justice. He is not only naive, but dangerous. Common sense is a notoriously unreliable source of guidance for practical affairs. In the pluralistic society of Canengus, its identity is vague and indeterminate, if not by design at least by inclination. Causation is a labyrinth for which Wright J. offers no realistic through-route. At bottom, he has to smuggle in basic value judgments as formal causal criteria. Recall the memorable words of Andrews J. in *Palsgraf* v. *Long Island Rly. Co.*, 248 N.Y. 339 at 352 (1928):

> Any philosophical doctrine of causation does not help us. A boy throws a stone into a pond. The ripples spread. The water level rises. The history of that pond is altered to all eternity: it will be altered by other causes also. Yet it will be forever the resultant of all causes combined. Each one will have an influence. How great only omniscience can say. You may speak of a chain, or, if you please, a net. An analogy is of little aid. Each cause brings about future events. Without each the future would not be the same. Each is proximate in the sense it is essential. But that is not what we mean by the word. Nor on the other hand do we mean sole cause. There is no such thing. . . .
>
> As we have said, we cannot trace the effect of an act to the end, if end there is. Again, however, we may trace it part of the way. A murder at Sarajevo may be the necessary antecedent to an assassination in London twenty years hence. An overturned lantern may burn all Chicago. We may follow the fire from the shed to the last building. We rightly say the fire started by the lantern caused its destruction.
>
> A cause, but not the proximate cause. What we do mean by the word "proximate" is that, because of convenience, of public policy, of a rough sense of justice, the law arbitrarily declines to trace a series of events beyond a certain point. This is not logic. It is practical politics. . . .

Causation is and must always remain a choice; see *Kinderavich* v. *Palmer* 127 Conn. 85 (1940). If we are to abide by general rules, we must be prepared for arbitrary results. Each accident is unique and demands a unique causal inquiry — "cause and effect find their beginning and end in the limitless and unworkable. . ., [h]ence arbitrary limits have been set"; see *Atlantic Coastline Rly Co.* v. *Daniels* 8 Ga. App. 775 (1911). Indeed, in the present case, which Wright J. acknowledges as simple and straightforward, it is unclear to me why "common sense" necessarily burdens Allan with the whole costs of the accident. Surely Derek *was* an "active" factor in the accident and Martin *might* have been. Within any compensation scheme based on fault, the conundrum of causation represents an insuperable barrier to the achievement of personal or social justice. Only a shift to a no-fault regime can overcome this impasse.

As for a "negligence" regime, adhered to by Doctrin C.J. and championed by Mill J., it is unclear why rules laid down in the days of the horse and carriage should continue to govern us today. Having witnessed a phenomenal increase in the scale and gravity of destruction and havoc which modern technology can wreak, Baron Bramwell's decision "*to put up with* such mischief as reasonable care on the part of others cannot avoid" is no longer acceptable; see *Holmes* v. *Mather* (1875), L.R. 10 Ex. 261 at 267. At the end of the second millenium, the victims of society's collective progress deserve more protection and compassion. The time has come in which obeisance to the benefits which the internal combustion engine have brought has to be accompanied by a recognition that we are also, if not rather, the children of a lesser god. Our society is not that which is dominated by subservience to either a thoroughgoing holistic or atomistic ideology. The law of torts may indeed be the paradigmatic law of the mixed society. It is our responsibility as Justices to ensure that the balance is correct.

The mixture as perceived by Beveridge in 1942 (*Report on Social Insurance and Allied Services* (Cmnd. 6904)) is in need of titration. We should add a touch of concern and compassion for our fellow human beings to the tort system and see what result is produced. But the hotch-potch of add-on or modified plans used to bolster up the private tort action needs comprehensive reconsideration and amendment. Such makeshift tactics can no longer be regarded as adequate. I cannot, of course, hope to canvass in the space of this short opinion all the elements of a wholesale replacement. My judgment today should be read as though a set of guidelines for a long overdue experiment in social reform.

As long ago as 1932, when other jurisdictions were remodelling their common law of tort around snails in bottles of ginger beer and exploding parcels, the Columbia Committee to Study Compensation for Automobile Accidents was completing its study which was to recommend that compensation for motor accident victims should be removed from the ambit of tort liability altogether. When the initiative was boldly taken to try to introduce a no-fault scheme in England in 1934, through the Road Traffic (Compensation for Accidents) Bill, the speeches that defeated that legislation might well and appropriately have spoken to the contemporaneous Lotteries Bill before the House. As *Donoghue* v. *Stevenson* wound its way to the House of Lords' judicial committee, so the *Jand'Heur* case was heading towards the plenary session of the Cour de Cassation, where they confirmed the impetus of the movement which had given rise to the prescription of strict liability in accident cases.

We now have an overwhelming body of statistical data that catalogues in precise detail the litigation lottery. The cost of accidents is astronomical. In Canada, for instance, out of a population of 25 million, 3.5 million sustain product-related injuries annually, 4,000 are killed and 11,000 permanently disabled. This amounts to losses of over $2 billion in product-related injuries alone. Of these victims, forty-five percent never recover anything. Further, only one percent reach the courts and most of those are settled on the courthouse steps. Over fifty percent of the compensation ultimately paid out is lost in administering and financing its recovery. These statistics are repeated in every common law jurisdiction, but, revealing as they are, they are the more disturbing when it is remembered that "negligence" is a feature endemic to modern life. Strong evidence suggests that a "good driver" makes about nine mistakes every five minutes; see 1 *Royal Commission on Civil Liability for Compensation for Personal Injury* (1978) at 210. Against such statistics, the efficacy of tort law as a compensatory or deterrent device is illusory.

Dissatisfaction with existing tort law is now a *universal* phenomenon. Committees, commissions, courts and commentators have railed for long enough. Unhappily, this court does not today speak with one voice. I refrain today from moving in advance of the legislature only after long, hard and sustained reflection. I have kept in mind what was said in the related context of vicarious liability by Lord Wilberforce in *Launchbury* v. *Morgans*, [1973] A.C. 127 at 136:

> I do not know on what principle your Lordships acting judicially can prefer one of these systems to the others or on what basis any one can be formulated with sufficient precision or its exceptions defined. The choice is one of social policy. . . . Whatever may have been the situation. . . in the youth of the motor car, it is very different now, when millions of people drive for a vast variety of purposes and when there is in existence a complicated legislative structure as to insurance — who must take it out, what risks it must cover, who has the right to sue for the sum assured. Liability and insurance are so intermixed that judicially to alter the basis of liability without adequate knowledge (which we do not have the means to obtain) as to the impact this might make on the insurance system would be dangerous, and in my opinion, irresponsible.

Today, I hesitate to remind the legislature that we are all better informed. The evidence that I intend to review is clear. Mill J. is correct to remind us that the judicial application of existing rules reaffirms and enforces previous policy choices. My view is that these old choices are no longer sufficient, adequate or desirable for contemporary society. As has been frequently said, the life blood of the common law is not logic, but common sense. However, it can also be its death-knell. To plod along as we have done, rather like the horse and carriage, treating automobile accidents within the same clumsy legal parameters as those of the nineteenth century is to fail to keep the law up to date. Yet, as if this tardiness is not enough, many suggest that only the legislature can step in. This is impractical and unnecessary. The difficulties of legislative action, of weighing and balancing competing political forces, is so great that even urgent law reform may be frustrated. Throughout our legal system, legislation overtakes and overwhelms the common law. For many, this may seem undesirable. But I think that this development brings with it hidden dangers and limitations of its own.

The age of statutes is upon us. The judiciary must respond, or at least belatedly acknowledge this shift. This does not mean a passive genuflexion to legislative wisdom. Judges must become constitutional partners in keeping the law in tune with contemporary society. The judicial timidity evidenced in cases like *Maki* v. *Frelk*, 40 Ill. 2d 193 (1968) does not benefit our democratic responsibilities. The common law must grow and develop with society. As the court concluded in *Alvis* v. *Ribar* 85 Ill. 2d 1 (1981):

> We believe that the proper relationship between the legislature and the court is one of cooperation and assistance in examining and changing the common law to conform with the ever-changing demands of the community. There are, however, times when there exists a mutual state of inaction in which the court awaits action by the legislature and the legislature awaits guidance from the court. Such a stalemate exists and the legislature has, for whatever reason, failed to act to remedy a gap in the common law that results in injustice, it is the imperative duty of the court to repair that injustice and reform the law to be responsive to the demands of society.

With their training and experience, the judiciary as a body may properly be entrusted with this democratic responsibility. It is not *the* responsibility, but an important one to prompt and, ultimately, to cajole the legislature to action. Of course, greater power correctly lies with the legislature than with the judiciary. But this does not mean that the legislature has exclusive power or that the judiciary is relegated to the role of constitutional ciphers.

My judgment today is a clarion call for action. It may give the legislature the opportunity for a second look, not a passive glance, but an active investigation. Failing this response, under our democratic duty to keep the common law alive, I propose that this court snatch accident compensation from under the crushing weight of the technological machine and establish it firmly in the driving seat of the law. Canengus must embrace and implement a thoroughgoing and comprehensive scheme of accident compensation.

The implementation of such a scheme is not a revolutionary or radical step. It simply approves of and makes universal a mode of relief that underpins the real world of accidents. Through a combination of compulsory and voluntary insurance schemes, society has generally considered it appropriate to spread the economic consequences of accidents over the whole community. Within such practices the search for negligent or strictly liable defendants is fictional and is really a weak attempt to control the aggregate sum payable by society. If loss-distribution is our intended goal, a patchwork of a tort system and private insurance is a less than efficient way to proceed. Beyond a certain point, the two are incompatible and hostile. Indeed the resort to insurance undermines the "rationality" assumptions of Doctrin C.J., Mill J. and Wright J. People lack sufficient ability to make rational judgments about accident prevention. Therefore, they insure if risk-adverse. Behaviour in the face of danger is not motivated by concern for personal safety, but for the financial consequences. Moreover, to seek, as Mill J. might, to explain differences in the distribution of accident insurance purchased as a function of individually optimal decisions is absurd. It reflects and corresponds to the maldistribution of information and resources. My plea is to introduce minimal levels of compensation below which we do not consider it morally justifiable to allow anybody to fall. Private insurance can still exist and prosper. Market forces can provide a cushion for the wealthy who fall heavily or awkwardly on the state safety-net.

To introduce such a scheme of comprehensive accident compensation, allied to a programme for the alleviation of the fiscal consequences of disease is a tall order for the Exchequer. But we would be less than candid if we failed to recognize, as Justice Lefft does, that the notion of communal responsibility is a two-edged sword. Not only does the community have a duty to safeguard its members, but it must do so in a way that best suits the community's interest. If the population is daily subjected to the dangers of modern technological life, it follows that its productive capacity is constantly at risk. To be sure, this requires me to equate the individual human being to a societal asset. But, because society views individuals as producing entities, any injury to a human being is a loss to society. The loss occasioned to the injured person cannot be recouped; it is a net social loss. Once it is conceded that this loss can *never* be made good, the problem becomes whether any one person should be required to bear the full impact of the loss. For instance, Doctrin C.J. perceives the harm suffered in a one dimensional fashion; the harm inflicted is solely on Derek. But it seems to me that where a person suffers injury, so does the economy. That amounts to a *real* social cost. Thus, the community has not only a clear duty, but a vested interest in urging forward the physical and fiscal rehabilitation of every person whose activities bear upon the general welfare. That is what maximizing social welfare truly means; it is not to be hedged in some limited or constrained utilitarian fashion nor swamped by some hedonistic fervour, but is a programme that eschews slogans and tokenism and encourages care and responsibility. If the net result of this proposal is that some minor injuries have to forego some compensation so that the most serious, lasting and debilitating injuries are fully compensated (the complete converse of the present system), if it means that there are those whose pre-accident earnings cannot be fully reimbursed from the state fund and they must forego the last few drops in order to allow the blood to flow more freely to all parts of the body politic, then so be it. There are no simple or perfect solutions, only difficult choices.

The most persistent argument made against "faultless" insurance schemes is that the deterrent effect of tort law is lost. I have never been persuaded of the efficacy of this deterrent function. For the law to be an effective deterrent, there must exist a correlation between the sanction and an individual's behaviour. Yet, while there may be a massive award of damages based on a minor deviation from the behavioural norm, there will be no liability, no matter how heinous the breach, so long as no one is injured. And, the prevalance of insurance as a means to spread the loss substantially diminishes the impact of tort law. Insurance, like an increase in oil prices, is merely another cost of doing business or owning a car. Allan knows this well. Furthermore, the existence of criminal regulation undermines the deterrence argument. Why would overworked legislators deliberate over and introduce manifold regulations to control careless conduct, if this merely duplicated results and outcomes already operational under a tort system? The probability of criminal sanction better encourages pre-accident safety measures than possible post-accident liability in tort.

The vision of social justice I have argued for will offend my colleagues. Mill J. will recall those "eccentric principles of socialist philanthropy" which so fatally offended his predecessors sixty years ago; *Roberts* v. *Hopwood*, [1952] A.C. 578 at 594. Lefft J. will be dismayed because an insurance scheme requires society, on behalf of injured persons, to enter the marketplace of compensation. But its strengths are that it makes some effort to recognize the levelling quality of injury and death. Within the structure of administrative bureaucracy, it seems to restore to the law of tort its paradigm nature in a mixed society and not, as would the despair of Justice Lefft and the agnosticism of Justice Mill, destroy it. They are equally in danger of losing sight of the mixed society which demands a mixed law. But, as I have said before, the mixture needs to be constantly checked and reviewed. Our natural and proper feelings of compassion for injured persons must not lead to a state guarantee against misfortunes of all or any kind which might bankrupt the strained resources of the Exchequer. Nor must our concern for fiscal logic neuter our compassionate response to injury. In a mixed society the lodestar of any such compensation scheme must be incentive to avoid injury, the natural descendent of the ethic which guided our troubled passage through the turbulent seas of the industrial revolution. We are too well schooled in that spirit for the utopian schemes envisaged by Justice Lefft. We must take into the post-industrial age some incarnation of essential principles which have served us well, but whose present forms have now outlived their usefulness.

There must be an incentive to recovery offered by effective rehabilitation. To encourage a return to productive and gainful employment, there must exist a fair margin of return on independent effort. This incentive must not itself be handicapped by the current favour for levelling state benefits or begrudging or denying effective help for long-term incapacity. Real compensation must be the goal. Full and adequate financial assistance, carefully tailored to the severity of injury, and to the needs of all people at whatever level of employment and every normal level of income, must be our aim. The result will be a system that will be able to provide a direction, an objective for individuals that will divert and subvert charges of state paternalism.

Naturally, any change in our present compensation schemes will depend ultimately on two things which have been implicit throughout my judgment: the cost of compensation to the community and its willingness to pay that price. These draft guiding principles are offered as a foundation for building such a scheme. First, it must be regarded and accepted as a matter of community-wide obligation that the community itself must bear responsibility for protecting all citizens who suffer sudden, individual, personal loss which impairs or interrupts their ability to participate fully in the life of the community. Of course, there would ultimately be no room for distinctions based upon accidental injuries as opposed to "natural" diseases; such categorization depends as much upon contemporary social mores as upon some rational, self-evident scheme. Radicals will no doubt object to this apparent relegation of the individual to a productive unit of society. But, no less than Mill J., that would seem to sacrifice the individual to the intellect. We all persist in following community activities; done for the benefits of all. Each year these activities, whether they be transport, manufacturing, leisure or whatever, exact a predictable and almost inevitable toll. Thus, we should all share in sustaining and nurturing those who become the random, but statistically necessary victims of modern life. That is the second face of community responsibility. From this flows the second guiding principle.

The coverage which such a scheme offers must be properly comprehensive. Injury, not cause, is at issue. I recognize that this raises in the most acute manner possible what is to be counted as an injury. Objectors will point to the potentially arbitrary lines which this formulation might require. I am sensitive to those criticisms, but they do not, for me, carry the day. These critics are the intellectual Luddites of the litigation system. Their objections are based either, in good faith, on the redistributive questions which accident compensation throws up or, more mischievously, on a secret desire to return to the formalities of a system of pleading which relied on trespass to the satisfaction only of lawyers and to the glorification of none. Both are mistaken. A comprehensive accident insurance scheme is such an enormous leap forward from our present haphazard, arbitrary and capricious tort scheme that it cannot and ought not to be jeopardized by the sensibilities of the radical reformers or the conservative critics.

Finally, comprehensive coverage is meaningless unless it provides *real* compensation. We have to look closely and carefully at how we define "need" in our system. Clearly, not every imaginable loss is one which ought to or need be compensated. However, we must recognize that physical injury or death has economic consequences above and beyond the injury itself. Commitments which most households accept today as regular and justifiable may have been considered luxuries in the recent past. It seems entirely appropriate that compensation keeps pace with the increasing affluence we enjoy today; a realistic assessment of compensation should take this into account. Justice, unless humanely and speedily rendered, is just a hollow tag if it fails to deliver people from the total consequences of misfortune following accidental injury.

Why have such schemes not been introduced if they are so desirable and workable? The answer is simple: there are no votes in accident compensation. Legislators daily make rules with little expectation that they will have any substantial impact upon people's lives; they are directed towards the winning of the next election. Accident victims are a diffuse class and lack an effective lobbying status. As has been astutely noted, "the average man is not greatly stimulated by potential difficulties: until they actually beset him he remains an optimist and a sturdy supporter of what is familiar"; see *Compensation for Personal Injury in New Zealand* (1967) s. 14. Like the New Zealanders, I believe the people of Canengus have begun to realize that accidents regularly befalling large numbers of their fellow citizens are not so much due to human error as to the complicated and uneasy environment in which we live. It is the risk of social progress; its cost ought to be shared among society. As Judge Fuchs said in *Montgomery* v. *Daniels* 38 N.Y. 41 (1975):

> I believe that the concept that the individual is the basic and ultimate unit in society must be supported by recognition of the value of one's physical, mental and emotional integrity, including freedom from pain and suffering and the ability to live an uncrippled life. The automobile, a modern bane and boon, daily threatens that integrity for millions of people.

It is now long past the time when our legal system ought to meet this challenge squarely.

There is yet the moral and legal dilemma of the rescue situation. Of course, the introduction of the proposed scheme ameliorates the situation of those injured. Yet it does not offer an exclusive solution to accidents. Our concern must be not only to compensate those injured, but to reduce the incidence of injury. The attempt to increase safety and reinforce moral standards of care through the tort system has been an unmitigated disaster. The appropriate device for such control is the criminal law. It focuses on and punishes behaviour that is morally culpable. The offences of careless driving and unhygienic preparation of food are obvious illustrations. Similarly, the failure to effect an easy rescue can be dealt with in this way. As in Vermont and Czechoslovakia, it ought to be a criminal offence to fail to rescue someone who is in imminent and serious danger when there is no serious danger to the potential rescuer; see Vt. Stat. Ann. tit. 12, § 519 (supp. 1971) and C.S.R. 1964, Oblansky Zakonik, ss. 415-19.

Not only is criminal law a more efficacious deterrent than tort law, but it encourages us to take a more caring, less alienated attitude towards our fellow citizens. As such, it is a natural corollary to a comprehensive insurance scheme. Anyone who is injured in a rescue attempt will automatically be compensated. Also, it seems entirely proper, and accords with common law morality, that the "rescuer" ought to be criminally liable whether or not the victim is injured as long as there existed a serious possibility of injury. Finally, we should not underestimate the moralizing power of the criminal law. Law must not only keep up with morality, but often is itself looked to for moral guidance by the less sure or weaker among us.

My support for the early implementation of a new compensation scheme has created a dilemma for me in disposing of the present case. Do I act today as a legislator and introduce such a scheme or give the legislators one last chance? Reluctantly, I have decided to stay my hand. This is not for fear of upsetting the insurance markets or because all existing mechanisms for compensation would grind to a halt. Rather, out of deep respect for our constitutional traditions, I defer to the legislators this one more time. Accordingly, I will uphold the decision of the lower court. The patent absurdity and inequity of that result is not lost on me. I can only hope it is not lost on others too.

* * *

LEFFT J.: The writing of this judgment has been an occasion of very mixed blessings. It is very sad in that it is the last judgment I ever intend to give. It concludes a legal career that I now view as being an embarrassing and inexcusable dissipation of energy and time. Yet it is an occasion of happiness for me as well. I have finally realized and come to accept the true nature of the enterprise that I have participated in as lawyer and judge for the past forty years. I have moved from the shadows into the light. I have stepped through the veil of my ideological ignorance and seen the existing world for what it is. What I see is extremely horrible, depressing and unnerving. Yet the fact that I now see things as they really are is cause for some hope. It is a small, yet important first step. The circumstances of my "conversion" may provide some explanation and offer some encouragement to others.

While strolling through Memorial Park recently, my attention was caught by a young group of enthusiasts, railing against our present society. They were distributing leaflets. Out of idle curiosity, I went over to listen and to accept a leaflet. The pamphlet contained a battery of staggering statistics and information: every minute the world spends $1.3 million on military objectives and thirty children die through lack of food or health care; one nuclear submarine costs more than the annual education budget of twenty-three developing countries with 160 million school children; the United States government paid farmers to take over forty million hectares of land out of production while 450 million people in the world starve. These figures went on in nauseating detail. As I left the Park, I walked through a run-down part of Ottlonwash. Ragged children played in the dirty streets asking me for money as I passed. Families lived in dilapidated buildings. People lined up at hostels for food and shelter. Deprivation and degradation were everywhere. The contrast with my own pleasant neighbourhood was stark and sickening.

That night and over the following days, I agonized over that experience. Whichever way I looked at it, I could not avoid the conclusion that I had previously rejected, but always feared; that the legal process is a major force in creating, sustaining and justifying our social situation. As organs of state power, the courts must accept their share of responsibility for the plight of the homeless and the poor. Judges hold in place the deep structure of society that sacrifices people for profits.

The vast paraphernalia of legal rights and entitlements amounts to nothing more than a sugar coating on a bitter pill. Although suffering and domination are rife within society, the ideal of governance according to the rule of law masks these offensive facts. Far from being a vehicle for social justice, the law represents a formidable barrier to significant social change.

The ideological potency of the law is subtle and profound. It contrives to be both friend and enemy. It persuades us that contemporary life is almost rational and just. Although there are blemishes and sores, this is the best there is. It is the natural and, therefore, inevitable form of social life. In the constant clash between individual interests and communal concerns, the law offers itself as a real and genuine compromise. The judicial process is portrayed as an objective and non-arbitrary enterprise, distinct from the naked power play of party politics. The judge becomes a passive conduit of an elusive rationality. A complex scheme of legal rights and entitlements controls the interaction of citizens; each is considered a rational and equal actor in the economic and moral order. The law claims to be neutral between individuals who self-interestedly determine their own social universe. Yet this simplistic process hides substantial and manifest injustice. The legal process places society in a condition of bondage. It is a powerful instrument of mystification that maintains the status quo; it operates so as to convince the oppressed *and the oppressors* of the relative freedom and inevitability of modern life. It breeds a false sense of moral security and political resignation. Yet its continued success depends on our acquiescence. Like Canengusian Railways, the legal and political process is sustained in bankruptcy by a sinister combination of naivety, self-interest and fear of alternatives; see, for example *Bromley L.B.C.* v. *Greater London Council*, [1982] 2 W.L.R. 92.

Of course, judges are not neutral or neutered political agents. Judgments are rationalizations of our ideological prejudices. The legal order is not a coherent moral scheme, but an elaborate regime to facilitate and protect concrete economic interests dressed up in doctrinal gibberish; see, for example *Rondel* v. *Worsely*, [1969] A.C. 191. The laws are perfectly egalitarian insofar as they allow both rich and poor to sleep under bridges; see A. France, *The Red Lily* (trans. W. Stephens, 1908) at 95. Furthermore, legal doctrine is an open-ended and indeterminate exercise. Law moves from one doctrinal peak to another through the misty vales of fiction. This is necessitated by the fundamental and often unconscious rationality of the contradictory relations which characterize and underpin the hierarchical society in which we live. Throughout tort law, two background and contradictory visions, individualism and collectivism, compete for control and manifest themselves in matching bundles of principles and counterprinciples.

For instance, tort law is generally based on broad individualistic principles. A person is only liable for what could be reasonably foreseen, albeit objectively ascertained; see *Overseas Tankship (U.K.) Ltd.* v. *Morts Dock & Engineering Co.*, [1961] A.C. 388. However, there exist certain counter principles which ensure that the less fortunate in society are not excluded from relief. The rule that a tortfeasor takes a victim as she finds him incorporates an element of communal concern to check on over-zealous adherence to individualistic principles; see *Smith* v. *Leech Brain & Co.*, [1962] 2 Q.B. 405 and *Marconato* v. *Franklin*, [1974] 6 W.W.R. 676. Similarly, in rescue situations, there is a robustly individualistic principle which does not require rescue, but this is being constantly eaten into by a communally-inspired requirement to act in cases of a special relationship; see *Mathews* v. *MacLaren* (1971), 22 D.L.R. (3d) 545. Insofar as traditional legal (and political) thought is premised on the necessary and realizable reconciliation of the competing interests of individuals and community, it would be the negation of its very *raison d'etre* to opt completely for either extreme. Doctrine vacillates. Neither legal logic nor policy analysts can provide objective guidance as to where doctrine ought to position itself along the continuum. As there is an in-built contradiction, there is no meta-solution; it is a matter of choice. Once a valid and necessary communal competent is admitted, it must be arbitrarily held in check or else it will consume the whole doctrine. At any time, the discrete legal pieces could be arranged into a completely different doctrinal jigsaw. Determinancy is contrived, superficial and ephemeral.

Although this enterprise is carried on in diverse, ingenious and sophisticated forms and often with genuine and well-intentioned sincerity, as the judgments of my former colleagues amply demonstrate, the judiciary cannot escape indictment in this grand affair. Doctrin C.J., Mill and Wright JJ. may be the chief culprits, but Prudential J. is fully implicated. Her criticisms of the others are valid as far as they go, but she remains firmly within this unfortunate tradition. Although variously expressed and disguised, their judgments are nothing more than a crutch for terminally ill society. Each one legitimates the tragic toll of human life in our industrialized society. They present accidents and injuries as an inescapable and natural feature of modern life. Life and death is treated as another commodity to be traded in our market economy.

This obscene reduction of people to a piece of property reaches its most egregious form in the arguments of Mill J. His bottom line is that it does not pay to be too careful. Indeed, he seems committed to the view that the taking of certain safety precautions will be unjust as they will squander valuable social resources. Also, it is ludicrous and despicable to talk of a market in accidents. The legal process is concerned with particular accidents and, if "efficiency" has any value, it is only over the totality of accidents; see *O'Shea* v. *Riverway Towing*, 677 F. 2d 1194 at 1201 (1982). Further, the very notion of "efficiency" is an anathema. We would not contemplate using "efficiency" to justify tortured confessions, slavery or baby markets, so why rely on it to determine the incidence of death and injury? While characteristically extreme, Mill J.'s supposedly rational scheme shows the political bias of his colleagues. Rationality is not a formal device, but embodies a deep structure of values. Although the courts would not enforce a $1 million bargain to undergo a .000001 chance of death, they would enforce the payment for a $1 bus ride which, statistically, offers a far higher risk of injury.

Nonetheless, the excesses of Mill J. must not be allowed to deflect criticism from his colleagues. All combine in their treatment of injury and death as economic events. Each accident is considered remedial by the payment of money. People are simply their property; their worth is measured by the value of that property. As Oscar Wilde might have said, "the law knows the price of everybody, but the value of nobody." For instance, the bulk of a damages award consists of a sum for discounted future earnings; see *Andrews* v. *Grand & Toy Alta. Ltd.*, [1978] 2 S.C.R. 229 and *Seffert* v. *Los Angeles Transit Lines* 56 Cal. 2d 498 (1961). This means that, for exactly the same injuries, an infant may get $100,000, a young adult $250,000, and a senior citizen $30,000. Clearly, a victim's worth is his income loss. Moreover, by preserving the income of claimants, it perpetuates the existing unequal distribution of wealth.

In all its guises, the whole process of accident compensation serves to dehumanize. It encourages the maker of Pintos to act as it does and, more, to claim moral and political legitimacy for its economic endeavours. Compensation for injury simply pays off our collective conscience. We can ignore the injured by pretending to have taken care of them, as typified by our attitude to rescue; see *Gautret* v. *Egerton* (1867), L.R. 2 C.P. 371. Our law reflects a profound indifference to life and suffering. The sentiments of Esher M.R. in *Le Leivre* v. *Gould*, [1893] 1 Q.B. 491 at 497 that "a man is entitled to be as negligent as he pleases towards the whole world if he owes no duty to them" still inform the law. In 1969, Breitel J. in *Tobin* v. *Grossman* 24 N.Y. 2d 609 (1969) held that a mother who did not see, but heard and came upon the aftermath of a bad accident to her son could not recover; "this is the risk of living and bearing children."

No matter how comprehensive or generous, compensation schemes only address part of the problem. They are all cure and no prevention. Compensation must be subordinated to safety and health. The overriding objective of the law must be to equalize risk throughout society and restore control of those risks to those who undergo the dangers flowing from such risks. Of course, it will never be possible to *eliminate* risk in our lives. But the second-best alternative is to ensure that all persons can decide the risks to which they are individually exposed. We must share risk collectively and equally. In place of the present unjust distribution, we must radically democratize risk-control. Achieving this objective demands a complete restructuring of all aspects of social life. The time to begin such an heroic effort is well past.

The first step must be to redistribute knowledge and information, for knowledge is power. The elite in our society hold a monopoly on knowledge which comprises the foundation and guarantee of its power. Indeed, this very assumption of information-deprivation is the motive force of Mill J.'s "efficiency" scheme. He treats transaction costs as a natural given rather than a political choice. The debacle of the Ford Pinto case illustrates the pernicious operation of a system based on an unequal distribution of knowledge. Moreover, the possibility of bargaining with a manufacturer over the safety of a car you wish to buy is fanciful. What does a consumer know of a product compared to its manufacturer? For instance, the purchaser of the thalidomide drug lacked adequate resources to discover information about it in order to make a truly informed choice about using it. The fact that the manufacturer possessed, but concealed the available information compounds the injustice; see H. Teff and C. Munro, *Thalidomide: The Legal Aftermath* (1976).

Throughout our lives we are constantly exposed to risk, but starved of proper information as to the extent of that risk. Moreover, exposure to risk is thoroughly maldistributed. White and blue collar workers do not face the same risk of injury. Whereas a manager of a quarrying company has a .004 chance of injury, a quarryman has a .098 chance; see 2 *Royal Commission on Civil Liability and Compensation for Personal Injury* (1978). Furthermore, the quarryman does not receive compensation for this exposure in his wages, but earns substantially less than the manager. As regards domestic injuries, incidence of injury depends on the quality of the product bought which, of course, is a function of wealth. In the instant case, Derek is more exposed to injury in his old jalopy than is Allan in his expensive sports car. Also, the level of environmental pollution to be endured is higher in poorer residential areas than in richer ones; there is a strong inverse relationship between smog levels and property values.

To remedy this unequal distribution of information and risk, we must administer a strong dose of democratization. As presently practiced, democracy is a sham and operates as a mild sedative or anaesthetic. It is an apologetic device for the prevailing power-structure. Participation is reduced to a formal and sporadic ritual. Political equality is rendered meaningless by economic inequality. Moreover, such notional participation is confined to governmental activity. Politics is not seen to embrace the exercise of private power and corporate decision-making. Insofar as government is suffocated by corporate and private power, popular participation has no impact on the real decision-makers. It merely allows contemporary social arrangements to be presented as the outcome of citizen choice rather than as the produce of elite imposition. The forums of popular choice — legislature and market — are deadlocked.

The offensive symbolism and injustice of modern democracy must be replaced by a substantive and just vision of democratic society. Democracy is much more than a formal theory of political organization; it is a potent way of daily life. It is not about process, but about action. Democracy means the greatest possible engagement by people in the greatest possible range of communal tasks and public action. Self-determination, individual freedom and personal involvement are the watchwords of the truly democratic culture. A genuine commitment to its unadulterated practice will represent the most powerful challenge to the hierarchical elite. For domination arises and thrives when people lose the sense that society and its institutional paraphernalia are created by people and can be changed by people. Furthermore, participatory democracy is addictive; it educates the political mind. As people begin to reclaim control over their own lives, they will develop an appetite and a capacity for more. Increased political engagement will create and sustain its own momentum. A system of democratic participation in *all* communal life exploits the vast untapped resources of popular power. The agenda of political debate and action is constantly being redrafted. While promoting the common and the communal, true democracy preserves the unique and the individual. In time, a profound and sensitive understanding of the dialectic tension between individual and community will emerge. Of course, there are no guarantees, but true democracy offers a chance that its stunted contemporary practice can never imagine or realize.

It is clear that the increasing public and private bureacratization of society places a divisive barrier of formal institutions between individuals. It dulls the democratic imagination and suppresses the participatory initiative. Further, it distances people from the political decisions which pervasively affect their lives. At every turn, citizens encounter non-democratic institutions. There is a prevalent feeling of impotence and hopelessness. Yet this very process of bureacratization opens up opportunities for democratic involvement. As both the dominant and dominated groups come to rely increasingly upon such bureaucracies, there emerges a shared focus for their opposing claims and objectives. Accordingly, the democratization of bureaucracy offers the possibility for meaningful control over the actual centres of social decision-making. Popular control over policy-making and risk-exposure is vital. In this struggle, the work of the environmental and anti-nuclear movements exemplify the present despair and the future hope. Excluded from the decision-making process, such activists testify to the true democratic spirit which, repressed and subdued for so long, strains for recognition and fulfillment. Aroused and unleashed, its power is sufficient to fracture the boundaries between bureaucracy and its constituencies and to bridge the gap between bureaucrats and citizens. To entrust such responsibilities to the judiciary is to strengthen the very boundaries and extend the very gaps that are to be removed. Sadly, the Orwellian dystopia is with us; his black prophecy has been almost tragically fulfilled. If 1984 is to be the dark year of the bureaucracy, let 1985 be the dawn of the movement toward a new democracy.

Finally, the notion of risk-sharing proposed is neither novel nor radical. Although its pervasive implementation would revolutionize society, its general validity is recognized and upheld by existing doctrine. Although artificially confined to medical situations, a clear feature of tort law is "informed consent"; see *Cobbs* v. *Grant* 8 Cal. 3d 229 (1972) and *Reibl* v. *Hughes*, [1980] 2 S.C.R. 880. Doctors are required to supply their patients with all the necessary and available facts of the material risks of a procedure in order for there to be intelligent consent. As the court declared in *Canterbury* v. *Spence* 474 F. 2d 772 at 780 (1972):

> The root premise is the concept. . . that "every human being of adult years and of sound mind has a right to determine what shall be done with his own body. . . ." True consent to what happens to one's self is the informed exercise of a choice, and that entails an opportunity to evaluate knowledgeably the options available and the risk attendant upon each.

This requirement rests upon a person's right of self-determination. Founded on the need to promote individual autonomy and to encourage rational decision-making, it is impliedly defended and espoused by all of my former judicial colleagues. Yet it remains arbitrarily and illogically confined to peripheral situations. If it were not held in check, it would consume the whole of the tort law. Its present constriction highlights the arbitrary character and deep indeterminancy of the law and reveals the illegitimate hierarchy of power its confinement serves to perpetuate and sustain.

In taking my leave of this court, I implore you to follow my lead. I dedicate my remaining years to this struggle. Humanity stands on the edge of the abyss. We must regroup and make good on our commitment to ourselves. Love and power must converge. We must give voice to the inarticulate speech of the heart. Victims of the world unite. In the eternal words of John Donne:

> No man is an Island, entire of itself;
> Every man is a piece of the Continent, a part
> of the main.
> Any man's death diminishes me,
> Because I am involved in Mankind;
> And therefore never send to know for whom the
> bell tolls;
> It tolls for thee.

BIBLIOGRAPHY

ABEL, *A Critique of American Tort Law* (1981), 8 Brit. J. Law & Soc'y. 199.

ABEL, *A Socialist Approach to Risk* (1982), 41 Md. L. Rev. 695.

ATIYAH, *Accidents, Compensation and the Law* (3rd ed., 1980).

BELOBABA, 1 *Products Liability and Personal Injury Compensation in Canada: Towards Integration and Rationalization* (1982).

BROWN, *Towards an Economic Theory of Liability* (1973), 2 J. Leg. Stud. 323.

CALABRESI, *The Costs of Accidents* (1970).

CALABRESI, *Torts - The Law of The Mixed Society* (1978), 56 Tex. L. Rev. 519.

CALABRESI AND HIRSCHOFF, *Toward a Test for Strict Liability in Torts* (1972), 81 Yale L.J. 1055.

CANE, *Justice and Justifications for Tort Liability* (1982), 2 Ox. J. Leg. Stud. 30.

CHAPMAN, *Ethical Issues in the Law of Tort* (1982), 20 U. W. Ont. L. Rev. 1.

D'AMATO, *The Bad Samaritan Revisited* (1975), 70 Nw. U. L. Rev. 798.

DWORKIN, *Taking Rights Seriously* (1979).

DWORKIN, *Is Wealth a Value?* (1981), 9 J. Leg. Stud. 191.

DWORKIN, *Political Judges and the Rule of Law* (1981).

DWORKIN, *Law as Interpretation* (1982), 52 Tex. L. Rev. 527.

ENGLARD, *The System Builders: A Critical Appraisal of Modern American Tort Theory* (1980), 9 J. Leg. Stud. 27.

EPSTEIN, *A Theory of Strict Liability* (1980).

EPSTEIN, *Automobile No-Fault Plans: A Second Look at First Principles* (1980), 13 Creighton L. Rev. 769.

FLEMING, *The Law of Torts* (6th ed., 1983).

FLETCHER, *Fairness and Utility in Tort Theory* (1972), 85 Harv. L. Rev. 537.

FRANKLIN AND RABIN, *Cases and Materials on Tort Law and Alternatives* (1983).

FRIED, *Anatomy of Values* (1970).

FRIED, *Right and Wrong* (1978).

GLASBEEK AND HASSON, "Fault - The Great Hoax," in Klar, ed., *Studies in Canadian Law* (1977) at 395-424.

GOLBERT AND LOWENSTEIN, *The Court and the Market Place: Who Should Regulate Whom?* (1981), 34 Baylor L. Rev. 39.

GRIFFITHS, *The Politics of the Judiciary* (2nd ed. 1981).

HUTCHINSON AND MONAHAN, *Law, Politics and The Critical Legal Scholars: The Unfolding Drama of American Legal Thought* (1984), 36 Stan. L. Rev. 199.

HUTCHINSON AND MONAHAN, *The Rights Stuff: Roberto Unger and Beyond* (1984), 64 Tex. L. Rev. (forthcoming).

ISON, *Accident Compensation* (1980).

KENNEDY, *Form and Substance in Private Law Adjudication* (1976), 89 Harv. L. Rev. 1685.

KENNEDY, *The Structure of Blackstone's Commentaries* (1979), 28 Buffalo L. Rev. 205.

LANDES, *Compensation for Automobile Accident Injuries: Is the Tort System Fair?* (1981), 11 J. Leg. Stud. 253.

LANDES AND POSNER, *The Positive Economic Theory of Tort Law* (1981), 15 Ga. L. Rev. 851.

LINDEN, *Canadian Tort Law* (1983).

LOWI, *The Politics of Disorder* (1971).

MANSBRIDGE, *Beyond Adversary Democracy* (1980).

MARCUSE, *One-Dimensional Man* (1974).

MENSCH, *Freedom of Contract as Ideology* (1981), 33 Stan. L. Rev. 753.

MCCLUNG, *In Defense of Reasonableness: A Critical Analysis of Monolithic Theories of Tort Law*, [1981] S. Tex. L. J. 1.

NEW SOUTH WALES LAW REFORM COMMISSION WORKING PAPER, *A Transport Accident Scheme for New South Wales* (1983).

NOEL AND PHILLIPS, *Torts and Related Law* (1980).

Note, *Stalking the Good Samaritan: Communists, Capitalists and the Duty to Rescue* (1976), 3 Utah L. Rev. 529.

NOZICK, *Anarchy, State and Utopia* (1974).

O'CONNOR, *The Democratic Movement in the United States* (1979), 7 Kapitalistate 5.

PATEMAN, *Participation and Democratic Theory* (1970).

POSNER, *A Theory of Negligence* (1972), 1 J. Leg. Stud. 29.

POSNER, *The Economic Approach to Law* (1975), 53 Tex. L. Rev. 757.

POSNER, *Economic Analysis of Law* (2nd ed., 1977).

POSNER, *Some Uses & Abuses of Economics in Law* (1979), 46 U. Chic. L. Rev. 281.

POSNER, *The Economics of Justice* (1980).

POSNER, *Tort Law: Cases and Economic Analysis* (1982).

PRIEST, *The Common Law Process and the Selection of Efficient Rules* (1978), 6 J. Leg. Stud. 65.

RAWLS, *A Theory of Justice* (1970).

AUST., REPORT OF THE NATIONAL COMMITTEE OF INQUIRY, *Compensation and Rehabilitation in Australia* (1974).

N.Y., REPORT OF THE NEW YORK DEPARTMENT OF INSURANCE, *Automobile Insurance . . . For Whose Benefit?* (1970).

Report of the Royal Commission on Civil Liability and Compensation for Personal Injury (Cmnd. 7054, 1978).

NEW ZEALAND, REPORT OF THE ROYAL COMMISSION OF INQUIRY, *Compensation for Personal Injury in New Zealand* (1967).

RUBIN, *Why is the Common Law Efficient?* (1978), 6 J. Leg. Stud. 51.

SAGOFF, *On Markets for Risk* (1982), 41 Md. L. Rev. 755.

STEINER, *Justification and Social Vision in Modern Tort Law of Accidents* (unpublished manuscript, June 1982).

STEINER, *Economics, Morality and the Law of Torts* (1976), 26 U. Toronto L. J. 229.

STEINER, *Putting Fault Back Into Products Liability: A Modest Reconstruction of Tort Theory* (1982), 1 Law & Phil. 419.

THOMPSON, *Whigs and Hunters: The Origins of the Black Act* (1978).

UNGER, *Knowledge and Politics* (1975).

UNGER, *The Critical Legal Studies Movement* (1983), 96 Harv. L. Rev. 561.

URSIN, *Judicial Creativity and Tort Law* (1981), 49 Geo. Wash. L. Rev. 229.

WEINRIB, *The Case for a Duty to Rescue* (1980), 90 Yale L. J. 247.

WHITE, *Tort Law in America: An Intellectual History* (1980).

A FINAL LETTER

Allan C Hutchinson[1] and Derek Morgan[2]

What a generous invitation! I am delighted to make a small contribution to your symposium. Although I am not as strong or fervent as I once was (and, if truth be told, spend a large part of my energy simply 'raging against the dying light'). I welcome the opportunity to share some of my modest thoughts on the related events and developments in the law of torts generally and accident compensation more specifically of the last quarter century.

Having glanced through the Derek case in the past weeks and annotating it, I returned to re-read the whole – though not in the order in which the judgment was originally drafted and written – on Saturday morning in a more salubrious cafe some mere seven miles removed from Francis Minchella's cafe where the facts of May Donoghue's now notorious case are alleged to have occurred. It took about an hour to read and to annotate sketchily. It reminded me, as it were, that while art may be short, work is long, but that that work is the art of selection as much as of reflection. We judges are engaged in the construction of hard cases and borderline cases, we make them in the way we select and recount salient facts; review and discount 'applicable' norms; and then weave our own legal threads into the garment that we have designed

What did I find there? Three questions, at least; two assumptions, four typos, and one, maybe two, possible mistakes. And, of course, a number of reflections and reservations were prompted.

First, it is hard to believe that twenty-five years have passed since the judgment in the rather run-of-the-mill Derek and Charles v. Anne and Martin. We are all older, but if my own experience is anything to go by, not necessarily any the wiser. Although I have sought to resist the fall-back temptation of the older author, it does seem to me that the truth of Jean-Baptiste Kar's epigram plus ca change, c'est plus ca meme remains more telling than ever. There has been a lot of 'chatter' (judicial and academic), but very little action for the better when it comes to tort law. We are

[1] Distinguished Research Professor, Osgoode Hall School of Law, Osgoode Hall University.

[2] Sometime Professor of Law, The University of Sheffield, and Editor, The Journal of Professional Negligence.

running on the spot, utilising much intellectual effort, but getting nowhere fast. It is not a very edifying condition.

However, I am both delighted and despondent with the knowledge that this judgment of the Canengus Supreme Court has achieved such notoriety that it warrants recollection and even celebration so many years later. The fact that it is used as both fodder for the academic mill and as a teaching tool for young lawyers is both a blight and a blessing. I am genuinely flattered that people think it retains a certain relevance and can still open up readers' eyes to the problems and plights of tort law and common law adjudication generally. However, its continued usage confirms to me that we have not really come very far in the intervening years and made much of a success of addressing, let alone resolving, the problems that pervade both enterprises.

With that said, what can I offer? Having read and re-read that case and the contributions of my colleagues, I was more than slightly embarrassed by the rather self-righteous and almost sanctimonious tone of my own contribution. It would seem that I had a very high opinion of my own importance and clearly thought that I was making a grand gesture that would stir my colleagues, myself and the rest of the legal world to make some significant changes in what they did. This, of course, was a pious hope.

Nevertheless, although suitably chastened by age and further experience, I still hold to much of what I said in my judgment. I might have expressed it in less alienating and slightly more accommodating terms, but I think that my fit of pique likely served some purpose, if only as an outlet for my own sense of disillusionment and felt need to do something. Since then, I have sought in my writings and public actions to remain true to that commitment to making the world and its legal community a better place. That I have not done close to enough or had sufficient impact is something that I have to live with.

Even though a quarter century has passed, how little has changed. The ghosts of poverty are ever-present. Nearly half of all human beings presently live in severe poverty; many of them fall far below that threshold: people of colour, women and the very young are heavily over-represented among the global poor. Almost a billion people are chronically under-nourished and lack access to safe water; more than two billion cannot rely on basic sanitation and essential medicines are out of their reach. Illiteracy is rampant and children are obliged to work as soldiers, prostitutes, or domestic servants. These circumstances are depressing and are getting worse, not better.

What is equally depressing is that extreme forms of poverty exist not only in the Third World, but also in so-called 'advanced' and wealthy societies like Canengus and other similar societies. Nearly one in ten Canengusians experienced conditions of 'absolute poverty' without basic human necessities such as enough food, safe drinking water and proper sanitation. And a similar number live in conditions of relative poverty and deprivation; it is the old, the young, and single parents who carry the heaviest burdens. The gap between the haves and the have-nots continues to grow wider. This is an affront to all decency and an insult to humanity.

I still tend to agree with what John Maynard Keynes (now slightly back in favour after being intellectually exiled by the Chicagoan marketeers) said almost 100 years ago that "we assume some of the most peculiar and temporary of our late advantages as natural, permanent, and to be depended on, and we lay our plans accordingly." Moreover, "on this sandy and false foundation we scheme for social improvement and dress our political platforms, pursue our animosities and particular ambitions." Lawyers, judges and jurists do not seem to appreciate (or simply refuse to accept) that the judgments and processes in the Derek case have built on the same sandy and false foundations. We continue to contribute to that state of affairs if we proceed with mere hand-wringing at these unpardonable facts. It may be that prevailing economic regimes need the poor, but moral communities do not. As stark as it seems, the legal community is contributing to perpetuating this travesty as long as it fails to do something significant and sustained to change things.

Many will find this implied vision of the judges as moral and political activists to be very much beyond the pale. I obviously do not. The voice of the judiciary is moral and political whether it likes it or not. The only choice is about what morality and whose interests it wants to serve. There is no place of neutrality or indifference to stand. Like other political actors, the judges have a singular responsibility to forge a moral identity that is worthy of their power and influence. To do otherwise, as many of my colleagues did in Derek, is to institutionalize Hannah Arendt's notion of the 'banalization of suffering'. It is the privileged position that courts claim in our system of governance that behoves them to assume this crucial role and hold communities up to a better vision of themselves. There can be no more noble or fitting ambition than to defend and promote the values of a common humanity. This applies in the doctrinal details of tort doctrine as much as it does in the grander issues of constitutional politics.

When courts engage in the arena of moral politics, as they must, the questions of boundaries become important; there is a prima facie understandable caution in straying from the High Court to the High Court of Parliament and into the High Street. The currencies of legitimacy and credibility mean that judges cannot afford to be thought of as toxic assets on the ideological balance-sheet of democratic politics. However, the Canengus judiciary seems to have frittered away much of its political capital by granting a much higher credit-rating to the courts in the new moral economy of rights-based adjudication. Like so many other countries, Canengus has adopted a Bill of Rights with all its attendant institutional paraphernalia. That some judges have invested this new capital more keenly or rashly than others should be no surprise; there have always been 'brave souls' and 'timorous spirits'. But even the most bold of judicial spirits has refused to utilise their dubious powers to greet the moral clarion-call of poverty's eradication. If they are to have any chance of gaining the support of their citizens, they must act to enhance the welfare, in its broadest sense, of all those who are presently disempowered and disenfranchised (except in the most formal terms). Judges can only help to make politics safe for democracy by instantiating the kind of civic dialogue and action that is needed. Any other way of proceeding is a betrayal of themselves and the society that they represent. Judges need to reconfigure law so that it sharpens, not dulls the 'conscience' of society, a task I set out to accomplish in my judgment in Derek but lacked, as I now see, the moral will to complete, choosing instead to resign my commission and abandon my responsibility to the wider social interests that I was trying to articulate.

As for academic lawyers, I offer my comments and suggestions with even greater hesitation. I have followed the agonies of legal scholarship from the relative sidelines in the past few decades. The American professor, Bruce Ackerman, famously noted that "philosophy decides cases and hard philosophy at that." This strikes me as both a challenging insight and also a dangerous distraction. It seems to me absolutely correct that it is impossible to resolve difficult cases without some resort to a broader set of principles and values; the idea that judges can get by without appreciating the broader theoretical context in which a case or legal doctrine falls is badly mistaken. The only choice is whether you are to have a genuine and defensible knowledge of what your animating theory is or not. Any craft worth its name has to be guided by some more general vision or ambition of social justice. As that quotable jurist, Karl Llewellyn, opined "technique without ideals is a menace; ideals without technique are a mess." And, I would add, that they are not simply a mess, but also a menace. But, even though a resort to hard philosophy is inevitable it also self- deluding to think that such theories can relieve judges of the painful burden of choosing. At best, philosophical theories can provide an important context or orientation with which they can frame and answer the problems that cases throw up at them. What they cannot do is to lead from abstract elucidation to practical resolution in one fell swoop. As another American, the inimitable Oliver Wendell Holmes, Jr., said, "general propositions do not decide concrete cases." There are many staging-posts from reflection to decision and so many variables to consider. It is little more than a sleight of the hand to propose or pretend that 'philosophy decides case' of its own exclusive and unaided motion. Judges must be philosophers, but they must also be practical men and women of the world. Like all other realms of human interaction, philosophy is one more venue where vested interests, special affiliations and other local enthusiasms are given universal clothing. Law does not need dogma, philosophical or otherwise, but a more pragmatic sensibility and hands-on bent. If I may so, that is exactly why my former colleagues Justices Mill and Wright went so awry.

One theorist who seems to have grasped this is the prolific scholar, Cass Sunstein. He recognises that the retreat to philosophy will not resolve much. As tort law shows, there are almost as many philosophical theories on offer as there are theorists. So, instead of withdrawing to some lofty aerie of pure philosophy, he recommends that progress can be made if we settle for a more modest climb and occupy a ledge on which those who disagree at a greater height can nonetheless find sufficient commonality closer to the ground. Not surprisingly, this innovation has appealed to common law judges and jurists. These 'incompletely theorized agreements' can afford a temporary relief, but their lasting appeal is more elusive. They tend, if I may mix my metaphors, to fall in that uncomfortable spot between an abstract rock and a practical hard place. It only works when there is already ample uniformity and conformity between the philosophical high-fliers; there is no real space for genuine conflict in this middle-of-the-road ideology. It is a band-aid that does little to heal the real source of conflict.

In the face of these salutary truths, it would seem that judges have little choice but to go on doing what they have always done – trek from one case to another in the hope that they will stumble upon some temporary nostrum that will get them out of the doctrinal binds that they so often find themselves in. And the fact is that this might be the best that we can do. If we look for greater consistency or coherence, we will be forever condemned to the hellish fate of other disappointed or frustrated absolutists. Somewhat perversely, I now realise that, for all my criticisms of the judicial process and my premature retirement from it, there is no other mode of practice that can do much better than the common law format.

Rather than see the common law as a fixed body of rules and regulations, it is preferable to view it as a living tradition of dispute-resolution. Because law is a social practice and society is in a constant state of agitated movement, the common law is always an organic and hands-on practice that is never the complete or finished article; it is always situated inside and within, not outside and beyond, the society in which it arises. In short, the common law is or should be a work-in-progress -- evanescent, dynamic, messy, productive, tantalizing and bottom-up. The common law is always moving, but never arriving, is always on the road to somewhere, but never getting anywhere in particular, and is rarely more than the sum of its parts and often much less. And judges play the role of its itinerant travelers-cum-guides. But – and this is a very large 'but' – this is not to be taken as a complete or uncritical vindication of the status quo. Much less is it a recantation of my earlier criticisms. Far from it. If we are to make good on this depiction of the common law, we must appoint men and women who understand this and who bring to it a wealth of not only legal experience, but also social sensitivity and political insight. [The great judge is not someone who knows more about law than anyone else. Not only do we need judges who are humble and honourable, but also those who are committed to advancing a set of values that are compatible with the best traditions of a truly human and humane society. A great judge should be acclaimed because of their values, not in spite of them. The difficulty comes of course when we come to address what those values are and how they compete one with the other, or one set of values with another set. There is a powerful illustration of the irresolvable difficulties that competing moral and philosophical values pose for common law adjudication in the recent High Court of Australia litigation of Cattanch and Harriton, cases involving so-called 'wrongful life' actions

Actions for wrongful life, as they have come unfortunately to be styled encompass various types of claim. These include claims for alleged negligence after conception, those based on negligent advice or diagnosis prior to conception concerning possible effects of treatment given to the child's mother, contraception or sterilisation, or genetic disability. This distinguishes such claims from those for so called wrongful birth, which are claims by parents for the cost of raising either a healthy or a disabled child where the unplanned birth imposes costs on the parents as a result of clinical negligence. Two of the more controversial cases to have reached the High

Court in the past decade are Cattanach v Melchior where the Court, by a narrow majority (McHugh, Gummow, Kirby and Callinan JJ; Gleeson CJ, Hayne and Heydon dissenting) acknowledged recovery for wrongful birth. In the second joined appeals of Harriton v Stephens and Waller v James; Waller v Hoolahan the Court overwhelmingly precluded a 'wrongful life' claim (Gleeson CJ, Gummow, Hayne, Callinan, Heydon and Crennan JJ; Kirby J dissenting). Both cases raised issues around the sanctity and value of life and the nature of harm and the assessment of damages, Harriton and Waller both involve three questions. First, how is the loss in a 'wrongful life' case to be characterised? Is the 'loss' indeed properly regarded as 'life'? Second, once that loss has been characterised, does legal principle or public policy permit recovery? Third, if principle or policy permit recovery, is that loss capable of being ascertained. Of course, these three questions are not considered in isolation from each other – for example, the characterisation of the loss and the views on public policy are obviously interlinked. In Harriton, Crennan J, giving the leading judgment, emphasises the need to preserve the coherence of legal principles ironically using aspects of policy to do so.

In Cattanach, McHugh and Gummow JJ observed that the law should not shield the appellant doctor or hospital from 'what otherwise is a head of damages recoverable in negligence under general and unchallenged principles' for what was a breach of duty of care by Dr Cattanach. They argued that what was wrongful was not the birth of the child but the negligence of Dr Cattanach. Hence, as future expense was a reasonably foreseeable loss, albeit financial, it was recoverable. A similar view was also taken by Justice Kirby. Justice Hayne in dissent acknowledged that financial expenses associated with a child were reasonably foreseeable, but rejected any notion that this automatically entitled parents to recover, arguing that it was against public policy to encourage parents to assert that their child represented a net burden. Justice Heydon also appealed to public policy considerations; child-rearing costs should not be recoverable as this would transform children into objects and create a 'commodification' of life. Chief-Justice Gleeson appealed to international instruments protecting the rights of the child to support this same conclusion while Justice Heydon believed such 'commodification' would be contrary to human dignity.

In a phrase that was later to be reflected on in Harriton and Waller at greater length, responding to the appellant's argument that it was wrong to try to place a value on human life 'because it is invaluable – incapable of effective or useful valuation' - McHugh and Gummow replied that it would be wrong

– simple but wrong – to call upon values such as the importance of respecting human life to conclude that that should shield the appellants from the full consequences in law of Dr Cattanach's negligence. Similarly, it was inappropriate to require set off of the benefits that the Melchior's could be expected to enjoy from the birth and development of the child, as the financial damage directly consequent upon damage to the physical interests of Mrs Melchior were an unrelated head of damage. The Court had been urged to follow a distributive justice approach that requires a focus on the just distribution of burdens and losses among society, as held in the English House of Lords decision in McFarlane v Tayside Hospital Board. There Lord Steyn had argued that 'tort law is a mosaic in which principles of corrective justice and distributive justice are interwoven and in situations of uncertainty and difficulty a choice has to be made between the two approaches.' In Cattanach the High Court narrowly settled on the corrective justice approach, without recourse to subjective judicial notions of community conscience. The community conscience has spoken loudly since however, as, responding to political lobbying from the powerful medical professional organisations in Australia, each state jurisdiction has passed legislation reversing the effect of the High Court's decision.

Harriton and the conjoined case of Waller involved claims for so-called 'wrongful life,' previously derided in a leading English case as entailing the conclusion that 'to impose such a duty towards the child would, ... make a further inroad on the sanctity of human life which would be contrary to public policy.' Alexis Harriton was born 25 years ago with severe physical and intellectual disabilities; she is blind, deaf, has mental retardation and physical disability. She is unable to care for herself and will require continuous care for the rest of her life. She argued that all this could have been avoided or averted if her mother, who had rubella during the first trimester of pregnancy, had been properly advised, which it was accepted that she was not, thus allowing her lawfully to terminate the pregnancy. The doctor's failure to order a second blood test on the appellant's mother led him wrongly to advise that the illness with which she had been suffering had not been rubella.

Keeden Waller (K), on the other hand, was born following his parents use of IVF. Mr Waller had a low sperm count and poor motility; examination disclosed that he also suffered from a blood disorder known as anti-thrombin or Factor III deficiency, the effect of which is to raise the likelihood that blood will clot in the arteries and veins. It was agreed that had the Waller's been told – which they were not – that the AT3 deficiency was genetic they would have either deferred undergoing insemination until methods were available to ensure only unaffected embryos were transferred, or used donor sperm or terminated an affected pregnancy, such as K's Soon after birth K was diagnosed as suffering from a cerebral thrombosis as a result of which he suffers permanent brain damage, cerebral palsy and uncontrolled seizures. He sued the IVF practitioner, the diagnostic service that analysed K's father's sperm and a specialist obstetrician to whom K's mother was referred after embryo transfer for antenatal care arguing in each case that, but for the negligence of the defendants [comma here] he would not have been born suffering with disability. The High Court finally dismissed both claims and in each case both cases by a majority verdict 6 -1. Justice Crennan, in Harriton and Waller, wrote the leading judgment; Kirby J was the sole dissentient in both appeals. Crennan J (with whom Gleeson CJ, Gummow and Heydon J agreed in both cases) advised that the two main issues in H's appeal were whether there was legally cognizable damage and secondly whether there was a relevant duty of care. Even if both these questions were answered affirmatively, she would have apparently denied the suit 'if calculating damages according to the compensatory principles was virtually impossible ... .' Crennan J observed that to superimpose a further duty of care on a doctor to a foetus (when born) to advise the mother so that she can terminate a pregnancy in the interest of the foetus in not being born, (which may or may not be compatible with the same doctor's duty of care to the mother in respect of her interests), has the capacity to introduce conflict, even incoherence, into the body of relevant legal principle.

Kirby J in contrast contended that what is involved is an "unremarkable" case of a medical practitioner's duty to observe proper standards of care when the plaintiff was clearly within his contemplation as a fetus, *in utero*, of a patient seeking his advice and care. He cautioned against the use of the 'emotive slogan' of 'wrongful life' and, as he sees it, the importation of 'contestable religious or moral postulates.' The reality of the 'wrongful life' concept is such that a plaintiff both exists and suffers, due to the negligence of others. A further disagreement coloured the approaches to the question: 'what is the damage in a 'wrongful life' suit'? According to Hayne J the relevant question, and problem, is that in order for the appellant's life to be viewed as an "injury" or "harm", 'it is logically necessary to compare her life with another person' and not, as she had contended with not having been born at all. 'It is because the appellant cannot ever have had and could never have had a life free from the disabilities that she has that the particular and individual comparison required by the law's conception of "damage" cannot be made.' Crennan J suggests that the appellant's argument that her life with disabilities is actionable clashes with arguments about the value (or sanctity) of human life and evoke 'repugnance.' It is 'odious and repugnant' to devalue the life of a disabled person by suggesting that such a person would have been better off not to have been born into a life with disabilities But this is to mischaracterise the debate. The plaintiff in a wrongful life action does not maintain that his or her existence is wrongful. Nor does the plaintiff contend that his or her life should be terminated. Rather, the "wrong" alleged is the negligence of the defendant that has directly resulted in the present suffering.

This much seems to be at the heart of the acknowledgement by McHugh and Gummow in Cattanach that what was wrongful was not the birth of the child but the negligence of Dr Cattanach. As alternatively expressed in Waller, "'wrongful life" actions do not literally involve the complaint that life per se is wrongful. As in everyday personal injury actions, the complaint rather is that particular suffering and loss caused by the tortfeasor is legally wrongful. As Tony Weir has nicely expressed it; to damage is not always to make worse in the law of tort; '… it can consist of not making things better when there was a duty to do so.' The fact that the doctor did not cause the rubella damage does not mean that he did not cause the plaintiff to suffer under the rubella damage. What is 'wrongful' is not the life but the life of foreseeable suffering in the event of breach of a duty of care. This is not a wrong with no name; it is a wrong with the wrong name.

The legal action is a limited exercise constructed only in order to attempt to recover damages to support the life that is now being lived, one which, as described, involves total dependence and continuing care, a life of suffering. This case is, evidently, as with many torts cases, about other and wider issues than the presenting issue; it is about who cares, literally and metaphorically, for Alexia Harriton. 'It is hard to see, as Justice Kirby puts it, how an award of damages to a severely handicapped or suffering child would 'disavow' the value of life or in any way suggest that the child is not entitled to the full measure of legal and nonlegal rights and privileges accorded to all members of society. The hope expressed in the majority judgments is that that will be done by or provided for by the state, rather than the insurance company standing behind Dr Stephens. Yet daily, we read of the general reluctance of all publics to pay for state of the art treatment and care for those who really need it; in terms of health care dollars, we want more and more for less and less. In everyday life there are those who live – literally and metaphorically – on the edges of existence. In this world, the Alexia Harriton's of our societies are likely to be towards the back of a very long queue. That is not, of course, the same as saying that they should be at the head of it. But the metaphysical argument that the High Court constructs and then eschews (life v non existence) are no more than a convenient screen deflecting away from the core issue; should an admittedly negligent insured doctor's insurers be asked to absorb the costs of the long term consequences of the negligence, or should that be left either to general taxation or the private and philanthropic interest of the appellant's family and friends?

In Waller Crennan J (with whom Gleeson CJ, Gummow and Heydon JJ again agreed) averred that the plaintiff alleged that the defendants caused or materially caused his life with disabilities, flowing from the implantation of the embryo 'which became him,' by failing to investigate and advise his parents that the AT3 deficiency was liable to be transmitted to offspring. It was agreed that such advice would have enabled the parents to make lawful decisions about starting or continuing the pregnancy which would have resulted in K not being born. According to Crennan J the claims involved an assertion that it would have been better if he had not been born, 'irrespective of whether the conduct about which he complains occurred prior to, or during, his mother's pregnancy with him.' That this is not legally cognisable damage, was held in Harriton. Justice Hayne (concurring) said that there was no relevant damage and Callinan J added that Waller (like Harriton) 'cannot be heard as a matter of logic, to say that he "should never have been brought into existence", in which event he would not have been able to say anything at all.'

Again Justice Kirby was straightforward in his explication of the relevant law: 'the established duty of care which health care providers owe to the unborn in respect of pre-natal injuries requires the exercise of reasonable care in investigating risks of disability that might afflict prospective children and warning those in relevant relationships with the provider of such risks.' K was 'unquestionably foreseeable' and vulnerable to the consequences of the defendant's negligence. The first and second respondent 'enjoyed special control' over the circumstances that occasioned the damage caused. And none of the public policy arguments 'furnishes a convincing reason for refusing to provide relief for which ordinary negligence doctrine would otherwise provide.' The strongest argument against recognising a duty or imposing liability if it were breached, Kirby acknowledged, is that comparing existence with non-existence is an impossible exercise because it would involve unknowables or immeasurables, incommensurables as it were. But as Kirby objects in both Harriton and Waller 'these cases demonstrate that this is not so.'

From Cattanach, Harriton and Waller we learn that while birth is not always a blessing for those caring for the born, life is always a boon for the person living it, irrespective of the cost or burden of that life to or on others. There is something in these cases – especially Waller and Harriton – that discloses much about the nature of common law adjudication, and, incidentally, of modern medicine. In applying what he calls the ordinary principles of the law of negligence to Waller, Kirby J comes closest to an appreciation that IVF and its associated genetic technologies are part of an industry – a very particular and special industry to be sure – that operates on commercial lines. And that industry is heavily backed by insurance and services for which consumers are willing to pay. For some, that might in itself be thought to be a cognisable moral objection to the practices of IVF and genetics; that increasingly it looks like the child is being treated in some way as a commodity (not just as a means to another's ends in the Kantian formulation – at least no more than any child may be when conceived) IVF may itself be a part – a large part – of the commodification of the child, but a child who is no less loved and valued by its parents when it is a member of their family. In other words the commodification or commercialisation of part of the process of conception does not deleteriously affect the child after its birth. In the same way in the 'wrongful life' cases, the reality of a case such as this is that the wrongful life action like that of wrongful birth 'are about money rather than love or family feelings.' And, the High Court has held, there is no ground for believing that upholding a claim for damages following the birth of a healthy but originally unwanted child is likely to do any more to commodify that child as a matter of law rather than unwarranted social sentiment (or values) that the Court was not prepared to admit to the bar. Strange then, that it does precisely that in Harriton and Waller, relying on the emotional linguistic appeal of the notion of wrongful 'life' rather than as Kirby suggests the less negatively valued - laden (but not value free) notion of 'wrongful suffering.' In the first case the damages are awarded for the unlooked for expense of damage flowing directly from the physical harm to the mother in the unwanted pregnancy and childbirth, a fact virtually indistinguishable from the real harm in Harriton.

The changing catalogue of the doctrine of sanctity of life in the library of the common law, holds now that it should be shelved below other valuable principles, notably autonomy and in some libraries human dignity. This fundamental shift is a steady and growing if sometimes reluctant acceptance that life may be sometimes more of a burden than a benefit. This has found notable judicial expression in the past two decades in cases such as those involving the dying of patients in persistent vegetative state, of the withholding or withdrawal of treatment from severely disabled adults and neonates and from the terminally ill, and of the judicial authorisation of operations when the known or sometimes intended result is that one person will die, as in the sanction of operations on conjoined twins. These legal confrontations of the endings of life, notably in England & Wales in the case of Airedale NHS Trust v Bland (1993), are almost paradigm cases of the incommensurability of values. Each evidences a radical rethinking of the doctrine of the sanctity of life in modern law, and is one of the most significant shifts in the common law for centuries, if not, arguably, ever.

Whatever its rhetoric, however, the common law has never in fact been umbilically joined to the sanctity of life doctrine. The tort law system itself is one of regulating risk; certain activities entail risks that may be outweighed by the benefits resulting from them to the community as a whole. 'It is no less plausible to assert that rather than treating life as sacrosanct, the courts are inexorably involved in a system which cheapens life by exposing some lives to threat for comparatively trivial rewards for other people.' As Guido Calabresi has taught, the law of torts entails choices in everyday life. Cases at the edges of existence are sometimes thought to demand as much judicial precision as achievable in the controversy at bar, yet they disclose some of the fundamental values at stake in a legal system. It is unsatisfactory, then, to approach these cases as an exercise in misreading based on mislabelling.

So, in closing, I thank you for presenting me with this opportunity to share these few thoughts with you. In particular, I offer my apology for not having conveyed to you a more enlightening and compelling set of insights. However, I see little that gives me any great optimism that the next twenty-five years will be much different than the previous twenty-five years. As the English causation cases of Hotson, and others, show, the judges still put abstract principle above social justice it is a sad and wasteful process. Hotson tells us much that we need to know about the common law: principle is prioritised, but there is no escape from politics; indeed the invocation of principle impedes social progress and serves sectional interests. We will continue to make our way through the fog that rolls in from the shores of the future. At a minimum, it is our judicial duty to ensure that we do not add to that murkiness with intellectual smog of our own making.

I ended my judgment in Derek with a few words from John Donne. I will close now, if I may, with the more daunting words of James Fitzjames

Stephen. The tone is more gloomy and downbeat, but no less compelling for that:

"We stand on a mountain pass in the midst of whirling snow and blinding mist, through which we get glimpses now and then of paths which may be deceptive. If we stand still, we shall be frozen to death. If we take the wrong road, we shall be dashed to pieces. We do not certainly know whether there is any right one. What must we do? 'Be strong and of a good courage.' Act for the best, hope for the best, and take what comes. Above all, let us dream no dreams, and tell no lies, but go our way, wherever it may lead, with our eyes open and our heads erect."

Yours truly,

Derall Leftt

References

B Ackerman, Private Property and the Constitution, (1977) at 5
C Sunstein, 'Incompletely Theorised Agreements,' 108 Harvard Law Review 1733(1995)
International Covenant on Civil and Political Rights 1966, arts 23 and 24. International Covenant on Economic, Social and Cultural Rights 1966, art 10. Convention on the Rights of the Child, 1989, art 18.
Cattanach v Melchior (2003) 77 ALJR 1312,
MacFarlane v Tayside Health Board [2000] 2 AC 59
Curlender v Bio-Science Laboratories 165 Cal Rptr 477 at 488 (1980) per Jefferson PJ
G Calabresi, 'The Law of Torts and the Evil Deity' in, Ideas, Beliefs, Attitudes, Values and the Law, (1985) at 1
Harriton v Stephens [2006] HCA 15
Waller v James; Waller v Hoolahan [2006] HCA 16
J M Keynes, The Economic Consequences of Peace, (1919) at 1
K Llewellyn, 'On What Is Wrong With So-Called Legal Education' 35 Colum. L. Rev. 651, 662 (1935).
Justice Holmes, Lochner v. New York, 198 U.S. 45 (1905) (in dissent)
J F Stevens, Liberty, Equality, Fraternity, (1873)
Hotson v East Berkshire HA [1987] AC 750

THE TORTOLOGICAL QUESTION AND THE PUBLIC-PRIVATE RELATIONSHIP IN TORT LAW

TT Arvind*

1. Introduction

Part of the enduring value of Hutchinson and Morgan's 'The Canengusian Connection'[1] lies in the light it sheds on how significantly scholars or judges' theoretical views shape their views as to what the outcome of a particular tort case should be, and just how much these theoretical positions can diverge. Through the words of the Canengusian judges, Hutchinson and Morgan explore a number of points on which tort theories diverge – including the purpose of tort law, the principles that inform it, the interests it protects, and the manner and extent to which it assigns blame and transfers responsibility for wrongs to another.

However, quite apart from the issues on which the judges directly speak their minds, 'The Canengusian Connection' also sheds significant light on an issue which none of the judges directly addresses, but on which each of them nonetheless implicitly takes a strong position – namely, the question of whether tort law's essential nature should be seen as being purely private, or whether it should be seen as being principally public. Both positions have long pedigrees and vocal defenders, both amongst the Canengusian judges and amongst academics in the real world. The proponents of the private approach argue that tort law is entirely private in that it remedies harm caused by one individual to another through providing a private right of action.[2] The proponents of the public approach, by contrast, argue that tort law is primarily public, in that the actions it provides and the rights it protects have the effect of allocating risk and of shaping conduct by incentivising or disincentivising particular types of action and hence,

* York Law School, University of York. email: tta500@york.ac.uk. I am grateful to Richard Mullender and Lindsay Stirton for their comments on earlier drafts of this essay. Any errors that remain are my own.

1 Allan C Hutchinson and Derek Morgan, 'The Canengusian Connection: The Kaleidoscope of Tort Theory' (1984) 22 *Osgoode Hall Law Journal* 69–113.

2 The classic examples of this approach are theories centred around the idea of corrective justice. See e.g. Jules Coleman, *The Practice of Principle* (Oxford: Clarendon Press, 2001); Allan Beever, *Rediscovering the Law of Negligence* (Oxford: Hart, 2007)

ultimately, affect society more broadly.[3] There is also a middle way, adhered to by some tort theorists which holds that tort law should be conceptualised in a more pluralistic way as incorporating elements of both private and public purposes.[4]

In this essay, I argue that Hutchinson and Morgan present an accurate overview of the range of academic positions on the public-private relationship in tort law, but fall significantly short of capturing the complex nuances of the positions taken by common law judges on this relationship. This oversight highlights a serious lacuna in modern tort theory, namely, the failure of tort theorists to engage with the position – repeatedly expressed by the senior judiciary – that tort law intrinsically combines public and private aspects, and to do so in a manner that encompasses a broad range of sources and perspectives.

I elaborate on this lacuna through a comparison with the debates surrounding a particular issue in Christian theology, namely, the combination of human and divine natures in Christ. Christian theologians often speak of what they call the 'Christological question,' traditionally presented in the words of the gospel, as Christ asking 'Who do you say I am?'[5] Its central point, however, is understanding what it means to say that Christ is both wholly man and wholly God, and what it means to say that these two natures meet and are united in his person.[6] Most Christian theologians agree that the Christological question lies at the heart of Christian theology, and many theological differences were traditionally depicted as having their roots in differing Christologies, for the manner in which one understands who Christ is will necessarily determine what we understand his significance for the individual believer to be.

---

3 The classic example of this approach is the law and economics school. See e.g. Richard A Posner, *The Economic Analysis of Law*, 6th edition (New York: Aspen Publishers, 2003) 383-385, Steven Shavell, 'Liability for Accidents', chap. 2 in: A.M. Polinsky and S. Shavell, editors, *Handbook of Law and Economics* (Amsterdam: Elsevier, 2007) 139–182

4 For instance, those who argue that tort law should be seen as incorporating elements of both corrective and distributive justice. See e.g. James Gordley, *Foundations of Private Law: Property, Tort, Contract, Unjust Enrichment* (Oxford: Oxford University Press, 2006)

5 See e.g. Jacques Dupuis, *Who Do You Say I Am? Introduction to Christology* (New York: Orbis Books, 1994).

6 Oliver Crisp, *Divinity and Humanity: The Incarnation Reconsidered* (Cambridge: Cambridge University Press, 2007) 1-5, 118-20.

The problem of the private-public relationship in tort law can be conceptualised through an analogous question – which I here call the 'tortological question' – that, like the Christological question, ought to be at the centre of tort theory. As several scholars have pointed out, tort law can only be understood if we acknowledge that it is both wholly private and wholly public, and that it is consciously so, because through the history of tort law, both its private and public aspects have been deliberately made use of by legislatures and judges.[7] It is the fact that these two very different natures can, and frequently do, combine in one institution that creates the dilemma of tort theory. The private nature of tort law pushes it in the direction of doing justice on the facts of a case, of a focus on moral principles and of flexibility; the public nature of tort law pushes it in the direction of setting principles which guide the conduct of individuals in society, of an express focus on regulating conduct by promoting the desirable and acting against the undesirable, and of a focus on policy.[8] The thrust of the tortological question, then, is to understand the extent to which, and the manner in which, these two natures actually combine in modern tort law, and what this combination means for our understanding of tort.[9]

In the following pages, I present a tortological reading of 'The Canengusian Connection' and of the trends in modern tort scholarship on which it is a commentary. I seek to make three points through this reading. First, I seek to demonstrate that the differences between the judges as to the purpose and content of tort law are rooted in profound differences of tortology, which represent fairly accurately the varying tortological positions prevalent in modern academic scholarship. Secondly, I argue that the positions taken by the Canengusian judges also illustrate several problems with modern tortology, most importantly, the limited range of tortological positions it takes, its refusal to expressly consider the tortological question, and the growing divide between judicial and academic perspectives on tortology.

7 See e.g. Steve Hedley, 'Looking Outward or Looking Inward? Obligations Scholarship in the Early 21st Century', in: Andrew Robertson and Tang Hang Wu, editors, *The Goals of Private Law* (Oxford: Hart, 2009) 193–214

8 Hanoch Dagan, 'The Limited Autonomy of Private Law' (2008) 56 *American Journal of Comparative Law* 809–833 at 811-819.

9 In the following discussion, I equate the 'private' tendency in tort law with the aspects of Christology oriented towards the 'divine' aspect of Christ, on the basis of the strong tendency towards transcendental arguments found in that school. Similarly, I analogise the 'public' tendency with the aspects of Christology oriented towards the 'human' aspects of Christology on the basis of its tendency to historical and empirical argument.

Finally, I draw upon twentieth century typologies of Christology and the Christological theories of Dietrich Bonhoeffer to examine how we might articulate a more nuanced theory of the law of tort.[10]

2. Modern tortology and 'The Canengusian Connection'

Although the tortological question is rarely expressly asked, most theoretical work in tort law implicitly takes a position on the question in the course of discussing the nature of tort law. Unlikely in Christology, however, positions in tortology tend to cluster around the extremes. At one extreme, we have certain theorists of the corrective justice school who, in an argument that would have been worthy of Eutyches,[11] declare that tort is wholly private, and that to impute even a semblance of public character to it violates its integrity and renders it incoherent. Any public purposes it may seem to serve are fully subsumed within the private, and to endow them with an existence independent of the private is to fundamentally misunderstand the form of tort law:[12] whilst tort law may *enable* the pursuit of public goals, it is not *about* the pursuit of public goals.[13] Not all who see the nature of tort law as being principally private see this type of corrective justice as being at the heart of tort law – some scholars prefer to view it as a means for vindicating rights against their wrongful infringement,[14] or of protecting the interests of one against encroachment by another[15]. All, however, agree that the nature of tort law must be sought in analysing the manner in which it relates the claimant with the respondent.

---

10 Dietrich Bonhoeffer was a priest and theologian in the German Lutherean Church in the inter-war period. In addition to his theology – regarded as one of the most original of the 20th century – he also played a leading part in organising church and civic resistance to Hitler. He was executed by the Nazi government in 1945.

11 Eutyches of Constantinople, the chief proponent of what eventually came to be known as the Monophysite heresy, took the Christological position that Christ had only one nature - divine - and that any humanity he seemed to have was fully subsumed within the divine.

12 Ernst Weinrib, *The Idea of Private Law* (Cambridge, MA: Harvard University Press, 1995).

13 See e.g. Jules Coleman's discussion of whether tort law can properly be said to have a risk-spreading or insurance function Jules Coleman, *Risks and wrongs* (Cambridge: Cambridge University Press, 1992) 207-208

14 Robert Stevens, *Tort and Rights* (Oxford: Oxford University Press, 2007).

15 Peter Cane, *The Anatomy of Tort Law* (Oxford: Hart, 1997).

At the other extreme, we have the neo-Arians of the law and economics movement,[16] to whom tort law is entirely about the regulation of behaviour through providing appropriate incentives and disincentives with a view to achieving an efficient distribution of resources. This, they argue, is the primary function of tort law. Any private purposes are at best incidental to, or side-effects produced by, this overarching goal.[17] Once again, not all tort theorists on the public end of the tortological spectrum assign such a prominent role to efficiency. Others see the goal as being permitting private enforcement of legal rules,[18] a combination of risk-spreading, loss-distribution, and loss-prevention,[19] or even a mix of different policies reflecting the "desires and interests" of the general public.[20] But all are agreed that the key to understanding the nature of tort law is to analyse the intersection between its domain and the domain of the broader social or public interest.

Our views as scholars on whether the character of tort law is principally public or private, and of the precise private or public goals it serves, have a significant influence on the manner in which we describe, interpret and apply the rules of tort law, as well as our normative views as to which rules are desirable and which are not. The Canengusian judges follow this pattern. Like many modern tort theorists, they do not directly engage with the question of the public-private relationship in tort law, but a reading of their texts can nonetheless reveal a lot about their views and, in the process, about modern tort scholarship.

Doctrin J, for example, tells us that issues of policy are for the legislature, and not for judges. The separation of powers demands that judges not search for whatever principles may lie behind or be immanent in the rules of

---

16 Arianism, based on the teachings of Arius of Alexandria, denied that Christ had two natures, and took the Christological position that Christ was a created being - not an eternal one - of the same substance as other created beings and lacking the divine attributes of God. Law and economics, similarly, rejects the idea that tort law can have any transcendental or purposes of the sort championed by proponents of the private perspective, but must be seen as simply a political human institution no different from other political institutions.

17 See e.g. William Landes and Richard Posner, *The Economic Structure of Tort Law* (Cambridge, MA: Harvard University Press, 1997).

18 Edward Rubin, 'Punitive Damages: Reconceptualising the Runcible Remedies of Common Law' (1998) *Wisconsin Law Review* 131–156.

19 Guido Calabresi, 'Some Thoughts on Risk Distribution and the Law of Torts' (1961) 70 *Yale Law Journal* 499–553.

20 Leon Green, 'Tort Law Public Law in Disguise' (1959) 38 *Texas Law Review* 1–13.

law. Their job is simply to determine what the rules are and intelligently apply them.[21] What does this tell us about Doctrin J's views on the private-public divide? Quite a bit. Although Doctrin J's name might suggest that she speaks for doctrinal scholarship generally, her views in reality represent only one side of what is a deep divide within doctrinal scholarship, one whose origins lie in the public approach and whose popularity has been on the wane in Commonwealth jurisdictions as the popularity of more private-oriented approaches has risen. The roots of the divide go back at least as far as the late eighteenth century, but they become most visible in the mid-nineteenth century in the form of two competing approaches taken by treatises about tort law. These are best embodied, respectively, in the tort treatises of Charles Addison[22] and Fredrick Pollock.[23]

Addison's *Wrongs and their Remedies* was the first book on English tort law (it had been preceded a few years earlier in the US by a work by Francis Hilliard). Tort law, Addison declared in the preface to the first edition of his work, was concerned with the invasion of legal rights, and its object was "the protection of our property, and the security of our persons and reputation."[24] Having made this point, Addison concerned himself no further with attempting to detect any general principles – instead, he presented a litany of torts, subject by subject, whose only connection with each other, as far as the book tells us, appears to be the conjunction of a wrongful act and legal damage.[25]

Addison's approach is quite clearly rooted in the Austinian theory that law is simply a command issued by the sovereign, backed by the threat of a sanction, and entirely separate from morality. As such, it belongs to the public end of the spectrum: the state chooses to provide a party with an action in tort for its own purposes, and it is for the courts to give effect to that, not to enquire into the nature or desirability of those purposes or even what they might be. Doctrin's position is that of Addison, and as such it presents a sharp contrast with the dominant approach in contemporary doctrinal scholarship in the Commonwealth, namely, the approach begun by

21 Hutchinson and Morgan (n. 1) 71.

22 Charles Greenstreet Addison, *Wrongs and their Remedies, being a treatise on the law of torts* (London: Stevens and Sons, 1860).

23 Frederick Pollock, *The Law of Torts: a treatise on the principles of obligations arising from civil wrongs in the Common Law* (London: Stevens and Sons, 1887).

24 Addison, *Wrongs 1st ed* (n. 22) i-vii.

25 Charles Greenstreet Addison, *Wrongs and their Remedies, being a treatise on the law of torts*, 2nd edition (London: Stevens and Sons, 1864) 1-17.

Peter Birks and continued by others of his school which, in its Romanist influences and search for organising taxonomic principles, belongs firmly within the private-oriented approach to the nature of tort law.[26]

The Birkisian approach to tort has, however, much in common with the approach taken by Pollock. Pollock, and others of his school, deeply disliked Addison's strong positivism. Holmes' review of Addison's book in the *American Law Review* was unfavourable. He criticised the book's lack of cohesion and its organisation, and said that the subject could only be treated properly by a writer who could deal with it philosophically.[27] Pollock was even more scathing – in a review of Winfield's *Province of the Law of Tort* written some years after Addison's death, he dismissed Addison as someone "for whose judgment nobody now cares a farthing", declared that Addison's "book on Tort was only less bad than his book on Contracts," and went on to take a swipe at those "who see nothing but shreds and patches in the law of civil wrongs."[28]

Unlike Addison, the framework of whose treatise evidences no search for any overarching principle in tort law, Pollock's chief concern was identifying precisely such a principle, which he found in Ulpian's *alterum non laedere*[29] and the Church Catechism's 'hurt nobody by word or deed' (both expressed, he stressed, as legal and not moral principles).[30] Pollock was not the first to advocate such an approach – Francis Buller had taken a very similar view nearly a century previously in his treatise on Nisi Prius.[31] Nor was it the only candidate competing to be named the underlying principle of tort law. William Jones had in 1781 argued that the common law should be understood in terms of a tripartite division of standards of liability, analogous to the divisions of Roman law (and, although he does not mention it, also to the approach that came to be codified in the *Allgemeines Landrecht*, the late 18th century Prussian code of laws prepared by Fredrick

26 See e.g. Peter Birks, 'Definition and Division: A Meditation on Institutes 3.13', in: Peter Birks, editor, *The Classification of Obligations* (Oxford: Clarendon Press, 1997) 1–35, esp. pp. 2-4, 21ff.

27 Oliver Wendell Holmes, 'The law of Torts. By C.G. Addison, Esq.' (1871) 5 *American Law Review* 340–341 at 341.

28 Frederick Pollock, 'The Province of the Law of Tort. By Percy H. Winfield' (1931) 47 *Law Quarterly Review* 588–589 at 589.

29 Pollock, *The Law of Torts* (n. 23) 9.

30 Pollock, 'Province' (n. 28) 589.

31 Francis Buller, *An Introduction to the Law relative to Trials at Nisi Prius* (London: C. Bathurst, 1772) 35.

the Great and Fredrick William II).[32] Jones' approach enjoyed a brief period of popularity and continues to have its proponents to this day, but it is Pollock's approach that is characteristic of the private approach in modern doctrinal tort scholarship in the common law world, down to his emphasis on Romanist sources.

The two judgments that follow Doctrin J's in 'The Canengusian Connection' also follow on from these two threads within doctrinal scholarship. Mill J follows in the tradition of Addison – from the perspective of tortology, he is Doctrin J. without the latter's insistence on the separation of powers, and it is only to be expected that he and Doctrin J agree on so much in their respective judgments. Like Doctrin J, his judgment places him firmly at the public extreme of the tortological spectrum. Unlike Doctrin J, however, he does not conceal his position behind the mystery of the law. Negligence, he argues, fulfils an important social function. This social function, the purpose of tort law, he declares, is to promote the efficient allocation of resources in society.[33] The way to do this is by minimising risk and uncertainty at a level that encourages individuals to take the "socially efficient level of precautions."[34] Legal rules should be framed and applied in a manner that achieves this purpose.

Mill J's argument is framed in terms that, to the modern reader, invoke the early work of Richard Posner and the law and economics movement that grew out of it. The approach itself, however, is much older. As Englard points out, the direct ancestors of the economic approach to law are the late 19th century works of Otto van Gierke and Victor Mataja,[35] and can be traced back even further to the utilitarians (as Mill J's name was probably intended to suggest). The economic approach is, of course, not the only theory that regards tort law as being mainly public in nature. Other public-oriented approaches that have been popular in the twentieth century include Roscoe Pound's sociological jurisprudence, accounts that focus on tort law's role as a means to achieve distributive justice in the Aristotlean sense,[36] or

32 Jones, Buller and their relationship to early nineteenth century legal thinking are discussed in David Ibbetson, *A Historical Introduction to the Law of Obligations* (Oxford: Oxford University Press, 1999) 164-174.

33 Hutchinson and Morgan (n. 1) 82.

34 *Ibid.* 79.

35 Izhak Englard, *The Philosophy of Tort Law* (Aldershot: Dartmouth Publishing, 1993) 97-100.

36 Gregory C Keating, 'Distributive and Corrective Justice in the Tort Law of Accidents' (2000) 74 *California Law Review* 193–224.

equality more generally,[37] those who see it as a tool to restrain abuses by the rich and powerful (such as large corporations)[38] and more recent scholarship that focuses on tort law's role in distributing risk and responsibility across society in a more equitable way.[39]

Wright J takes his cue from the other, more private-oriented thread within doctrinal scholarship – that represented by Buller and Pollock, and their search for a unifying principle behind tort law. He places the focus squarely on the individual, and on the harm suffered by an individual as a result of another's act. The "deep sense of morality and rights" which "pervades the common law" demands that such a violation of an individual's integrity and autonomy be rectified. This, and nothing less, is the purpose of tort law.[40] In placing this principle at the centre of his account, Wright J is very close to Pollock, but where the two diverge is in Wright's willingness – indeed, insistence, invoking Cicero[41] – that consideration be taken of the moral and philosophical basis of the no-harm principle, in contrast to Pollock who insists on distinguishing and dissociating the legal principle from a mere moral imperative[42] although he was willing to concede that it had a moral basis.[43] His approach most closely approaches that of the corrective justice theorists, and in particular the more philosophically inclined amongst them, such as Ernst Weinreb.

The main difference between Mill and Wright JJ and their doctrinal counterparts lies not so much in their tortological views as in extent to which they are expressly discuss the basis of their positions and demonstrate a willingness to take these into account in determining the outcomes of actual cases. The position of the last two judges is, however, substantially different, in that they fundamentally question whether tort law has any role at all to play in the modern legal system, and come to the conclusion that it does not. Nonetheless, their judgments reveal fairly strong positions on the

37 Tsachi Keren-Paz, *Torts, Egalitarianism and Distributive Justice* (London: Ashgate, 2007).

38 Thomas H Koenig and Michael Rustad, *In Defense of Tort Law* (New York: NYU Press, 2001).

39 Arthur Ripstein, 'Private law and private narratives', in: Peter Cane and John Gardner, editors, *Relating to responsibility: Essays for Tony Honore on his eightieth birthday* (Oxford: Hart, 2001) 37–59.

40 Hutchinson and Morgan (n. 1) 90.

41 *Ibid.* 87.

42 Pollock, 'Province' (n. 28) 589.

43 Pollock, *The Law of Torts* (n. 23) 9.

question of whether the nature of tort law – or the system that each of them believes ideally ought to take its place – lies towards the public or the private ends of the spectrum.

Prudential J. argues that tort law is outdated, that it does not achieve the balance between social purposes and individual purposes that it needs to,[44] and that it must therefore be replaced – his favoured solution is a comprehensive insurance-based compensation scheme for traffic accidents.[45] This speech reveals little about what he believes the nature of contemporary tort law to be, but it reveals much about what he believes it *ought* to be – namely, ensuring that the balance between individual and social interests remains at an appropriate level, and that the individual is shielded from the dangers attendant upon modern life in a manner that meets the interests both of the individual and society.[46] This, too, is a public-oriented perspective on the tortological question, but one which differs significantly from those traditionally associated with the common law. Prudential J's perspective owes, instead, much more to twentieth century notions of the role of the welfare state that first appeared in the writing of political philosophers, and to ideas as to risk and blame that were first articulated in the middle of the twentieth century by sociologists and anthropologists. These ideas ultimately found their way into the realm of legal scholarship, both through policy documents such as the Pearson Report in the UK[47], which sought to re-conceptualise the relationship between the tort system and the welfare state by replacing significant parts of tort with no-fault insurance or strict liability regimes, and the work of legal scholars. As a result, they have little sympathy for or connection with the preservation of traditional doctrine as an end in itself and, unsurprisingly, Prudential J would overthrow not just the notion of fault, but most of the theoretical apparatus that supports modern tort law, including the notion of harm and legal injury. Yet, ultimately, he does not do so. Because, he says, of his respect for the separation of powers – the reform he desires to see must be left to the legislature to action.[48]

44 Hutchinson and Morgan (n. 1) 96-97.

45 *Ibid.* 98-102.

46 *Ibid.* 99-100.

47 *The Report of The Royal Commission on Civil Liability and Compensation for Personal Injury* (1978) Cmnd. 7054.

48 Hutchinson and Morgan (n. 1) 103-104.

Lefft J, by contrast, spends much of his speech discussing the role that tort law plays. His view is not positive. Tort law's role is principally ideological – to create an illusion of justice and objectivity that in reality places society in bondage.[49] Like Prudential J, he too sees a balance between the interests of society and the individual as having an important place in tort law, but the practical result he sees is vacillation, indeterminacy and arbitrariness.[50] Tort law suggests that it is appropriate to treat life and death as economic events, and that any injury can be remedied by money – a thought he finds dehumanising and repellent.[51] The only solution is completely to restructure the institutions of society, to redistribute information and knowledge so all are aware of the nature and extent of the risks to which they are exposed, and to democratise society at the level of everyday life and not just political organisation.[52] This view, which owes much to the Critical Legal Studies movement of the 1980s, is once again clearly rooted in a view of the nature of tort law as being public.[53] The purpose it actually serves is upholding existing social structures through legitimising them,[54] whereas the purpose it – or its replacement – *ought* to serve is the creation of a just society where each individual is given the means to let them attain their innate potential,[55] both of which demonstrate a view of tort law as being principally a tool that should serve the public or social interest. There is very little room in his theory for tort law to be regarded as principally about the protection of private interests, except where the public interest demands the protection of a private interest – as, for example, in the free availability of information and knowledge that he espouses.

These, then, are the tortologies we see in 'The Canengusian Connection.' One which pretends not to exist, but leans towards the public; one which unashamedly treats tort law as having a public nature; one which treats it as having a purely private nature; and two more who treat it as having a public nature, but deny that it plays any desirable role and would do away with it altogether to be replaced by something radically different. In the next

49 *Ibid.* 105.

50 *Ibid.* 106.

51 *Ibid.* 106-108.

52 *Ibid.* 108-109.

53 The Critical Legal Studies movement strongly criticised the public-private distinction as being an atavistic remnant of legal formalism. See e.g. Duncan Kennedy, 'The Stages of the Decline of the Public/Private Distinction' (1982) 130 *University of Pennsylvania Law Review* 1349–1357

54 Hutchinson and Morgan (n. 1) 105.

55 *Ibid.* 109.

section, I discuss some key themes which these tortologies illustrate. As I show, these themes are of continuing relevance in pointing to a fundamental flaw in academic debates about tort law.

3. Academic and judicial tortologies

Three features of the judgments in 'The Canengusian Connection' deserve special comment.

First, as I discussed in the previous section, each of the Canengusian judges has a very clear position on the private-public relationship in tort law, yet in sharp contrast to writings in theology, none of the judges expressly discusses his or her position in these terms. It is left to the reader to infer from each judge's decision whether he views tort law as being principally public or principally private. In consequence, none of the judges explains why they believe that tort law should properly be regarded as being, as the case may be, either wholly private or wholly public. Their views on the private-public relationship in tort law are the postulates from which they start – the judgments give no suggestion that they are the produce of reasoned consideration. For all the room Mill devotes to refuting the arguments of his fellow judges, he does not question his fundamental assumption that tort law principally serves a public function, not a private function. Wright J's Aristotlean ethics-based argument is perfunctorily dismissed because it offers no insights "into the source of the norms by which the conduct was judged wrongful."[56] The same holds, in reverse, for Wright J. He finds Mill J's argument morally unacceptable,[57] but fails to explain why a morally acceptable account of tort law is to be preferred over an account of tort law that is centred on social efficiency, or why rights are trumps over social welfare.

Unfortunately, although this particular type of discourse is by no means universal, it is the rule rather than the exception in academic tort scholarship. We regularly assert that tort law is a part of private law, but rarely explain what, precisely, it is about tort law that would make it wrong of us to classify it as yet another a branch of public law – a species of regulation, for example – and vice versa.[58] Much like Mill J and Wright J, we

56 Hutchinson and Morgan (n. 1) 77.
57 *Ibid.* 87.
58 Cf. Steve Hedley's criticism of internalist accounts of law in Hedley (n. 7).

are prepared to justify and explain the attractiveness of our position on the public-private relationship in tort law, but seldom explain why the contrary position could not provide just as effective a set of postulates to start with.

Secondly, the positions taken by the Canengusian judges cluster around the ends of the spectrum. Without exception, each judge bases his or her decision either on the postulate that the law of tort is wholly private and *not* public, or that the law of tort is wholly public and *not* private. There is no concession to the idea that it might in some way represent a combination of both. The only judge who comes close is Wright J. But he does this, in a manner reminiscent of Weinrib, from whose corrective justicist theories his views seem to be drawn. And, like Weinrib, he ultimately dismisses the public aspects he discusses: tort law, on his conceptualisation, remains clearly and exclusively private. Equally, it is notable that the majority of opinions cluster around the public end of the spectrum – even the spokeswoman for doctrinal jurisprudence puts forward a version rooted in a public, not private, view of the public-private relationship in tort, and the only judge who takes a private-leaning position, Wright J, too, finds it necessary to grant some concession to the public-oriented approach, even if he rejects Mill J's version of this approach.[59]

In both these points, 'The Canengusian Connection' again stands in sharp contrast to modern theological writing about Christology which rarely takes an extreme position. And, once again, it accurately captures features of modern academic tort scholarship, certainly as it stood when the piece was written but to a significant extent also today. This view is not universal. Some writers – such as James Gordley[60] and Richard Wright[61] – accept that tort law must be discussed and analysed in terms both of public and private functions, which they categorise as reflecting, respectively, distributive justice and corrective justice. But they are in a minority. The majority insist dogmatically that one, and only one, of these can represent the true nature of tort law. Partisans of tort's private nature may concede that tort law as actually practised by the courts sometimes does incorporate features of public law, but these, they argue, are errors that rob tort law of its coherence and which should be eliminated to preserve its intelligibility and coherence

59 Hutchinson and Morgan (n. 1) 93-94.
60 Gordley (n. 4).
61 Richard Wright, 'Substantive Corrective Justice' (1992) 77 *Iowa Law Review* 625–664 at 707-709.

as a distinct body of law.[62] Similarly, those who hold the nature of tort law to be principally public might concede that judges do sometimes base their decisions on their idea of what is a 'just' outcome without regard to economic efficiency or the public purpose of tort law, but argue that courts who do this are making a mistake, and preventing tort law from discharging its true social function – whether that be redistribution or wealth maximisation.

Equally, at the time the piece was written, theoretical accounts of tort law (and obligations in general) grounded in public approaches were by far the dominant ones in academic writing, a situation described by Peter Birks as "the long unchallenged hegemony of the welfare aspect of civil wrongs" in which "the normative purposes of civil wrongs have been forced into an incidental or subsidiary role" – a balance he sought to correct.[63]

Thirdly, and most significantly, although the article takes the form of five judgments, the five perspectives on tort law do not actually come anywhere near resembling real decisions. In part, as Mullender points out in his contribution, this is because they are far more dogmatic in describing their positions than judges are. But more fundamentally, the reason the five perspectives strike us as being so different from what real judges would say is that real judges, as discussed below, take a far more nuanced view of the public-private relationship in tort law than do any of the five fictional judges in 'The Canengusian Connection.'

Consider, for example, the statement of Lord Denning which Mill J. invokes in his opening salvo: that common law adjudication is "a matter of public policy" which judges must resolve.[64] This, he believes, justifies and supports his view that tort law is, at its core, an instrument with which to pursue socially desirable goals. Yet Lord Denning, whose own concern to do justice on the facts of a case has been much remarked on,[65] is an unlikely poster-boy for the sort of approach Mill J advocates, and he himself did not take such a narrow view of public policy. 'Policy', as he used it, simply meant the reason behind a rule, which could just as easily be the private one of doing

62 Ernst Weinreb, 'Understanding Tort Law' (1989) 23 *Valparaiso University Law Review* 485–526 at 492.

63 Peter Birks, 'Editor's Preface', in: Peter Birks, editor, *Wrongs and Remedies in the Twenty-first Century* (Oxford: Clarendon Press, 1996) v–x at vi-vii.

64 *Home Office v Dorset Yacht Co Ltd* [1969] 2 QB 412, 426.

65 See e.g. Francis Bennion, 'Lord Denning and the Judicial Role Part 2' (2005) 169 *Journal of Professional Negligence* 74–77

justice by a wronged individual, as the sort of public reason Mill J had in mind. He did not always distinguish 'policy' from 'principle' as carefully as the Canengusian judges do, and indeed, he himself used the two somewhat interchangeably. Compare, for example, his statement in *The Road to Justice* that contract cases frequently involved "divergent public policies: the one which demands the enforcement of contracts: the other which seeks to prevent the abuse of it"[66] with his famous holding in *Bishopsgate Motor Finance v Transport Brakes Ltd*[67] that, in English law, "two principles have striven for mastery. The first is for the protection of property... The second is for the protection of commercial transactions."[68] As these quotes should make apparent, the two terms are, to him, not very different in their import. And, equally, in each case the contrast Lord Denning sets up is not between two competing *public* goals, but between one goal of the sort that a system of tort law whose nature was public might be expected to pursue, and another goal that can only be pursued by a system of tort law that is private. Nowhere is there any hint of the postulate Mill J holds to be self-evident – that the public goal is the only one that matters, not the private one. To the contrary, Lord Denning's view of policy, where public-oriented and private-oriented objectives both form part of the law, to be balanced in coming to a conclusion, is very far removed from Mill J's far more simplistic notion, which simply assumes that the public interest overrides any private claims to justice.

In a similar fashion, Wright J's reading of Lord Scarman's holding in *McLoughlin v O'Brian*[69] reflects a far narrower and far more straitjacketed approach than Lord Scarman himself took. Lord Scarman did indeed contrast 'principle' and 'policy' and hold that the courts' role was restricted to questions of principle, and did not encompass questions of "social, economic, and financial policy."[70] Yet what Lord Scarman appears to have understood by 'principle' does not fit neatly into the private end of a private-public dichotomy. According to Lord Scarman, the application and expansion of principle by the courts was necessary and desirable to keep the common law *socially* relevant. In words that echo the comments of Mill J[71]

66 Alfred Thompson Denning, *The Road to Justice* (London: Stevens and Sons, 1955) 95.
67 [1949] 1 KB 332.
68 *ibid.* 336-7
69 [1983] 1 AC 410
70 *ibid.* 431
71 Hutchinson and Morgan (n. 1) 78.

rather than Wright J, he explained that the law must meet the demands of contemporary society. Courts must ensure that that the law does not become "irrelevant to the consideration, and inept in its treatment, of modern *social* problems" (emphasis supplied).[72] The application of principle, Lord Scarman went on to add, had within it the flexibility to take account of imperatives such as certainty, and of the risk of opening the floodgates, both of which could be applied in a manner that was in keeping with the area of law with which the courts were concerned.[73] Although he believed that certainty and the 'floodgates' argument had little role to play in negligence, his willingness to recognise the principles, coupled with his emphasis on the necessity of ensuring that law was able to respond to modern social problems, strongly suggest that Lord Scarman's juxtaposition of 'principle' and 'policy' was not intended to exclude the possibility that tort law could or did have a public aspect. Arguably, the circumstances he discusses in the course of explaining his views on 'principles' fall quite squarely within what Lord Denning described as 'policy.' They also bear a strong resemblance to the idea of "renewal and adaptation of the law to meet changing social needs," which Bell refers to in his analysis of the use of policy arguments in judicial decisions[74] and, as Bell goes on to argue, there are clear reasons to view the duty of care as a means of incorporating policy considerations into discussions of the limits of the tort of negligence[75]

What, then, did Lord Scarman mean by saying that policy was not the province of the courts? The conclusion of his judgment offers us an insight as to what his concern was. Why, he asks, should the courts leave the question of drawing lines of 'policy' to exclude "socially undesirable" outcomes to Parliament and not take on the role themselves? Because, he answers. the issue is not justiciable, because "the considerations relevant to a decision" of social, economic or financial policy "are not such as to be

---

72 *ibid.* 430

73 *ibid.* 431

74 John Bell, *Policy Arguments in Judicial Decisions* (Oxford: Clarendon Press, 1983) 40. It is worth noting that the narrower meaning of policy adopted by Lord Scarman is used by some academics. See e.g. Andrew Robertson, 'Constraints on Policy-Based Reasoning in Private Law', in: Andrew Robertson and Tang Hang Wu, editors, *The Goals of Private Law* (Oxford: Hart, 2009) 261–280 at 262-267, who unlike Lord Denning excludes considerations of justice between the parties from the scope of 'policy'.

75 Bell (n. 74) 43. There is some historical support for this in, e.g., Ibbetson's discussion of the use by 19th century judges of the duty of care to control what they believed to be excessive findings of liability by juriesIbbetson (n. 32) 170-5.

capable of being handled within the limits of the forensic process."[76] This view of the reason why the courts should avoid assuming a role in determining policy would seem to have more in common with Lon Fuller's idea of polycentricity[77] than with the absolute exclusion of anything not directly connected with identifying or correcting wrongs that one associates with the ideas of corrective justice in whose service Wright J invokes it.

This approach, which assumes that tort law has both private and public functions, is characteristic of the common law judiciary. A number of cases decided since the writing of 'The Canengusian Connection' have made it very clear that this is now the dominant judicial approach in the common law. Examples include Lord Hoffmann's express statement in *White v. Chief Constable of South Yorkshire*[78] that the earlier view that tort law should "aspire to provide a comprehensive system of corrective justice" had now been abandoned "in favour of a cautious pragmatism,"[79] and the statement of Lord Steyn in *Macfarlane v Tayside Health Board*[80] that tort law is "a mosaic in which the principles of corrective justice and distributive justice are interwoven."[81]

From elsewhere in the Commonwealth come cases such as *Haris v Bulldogs Rugby League Club*[82], a negligence action brought by spectators who had been hit by fireworks set off during a football match, in the course of considering which the court expressly took into account the social utility of holding football matches. Within this category also belong the two-stage test in *Anns*,[83] with the room it gave to the court to take into account 'any factors' in determining whether or not a duty of care existed. The three-part test set out in *Caparo*,[84] although significantly different from the *Anns* principle, also reflects an acknowledgment of the co-existence of public and private aspects in tort, if the principle is interpreted through the lens of the cases applying it. In *Marc Rich v Bishop Rock*,[85], for example, the court considered whether it

76 *ibid.* 432

77 Lon L. Fuller, 'The Forms and Limits of Adjudication' (1978) 92 *Harvard Law Review* 353–409.

78 [1999] 2 A.C. 455

79 *ibid* 502

80 [2000] 2 A.C. 59

81 *ibid.* 83

82 [2006] NSWCA 53

83 *Anns v Merton LBC* [1978] AC 728.

84 *Caparo Industries Plc v Dickman* [1990] 2 AC 605.

85 [1994] 1 W.L.R. 1071

would be "just, fair and reasonable" to impose a duty of care on a voluntary classification society in relation to the certificates of seaworthiness it granted. It answered the question in the negative, and took into account a broad range of factors – including the availability of insurance and the potential effect of finding a duty on what was clearly a socially desirable activity. These can only be described as rooted in the public aspect of tort law.

This approach is also evidenced in the long line of decisions of the House of Lords involving public authorities or bodies exercising statutory powers, in which the court balanced the private interest of the claimant against the public interest involved in permitting the authority in question to discharge its functions properly,[86] and by the cases where the courts have spoken about the prevailing "compensation culture"[87] – an approach that has since received statutory recognition in the Compensation Act 2006. In none of these cases did the court automatically conclude that public or private function of tort law automatically overrode the other – they spoke, rather, of the need to balance the two, and appear to view this as being intrinsic to tort law. In harder cases, a choice may have to be made between the two, as Lord Steyn pointed out in *Macfarlane* but this choice is made *on the specific facts of a case*, and does not reflect a general rule that the one or the other must always be the one that is chosen. The judicial view of the public-private relationship in tort law is thus far more nuanced then the polarisation of the Canengusian judges on a public-private axis would suggest or support.

Yet judicial tortologies, taken by themselves, present an unsatisfactory account of tort law. In the cases cited above and in other cases where courts have considered the question of the relationship between public and private purposes in tort law, they have tended to speak in terms of a balance, or of the need to make a difficult choice between the two in specific cases. What principles one applies in making this choice, the decisions do not tell us. In a legal system which values consistency, this silence is problematic. If the rules and principles on which a choice is made are unclear, it is difficult, if not impossible, to determine whether the courts have, in fact, been consistent in deciding similar cases – or, indeed, whether two cases were in fact similar in

86 See e.g. *JD v East Berkshire Community Health NHS Trust* [2005] UKHL 23, where the court held that there were "cogent reasons of public policy for holding that no common law duty of care should be owed" (*ibid.* [115] per Lord Rodger)

87 See e.g. *Tomlinson v Congleton Borough Council* [2003] UKHL 47 and *Gorringe v Calderdale Metropolitan Borough Council* [2004] UKHL 15

substance.[88] It is for this reason that the growing divide between academic and judicial approaches to the public-private relationship in tort law is a cause for concern – not so much because it would, if it continues, consign to irrelevance the role of academic tort scholarship, but also because it produces an impoverished vision of tort law where judges, deciding from case to case, lack the professional space to articulate a framework for tort that goes any way beyond "shreds and patches", and the majority of academics, clinging to their singular visions of tort law, refuse to do so.

What, then has prevented the emergence of more closely integrated accounts in tort law? Why have we, made so little progress in capturing the "modern interweaving of public and private", as Steve Hedley put it, within our theoretical frameworks?[89] And how can we present a theoretical account of the relationship between tort law's private and public functions that avoids the monist dogmatism that is so accurately captured in 'The Canengusian Connection' but, at the same time, also avoids lapsing into a purely case-by-case approach with little role, if any, for the formulation or articulation of principles, as a simple reading of judicial decisions would suggest? In the next section, I return to the analogy with christology with which I began this essay and argue that it provides a framework which lets us analyse the roots of this problem, and which points the way towards an approach that lets us start bridging this gap.

4. Rethinking tortology

The core problem of understanding how one entity can have two very different natures is one which Christian theology has had to deal with for a very long time. In sharp contrast to tort theory, there is a virtual consensus in contemporary Christian thought that these two natures coexisted and were united – schools that held otherwise have for the most part been consigned to the category of extinct heresies. There is also a consensus that the study of the nature of Christ must be informed by his works – what he actually said and did.[90] It is not identical to the study of his works – that is

88 Cf. Englard's criticism that this would render the law incoherent. Izhak Englard, 'The Idea of Complementarity as a Philosophical Basis for Pluralism in Tort Law', in: David G. Owen, editor, *Philosophical Foundations of Tort Law* (Oxford: Clarendon Press, 1995) 183–195 at 186

89 Hedley (n. 7) 203.

90 Gerald O'Collins, *Christology: A Biblical, Historical and Systematic Study of Jesus* (Oxford: Oxford University Press, 2009) 1.

the subject of another sub-discipline within theology called soteriology – but it is inseparable from it, because the gospels – and Christian doctrine – identify him through his words and actions.[91]

The differences that continue to exist in christology, and which underlie contemporary debate, are rooted in differing perspectives as to the role and importance one ought to assign to historical and social scientific argument as opposed to arguments from scripture. The similarity of this dichotomy to the internalist–externalist dichotomy in tort scholarship – the phraseology of 'external' and 'internal' accounts is also used to describe christological positions – makes a comparison particularly relevant. As I discuss in this section, an examination of the various positions represented in modern christological debate sheds a significant amount of light on what exactly is missing in the five opinions that make up 'The Canengusian Connection' – and, more generally, in modern academic tort scholarship. This, in turn, points to the reasons why academic scholarship is so poor a mirror of actual judicial attitudes to tort, and to reasons behind the growing gap between academic and judicial accounts of the public-private relationship in tort law.

David Ford classifies modern christological positions into five typological categories, based on their positions on historical and scriptural argument.[92] At one extreme (Type 1) are the theorists whose starting point is in modern thinking, to which they try to fit traditional scriptural teaching, rejecting the portion of those teachings that do not fit. At the other extreme (Type 5) are the theorists whose starting point is scripture, and who reject all external frameworks as having no relevance to understanding the nature of Christ. In between these two extremes are three other, more moderate frameworks. Type 2 – typified by the theology of Rudolf Bultmann – seeks to reinterpret traditional teaching in modern terms, and to present theological claims in "rational, general, universal" terms – in other words, stripped of the traditional 'mythological' language and the world-views that were prevalent at the historical moments when key doctrines were formulated. Type 3 sees the possibility of a range of external and internal descriptions of Christ – for example, the Christ of history and the Christ of faith – which are in harmony, but as at the same time so distinct that it is impossible to integrate them within a general all-encompassing framework. Type 4 agrees with the

91 David Ford, 'Christology', in: Adrian Hastings, Alistair Mason and Hugh Pyper, editors, *The Oxford Companion to Christian Thought* (Oxford: Oxford University Press, 2000) 114–118 at 114.

92 Ford (n. 91) 117-118.

preceding type as to the existence of a variety of frameworks, but takes the view that external frameworks – of the sort espoused by Types 1, 2 and 3 – cannot be permitted to dictate our understanding of Christ. The essential framework for this must come from traditional Christian testimony; however, within this framework there is room for dialogue with other disciplines.

In 'The Canengusian Connection', by contrast, the positions taken by the judges cluster around the extremes. Doctrin CJ, with her emphasis on the law, and the law alone, rejecting all considerations of policy or, indeed, of the possibility of external insight, is the precise counterpart of Type 5 theorists, representing in this respect most 'internalist' theorists of law. But so, too, is Wright J, and the particular version of the corrective justice school his decision represents. His willingness to engage with the idea of rights might suggest a willingness to look to other frameworks – notably, Aristotlean ideas of commutative justice, Kantian notions of right and other similar ideas drawn from the Western tradition of moral philosophy. However, the writings of the corrective justice writers he represents make clear that this engagement is only possible to the extent these ideas are already immanent in the law. Purely moral arguments, even if non-instrumental in nature, must be held to be extrinsic to proper legal discourse – to do otherwise is to reject the law's coherence and autonomy.[93] External frameworks cannot and should not be permitted to dictate our understanding of tort law. There is, in other words, no representative of Type 4 theories amongst the Canengusian judges, in that none of them shows a willingness to engage in the trans-disciplinary dialogue that is its hallmark.

At the other extreme, Prudential J represents Type 1 almost perfectly, in treating modern thinking – in his case, risk avoidance – as being the appropriate starting point, and rejecting all of traditional doctrine that does not fit within this framework. And, once again, so does Mill J. Despite his seeming acceptance of the framework of tort law – unlike Prudential J, he does not recommend its abolition – he, too, rejects all traditional doctrine. There is no attempt to seek to reinterpret the traditional concepts or categories of tort law within the framework of his theory, or to restate the law in language that reflects modern, rational ideas, stripped of the terminology associated with older world-views. Instead, he calls for a

93 Weinrib (n. 12).

wholesale replacement of traditional tort doctrine with a new, efficiency-based principle.

Outside the limited world of 'The Canengusian Connection', things are slightly better, but not significantly so. Tort scholars in the real world do not show the disdain for other approaches that the Canengusian judges do. With the exception of a few extreme purists (such as the neo-Arian law-and-economists discussed above) scholars who principally focus on the public aspect of tort law acknowledge that it has a private aspect, pay attention to the work discussing it and acknowledge that it makes an important contribution to tort scholarship. Similarly, scholars who focus on the private aspect of tort law, too, frequently acknowledge the insights which studies of its public aspect have to offer (although, again, they too have their contingent of modern-day Monophysites who deny the possibility of there being a public aspect to tort law). There are even a small number of tort scholars who have attempted to present integrated theories of tort law that acknowledge its melding of public and private natures. Some – such as James Gordley[94] and Richard Wright[95] – have sought to do so within a broadly Aristotlean framework, or related frameworks that conceptualise the natures in terms of distributive and corrective justive.[96] Others have looked elsewhere. Izhak Englard, for example, has attempted to use the Copenhagen interpretation (of quantum mechanics) as a framework within which to integrate the public and private aspects of tort law.[97]

Yet this has not produced the tort law equivalents of the intermediate typologies discussed above. For all that public-oriented theorists acknowledge the importance of the theories exploring the private structure of tort law, they rarely attempt to produce their own doctrinal accounts, which reinterpret the traditional private-oriented doctrinal concepts in which the law is expressed in fresh, public-oriented terms, as Bultmann and other Type 2 theorists of christology have done. The same applies to private-oriented theorists. Even those who appreciate the value of studies of the public aspect of tort law seldom consider the implications of these studies for their understanding of the structure of tort law. It is not just the framework of their understanding of the nature of tort law that comes from

94 Gordley (n. 4).
95 Wright (n. 61).
96 See e.g. William Lucy, *Philosophy of Private Law* (Oxford: Oxford University Press, 2006) 376-418; Dagan (n. 8)
97 Englard, 'Complementarity' (n. 88).

traditional private-oriented approaches, but also the entire content. Integrated theories, too, have not found the place at the heart of mainstream academic tort theory that the judicial approaches discussed in section 2 suggest they should have.

Table 1, which locates the Canengusian judges and some of the theorists discussed in this paper on a tortological spectrum derived from the five Christological typologies, highlights this divide. All private theorists fall within Type 5 – the canonical internalist position. And whereas internalists (Type 5) are spread across the possible range of opinions on the private-private question, externalists cluster around the public end of the spectrum. Even worse, type 2 is not present at all, reflecting the failure (discussed above) of externalists to produce their own reinterpretations of tort doctrine, and types 3 and 4 are only present in a few, isolated 'thought' pieces rather than in a systematic literature.

Nature	Type 5 (internal)	Type 4	Type 3	Type 2	Type 1 (external)
Private	**Wright J** Pollock Birks 'Corrective Justice'				
Mixed	Gordley Wright		Englard		
Public	**Doctrin CJ** Addison	Green			**Mill J** **Lefft J** **Prudential J** Posner

Table 1: The modern tortological spectrum
The Canengusian judges are highlighted in bold.

The result is an academic tort scholarship that suffers from many of the flaws that led the German theologian Dietrich Bonhoeffer to produce his famous critique of twentieth century Christian theology. Bonhoeffer's starting point was his argument that the Christian theology of his day was complicit in reducing the role of God to those few gaps that science could not fill. As the world increasingly came of age, Bonhoeffer said, man found that he was increasingly able to do without God. Liberal theology reacted to this by accepting the increasingly limited role that was assigned to God, whereas conservative theology reacted by attempting to convince the world that it in reality could not live without God. Bonhoeffer took the view that both approaches were deeply flawed. They produced a God inhabiting the ever-shrinking domain of areas which modern secular knowledge could not answer. When the day came when secular knowledge was capable of answering the 'ultimate questions', no role would be left for God. This sort of theology, he said, misunderstood and misrepresented the nature and role of Christ.[98]

Bonhoeffer's idea of a 'God of the gaps' should be familiar to tort scholars. Common law scholars, lawmakers and judges have struggled to define the scope of tort law almost since the time of its recognition as an independent area of law. Broom in his commentaries on common law faithfully followed the wording of the Common Law Procedure Act 1852, and defined a tort as "a wrong, independent of contract."[99] This phrase was also adopted by Underhill as the title of his treatise on tort, and with modifications continues to be used to this day. Salmond on Torts, for example, defines a tort in the following terms: "A tort is a civil wrong for which the remedy is a common law action for unliquidated damages and which is not exclusively the breach of a contract or a trust or other merely equitable obligation." Attempts to remedy the negative phrasing of this definition have usually ended up arguing for erasing the distinction between a breach of contract and tort, and treating the former as part of tort law rather than contract law. Whatever the academic merits of this argument, it tells us very little about what distinguishes what we today commonly understand as tort law.

Negative definitions of this type suffer from the same problems for which Bonhoeffer criticised accounts of theology which led to a "God of the gaps", namely that they tell us very little positive about what tort is for. But so, from the perspective of Bonhoeffer's critique, do accounts of tort law that treat it as being principally a means for the enforcement of rights or principles whose existence is independent of tort law. Tort law, in these accounts, occupies whatever domain the law at any moment chooses to assign to it by deciding to create, or withhold, particular rights. This domain

98 Dietrich Bonhoeffer, *Letters and Papers from Prison: The Enlarged Edition* (London: SCM, 1971) 325-327.

99 Herbert Broom, *Commentaries on the common law, designed as introductory to its study* (London: W. Maxwell, 1856) 658.

shrinks or expands at the choosing of the legislature (or other system that is claimed to be the source of the rights upheld by tort law). If, for example, the law chooses to remove accidents from the domain of tort law and assign them to some other branch of law, as Prudential J so strenuously argued it should, then so it will be. There is nothing that we can deduce from tort law itself about its proper role. It has been reduced to the status of a mere means of enforcing principles obtained from elsewhere, not a source of principle in its own right. Yet, much as Bonhoeffer argued that contemporary theologies misrepresented the true nature and role of Christ, and as the account of judicial tortologies in the previous section demonstrates, this is patently not how judges view tort law and does not reflect the nature of tort law as practised in the courts.

How, then, might we structure a theoretical framework that is capable of representing the interwoven character of public and private in tort law, by re-integrating the academic study of the structure of tort law and of the public impact of tort law? Bonhoeffer took the view that the problem was, fundamentally, a problem of christology. Christology, Bonhoeffer argued, frequently asked the wrong questions. It either spent too much time considering the question of 'how' or 'whence' – how it could ever be possible for two natures to be united in one person, or whence these two natures came. Bonhoeffer dismissed these as, fundamentally, being concerned with the 'alchemy of the incarnation' rather than with the central question of Christology.[100] To get to the root of this question, Bonhoeffer said, requires a more nuanced and positive Christology, and a positive definition of the role of the church and Christ which placed Christ at the centre of human existence, not its margins. Part of the answer, according to him, lay in realising that a focus on Christ's works as a means of understanding his nature was in effect an evasion of the central questions of christology. Rather than starting with the works and proceeding from there to the nature, therefore, Bonhoeffer argued that 'act' and 'being' must be seen as part of an integrated whole. Christology must draw upon the study of Christ's words and deeds, but it must never be reduced to the study of his words and deeds – its questions are more fundamental.[101] Christ must, instead, be understood through his presence in the world and through his presence in history, and in either case must be placed at the centre of our

100 Dietrich Bonhoeffer, *Christology* (London: Collins, 1966) 27-37.
101 *Ibid.* 37-40.

interpretation. Whilst other disciplines must be engaged with, it is Christ that must be the starting point, not the world.[102]

There are analogies between Bonhoeffer's approach to the problem of the union of divine and human in Christ and the general problem of the union of public and private natures in tort law, which point to how and why tort theory falls short. The Canengusian judges – again, like many academic theorists – either start with a focus on the functioning of tort law, i.e. its works (Prudential J, Lefft J and Mill J), or on its structure, i.e. its nature (Doctrin J and Wright J). The result is that none of them considers the works and structure as aspects of an integrated whole, as Bonhoeffer suggests in the context of theology. This then influences the manner in which they relate to insights offered by other disciplines. Mill J and Prudential J are led by the findings of other disciplines to the extent that these disciplines, rather than tort law, form their starting points. Wright J and Doctrin J, by contrast, reject other disciplines altogether in their eagerness to place an autonomous understanding of tort law at the centre.

Courts, by contrast, are less susceptible to this problem. Of their nature, courts deciding cases are both embedded in the structure and doctrine of tort law, and at the same time form an inseparable part of the working of tort law and of its effect on society. As a result they are, intrinsically, far likelier to view tort law as a combination of its works and its nature. The absence of an equivalent bridge in academic tort scholarship is a major factor contributing to the growing divide between academic and judicial perspectives on the public-private relationship in tort law. In drawing our attention to this existence of this divide and the breadth of this gap, 'The Canengusian Connection' both highlights the limits of academic tort theory and gives us tools to diagnose the reasons for these limits.

5. Conclusions

The discussion thus far has focused on using christology to highlight the reasons behind the problems in modern academic tort theory to which 'The Canengusian Connection' draws our attention. Much more work needs to be done before we can attempt to outline a theory that makes positive use of Bonhoeffer's insights, but I conclude by offering an example from legal history to suggest how we might go about formulating an integrated model.

---

102 *Ibid.* 43-47, 71-77.

Around fifty years ago, Vilhelm Lundstedt – a Swedish jurist who was a leading proponent of Scandinavian Legal Realism – in the course of a critique of American realist theories of the law of tort pointed out that Anglo-American writers rarely asked the question of why the *state* was at all involved in tort law. He argued that they tendend to put forward various theories as to what they believed the purpose of tort law to be – the protection of certain interests, the achieving of corrective justice, and so on – but they hardly ever bothered to investigate the extent to which these theories were supported by the historical record. This, he argued, fundamentally hampered the ability of Anglo-American jurisprudence to present a theory of tort law that conformed to the experience of the law in the real world.[103]

With some exceptions (e.g. James Gordley), this criticism remains valid today. Whilst a number of theorists have attempted to identify and describe the principles or logic inherent in tort law, less attention has been paid by these theorists to the question of why the state chooses to give effect to these principles or to a system based on this logic[104] – in other words, to what Dorfman in a recent paper described as the "public morality" of tort law.[105] This question is, however, much more frequently asked in legal history, and the picture when we examine specific moments in legal history is of close integration between the public and private aspects of the law.

Consider, for example, the mediaeval writ of trespass, which was the earliest discernable direct ancestor of the modern law of tort. 'Trespass', as numerous historians have pointed out, in those days simply meant 'wrong.' The wording of the writ of trespass tells us that an action in trespass lay where the wrongful act constituted a breach of the king's peace. By the thirteenth century, this phrase had lost all practical significance. In theory, it meant that the litigant had to demonstrate that the wrong was done to him *vi et armis*, but histories of the law of obligations record how litigants creatively

103 A Vilhelm Lundstedt, *Legal Thinking Revised* (Stockholm: Almqvist and Wiksell, 1956) 337-396.

104 Even where the question is considered, it is usually in the form of an ought – why *might* a state justifiably be entitled to create a system of tort liability – rather than the question of why states *actually* create systems of tort liability. See e.g. Tony Honore, 'The Morality of Tort Law', in: David G. Owen, editor, *Philosophical Foundations of Tort Law* (Oxford: Clarendon Press, 1995) 73–95 at 76-78

105 Avihay Dorfman, 'Can Tort Law be Moral?' (2010) 23 *Ratio Juris* 205–228 at 206.

presented their facts to satisfy the formal requirement of force.[106] In origin, however, the term had a much more profound meaning, which gives us a clue as to why the mediaeval state concerned itself with the redress of private disputes. Amongst Germanic tribes, one way for a strong leader to legitimate his authority was by offering the protection of his peace. This was originally confined to protecting a favoured few, but it grew from there to cover the entire body of the king's 'subjects'[107] This idea eventually crystallised into the notion of the "king's peace," a peace that extended over everyone within the kingdom.[108] That, then, was the original idea behind the condition that a writ of trespass would only lie for a breach of the king's peace. The state, such as it was in mediaeval times, began to provide a remedy against certain serious private wrongs to reinforce the idea of his protection of the populace, and with a view to preventing them from escalating into worse disputes that threatened the peace of the community, from the maintenance of which the king drew his legitimacy. The king was, however, originally not the only source of peace that existed. There was also a notion of a local or communal peace, which was preserved by local institutions – such as local courts – which also included the protection offered by a local noble to places and individuals under his control.[109] Until the centralisation of authority in the thirteenth and fourteenth centuries turned them into inferior fora that only dealt with relatively minor matters, these courts had heard a range of matters.[110] The emphasis that the king's courts would only hear cases that involved a breach of the *king's* peace, therefore, served to separate the matters that properly fell within his domain – that were the subject of his interest, because they involved force or affected property or had some other relevant impact – from those that did not.[111] There were, here, a complex mix of public factors that lay at the heart of the decision to offer a private remedy of the particular scope that was offered.

---

106 Ibbetson gives the example of a case where the negligence of a smith in shoeing a horse was described as an attack by the blacksmith, *vi et armis*, with swords and arrows, upon the claimant in which the blacksmith killed the horse by driving a rusty nail into its hoof. Ibbetson (n. 32) 45.

107 Alan Harding, *Medieval Law and the Foundations of the State* (Oxford: Oxford University Press, 2002) 26-27.

108 *Ibid.* 28-30.

109 Harding (n. 107) 79-81.

110 Robert C Palmer, *The County Courts of Mediaeval England, 1150-1350* (Princeton: Princeton University Press, 1982) 220-296.

111 Robert C Palmer, *English Law in the Age of the Black Death, 1348-1381* (Chapel Hill: University of North Carolina Press, 1993) 160.

Less benignly, as Palmer has argued, public factors also lay behind the expansion of the jurisdiction of the king's courts through the introduction of the action on the case. The action on the case was largely a product of the Black Death which, by wiping out a large proportion of the population of England, created serious threats to social stability and had the potential to radically alter the relations between the upper and lower orders of society. The upper orders responded to this threat by drawing together and by altering the law to permit themselves to more easily enforce obligations as against themselves, and more vitally against the lower orders. The action on the case was one of the tools introduced as part of this reaction, along with other devices as diverse the Statute of Labourers, the regulation of the church and the action of covenant, as the result of a deliberate social policy.[112] Once again, therefore, the provision of a private remedy had at its heart a public purpose.

As these examples show, the interweaving of the public and private aspects of tort law is not simply modern, but has roots that go to the origins of the actions that evolved into tort. The starting point in the formulation of integrated theories must, therefore, be the realisation that the public and the private natures of tort law cannot realistically be regarded as being totally separate, as some extreme theorists would have it. At the same time, however, it is also insufficient to acknowledge the combination, but regard it as a mere mixture caused by the fact that legislative intervention has introduced policy considerations into tort law. The private and public aspects of tort law must, instead, be understood as being inextricably combined, such that the public flows from the private and the private from the public, with each present and fulfilled in the other.[113] Any discourse on tort law which fails to understand this or place it at its centre will end up presenting a partial and ultimately unhelpful account of this branch of law law that can see nothing more than "shreds and patches". Drawing our attention to the fragmented nature of such tort discourse is the most important – and most enduring – insight 'The Canengusian Connection' has to offer.

112 See *Ibid.* and esp. 9-27 and 220-293.

113 Cf. Robertson (n. 74) 279-280, which emphasises the need to understand private law's bipolarity and the role of policy considerations in shaping its rules.

DIVERSITY, DISSONANCE AND DENIAL: EXPLORING THE CANENGUSIAN ENVIRONMENTAL CONNECTION

Ole W. Pedersen*

Introduction

This essay seeks to highlight the broad application of Hutchinson and Morgan's analysis of tort law as this is put forward in 'The Canengusian Connection', by showing its relevance to environmental law (a body of law that intersects in a variety of ways with tort law).[1] This seems worthwhile since Hutchinson and Morgan's analysis, masterfully dissecting a fictitious traffic accident and the tort claims that it gives rise to by way of a written decision by the Canengusian Court of Appeal, can be applied to debates on the role and form of environmental regulation. The aim of this essay is to illustrate how the deliberation of the five Canengusian Court of Appeal judges along distinct lines (doctrinal, consequentialist, deontological, socio-legal and critical legal scholarship (CLS)) alerts us to the inherent diversity in law, while highlighting a number of critiques.

In addition to linking 'The Canengusian Connection' to environmental issues, this essay also discusses the themes of diversity and denial as these are identified as subtle premises lurking underneath the deliberations of the five Canengusian Appeal Court judges. As a way of elucidating these themes, we will partly rely on the concept of cognitive dissonance. In the course of developing these themes, this essay argues that the response of the five judges to the diversity identified in 'The Canengusian Connection' is one of denial. This essay argues that the issues of diversity, dissonance and denial are equally applicable to environmental issues. In light of this, this essay seeks to demonstrate that such denial and dissonance may give rise to so called group polarisation, which in turn can be countered by reliance on concepts of open deliberation and critical rationalism, as these are elaborated by John Dewey and Karl Popper respectively.

The Canengusian Connection

In 'The Canengusian Connection' we learn how tort law as a legal discipline is highly susceptible to judicial discretion and can be moulded in a number

* Lecturer, Newcastle Law School. I am grateful to Richard Mullender for helpful suggestions and encouragement. Usual disclaimer applies.

[1] A. Hutchinson and D. Morgan, 'The Canengusian Connection: The Kaleidoscope of Tort Law' (1984) 22 *Osgoode Hall L. J.* 69.

of different directions. 'The Canengusian Connection' plays out on the fictional island of Canengus, situated somewhere in the mid-Atlantic, with a legal system which is a "unique blend of Canadian, English and American sources".[2] The central focus in 'The Canengusian Connection' is a series of negligence claims before the Canengusian Court of Appeal following a traffic accident. Presented with the question of whether the accident gives rise to liability on behalf of another driver (whose faulty headlight caused the applicant to break abruptly and skid off the road) and/or a local farmer (who overheard the accident from the front porch of his house but failed to investigate it, further resulting in the applicant receiving belated medical attention), the five Court of Appeal judges follow their distinct judicial philosophies when rendering their judgements. Thus, Hutchinson and Morgan foreground the fact of diversity without, however, doing so explicitly and without overtly stating their intentions for doing so. We are hence left to assume that they are seeking to achieve some degree of verisimilitude.

Chief Justice Doctrin emphasises that she is concerned only with "the legal aspects of this case alone" and will resolve the dispute in a manner which is "in accordance with the law as it is, and not as some think it ought to be".[3] Moreover, she interprets the constitutional arrangement of Canengus to be one of exclusive positivism where "arguments of law and morality are rendered mutually exclusive".[4] Mill J, on the other hand, favours a strong consequentialist orientation and considers the law's purpose to be that of economic efficiency. Mill J argues that "the law should seek to simulate an outcome that would be produced by market forces in a world which generates no transaction costs".[5] The consequentialist thrust of Mill J's thinking is found in his broad interpretation of "economic efficiency", which he considers to be one of overall welfare maximisation. To Mill J, efficiency is Pareto efficiency, whereby "there is no other pattern of allocation that would improve any one person's welfare without making any other person worse off".[6]

In contrast, Wright J finds such cost-benefit analysis deplorable and instead espouses a strong deontological approach to adjudication. Wright J argues that individuals are autonomous, deserve respect and "possess certain rights

[2] Hutchinson and Morgan above n. 1 at 69.

[3] *Ibid* at 70-71.

[4] *Ibid* at 71. See for a critique of this idea of separation between law and morals J. Gardner, 'Legal Positivism: 5 1/2 Myths' (2001) *American Journal of Jurisprudence* 199 at 222-225.

[5] Hutchinson and Morgan above n. 1 at 80.

[6] *Ibid* at 81.

that cannot be overridden by appeals to general utility".[7] Despite expressing intuitive sympathy with Wright J, Prudential J favours an approach to adjudication which takes into account personal (along corrective lines) and social justice.[8] He argues "we should add a touch of concern and compassion for our fellow human beings to the tort system".[9] This compassionate account can be likened to the idea of 'sympathy' developed by Adam Smith (although Smith's account of 'sympathy' was not restricted to one of compassion and pity).[10] Smith saw 'sympathy' as a technical term facilitating the situation whereby an impartial spectator imaginatively aligns himself/herself with the "fellow-feeling for any passion whatever", as this is experienced by an agent without necessarily experiencing the same loss or injury.[11] Accordingly, Smith's account of 'sympathy' is similar to Prudential J's attempt to have the Court put itself in the shoes of the tort claimant and appreciate the (to Prudential J) unjust situation and predicaments behind the accident. While Prudential J lets us know that he attaches importance to the doctrine of separation of powers, he emphasises the judicial obligation to "cajole the legislature into action" so the "judges must become constitutional partners", where the legislator fails to secure society's reflection in the law.[12] Prudential J hereby emerges as an advocate for the 'mirror thesis' which seeks to fashion a body of law that reflects societal norms and customs.[13]

Finally, Lefft J, who tells us that his judgment in the case is to be his last, fires a broadside at the legal establishment when announcing that the "vast paraphernalia of legal rights and entitlements amounts to nothing more than a sugar coating on a bitter pill".[14] Lefft J's judgment thereby echoes the arguments of the CLS movement, which claims that the law often serves the interests of the dominant classes. We can consider Lefft J's approach part of a wider left-of-centre movement, which, as a result of its discontent with the

---

[7] *Ibid* at 90.

[8] We may question whether the pursuit of corrective and social justice at the same time is at all feasible. The answer would to a large degree depend on the definition of 'social justice' and what goods we intend to distribute through such justice. See R. Mullender, 'The Scampering Discourse of Negligence Law' *infra* at n. 121 and 150.

[9] Hutchinson and Morgan above n. 1 at 96.

[10] See A. Broadie, 'Sympathy and the Impartial Spectator' in K. Haakonsson (ed), *The Cambridge Companion to Adam Smith* (Cambridge, Cambridge University Press, 2006) 158.

[11] For an analysis of Smith's take on sympathy see I. Ward, *Justice, Humanity, and the New World Order* (Aldershot, Ashgate, 2003) at 30-37.

[12] Hutchinson and Morgan above n. 1 at 98.

[13] See, for instance, B. Tamanaha, *A General Jurisprudence of Law and Society* (New York, Oxford University Press, 2001) at 1-3.

[14] Hutchinson and Morgan above n. 1 at 105.

status quo, seeks sweeping societal changes.[15] We thus see how each of the five justices on the Canengusian Court of Appeal makes explicit use of particular doctrinal or theoretical theories in reaching their respective judgments. While this is done in the context of tort and negligence law, the application of these theories and assumptions is broadly relevant to environmental law. Moreover, a central theme running through 'The Canengusian Connection' is that of diversity insofar as Hutchinson and Morgan draw our attention to the many ways in which one can approach tort law. In highlighting diversity by way of the vivid example of the five judges, Hutchinson and Morgan represent a challenge to those who seek to deny that diversity is fact of legal life.[16] It is to this point we will now turn.

Diversity and Denial

By highlighting the different legal approaches to the particular problem of negligence law, Hutchinson and Morgan alert us to the presence of diversity in law. In doing so, Hutchinson and Morgan tentatively fall in line with the CLS movement, which sought to challenge previously held assumptions emphasising consensus on values and the neutrality of law. Emerging from American universities in the 1970s, the CLS movement challenged and partly attempted to break the 'particular sense of consensus' which was prevalent in legal thinking.[17] Drawing inspiration from the political left, this movement, which has been labelled as a group of 'college Marxists', sought to highlight the differences between the law as it was taught in law schools and the law as it played out in the real world, where racial and sex discrimination was rife (thus rehearsing the theme of difference between law

---

[15] It is even possible to link the CLS movement to the American New Left movement which was prominent on American university campuses in the 1960s and which sought to challenge traditional liberal virtues on the ground that they were essentially repressive. See for instance, N. Duxbury, *Patterns of American Jurisprudence* (Oxford, Oxford University Press, 2001) ch. 6.

[16] For a discussion on indeterminacy in law see C. L. Kutz, 'Just Disagreement: Indeterminacy and Rationality in the Rule of Law' (1994) *Yale Law Journal* 997, who argues that "the conflict and indeterminacy that is inherent in the law is both ineradicable and deeply valuable to a self-scrutinizing moral and political culture" at 999. See also D. Price, 'Taking Rights Cynically: A Review of Critical Legal Studies' (1989) 48 *Cambridge L. J.* 271, who argues that "If a "real theory" is understood to refer to a unitary theory behind the actual doctrines, then there *is* no "real theory" [of contract law]...The conclusion to draw from this fact is not that the legal system is on the brink of destruction from without or within, but instead that legal doctrines are made by imperfect human institutions, are the result of high-minded and low-minded compromises, and must continually be elaborated further and revised in response to new situations. The argument that competing conceptions exist in the law has neither the novelty nor the destructive significance that the CLS adherents claim." at 288 (original emphasis).

[17] Duxbury above n. 15 at 424.

in the books versus law in action, as emphasised by the American Realist scholars).[18] A central theme of the CLS movement was the notion of 'trashing', which assisted CLS scholars in attacking legal discourses "to show their premises to be contradictory or incoherent and their conclusions to be arbitrary or based on dubious assumptions or hidden rhetorical tricks".[19] Unger thus notes that lawyers dogmatically assume a number of causes and effects when interpreting law while infusing the law with a particular purpose before deciding on what reasonable interpretation best conforms to this purpose.[20] We witness vivid examples of this throughout 'The Canengusian Connection' where the five judges each instil their interpretation of the case before them with their purposes ranking from Lefft J's 'informed consent' to Mill J's consequentialist emphasis on efficiency.

While the CLS movement was clearly much more than just a critique of the law and the workings of legal institutions, it would seem fair to say that a central (if not defining) feature of its work centred on critiquing existing legal discourses. One central critique pursued by the CLS movement was the Marxist inspired contemplation that the law often works in the interest of the powerful.[21] Law is consequently not considered apolitical. The CLS movement was very much alert to the political nature of law as are Hutchinson and Morgan in 'The Canengusian Connection'. A distinct feature of this alertness to law's political nature is that the CLS movement brings to the foreground the issue of denial, which was arguably present in the legal discourses that the movement criticised. Unger, for instance, highlights that the appeal to abstract categories of legal rights represents a truncation which is inherently silent with regard to the "divergent schemes

[18] Duxbury above n. 15, who uses the term 'campus Marxism' by virtue of it being "strong on exhortation, weak on practicalities" when describing Duncan Kennedy's 1979 critique of US law schools at 493.

[19] R. W. Gordon, 'Law and Ideology' (1986) 3(1) *Tikkun* at 17.

[20] R. M. Unger *The Critical Legal Studies Movement* (Cambridge, Harvard University Press, 1983) at 16. See also R. M. Unger, 'The Critical Legal Studies Movement' (1983) *Harv. L. Rev.* 561 at 571, where Unger criticises the 'sanctification of the actual': "For it would be strange if the results of a coherent, richly developed normative theory were to coincide with a major portion of any extended branch of law. The many conflicts of interest and vision that lawmaking involves, fought out by countless minds and wills working at cross-purposes, would have to be the vehicle of an immanent moral rationality whose message could be articulated by a single cohesive theory. This daring and implausible sanctification of the actual is in fact undertaken by the dominant legal theories and tacitly presupposed by the unreflective common sense of orthodox lawyers."

[21] Unger above n. 20. Unger notes how "established forms of economic and political organizations enable relatively small groups of people to control the basic terms of collective prosperity by making the crucial investment decisions" at 28.

of social life that are manifest in conflicting bodies of rules, policy and principle".[22]

In order to advance this argument, we can borrow an example touching on denial from 'The Canengusian Connection', notwithstanding that Hutchinson and Morgan never explicitly refer to the issue. The most striking example of denial in Hutchinson and Morgan's essay is arguably Doctrin CJ's strict adherence to legal doctrine. While Doctrin CJ's argument that judges interpret the law and that the legislature makes the law is simplistically appealing, it is fundamentally at odds with important parts of the common law. Her assertion that the "law is insulated from political controversy" arguably reveals a trait of denialism, which the CLS movement would waste no time in challenging.[23]

Wright J's strictly deontological approach to the law likewise represents a form of denialism, albeit to a lesser extent. His strong emphasis on individual freedom and intrinsic worth, while admirable, overlooks some of the qualifications which society places on deontological theories. For instance, few rights are absolute in the way that Wright J would seem to prefer and his dismissal of 'contributory negligence' ignores important statutory developments in English negligence law.[24] His criticism of acts of rescue likewise overlooks the fact that a large number of civil law jurisdictions maintain provisions on duty to rescue on their statute books.[25]

This subtle theme of denial which is arguably present in 'The Canengusian Connection' is, however, not unique to the essay nor to judicial decision-making in general. It is a phenomenon that is widespread and that we find in many contexts. In order to explain (at least in part) its presence, we can look to the concept of cognitive dissonance, as this is deployed in social psychology.[26] Cognitive dissonance seeks to explain the actions and thoughts people take and have when they are faced with dissonance that is psychologically uncomfortable. In other words, faced with dissonance, i.e. conflicting information, people seek to reduce such dissonance and avoid situations and information which are likely to increase the dissonance.[27] Smokers (faced with the dissonance that one of their basic enjoyments

[22] *Ibid* at 21.

[23] Hutchinson and Morgan above n. 1 at 71.

[24] See J. Steele, *Tort Law* (Oxford, Oxford University Press, 2010) at 277-278.

[25] See Art. 2 Chapter I of the Quebec Charter of Human Rights and Freedoms.

[26] See L. Festinger, *A Theory of Cognitive Dissonance* (Stanford, Stanford University Press, 1957), for some of the original studies and S. Plous, *The Psychology of Judgment and Decision Making* (New York, McGraw-Hill, 1993), for an overview of cognitive dissonance.

[27] Festinger *ibid* at 3.

constitutes a serious health risk), for instance, are notorious for seeking to reduce this dissonance by justifying their smoking, despite the evidence that smoking is bad for them.[28] One way in which cognitive dissonance relates to denial is the way in which persons take to ideas and statements that are dramatically different from the ideas they hold themselves.[29]

Research on cognitive dissonance indicates that people are more likely to not think about and dismiss arguments which cause dissonance.[30] This in turn leads to so-called information bias whereby people, when confronted with evidence that gives rise to a dissonance, often criticise, distort or dismiss disconfirming evidence.[31] These developments are strongly linked to what O'Callaghan, relying on Bakhtin, considers 'monologue creep'.[32] This is directly applicable to the 'theatre of roles' playing out in 'The Canengusian Connection'. Here it is evident that each of the five judges holds deep-rooted assumptions on the nature of negligence law (and, in Prudential J and Lefft J's judgments, accident compensation law more generally). These entrenched assumptions lead each of the five judges to dismiss the opinions and ideas of the other judges. Most strikingly this is seen in the judgment delivered by Mill J. He dismisses Doctrin CJ's emphasis on legal doctrine as "confused, schizophrenic, and altogether too restricted" before setting out his own and no doubt, in his eyes, more plausible account of negligence law.[33] This strongly dismissive utterance of disapproval is arguably a form of 'naive realism' (a desire for simplicity), whereby people are more inclined to believe that the opinions they hold themselves are the most reasonable ones. In other words, if people "disagree with us, they obviously aren't seeing clearly."[34] Thus, when scratching the surface of 'The Canengusian Connection', it becomes clear that it gives rise to a number of relevant lines of enquiry beyond the relatively narrow boundaries of negligence law. The

[28] See E. Aronson et al, *Social Psychology* (Upper Saddle River, Prentice Hall, 2002), discussing the smoking example at 176.

[29] See also C. Sunstein, *Going to Extremes: How Like Minds Unite and Divide*, (New York, Oxford University Press, 2009) on cognitive dissonance and conspiracy theories at 110-112.

[30] Aronson et al above n. 28 at 177, referring to a study by Jones and Kohler indicating that people in the study group were more likely to dismiss a sensible argument on the other side of the relevant debate than an implausible argument on their own side of the debate as this would minimise dissonance.

[31] See C. Tavris and E. Aronson, *Mistakes were Made (But Not by Me)*, (London, Pinter Martin, 2008) at 18.

[32] See P. O'Callaghan, 'Monologism and Dialogism in Private Law' *infra.*

[33] Hutchinson and Morgan above n. 1 at 76.

[34] Tavis and Aronson above n. 31 at 42. See also J. Ehrlinger, T. Gilovivh and L. Ross, 'Peering Into the Bias Blind Spot: People's Assessment of Bias in Themselves and Others' (2005) 31 *Per. Soc. Psychol. Bull.* 68.

aim of highlighting this undercurrent of dissonance and denial which runs through 'The Canengusian Connection' is to underline its applicability to other legal settings, including environmental law where issues of diversity, dissonance and denial equally form part of a 'theatre of roles'.

The Canengusian Environmental Connection

While Lefft J's doomsday pitch of humanity standing "on the edge of the abyss" resonates all too well with the tone of many environmental debates of the last four decades (Matt Ridley calls this the 'fashionable gloom'),[35] the five judgments each hold ideas and presumptions that are broadly applicable to environmental issues in general.[36] At the outset, we can argue that Prudential J's argument in favour of not only compensating the injured but "to reduce the incidence of injury" on grounds of safety has similar broad environmental law appeals along the lines of precaution. Lefft J's arguments for "equaliz[ing] risk throughout society", securing consent to any risks and access to proper information about risks, likewise intersect with environmental law in the broad sense.

Wright J's calls for strict liability can also be linked to the prominent polluter pays principle.[37] Originally the polluter pays principle emerged as a principle of cost-allocation, arising as a result of pollution; it has since been adopted as a principle of liability.[38] More to the point, Wright J's plea for a strict liability regime has already found its way into environmental legislation and s. 32-33 of the *Pollution Prevention and Control (England and Wales) Regulations 2000* provides for strict liability where the Regulations are contravened.[39]

What is more, the deontological leanings of Wright J are arguably echoed in the theoretical literature on foundations of environmental law discussing the relationship between man and the environment. Here, it is often argued that man owes a duty to protect the environment on deontological grounds.[40]

[35] M. Ridley, *The Rational Optimist* (London, Fourth Estate, 2010) at 283-297.

[36] For an analysis of the environmental movement's doomsdays prophecies see M. Sagoff, *The Economy of the Earth*, (New York, Cambridge University Press, 2008) ch. 6. See also B. Lomborg, *The Skeptical Environmentalist*, (Cambridge, Cambridge University Press, 2001) at 12-18.

[37] See in general N. De Sadeleer, *Environmental Principles: From Political Slogans to Legal Rules* (Oxford University Press, Oxford, 2002).

[38] *Directive 2004/35/CE of the European Parliament and of the Council of 21 April 2004 on Environmental liability with regard to the prevention and remedying of environmental damage*, Art. 1.

[39] S. 32-33 of *The Pollution Prevention and Control (England and Wales) Regulations 2000*. See also *Environment Agency v Empress Car Co.* [1999] 2 A.C. 22.

[40] For an overview of the theoretical foundations of environmental law, see in general J. Alder and D. Wilkinson, *Environmental Law and Ethics* (Palgrave Macmillan, Houndmills,

One such deontological base is found in the argument that non-sentient beings hold an intrinsic value regardless of the instrumental value which humans may attach to them. Advocates of such a theory include philosophers, such as Arne Naess and Holmes Rolston, among others. Most famous within this group is arguably Norwegian philosopher Arne Naess and his ideas on deep ecology.[41] Within this body of thought, Naess distinguishes between shallow and deep ecology. The former promotes fights against pollution and resource depletion, but has as its objective the health and rising affluence of people in the developing countries. The latter completely rejects any ideas of 'man in the environment' and dedicates itself to the environment only.[42] On various levels, the deep ecologists point towards an intrinsic value in non-human entities as a justification for their emphasis on the environment. A good example of this is Rolston's argument that "humans arrived so late on the evolutionary scene that to claim they brought all values with them shows a remarkable subjective bias."[43] Critics, however, could forcefully assert that these approaches overlook Hume's famous 'is/ought' distinction, stipulating that normative arguments cannot be derived from factual observations.[44] In other words, while ecologists are capable of ontologically observing the workings of nature and the environment, we cannot base any normative arguments as to the relationship between man and the environment, or other species and the environment, on these observations.

These ideas differ dramatically from the ideas of some of the earliest thinkers, who pondered the relationship between man and the natural environment. For example, Aristotle thought that animals existed for human purposes only. Thomas Aquinas argued that man's right to exploit animals was a matter of divine providence.[45] Once, however, intrinsic value has been ascribed to the environment and animals within it, such value forms a base on which we can grant normative theories establishing that harming the environment is inherently wrong, as non-sentient beings are deemed to have inherent worth on their own. A prominent example of such a deontological

1999) and S. Coyle and K. Morrow, *The Philosophical Foundations of Environmental Law* (Oxford, Hart Publishing, 2004).

41 A. Naess, *Ecology, Community and Lifestyle*, Translated and edited by David Rothenberg, (Cambridge, Cambridge University Press, 1989).

42 A. Naess, 'The Shallow and the Deep, Long-Range Ecology Movement. A Summary' (1973) 16(1) *Inquiry* 95.

43 H. Rolston, 'Value in Nature and the Nature of Value' in R. Attfield and A. Belsey (eds), *Philosophy and the Natural Environment* (Cambridge, Cambridge University Press, 1994) 25.

44 See D. Hume, *A Treatise of Human Nature* (London, Penguin Books, 1969) Book III, Part I.

45 See in general J. R. DesJardins, *Environmental Ethics* (Belmont, Wadsworth, 2006) at 96.

approach is found in the work of Regan, who favours the allocation of rights to animals on the basis that they are, in his words, subject to a life.[46] Regan accordingly considers it wrong to, for instance, carry out laboratory testing on animals not because they suffer any harm but because doing so violates their right to equal respect, which an animal is entitled to when it is subject to a life.[47]

Broadly similar ways of ascribing intrinsic value to inanimate objects are based on the aesthetic value the environment has, without being intentionally designed to hold such value, as is the case with, for instance, a building possessing incidental aesthetic value.[48] For example, Edinburgh Castle will, to most people, have some aesthetic value. This is in spite of it being intentionally designed by human beings, albeit for other non-aesthetic purposes (as a defensive stronghold). It may likewise be claimed that the extinct volcano upon which the Castle is resting has aesthetic value without having been intentionally designed.[49] Insofar as the objective is deemed to hold a value on its own, we can use this as a platform on which to ground intrinsic value.[50]

[46] T. Regan, *The Case for Animal Rights* (London, Routledge, 1983). To Regan a creature is subject to a life when it possesses beliefs, desires, perception, memory, sense of future, emotional life and feelings, pleasures and pains, preferences and interests, ability to initiate action in pursuit of desire.

[47] This contrasts with Kant's deontological theory. Kant argued that no direct duties could be owed to animals as these lack reason and are not rational beings able to judge or obey the moral law. This is not to say that animals cannot benefit from human duties and obligations. Kant thought, on the contrary, that animals would benefit from indirect duties owed to humans. See E. Kant, *The Metaphysics of Morals* edited by M. Gregor (Cambridge, Cambridge University Press, 2007) at 192-193 and E. Kant, *Lectures on Ethics* translated by L. Infield (London, Methuen, 1930) at 239-241.

[48] R. Elliot, 'Ecology and the Ethics of Environmental Restoration' in R. Attfield and A. Belsey (eds), *Philosophy and the Natural Environment* (Cambridge, Cambridge University Press, 1994) 36.

[49] See also R. Dworkin, *Life's Dominion: An Argument about Abortion. Euthanasia, and Individual Freedom*, (New York, Vintage Books, 1994) at 74-76.

[50] This kind of intrinsic value is what might be called the objectivist approach to valuation, where a subject is afforded value without a human valuer (see also Mullender, above n. 8). Examples of this could be the fact that history exists without historians, biology exists without biologists or the argument that the colour green remains green even where there are no humans to see it. This notion of value is contrasted by the subjective theory of valuation, where no values exist without a valuer. Examples of this could be the lack of thoughts without a thinker, lack of deals without a dealer or no religion without a believer. See Rolston above n. 43 at 29. Again, however, this is open to the Humean criticism on grounds of it conflating facts with values. See above n. 44 and accompanying text.

The legal implications for such theories become immediately clear when we consider Christopher Stone's epic essay *Should Trees Have Standing*.[51] In his essay, Stone argues, based on the intrinsic worth of the environment, in favour of giving natural objects human proxies, in the shape of a guardian, to serve the object's interests.[52] Stone argued that, for instance, NGOs can take upon them the role of guardians and make sure that when damage occurs to the natural object, it should be fully compensated for its 'own injuries' and not just property or monetary loss suffered by a human being.[53] More recently, the 2008 constitution of Ecuador affords nature a right "to exist, persist, maintain and regenerate its vital cycles, structure, functions and its processes in evolution".[54] This provision is a particularly strong deontological example in that it is not qualified – at least from a strict reading of the provision.

The deontological approach to environmental problems is likewise found in the increasing attention which is afforded environmental issues in human rights contexts. Here the deontological emphasis on principles and respect for particular virtues regardless of consequences is applied not to non-sentient beings but to human beings. The human rights approach to environmental problems essentially rests on the assumption that every human being has an equal right to environmental protection and the benefits that this gives rise to.[55] Hence, adequate environmental conditions are considered paramount to the extent that they deserve protection alongside the right life and privacy.[56] One important limitation here though is the fact that these rights are often limited. This throws into sharp relief the fact that

[51] C. Stone, 'Should Trees Have Standing? – Toward Legal Rights for Natural Objects' (1972) 45 *S. Cal. L. Rev.* 450.

[52] *Ibid.* To some, this 'instrumentalising' of the guardian/agent to serve the interest of the object/non-agent would, however, seem counterintuitive.

[53] *Ibid.* at 473. To critics, however, the idea that non-sentient beings can incur 'injuries' comes across as a category mistake. See for a critique of Stone P. S. Elder, 'Legal Rights – The Wrong Answer to the Right(s) Question' (1991) 22 *Osgoode Hall L. J.* 284.

[54] See website of Community Environmental Defense Fund which helped to draft the chapter on Rights of Nature on http://celdf.org/article.php?id=185.

[55] This reading excludes much of the case law emanating from the European Court of Human Rights on the environment. Although this case law recognises the increasing importance of environmental protection, many of the Court's decisions essentially relate to the enforcement of domestic environmental provisions where domestic authorities have ignored their responsibilities. See for this 'rule of law' approach: O. W. Pedersen, 'The Ties that Bind: The Environment, the European Convention on Human Rights and the Rule of Law' (2010)16(4) *European Public Law* (forthcoming).

[56] See D. Shelton, 'The Environmental Jurisprudence of International Human Rights Tribunals' in Romina Picolotti and Jorge Daniel Tillant (eds), *Linking Rights and the Environment* (Tucson, University of Arizona Press, 2003) 1 (for an argument on the normative compatibility between human rights and environmental protection).

qualified deontology informs the law in this area. The environmental jurisprudence of the European Court of Human Rights contains numerous examples of situations where violations by the State are justified by reference to executive discretion or economic importance.[57] In addition, a number of domestic constitutions contain rights to safe and healthy environmental conditions along the lines of, for instance, the 1988 *Constitution of Brazil*, which states that "[e]veryone has the right to an ecologically balanced environment".[58] Although such approaches are arguably more aspirational than effective, constitutionally entrenched environmental provisions can have positive effects where such provisions serve as an informative foundation for general legislation or serve as an instrument which the local population identifies with.[59]

In addition to the implicit environmental application of Lefft J's arguments on risk and informed consent noted above, the almost Unger-like call for a dramatic change in societal priorities made by Lefft J can be likened to the many similar assertions which have called for an entire re-thinking of man's relationship with the natural environment, often made within environmental ethics. One such prominent call was made by Aldo Leopold who, in his *Land Ethic*, favoured an eco-centric and holistic approach, considering the natural environment and its entire groups of species, of which man is just one, as one community of interdependent parts not dissimilar to the Gaia hypothesis developed by James Lovelock in the 1960s.[60] In this setup, man holds no special or higher position and the protection of particular species is not an aspiration. Instead the emphasis is on the protection of all species and biodiversity. This is because Leopold argues that "a thing is right when it tends to preserve the integrity, stability and beauty of the biotic community" and on the other hand "it is wrong when it tends to otherwise".[61] Leopold's idea of rethinking man's role in the wider

---

[57] See Pedersen above n. 55 and *Hatton and others v. United Kingdom*, (2003) 37 EHRR 28 (relating to the extension of Heathrow Airport) and *Fagerskjöld v. Sweden*, decision of 26 February 2008 (Appl. no. 37664/04) (concerning the noise from windmills).

[58] Constitution of Brazil Article 225 reprinted in H. Flanz, *Constitutions of the Countries of the World*, (Dobbs Ferry, Oceana Publications) Release 2000-2, March 2000 Articles 129 and 225. See J. R. May and E. Daly, 'Vindicating Fundamental Environmental Rights: Judicial Acceptance of Constitutionally Entrenched Environmental Rights' (2009) 11 *Oregon Review of International Law* 365, for a recent analysis of constitutional approaches to environmental protection.

[59] See C. Sunstein, 'On the Expressive Function of Law' (1996) 144 *U. Pa. L. Rev.* 2021, on the use of legal statements to change behaviour.

[60] Aldo Leopold, *A Sand County Almanac and Sketches Here and There*, (New York, Oxford University Press, 1949).

[61] *Ibid.* Again, this can be criticized on the ground that Leopold conflates facts with norms cf. above note 44.

ecosystem(s) of the earth is similar to the despairing call from Lefft J whose ideas are radically transformative.[62] While the outcomes sought by Lefft J and Leopold are significantly different from one another (informed consent and eco-centrism respectively), the point to be made here is that they share a common theme of unprecedented societal change. Again, this can be linked to the above discussion on diversity and cognitive disorder. Where we are faced with great difficulties, complexities and frustration as a result of this (as are Lefft J and Leopold), it is easy to be enticed by the comfortable prospects of radical (some would say utopian) transformation. In other words, when faced with a series of serious challenges it is easy to lose sight of the concrete problems at hand and automatically opt for the most drastic option in the hope that this would efficiently solve the difficulty.[63]

We may find further similarities to Lefft J's call for change within the context of global climate change. Here it is often asserted that what is needed in order for humanity to address the apocalyptic nature of the problem is wide-scale and unprecedented societal changes. The eminent scientist James Lovelock even speculates whether humanity is too stupid to handle the problem of climate change and if current democratic structures are in the way of effective solutions.[64] This questioning of existing structures is a telling example of the denial which is often equally present in environmental debates. Ever since Rachel Carson portrayed pesticides as the elixirs of death in *Silent Spring*, stories of environmental apocalypses have been abundant.[65] In the 1970s, Ehrlich predicted that human over-population would lead to environmental crisis which "will persist until the final collapse" and The Club of Rome likewise predicted that the world would run out of many of the natural resources which we continue to enjoy by the 1990s.[66] This is not to say that any of these accounts are wrong in their entirety but to highlight that what Lovelock, Carson, Ehrlich and The Club of Rome have in common is the questioning of existing social structures on grounds of sustainability. This echoes Lefft J's assertion that

[62] A related question is whether humans are at all capable of being radically transformative and if so to what extent. Critics may question whether the strong role played by social traditions limits our imaginative capacities.

[63] This may in turn foster so-called 'monologue creep'. See O'Callaghan, above n. 32.

[64] L. Hickerman, 'James Lovelock: Human Are too Stupid to Prevent Climate Change' *The Guardian*, 29 March, 2010.

[65] R. Carson, *Silent Spring* (Boston, Houghton Mifflin, 2002).

[66] P. Ehrlich, *The Population Bomb* (New York, Ballantine Books, 1971) at 47 and D. Meadows et al., *The Limits to Growth: A Report for the Club of Rome's Project on the Predicament of Mankind* (New York Universe Book, 1974). See for updated scenarios P. Ehrlich and A. Erhlich, *One with Nineveh* (Washington, Island Press, 2004) and D. Meadows et al, *The Limits to Growth: The 30-Year Update* (London, Earthscan, 2005).

humanity is facing descent into the abyss. Once again, this represents an example of the aversion to cognitive disorder. Arguably humans are prone to turning to the siren song of radical change as a result of vulnerability towards tempting appeals exerting influence on our emotions (Carson is a good example of this).

We find an altogether different analysis in the judgment rendered by Mill J, although it may be informed by a similar motive of aversion to complexity. The consequentialist tone of Mill J's judgment is equally detectable in environmental debates. Just as protection of non-human species is afforded along deontological lines, consequentialist theories have been used in support for protection of inanimate objects. Bentham, for example, questioned man's treatment of animals on the premise that, although animals could not reason or talk, they could suffer.[67] This line of thought has been continued most prominently by Peter Singer, who, in his *Animal Liberation*, argues that the ability to suffer should be taken as a premise that supports consideration for the interests of animals.[68] Under this approach, Singer argues that not affording animals protection amounts to speciesism akin to the arbitrary discrimination to which slaves were subjected prior to slave trading being outlawed.[69]

The consequentialist approach found in environmental law becomes apparent when we consider the strong role that cost-benefit analysis plays in decisions as to whether to adopt particular environmental regulations. When environmental officials consider whether to ban in whole or in part particular substances or actions presumed harmful to the environment, it helps to know the benefits and costs associated with these decisions.[70] Very simply, this entails a weighing of the total costs and benefits obtained by affording a value (usually ascertained through questions of willingness to pay or willingness to accept) on the benefits and costs allowing regulators to establish which option yields the most cost-effective outcome.[71] In the UK, we see this in *The Environment Act (1995)*, facilitating the creation of The

---

[67] H. Burns and H. L. A. Hart (eds), *An Introduction to the Principles of Morals and Legislation* (London, Athlone, 1970) at 283.

[68] P. Singer, Animal Liberation (London, Pimlico, 1995).

[69] See also S. W. Wise, 'Animal Rights, One Step at a Time' in C. Sunstein and M. Nussbaum, *Animal Rights: Current Debates and New Direction* (New York, Oxford University Press, 2004) 19.

[70] See F. Ackerman and L. Heinzerling, *Priceless: On Knowing the Price of Everything and the Value of Nothing* (New York, The New Press, 2004) (for a critical analysis of the role of cost-benefit analysis).

[71] See in general C. Sunstein, *The Cost-Benefit State: The Future of Regulatory Protection* (Chicago, American Bar Association, 2002).

Environment Agency and The Scottish Environment Protection Agency, which (in s. 39) makes it a statutory duty for the agencies to take into account the costs and benefits associated with them exercising their powers.[72] Support for such aggregation and consequentialism is likewise found in some of the decisions rendered by the European Court of Justice (ECJ) on nature conservation. In *Commission v. Federal Republic of Germany*, relating to the construction of dykes in a protected area, the ECJ partly relied on the fact that Germany was taking steps to offset the detrimental effect that the dykes would have by opening up other areas to flooding.[73]

A striking example of cost-benefit analysis applied to environmental discussion is seen in the work by Bjorn Lomborg. In his *The Skeptical Environmentalist*, Lomborg examines the aftermath of the Exxon Valdez spill while questioning whether the costly clean up was cost-effective.[74] Lomborg notes that the number of birds dying as a result of the spill was less than the number of birds killed by domestic cats every two days in the UK or the number of birds killed every day as a result of them colliding with plate glass in the US.[75] Lomborg moreover cites a report from the *Scientific American* stating that "the public wants the animals saved – at $80,000 per otter and $10,000 per eagle".[76] Cost-benefit analysis has likewise been used as a blueprint for how to get most value for money when policy-makers and governments are faced with a limited amount of money but a growing list of international problems, including climate change, access to education, malnutrition and armed conflicts.[77] The Copenhagen Consensus, a group of distinguished economists headed by Lomborg, has argued that the money currently invested in combating climate change could be spent more wisely on other problems such as, for instance, malnutrition.

Needless to say, this aggregation of benefits and costs is not popular among environmentalists who consider the reduction of the environment to mere numbers to be a violation of the inherent value which the environment possesses. In other words, the environment and monetary value are incommensurable insofar as by comparing and ranking one against the other

[72] *Environment Act 1995* s. 39.
[73] *Commission of the European Communities v Federal Republic of Germany* Case C-57/89.
[74] Lomborg above n. 36 at 193-194.
[75] *Ibid.*
[76] *Ibid* at 194.
[77] B. Lomborg (ed), *Global Crises, Global Solutions* (Cambridge, Cambridge University Press, 2004. See also website of the Copenhagen Consensus project http://www.copenhagenconsensus.com/CCC%20Home%20Page.aspx and O. W. Pedersen, 'Benefits and Costs of the Environment: Copenhagen Consensus 2008' (2008) 20(3) *Journal of Environmental Law* 465.

we do violence to the "considered judgment about how these goods are best characterized".[78] The dislike which many environmentalists have of such aggregation is echoed in Wright J's critique of Mill J's consequentialist focus on cost-benefit. Wright J wastes little time in making it clear that he finds "cost-benefit analysis [..] deplorable".[79] Despite this and in light of the role which cost-benefit analysis plays in regulatory settings, environmentalists have increasingly joined the cost-benefit bandwagon and started to phrase their arguments for environmental protection in economic terms and begun to emphasise so-called ecosystem services.[80] As a consequence, cost-benefit analysis becomes almost hegemonic. Against this, however, are those who consider such services to be more than just a value to which we can attach an economic price. Sagoff considers ecosystem services to be of the same kind as concepts of liberty – worthy of protection but not something that can be priced.[81] Sagoff favours a religiously inspired deontological emphasis on moral and ethical obligations.

The theme pursued in Prudential J's judgement of social justice and compassion is likewise one we recognise in debates pertaining to that of environmental regulation. This is most clearly seen in the concept of environmental justice, which seeks to address the perceived injustices that certain population groups face when it comes to enjoying clean and healthy environments. One of the central tenets of the environmental justice argument is the observation that low-income groups often suffer from greater exposure to a number of environmental harms including high levels of air pollution, closer proximity to industrial pollution sources and fewer local amenities in general – a point which Lefft J is explicitly alive to.[82] Environmental justice questions the distribution of and effects of environmental harms, along the same social justice lines as Prudential J questions the current Canengusian regime of negligence law.

---

[78] C. Sunstein, 'Incommensurability and Valuation in Law' (1994) 92 *Mich. L. Rev.* 779 at 796.

[79] Hutchinson and Morgan above n. 1 at 88.

[80] See G. C. Daily (ed), *Nature's Services* (Washington, Inland Press, 1997) (for an introduction to the concept of ecosystem services).

[81] Sagoff above n. 36 at 89.

[82] Hutchinson and Morgan above n. 1 at 108-109. For some of the empirical environmental justice data see G. Walker, G. Mitchell, J. Fairburn and G. Smith, 'Industrial Pollution and Social Deprivation: Evidence and Complexity in Evaluating and Responding to Environmental Inequality' (2005) 10(4) *Local Environment* 361-377, and J. Fairburn, G. Walker, G. Smith, 'Investigating Environmental Justice in Scotland: Links between Measures of Environmental Quality and Social Deprivation' Scottish Executive (2005).

The environmental justice argument differs dramatically from the approach which emphasises a strict adherence to the text of the law regardless of whether this may have unwarranted distributive consequences. We find evidence of such an approach in the US decision of *Bean v. Southwestern Waste Management Corp.*, where plaintiffs alleged that the siting of a solid waste site near a high school predominantly servicing African-American students was racially motivated.[83] Although a previous application for the waste site had been turned down years earlier when the area was predominantly White, the court found no discrimination noting that "this court has a different role to play, and that is to determine whether the plaintiffs have established a substantial likelihood of proving that TDH's [Texas Department of Health's] decision to issue the permit was motivated by purposeful discrimination in violation of 42 U.S.C. s 1983 as construed by superior courts".[84]

The decision reached in *Bean* would clearly upset Prudential J, who would likely consider the strict adherence to precedence as going against the need for "concern and compassion for our fellow human beings".[85] Moreover, Lefft J and critical legal scholars would find in decisions like *Bean* evidence to support the claim that the law merely secures the interests of the powerful.

One way to further our analysis of the Canengusian environmental connection and the associated themes of diversity and denial would be to consider how each of the above discussed theories may play out in the situation where an environmental decision has to be made.[86] If we imagine, for example, that an application for a housing development in an area of outstanding natural beauty has found its way to the court, we can (albeit somewhat simplistically) apply the five different theories to how we might solve this application. Firstly, we can consider that the deontological approach may start by questioning whether the development will threaten any of the many endangered species found in the area. If so, the deontologist may, by reference to the intrinsic value of such species, be hesitant to grant permission. Alternatively, the deontologist may favour an approach which emphasises aesthetic significance as a base for intrinsic value and find against the development.[87] On the other hand, a judge of a

[83] 482 F.Supp. 673 (S.D. Texas 1979).

[84] *Ibid* at 681.

[85] Hutchinson and Morgan above n. 1 at 96. Prudential J likewise argues that "it is unclear why rules laid down in the days of the horse and carriage should continue to govern us today" at 96.

[86] This example is partly borrowed from Alder and Wilkinson above n. 40 at 37.

[87] Support for this aesthetic approach can arguably be found in Lord Denning's dissent in *Miller v. Jackson* [1977] Q.B. 966, relating to the nuisance arising from a cricket ground,

consequentialist leaning would not rule out the development outright by reference to the harm suffered by an unspecified number of animals or plants. The consequentialist would instead seek to ascertain whether the suffering endured by the endangered species would be offset by the benefit gained from the development. Thus he/she would likely employ the above discussed cost-benefit analysis in the attempt to derive the overall benefits and costs associated with the development and its impacts.

The social justice-orientated judge, such as Prudential J and Lefft J, would likely discuss the social costs which the development will bring with it and seek to establish whether the development has a disproportionate effect on low-income groups. As a result, he/she would perhaps question whether the development will go towards securing affordable housing (advancing the cause of social justice), will it restrict access to the countryside for low-income urban families or whether the development would merely be another exclusive greenbelt development for the well-off. An adjudicator with a doctrinal inclination would, in the words of Doctrin CJ, be likely to interpret and apply the law before him/her with little regard to consequences in a manner alike to Pound's 'mechanical jurisprudence'.[88] This is likely to entail an examination of the statutory planning provisions and an assessment of the material considerations these give rise to. This may be followed by an argument laying down that in matters like these significant discretion is afforded local planning authorities as these are by far the best placed to make a decision like this. As long as these authorities have not fettered any discretion, taken into account irrelevant considerations or neglected material considerations, the separation of powers considerations urge the judge to refrain from imposing his/her inclinations as to the desirability of the development.[89] This contrasts with the stance which the followers of Lefft J's views may take. They may lament the status quo approach favoured by the doctrinally inclined judged when in fact humanity is under threat from

where Lord Denning argues "After all they have their rights in their cricket ground. They have spent money, labour and love in the making of it: and they have the right to play upon it as they have done for 70 years. Is this all to be rendered useless to them by the thoughtless and selfish act of an estate developer in building right up to the edge of it? Can the developer or a purchaser of the house say to the cricket club: "Stop playing. Clear out." I do not think so." at 978. Arguably there is a consequentialist element to Lord Denning's dissent as well as he ponders the consequences of the cricket club seizing to exist: "The cricket ground will be turned to some other use. I expect for more houses or a factory. The young men will turn to other things instead of cricket. The whole village will be much the poorer. And all this because of a newcomer who has just bought a house there next to the cricket ground." at 976. See for a very useful analysis D. Klinck, 'The Other Eden: Lord Denning's Pastoral Vision' (1994) 14(1) *OJLS* 25 at 44-45.

[88] R. Pound, 'Mechanical Jurisprudence' (1908) 8 *Colum. L. Rev.* 605.

[89] *Associated Provincial Picture Houses, Limited v Wednesbury Corporation* [1948] 1 K.B. 223.

the evil of climate change which requires us to make drastic changes in our lifestyles. Instead, what is needed is not more development in out-of-town greenbelt areas but an entirely new approach to the way we live our lives, build and sustain our communities, grow our food and consume it on this planet. We can imagine Lefft J and his supporters arguing that facilitating these changes is the real purpose of the planning system.

Another brief example that can illustrate how the different theoretical foundations can serve as justifications for a particular outcomes is the decision reached by the New York Court of Appeal in *Boomer v. Atlantic Cement Co.*[90] In *Boomer*, the Court allowed an injunction against a cement factory which would be vacated upon payment of permanent damages to the plaintiffs as a result of the nuisance caused to the plaintiffs. In allowing the injunction to be vacated by payment ($185,000 to all plaintiffs), the Court relied on the "the large disparity in economic consequences of the nuisance and of the injunction."[91] Hence, the Court weighed the costs of closing the plant against the damages incurred by the plaintiffs. From this short description of the facts, it is evident that Mill J would wholeheartedly endorse the Court's decision, whereas Wright J would in all likelihood be outraged that such efficiency calculations may set aside the moral entitlement that the plaintiffs enjoy to an environment that is not polluted. Prudential J would perhaps seek to cajole the cement company into changing and updating its practices and techniques in order to avoid further damage.

These examples highlight how the 'theatre of roles' on display in 'The Canengusian Connection' is easily applicable to environmental issues. Needless to say, this is done in an overstated way here in order to underline the overall argument of Hutchinson and Morgan's methods being applicable outside negligence law. Likewise, the problem of denialism has obvious relevance in environmental debates where answers to environmental problems are often seen as black and white. Thus, diversity, dissonance and denial are a fact of life in environmental issues as much as when it comes to negligence law and tort law more generally.[92] While this is hardly surprising, we still need to contemplate how to cope with such pluralism and uncertainty. It is to this question we will now turn.

[90] 26 N.Y.2d 219, 257 N.E.2d 870 (N.Y. 1970).

[91] *Ibid* at 223.

[92] See also G. Turton, 'Connecting Canengus to the University Curriculum' *infra*, noting how the quest for certainty and the 'answer' has made it into the teaching at law schools.

Coping with Dissonance and Denial

While we should be grateful to Hutchinson and Morgan for pointing us in the direction of the themes of denial and cognitive dissonance, we ought to be critical of their silence on the issue of how we best deal with these problems. Hutchinson and Morgan offer little in the way of assistance when it comes to striking a path through, firstly, diversity of theory and, secondly, denial.[93] Hence, we need assistance when responding to (a) the fact that there are a number of discordant views within a particular field of law (e.g. tort or environmental law) and (b) what are we to do about the associated problem of denial which manifests itself as a result of this?

In addressing this question, our reliance on the ideas of the CLS movement will cease. In fact, we may question whether one of the movement's foremost proponents himself is inclined towards denialism when faced with challenges bordering despair as he emphatically calls for divine intervention.[94] Instead we will briefly turn to the works of Karl R. Popper, John Dewey and Richard Rorty.

From the outset, it is worth emphasising that the plurality and diversity in opinion and theory which is highlighted by Hutchinson and Morgan should not be suppressed nor be avoided. In fact, such diversity is often useful in that it assists us in advancing our understanding of legal concepts, practices and institutions.[95] But how may we best achieve these gains? Here we could start by looking to Karl Popper's concept of critical rationalism. The central tenet of Popper's understanding of critical rationalism is that proposed solutions to a particular problem should be subject to vigorous attempts at overthrowing the proposed solution.[96] In other words, theories and propositions should be open to criticism and falisifiability. This should be done through critical discussion in order to ascertain the plausibility and robustness of a proposed solution.

The main application of this idea to this essay is the fact that Popper's theory provides a way in which to counter the problem of denial. A feature

---

[93] Here we can once more link Hutchinson and Morgan to the CLS movement which was likewise criticised for doing a lot of trashing without necessarily offering any viable solutions. See Price above n. 16 at 292-298.

[94] R. M. Unger, *Knowledge and Politics* (Free Press, New York, 1975) at 295.

[95] See C. Sunstein, 'Legal Reasoning and Political Conflict' (New York, Oxford University Press, 2000) at 58 (arguing that, in "law, as in politics, disagreement can be a productive and creative force, revealing error, showing gaps, moving discussion and result in good directions") and Kutz above n. 16..

[96] K. R. Popper, *The Logic of Scientific Discovery* (Hutchinson, London, 1959) at 16.

of Popper's critical rationalism is that it is "bound up with the idea that the other fellow has a right to be heard, and to defend his arguments."[97] While Popper's arguments clearly have democratic and institutional tones, they are equally applicable on the micro level of individual deliberation.[98] Popper's account of rationalism, however, should be distinguished from the one described by Michael Oakeshott in his *Rationalism in Politics*.[99] Here Oakeshott describes the political rationalist (who, to Oakeshott, is a prominent and disturbing figure in European politics) as seeing 'reason' as the only authority worth adhering to. While this seems appealing, Oakeshott's portrait of rationalism has an individualistic streak which significantly hinders its application if we are seeking to reach a common ground between a series of different propositions. Oakeshott explains that the rationalist is prone to over-confidence insofar as he or she assumes that the requirements of reason are clear to him or her; the rationalist finds it "difficult to believe that anyone who can think honestly and clearly will think differently from himself".[100] Here, we can forge a link to O'Callaghan's essay in this collection.[101] For Oakeshott's rationalist may slide into 'monologue creep'. As we have seen, this 'naive realism' is not an uncommon feature in everyday life as people are often more likely to think more highly of their own beliefs and more likely to disregard the opinions of others as biased or wrongheaded.[102] In this light, a sense of humility and appreciation of falsifiability would not go amiss.

We can link this to John Dewey's work on the wider context of ethics and morals. Dewey argues that we must come to anticipate diversity in ethics and that the best way to deal with this is through tolerant inquiry and

---

97 K. R. Popper, A *Pocket Popper*, edited by D. Miller (Fontana Press, London, 1987) at 43. See also J. Alder, 'Dissents in Courts of Last Resort: Tragic Choices' (2000) 20(2) *OJLS* 221 (arguing that one purpose of law is to manage disagreement) as well as M. C. Siu, 'Conflict in Canengus: The Battle of Consequentialism and Deontology' *infra* (describing a similar process playing out behind Rawls' veil of ignorance while applying his to Prudential J's judgement).

98 Institutional is here used as a reference to describe the attempt, by a multiplicity of people, to capture some feature of the world or the requirements of a practice.

99 M. Oakeshott, 'Rationalism in Politics' in M. Oakeshott, *Rationalism in Politics and other Essays* (Liberty Press, Indianapolis, 1991) 5. We may further distinguish the rationalism pursued here from the one described by Rawls (who argues that rational agents lack the particular form of "moral sensibility that underlies the desire to engage in fair cooperation as such, and to do so on terms that other as equals might reasonably be expected to endorse"). J. Rawls *Political Liberalism* (Columbia University Press, New York, 1993) at 51 and 50-58 in general.

100 *Ibid* at 6.

101 O'Callaghan above n. 32.

102 Above n. 30 and accompanying text.

reflection.[103] Thus, preconceived ideas and theories become an instrument for more effective and open deliberation.[104] In line with Popper's falsifiability arguments, it becomes clear that in order to facilitate such deliberation the wisdom of the multitude plays a central role; "one needs many eyes, not just two", in the words of Jeremy Waldron.[105] And these eyes of others can serve as external constraints restraining 'monologue creep', partly facilitate falsifiability and save us from foolishness, hobby-horsicality, and the slippery slope of solipsism.[106]

This is important in the context of denialism as one significant consequence of denial is the danger it entails of group polarisation.[107] Group polarisation is the phenomenon used to explain the effect that in-group deliberation has on a group's belief towards a particular subject. Often, a group tends to move towards a more extreme position, while reducing diversity, as a result of in-group deliberation. One way to counter this would be through external constraints such as tolerant criticism and open deliberation which can assist us in ascertaining the plausibility and robustness of a particular approach.[108] Popper's idea of falsifiability is here applied more widely as this will help us to avoid dogmatic adherence to particular doctrines asserting claims of 'truth' and overly individualistic approaches to 'reason' before these turn hubristic and (worse still) hegemonic.

On this point, we ought to take Richard Rorty's advice in relation to truth to heart.[109] Rorty advises that caution should be exercised in attaching too much importance to it. To Rorty, "there is less to be said of truth than one might think".[110] We can link Rorty's aversion towards truth claims to his work on 'final vocabularies' which he describes as "a set of words which

---

[103] J. Campbell, *Understanding John Dewey* (Open Court, Chicago, 1995) at 118-120.

[104] *Ibid* at 119.

[105] J. Waldron, 'The Wisdom of the Multitude: Some Reflections on Book 3, Chapter 11 of Aristotle's Politics' (1995) 23(4) *Political Theory* 563-584 at 568.

[106] At this juncture we ought to note that, as far as constraints on such inquiries go, these ought to be conversational restraints only. See I. Ward, 'Bricolage and low Cunning: Rorty on Pragmatism, Politics and Poetic Justice' (2010) 28(2) *Legal Studies* 281.

[107] See S. Moscovici and M Zavalloni, 'The Group as a Polarizer of Attitudes' (1969) 12(2) *Journal of Personality and Social Psychology* 125 and in general Sunstein above n. 29. See also O. W. Pedersen, "Climategate', Group Polarisation and Hockey Tricks' (2010) 18(1) *Environmental Liability* 11, for an analysis of group polarisation and climate change.

[108] See also Ward, above n. 106, on tolerance noting that 'the only thing which a good society should not be prepared to tolerate is intolerance' at 302.

[109] R. Rorty, *Truth and Progress, Philosophical Papers Vol. 3*, (Cambridge, Cambridge University Press, 1998) at 1-42.

[110] *Ibid* at 22.

[humans] employ to justify their actions, their beliefs, and their lives."[111] Anyone who offers a final vocabulary, in Rorty's eyes, automatically assumes that they know the 'truth'. Assertive claims to 'truth' (whether asserted in Canengus or in or other legal debates) ought to set the alarm bells tolling.

Not surprisingly, to Rorty, vocabularies are contingent and reflect the particular problems and solutions which we are currently engaged in.[112] In the spirit of pragmatism, Rorty is critical of metaphysical claims and does not see truth *per se* to be the goal of inquiry. Instead he favours an emphasis on justifiability (which, however, is inevitably contingent on the particular audience at hand).[113] The validity of a particular assumption is not derived from its relationship to truth but by virtue of whether it has been adequately justified: "If I have concrete, specific doubts about whether one of my beliefs is true, I can resolve those doubts only by asking whether it is adequately justified – by finding and assessing additional reasons pro and cons".[114] While Rorty's argument of justification being contingent may strike some as relativism by the backdoor, Rorty reminds us that justification does not, unlike truth, have metaphysical implications. This takes us right back to our earlier point about diversity being a fact of life which denialism will do little to counter. In a sense, the job of the pragmatist is partly to highlight this. As Rorty observes: "The pragmatist regrets the prevalence of this representationalist picture and of the "realist" institutions that go with it, but

[111] Rorty defines 'final vocabularies' further by noting that these "are words in which we formulate praise of our friends and contempt of our enemies, our long-term projects, our deepest self-doubts and out highest hopes. They are the words in which we tell, sometimes prospectively and sometimes retrospectively, the story of our lives. [....] A small part of our final vocabulary is made up of thin, flexible, and ubiquitous terms such as "true," "good," "right," "and beautiful." See R. Rorty, *Contingency, Irony and Solidarity* (Cambridge, Cambridge University Press, 1989) at 73.

[112] Rorty associates the usage of 'final vocabularies' with the Western tradition of philosophy (which espouses a heavy emphasis on metaphysical questions) which he traces back to Plato. This Rorty contrasts with the "ironist" approach to philosophy which Rorty finds in Nietzsche among others. Rorty *ibid* at 76-83.

[113] Rorty notes that: "justification is relative to an audience and [...] we can [...] never exclude the possibility that some better audience might exist, or come to exist, to whom a belief that is justifiable to us would not be justifiable [...] For any audience, one can imagine a better-informed audience and also a more imaginative one – an audience that has thought up hitherto-undreamt-of alternatives to the proposed belief." above n. 107 at 22. It is worth noting, however, that the contingency of a particular audience may come down to no more than a 'local enthusiasm'. See R. Mullender, 'Law, Morality and the Egalitarian Philosophy of Government' (2009) 29(2) *OJLS* 389.

[114] Rorty above n. 109 at 19.

she cannot get rid of these unfortunate cultural facts by more refined analyses of contemporary common sense."[115]

Thus, the theme pursued here highlighting that diversity may lead to denial (which in turn can lead to group polarisation) is to be countered, first, by the observation that diversity is here to stay and not necessarily a bad thing, and, second, that the best way to avoid entrenchment is through open, tolerant and rational inquiry. Moreover, inquiry on the open, tolerant model described here affords a means by which to pursue falsifiability.[116]

Conclusion

While the tone of the five judges of the Canengusian Appeal Court is appropriately exaggerated in order to emphasise each position, it is clear that Hutchinson and Morgan's paper has a wider application beyond the boundaries of negligence and tort law. In this paper it has been underlined how some of the moral impulses which influence negligence and tort law equally influence environmental law and policy. This is not surprising given that the theoretical influences which are found in 'The Canengusian Connection' and in environmental law and policy, to a great degree are found in a long line of other social contexts. Debates as to whether we should favour a consequentialist or deontological approach are likewise found in debates relating to national security and foreign affairs.

This diversity, however, gives rise to associated dissonance as people are faced with a multiple of impressions. In turn, this may lead to a form of denial whereby the evidence causing the dissonance is deliberately ignored and discounted. One way to counter such developments would be to bear in mind that, first, diversity is inevitable and, second, that we can strike a way towards consensus by striving towards tolerant, critical and constructive deliberation without striding into solipsistic relativism. While such deliberation may be prone to 'monologue creep' and/or 'hobby-horsicality', we ought to at least seek a practice which is reflective and critically rational.[117] In this process, we could do a lot worse than taking inspiration

---

115 *Ibid* at 41. See also Ward above n. 106 at 289, noting that 'the liberal ironist appreciates two things. First, he or she appreciates that life is bifocal, a selfhood that is contracted by an ongoing relation of the private and the public; such a relation, of course being a matter of constant readjustment rather than demarcation. Secondly, the liberal ironist is, being ironic, also a poet, someone aware that the pretences of objective truth have been fatally crippled by the liberating play of metaphor.'

116 We might consider the model contemplated her as establishing a 'marketplace of ideas' as hinted at in *Gertz v. Robert Welch* 418 U.S. 323 (1974) per Justice Powell at 339-340. For a more recent application of the 'marketplace of ideas' see [2010] EWCA Civ 350.

117 On 'monologue creep' see O'Callaghan above n. 32 and R. Mullender above n. 8.

from Judith Shklar, who wrote that: "We all carry with us a mixed bag of *idée reçus*, and in order to travel with it through an everchanging world we must shift it around occasionally – drop something here and add something there."[118] Likewise, we must bear in mind that once we have embraced a particular view or made a particular choice, we must be open to the possibility that it is falsifiable and embrace the eventuality that we were wrong.

[118] J. Shklar, *Legalism: Law, Morals and Political Trials* (Cambridge, Harvard University Press, 1986) at 28.

MONOLOGISM AND DIALOGISM IN PRIVATE LAW

Patrick O'Callaghan*

1. Introduction

Since its publication in 1984, law students throughout the English-speaking world have become thoroughly familiar with Hutchinson and Morgan's 'The Canengusian Connection', [1] the subject of this special issue of *The Journal Jurisprudence*. The authors depict a hypothetical personal injury case featuring five fictitious judges, each of whom represents a major school of thought in legal theory, and, to this extent, the essay might be regarded as tort's version of Lon Fuller's 'Case of the Speluncean Explorers.'[2] In the vein of Fuller, Hutchinson and Morgan skilfully highlight the tensions between the various schools of thought, and, in so doing, capture the 'knock-about' character of much common law argument. But the authors sound a note in 'The Canengusian Connection' that may pain some lawyers trained in the 'grand traditions' of continental Europe, for it reinforces the standard view that the common law is nothing more than a chaotic mishmash of peculiar rules, procedures and accidents of history, lacking a sound systematic structure or core. Sceptical civilians single out the highest common law courts, in particular, on the grounds that their 'judicial monologues' sometimes give rise to vague and indeterminate decisions. The charge is that multiple voices breed incoherence; a court should speak with one voice (*la cour décide, elle ne discute pas!*), in the manner of the European Court of Justice or the French *Cour de Cassation*.[3] On this account, the province of a court is not to provide a forum for individual orations but rather to deliver the ultimate word, or, in the words of Leviathan, to arrive at a 'resolute and final sentence'.[4] While the members of a court might not unanimously agree on a particular course of action, they give the impression

---

* Lecturer, Newcastle Law School. I would like to thank John Alder and Richard Mullender for their comments.

[1] A.C. Hutchinson and D. Morgan, 'The Canengusian Connection: The Kaleidoscope of Tort Theory' (1984) 22 *Osgoode Hall Law Review* 69.

[2] L. Fuller, 'Case of the Speluncean Explorers' (1949) 62 *Harvard Law Review* 616.

[3] In fact, the *Code Civil* expressly prohibits judicial law-making. Article 5 *Code Civil* states: 'Il est défendu aux juges de prononcer par voie de disposition générale et réglementaire sur les causes qui leur sont soumises.' ('Judges are prohibited from declaring general and regulatory principles in the cases submitted to them'). On French formalism, see further V. Grosswald Curran, 'Formalism and Anti-Formalism in French and German Judicial Methodology' in C. Joerges and N.S. Ghaleigh (eds) *Darker Legacies of Law in Europe* (Oxford: Hart, 2003).

[4] T. Hobbes, *Leviathan* (J.C.A Gaskin, ed., Oxford: Oxford University Press, 1996), p 42.

of unanimity for the sake of legal certainty and the rule of law and, ultimately, to preserve a systematic structure where there is always a 'solution' to the *problematique*. In this way, while common lawyers might regard 'The Canengusian Connection' as an exaggerated (but nonetheless insightful) representation of the common law in action, to some sceptical civilians it is undoubtedly further evidence of the erratic and unpredictable nature of the common law.

This essay challenges the notion that the decisions of the highest common law courts can be reduced to mere monologues. Drawing on the work of Martin Buber, Mikhail Bakhtin, Isaiah Berlin and John Rawls, the essay argues that dialogism is the dominant feature of common law decisions. Nevertheless, courts should be on their guard against monologue-creep, a process in which an 'authoritatively persuasive voice', once embraced, begins to exert a stronger hold over the person or persons who have embraced it; thus, it becomes 'internally persuasive'.[5] Gradually, the voice attaches itself to those individuals and becomes part of their self-identity. As a phenomenon, monologue-creep is relatively common and can be partly explained by reference to various anthropological and psychological processes and pressures. In academic law, monologue-creep manifests itself in the desire to belong to a particular school of thought, even if that simply means describing one's approach as 'black-letter.' But the desire to 'belong' highlights another reason why scholars resort to monologue: more often than not, academics pursue an ideal; they latch onto the notion that they have found the 'correct answer' or, at the very least, that they are on the path to finding this answer. These ideals often encourage a utopian outlook in those who embrace them and Utopianism, with a capital 'U', thus pervades academia. This essay does not object to this practice in academic law; far from it – the pursuit of an ideal should be encouraged. For, as Berlin wrote, '[u]topias have their value – nothing so wonderfully expands the imaginative horizons of human potentialities.'[6] But he goes on to say that utopias are not quite as useful as 'guides to human conduct'.[7] On his account, a 'perfect solution' is not possible in practice and 'any determined attempt to produce it is likely to lead to suffering, disillusionment and failure.'[8] In order to illustrate this point, this essay examines the views of a group of lawyers we might label 'Strasbourg enthusiasts' and argues that their optimism concerning the impact of the ECHR and ECtHR judgments on English private law is misguided. Private law, as Hutchinson and Morgan

5 W.C. Booth, 'Introduction', in M. Bakhtin, *Problems of Dostoevsky's Poetics* (C. Emerson, ed. and trans., Minneapolis: University of Minnesota Press, 1984), p xxi.

6 I. Berlin, *The Crooked Timber of Humanity* (London: Pimlico, 2003), p 15.

7 *Ibid.*

8 *Ibid*, p 48.

recognise, is fundamentally dialogic and if human rights are to influence private law they must do so in a way that allows space for multiple voices, including those that are incommensurable. Before we move on to a discussion of these points, however, we must first carefully consider the meaning of 'monologue'.

2. The Meaning of Monologue

Is the sceptical civilian right to regard the decisions of the highest common law courts as collections of uncompromising judicial monologues? In response to this charge we must first carefully consider the meaning of monologue.

Consider the word itself: *monos* (singular/alone) and *logos* (voice/word). It is the *singular voice* or the *lonely word*, depending on one's etymological persuasion, but can be understood as both: a monologue is at once singular and lonely (*einzig und einsam*).[9] The Austrian-born philosopher, Martin Buber, attached significance to the loneliness evident in the monologist's life.[10] In his short book, *Ich und Du*, first published in 1923, Buber regards man as having a 'twofold attitude'[11] and hence makes a distinction between the *Ich-Du* and the *Ich-Es* relationships.[12] In the *Ich-Du* relationship, the 'speaker has no thing for his object',[13] the *Du* is not merely 'a thing among things'[14] but a unique Other. This relationship is 'open'[15] and 'direct.'[16] By contrast, *Ich-Es* is a subject-object relationship where the object is to be

---

[9] For Heidegger, language is monologue - it is the *lonely word.* Language 'spricht einzig und einsam, mit sich selber' ('speaks singularly and solitarily with itself'). See M. Heidegger, *Unterwegs zur Sprache* (1951), p 241, quoted by K. van Eikels 'Zwei Monologe: Die Poetik der sprechenden Sprache bei Heidegger und Novalis' in S. Jaeger & S. Willer (eds), *Das Denken der Sprache und die Performanz des Litarischen um 1800* (Würzburg: Verlag Königshausen und Neumann, 2000), p 229.

[10] For Buber, the monologist 'is incapable of making real in the context of being the community in which, in the context of his destiny, he moves.' M. Buber, *Between Man and Man* (R. Gregor Smith, trans., London: Routledge, 2002), p 23.

[11] M. Buber, *I And Thou* (2nd edn, Edinburgh: T. & T. Clark, 1958), p 3.

[12] *Ich-Du* and *Ich-Es* are frequently translated as *I-Thou* and *I-It* but some scholars criticise the use of the English versions. Vermes, for example, writes that the 'German word *du* implies an intimacy and familiarity admittedly not contained in 'you', but 'thou' in English is now addressed almost exclusively to the Deity. The impression is therefore that the book is about man and God, which is quite misleading, though it is *also* about man and God.' See P. Vermes, *Buber* (London: Halban, 1988), p 40.

[13] M. Buber, *I and Thou,* above n 11, p 4.

[14] *Ibid*, p 8.

[15] *Ibid*, p 6.

[16] *Ibid*, p 11.

'experienced' and 'used'.[17] Understood in these terms, the *Ich-Du* relationship represents dialogue whereas *Ich-Es* constitutes monologue. According to Buber, '[g]rowth of the self does not take place...through our relationship to ourselves but through being made present by the other and knowing that we are made present by him.'[18] Friedman explains that this process is called 'confirmation': one becomes confirmed as a unique person when one experiences 'the other side of the relationship so that one can imagine quite concretely what another is feeling, thinking, perceiving and knowing.'[19] When I 'open myself to the otherness of the person I meet', I engage not in dialogue but in monologue, the Other exists 'only as a content of my experience'.[20] Because the monologist refuses to experience the 'wholeness', 'unity' or 'uniqueness'[21] of the Other as is experienced in an *Ich-Du* relationship, he himself is never confirmed as a unique person. He remains a lonely, unheard *individual* rather than a confirmed, unique *person.*

Martin Buber's work inspired the Russian literary theorist, Mikail Bakhtin, to develop his own ideas on monologism and dialogism. He regarded Buber as 'the greatest philosopher of the twentieth century' and admitted that he was 'indebted' to him, especially for 'the idea of dialogue'.[22] The necessity of dialogism was the dominant feature of Bakhtin's work and he associated monologue with the single-mindedness found in authoritarian and totalitarian forms of government.[23] In what was arguably his most famous work, *Problems of Dostoevsky's Poetics*, he contends that monologue:

'denies the existence outside itself of another consciousness with equal rights and equal responsibilities, another *I* with equal rights (*thou*). With a monologic approach (in its extreme or pure form) *another person* remains wholly and merely an *object* of consciousness, and not another consciousness. No response is expected from it that could change

---

[17] *Ibid*, p 40.

[18] M. Buber, *The Knowledge of Man* (M. Friedman and R.G. Smith, trans., Atlantic Highlands, New Jersey: Humanities Press International, 1988), p 61, quoted in M. Friedman, 'Martin Buber and Mikhail Bakhtin: The Dialogue of Voices and the Word that is Spoken' in B.H. Banathy and P.M Jenlink (eds), *Dialogue as a Means of Collective Communication* (New York: Kluwer, 2005), p 29.

[19] *Ibid*, pp 29-30.

[20] *Ibid*, p 30.

[21] M. Buber, *On Intersubjectivity and Cultural Creativity* (S.N. Eisenstadt, ed., Chicago: University of Chicago Press, 1992), p 74.

[22] *New York Review of Books Interview* with Bakhtin from 1986 quoted in Friedman, above n 18, p 30.

[23] Gurevitch argues that Bakhtin's work has resonance beyond literature as it is 'the actualisation of what is primary and primordially human in us.' See Z. Gurevitch, 'Plurality in Dialogue: A Comment on Bakhtin' (2000) 34 *Sociology* 243, 244.

everything in the world of my consciousness. Monologue is finalized and deaf to the other's response, does not expect it and does not acknowledge in it any *decisive* force. Monologue manages without the other, and therefore to some degree materializes all reality. Monologue pretends to be the *ultimate word.* It closes down the represented world and represented persons.'[24]

Understood in this way, monologue is a wholly negative and destructive exercise because dialogue is vital for man's very existence. For Bakhtin, '[t]o be means to communicate dialogically...Two voices is the minimum for life, the minimum for existence.'[25]

But if monologue is so destructive,[26] what explains the tendency to engage in it, to treat the other as an 'object of consciousness' rather than an equal consciousness? Buber identified an historical trend and suggested that the 'history of the human race' indicates 'a progressive augmentation of the world of *It* [in the sense of the *Ich-Es*, subject-object relationship or monologue].'[27] Science is concerned with the acquisition of 'items of knowledge' and thus persons increasingly become objects of 'specialised utilisation.'[28] The same holds true for economic development. But while Buber's account is enlightening, there are at least three further explanations as to why we resort to monologue.

First, there is a potential anthropological or psychological dimension. In Bakhtinian theory, polyphony or heteroglossia is the ideal, but humans tend to gravitate towards monologic unity because we are not only influenced by centrifugal but also centripetal forces, a desire to bring about coherence or 'formal unity' rather than face the overwhelming chaos of multiple voices.[29] Booth argues that the 'centripetal' force 'provides us with the best experience we have of what Coleridge called "multeity in unity", a unity that does justice to variety. But we are always tempted to follow that drive too far in the direction of imposing a monologic unity.'[30] This latter idea chimes with those who point to the relevance of cognitive dissonance theories in

---

[24] M. Bakhtin, *Problems of Dostoevsky's Poetics*, above n 5, pp 292-293.
[25] *Ibid*, p 281.
[26] Not everyone sees monologue as a destructive force. Brown and Keller distinguish between two types of monologue: exploratory and narcissistic monologue. Exploratory monologue is a 'natural part of human development' while narcissistic monologue is for the 'purpose of self-adoration, rather than for the exploration of one's thoughts'. See C.T. Brown and P.W. Keller, *Monologue to Dialogue, An Exploration of Interpersonal Communication* (Englewood Cliffs: Prentice-Hall Inc, 1973), p 188.
[27] M. Buber, *I and Thou,* above n 11, p 37.
[28] *Ibid*, p 38.
[29] W.C. Booth, above n 5, p xxi.
[30] *Ibid*, pp xxi-xxii.

human psychology. As Pedersen explains, 'when faced with dissonance i.e. conflicting information, people seek to reduce such dissonance and avoid situations and information which are likely to increase [it].'[31] He points to research which demonstrates that individuals tend to dismiss those arguments which might lead to dissonance. On this account, when we engage in monologue we are in fact retreating to the comfort zone of our individual *Weltanschauungen*, for it is in this place, where we insulate ourselves against the 'overwhelming chaos' of the outside world, that we are seemingly most content. We shall revisit this argument later.

Second, monologue is particularly common among policy-makers and academics because it is associated with the pursuit of the ideal.[32] The Platonic ideal assumes that all genuine questions have one true answer and all other answers are simply erroneous.[33] The monologist convinces himself, and perhaps even others, that he has discovered the ideal, or is on the path to finding it, and this optimism can generate large ambitions, grand schemes of social engineering or enterprise association.[34] He knows how and where 'to drive the human caravan.'[35] But in the practical world, the monologist is confronted with other monologues, and this is where the third explanation for our tendency towards monologue comes into play. The lonely monologist defends his position against the world, but the more he becomes embattled, the more the monologue becomes an aspect of his self-identity and the stakes become ever-higher. The preservation of the singular voice becomes a necessity – *es muss sein*[36] – not only because the monologist seeks to preserve an ideological position, but also because the other voices have assumed the character of an existential threat. This also partly explains the phenomenon of denial: why some individuals refuse to give ground, even in the face of overwhelming evidence that their argument is wrong. The monologist endeavours to save face. To do otherwise, to give ground to multiple voices, would undermine his identity.

31 See O. Pedersen's essay in this issue, 'The Canenguisan Environmental Connection: Diversity, Dissonance and Denial.'

32 On the pursuit of the ideal, see I. Berlin, above n 6, pp 5-7.

33 *Ibid*, p 5.

34 On 'enterprise association', see M. Oakeshott, On History and Other Essays (Oxford: Blackwell, 1983). See also R. Mullender, 'Human Rights, responsibilities, and the pursuit of a realistic Utopia', (2010) 61 *Northern Ireland Legal Quarterly* 33.

35 I. Berlin, above n 6, p 15.

36 In light of these points, we can press the analysis further by drawing on Milan Kundera. Kundera, in *The Unbearable Lightness of Being*, captures the intensity of the struggle between multiple voices. When we take the view that a particular course of action is right, the assumption that 'es muss sein' (it must be so) looms to prominence in our minds. Thus we demonstrate an intransigence that, in practical contexts, may give rise to problems.

Each of us is familiar with monologue, whether the authoritarian and totalitarian ideologies of the twentieth century or examples from our own lived experiences. But to what extent is monologue a feature of our judicial system? Does 'The Canengusian Connection', as a representation of the common law in action, provide some insights?

3. Monologism in 'The Canengusian Connection'?

On reading this hypothetical case, the sceptical civilian might suggest that each judge expects to have the Bakhtinian 'ultimate word', that they seem intent on discrediting the arguments of their colleagues rather than acknowledging 'any decisive force' in them. Each judge views the other judgments as lacking in some way. Sometimes this is simply the result of misplaced optimism in the capacity of legal doctrine to provide solutions to disputes. Wright J, for example, speaks of the 'doctrinal swamp into which Doctrin CJ and Mill J have allowed themselves to be lured.'[37] But often the criticism is that there are mischievous ideological undertones in the judgments. The judges single out Mill J for particular criticism on this ground, but each engages in his/her own individual monologue and thereby pursues a distinct ideal. Lefft J attempts to set himself apart, arguing that all the other judgments are 'nothing more than a crutch for terminally ill society'.[38] However, this argument has hints of the Marxist thesis of 'false consciousness' and his CLS-informed ideal, arguably a type of purer egalitarianism, becomes apparent.

In each case, the judges highlight shortcomings in the other judgments in order to bolster their own arguments, to demonstrate why theirs is the 'correct', 'fairest' or most 'practical' judgment. Mill J, for instance, argues that 'it is readily...apparent that [Doctrin CJ's] conception of the judicial role is confused, schizophrenic, and altogether too restricted.'[39] By contrast, his own costs-and-benefits account of negligence law 'clears away the rhetoric behind which [Doctrin CJ's] cloak-and-dagger approach to public policy lurks.'[40] But this tendency to buttress an individual argument by pointing to the inadequacies of alternative positions does not necessarily add rational force to the argument. Instead, it emphasises the weaknesses of the other arguments, thus strengthening the individual argument's comparative attractions. The tendency is even present in situations where a judge appears to give ground; where he/she admits that another argument is ostensibly

[37] A.C. Hutchinson and D. Morgan, above n 1, 92.
[38] *Ibid*, 106.
[39] *Ibid*, 76.
[40] *Ibid*.

persuasive. Prudential J, for example, argues that Wright J's judgment has 'intuitive appeal; it seems ethical, practical and efficient.'[41] But on further analysis, Prudential J contends that Wright J 'still lives in the Platonic realm of abstract justice' and concludes that he 'is not only naïve, but dangerous. Common sense', he continues, 'is a notoriously unreliable source of guidance for practical affairs.'[42]

Faced with exchanges of this sort, the sceptical civilian might conclude that in discrediting alternative arguments, the judges acknowledge each other's existence but do not perceive 'equal consciousness', acting in a manner that undercuts any hope of reciprocal recognition. Whether the result of centripetal forces, the pursuit of an ideal or the exercise of denial, the other judgments become 'objects of consciousness'; they are not simply discarded, but are utilised by each individual judge to help carve out his/her own distinctive position. Wright J, for example, begins his judgment by focusing on Mill J's 'utilitarian ethic', a philosophy which Wright J views as 'incapable of furnishing sufficiently compelling reasons to deserve the allegiance and support of actual human beings.'[43] Positioning himself in this way, Wright J does not simply reject his colleague's argument but depicts Mill J's utilitarianism as an extreme position in order to highlight the more humane, deontological aspects of his own judgment.

Moreover, as further evidence of Bakhtinian monologism the sceptical civilian might argue that the Canengusian judges do not expect a response from their colleagues which 'could change everything in their world'. Do the judges – in any genuine sense – talk to one another? Take Wright J, for instance, who states:

'As is often the case, I have the dubious distinction of following Justice Mill. It will come as little surprise to those who follow the proceedings of this Court that Justice Mill and I do not see eye to eye on the proper basis for compensation for injuries.'[44]

The arguments become quotidian: we are left with the impression that the facts of the case may change, but the arguments remain the same.[45] This chimes with Buber's notion of 'speechifying' where 'people do not really speak to one another, but each, although turned to the other, really speaks

---

41 *Ibid*, 94-95.
42 *Ibid*, 95.
43 *Ibid*, 87.
44 *Ibid*.
45 See D. Kennedy, 'Legal Education as a Training for Hierarchy', (1982) 32 *Journal of Legal Education* 591.

to a fictitious court of appeal whose life consists of nothing but listening to him.'[46] Understood in these terms, speechifying is part of a wider phenomenon in contemporary society in which monologue increasingly disguises itself as dialogue; it is where 'two or more men, meeting in space, speak each with himself in strangely torturous and circuitous ways and yet imagine they have escaped the torment of being thrown back on their own resources'.[47] In a very real sense, then, it is a conversation 'in which each regards himself as absolute and legitimate and the other as relativized and questionable',[48] a type of behaviour which manifests itself on the Canengusian bench.

We thus see evidence of monologic tendencies in 'The Canengusian Connection', but we even see glimpses of 'pure' monologism, a type of monologism more intense than the everyday centripetal desire to bring about uniformity. In Bakhtinian theory, there are three principal elements to 'pure' monologism. First, it is a way of 'visualizing and representing the world'.[49] It is the principle that lies behind the choices we make and the way we unify material, the principle 'behind the ideological single-toned quality' of the work.[50] Second, the monologist presents his ideas 'as a more or less distinct or conscious deduction drawn from the represented material.' Finally, the monologist assumes 'the ideological position of the main hero.'[51]

In 'The Canengusian Connection', these features of 'pure' monologism are most apparent in Lefft J's judgment. Of all the judges, our impression of him is that he cuts a lonely figure on the bench; his oration or monologue is not just a 'singular voice', it is also a 'lonely' or 'solitary' word and he turns himself into the Other by abandoning the law. We are presented with his visualisation and representation of the world, a reality in which '[h]umanity stands on the edge of an abyss.'[52] It is a socially unjust world where 'deprivation and degradation' are commonplace. Like the other judges, Lefft

---

[46] M. Buber, *The knowledge of man: Selected essays*, above n 18, p 69, quoted in M. Cooper, '"I-I" and "I-Me": Transposing Buber's Interpersonal Attitudes to the Intrapersonal Plane', (2003) 16 *Journal of Constructivist Psychology* 131, 139.

[47] According to Buber, monologue disguised as dialogue can take the form of a 'conversation characterised by the need neither to communicate something, nor to learn something, nor to influence someone, nor to come into connexion with someone, but solely by the desire to have one's own self-reliance confirmed by marking the impression that is made, or if it has become unsteady to have it strengthened.' See M. Buber, above n10, *Between Man and Man* pp 22-23.

[48] *Ibid.*

[49] M. Bakhtin, above n 5, p 82.

[50] *Ibid*, p 83.

[51] *Ibid.*

[52] A.C. Hutchinson and D. Morgan, above n 1, 111.

J presents his conclusions as deduced from the social reality he describes, and defends his position against the other judges, regarding his colleagues as 'culprits' in legitimating this unjust society.[53] In doing so, he depicts himself as a hero, imploring us to follow him in this just cause:

'In taking my leave of this court, I implore you to follow my lead. I dedicate my remaining years to this struggle. ... We must regroup and make good on our commitment to ourselves. Love and power must converge. We must give voice to the inarticulate speech of the heart. Victims of the world unite.'[54]

While Lefft J's judgment has monologic characteristics in the Bakhtinian sense, we can also compare it a more familiar type of monologism: the literary genre of 'dramatic monologue'. The idea of monologue as a feature of literary works is not new, and, as Byron illustrates, it 'came into its own' as a genre in Victorian England, particularly with the work of Alfred Tennyson and Robert Browning.[55] According to Byron, dramatic monologue has 'survived Modernism and its aftermath in a more vigorous state than is generally believed,' but is now generally used as an 'instrument of social critique.'[56] Byron puts forward the examples of Duncan Bush's 'Pneumoconiosis' (1985), in which, against the backdrop of the miners' strikes, a coalminer speaks about the effects of his lung disease and Paula Meehan's 'The Statue of the Virgin at Granard Speaks' (1991) which addresses the question of abortion in Irish society.[57] The dramatic monologist tends to 'project and fantasise a listener'[58] and is 'concerned with persuasion of one kind or the other.'[59] Byron argues that the link between twentieth century political oratory and dramatic monologue is particularly noticeable and he goes on to remind us of Churchill's wartime speeches and Edward VII's abdication speech.[60] Rhetoric is undoubtedly a feature of these speeches, but also the 'political speakers assume specific personae for the purposes of specific occasions.'[61] Lefft J firmly belongs to this category of monologist. What this means, in effect, is that he is at once

[53] *Ibid*, 106.
[54] *Ibid*, 111.
[55] G. Byron, *Dramatic Monologue* (London: Routledge, 2003), pp 30-33.
[56] *Ibid*, p 120.
[57] *Ibid*, p 133.
[58] *Ibid*, p 23, quoting L.D. Martin, *Browning's Dramatic Monologues and the Post-Romantic Subject* (Baltimore: John Hopkins University Press, 1985), p 138.
[59] *Ibid*, p 145.
[60] *Ibid.*
[61] *Ibid.*

the Bakhtinian and the dramatic monologist, adopting the role of the 'hero' in the political struggle before him.

Does Lefft J's judgment then indicate that he is a monologist in the purest form and that 'The Canengusian Connection' is simply a collection of uncompromising judicial monologues? The sceptical civilian might reach this conclusion. On reading 'The Canengusian Connection', he/she might argue that the 'egocentric'[62] judges appear more concerned with defending their own individual philosophies than promoting legal certainty and defending the rule of law. But, as we will see in the next section, such a representation of common law judgments, and even 'The Canengusian Connection' itself, is altogether inaccurate.

4. Dialogism as a Feature of the Common Law

There are two reasons why the sceptical civilian is mistaken. First, as Mullender points out in his essay, the Canengusian judges 'exaggerate certain features that we might find in the responses made by common law judges to negligence claims'.[63] Hutchinson and Morgan employ a Dickensian approach – they ascribe a limited number of 'salient features' to the judges in an attempt to convey a sense of character to each. But in order to achieve coherence, the authors surrender, almost exclusively, to centripetal forces. While this is an understandable, if not an inevitable, feature of literary works, the centrifugal forces of real life mean that real judges are more eclectic. Consider, for example, Lord Steyn's judgment in *White v. Chief Constable of South Yorkshire*,[64] in which he recognises that the police officers have a plausible case and maintains that, ideally, 'all those who have suffered as a result of the negligence ought to be compensated.'[65] But these corrective justice sentiments are qualified by distributive justice concerns. For him, any alteration to the special rules on liability for psychiatric harm would 'greatly increase the class of persons who can recover damages in tort' and this may result in a 'burden of liability on defendants which may be disproportionate' to the initial wrongful act.[66] The eclectic nature of Lord Steyn's judgment contrasts markedly with the single-mindedness of the judgments in 'The Canengusian Connection' in which, as

[62] The Russian social theorist Lev Vygotsky regarded monologue as 'egocentric speech.' But according to him, this type of speech was a necessary stage in a child's development, when 'internalizing' language. See C. Emerson, 'Bakhtin, Vygotsky – the internalization of language' in H. Daniels (ed.), *An Introduction to Vygotsky* (1st edn., London: Routledge, 1996).
[63] See R. Mullender's essay in this issue, 'The Scampering Discourse of Negligence Law'.
[64] [1999] 2 A.C. 455.
[65] *Ibid*, at 491 (*per* Lord Steyn).
[66] *Ibid*, at 494 (*per* Lord Steyn).

Arvind notes, the 'positions taken by the judges cluster around the extremes'.[67]

We can further object to the sceptical civilian's argument by demonstrating that dialogism is in fact present in 'The Canengusian Connection'. On the face of it, the judges appear to have come to completely different conclusions. This is unsurprising given that each of us, as Rawls puts it, is 'shaped by our total experience, our whole course of life up to now; and our total experiences must always differ.'[68] But on the Canengusian bench, not only are there some points of agreement,[69] the tension between the judgments give them force – the contrasts between the various ideals make the judgments more vivid. In his essay, Mullender draws on the work of the physicist Niels Bohr and argues that 'complementarity', i.e. the notion that 'opposing views can augment – or complement – one another in practically significant ways', is a feature of 'The Canengusian Connection.'[70] A similar notion finds expression in Bakhtinian theory: there is 'constant interaction between meanings, all of which have the potential of conditioning others.'[71] In this way, even though each individual has been shaped by a different 'total experience' in the Rawlsian sense, there is, at the same time, a common, shared experience to a degree, because each statement we make, each 'utterance', is conditioned by both 'preceding voices'[72] and its 'addressivity'.[73] Whether we realise it or not, our speech is conditioned by the persuasive voices that have shaped our 'total experience' *and* by the real

---

[67] See T.T. Arvind's essay in this issue, 'The tortological question and the public-private relationship in tort law.'

[68] J. Rawls, *Political Liberalism* (New York: Columbia University Press, 1993), pp 56-57.

[69] For example, Mullender, above n 63, identifies that Doctrin CJ and Mill J agree with each other on one point. Both think that judges must 'be careful not to encourage or facilitate bogus claims'.

[70] *Ibid.*

[71] M. Bakhtin, *The Dialogic Imagination: Four Essays*, (M. Holquist, ed., Austin: University of Texas Press, 1981), p 426.

[72] Our own utterance is conditioned by previous utterances but in a 'complicated' manner. Bakhtin explains that '[u]tterances are not indifferent to one another, and are not self-sufficient: they are aware of and mutually reflect one another. These mutual reflections determine their character. Each utterance is filled with echoes and reverberations of other utterances to which it is related by the community of the sphere of speech communication. ... Each utterance 'refutes, affirms, supplements, and relies on the others, presupposes them to be known, and somehow takes them into account'. See M. Bakhtin, *Speech Genres and Other Late Essays*, (C. Emerson and M. Holquist, eds., V.W. McGee, trans., Austin: University of Texas Press, 1984), p 91. See further J.A. Cheyne and D. Tarulli, 'Dialogue, Difference and Voice in the Zone of Proximal Development', in H. Daniels (ed.), *An Introduction to Vygotsky* (2nd edn., Hove: Routledge, 2005). Cheyne and Tarulli note, at p 132, that in Bakhtinian theory our 'utterances are thereby inhabited by the voices of others.'

[73] M. Bakhtin, *Speech Genres and Other Late Essays*, above n 72, p 95.

or imaginary addressee who stands before us, as, 'from the very beginning, the utterance is constructed while taking into account possible responsive reactions.'[74] In a very real sense then, no matter how monologic the Canengusian judges may appear, they are in fact engaging in dialogue. For their 'unique speech experience' is 'shaped and developed in continuous and constant interaction with others' individual utterances'.[75] Bakhtin goes on to explain that:

'[i]n each epoch, in each social circle, in each small world of family, friends, acquaintances, and comrades in which a human being grows and lives, there are always authoritative utterances that set the tone – artistic, scientific, and journalistic works on which one relies, to which one refers, which are cited, imitated and followed. In each epoch, in all areas of life and activity, there are particular traditions that are expressed and retained in verbal vestments: in written works, in utterances, in sayings and so forth.'[76]

In this passage, we can identify some points of intersection with the communitarian 'embeddedness' thesis, which argues that a person's character is 'shaped', although not wholly 'determined', by the social context.[77] The distinguishing feature here is that *both* the 'preceding utterances' and the 'addressivity' of the utterance mould our identity and our speech.

Individuals, judges included, do not usually invent new philosophies on the spot; rather they carve out their distinctive positions over time and in reaction to the emerging or established philosophies of others. Booth explains that in Bakhtinian theory, individuals reach this point by first accommodating all those voices that are 'authoritatively persuasive' and then gradually learning to accept those that are 'internally persuasive'.[78] We therefore engage in what Bakhtin terms a 'process of assimilation';[79] over time we become more critical, we develop a 'reflective critical attitude' as Hart says of the internal point of view.[80] Bakhtin believes that we behave in this way because life is fundamentally dialogical:

---

[74] *Ibid*, p 94.
[75] *Ibid*, p 89.
[76] *Ibid*, pp 88 – 89.
[77] See S. Caney, 'Liberalism and Communitarianism: A Misconceived Debate', (1992) 40 *Political Studies* 273, 276.
[78] W.C. Booth, above n 5, p xxi.
[79] M. Bakhtin, *Speech Genres and Other Late Essays*, above n 72, p 89.
[80] H.L.A. Hart, *The Concept of Law* (2nd edn., Oxford: Oxford University Press, 1997), p 57.

'Life by its very nature is dialogic. To live means to participate in dialogue: to ask questions, to heed, to respond, to agree, and so forth. In this dialogue a person participates wholly and throughout his whole life: with his eyes, lips, hands, soul, spirit, with his whole body and deeds. He invests his entire self in discourse, and this discourse enters into the dialogic fabric of human life, into the world symposium.'[81]

To live is to 'participate in dialogue'. The impulse to engage in dialogue is such that monologism, in its purest form, is rare or perhaps even non-existent in real life. In common law systems we see several examples of dialogism, and we now move on to consider two of the most familiar: incrementalism and the notion of the community.

(i) Incrementalism

Incrementalism embodies dialogue.[82] In response to novel claims and changing social circumstances, judges articulate new legal rules by engaging in dialogue with pre-existing law. As we have seen, for Bakhtin, 'monologue manages without the other', but judges require the existence of 'another consciousness,' i.e. precedent, in order to 'go on'.[83] While precedent has 'decisive force', it never pretends to be the 'ultimate word' – there are ways and means of distinguishing or departing from precedent. When judges develop the law incrementally, they attempt to accommodate the voices of past decisions in a new coherent liability rule. Influenced by centripetal forces, judges attempt to achieve a 'multeity in unity.'

Frankfurter throws light on the process by which judges seek to achieve this type of 'multeity in unity.' Writing in 1923, he emphasised the 'creative power' exercised by judges in 'decisive cases' and explained that judges have to make 'great choices, which are determined in the end by their breadth of understanding, experience in affairs, imagination, intellectual humility, and insight into governmental problems.'[84] On this account, when faced with hard cases, judges draw on their past experience, those 'authoritatively' and

---

81 Bakhtin, *Problems of Dostoevsky's Poetics*, above n 5, p 293.

82 On the distinction between 'wide' and 'narrow' incrementalism see L. Dolding and R. Mullender, 'Tort Law, Incrementalism, and the House of Lords', (1996) 47 *Northern Ireland Legal Quarterly* 12.

83 See B. Bix, *Law, Language and Legal Determinacy* (Oxford: Clarendon Press, 1993), p 42, in which he refers to secs. 224-225 of L. Wittgenstein, *Philosophical Investigations* (3rd edn, G.E.M. Anscombe, trans., New York: Macmillan, 1968) and p 344 of L. Wittgenstein, *Remarks on the Foundations of Mathematics* (rev. edn., G.H. von Wright, R. Rhees and G.E.M. Anscombe, eds., G.E.M. Anscombe, trans., Cambridge: MIT Press, 1978).

84 F. Frankfurter, 'Twenty Years of Mr. Justice Holmes' Constitutional Opinions' (1923) 36 *Harvard Law Review* 909, 911.

'internally' persuasive voices that have helped to carve out their distinctive philosophies. They exact, what Unger calls, 'revisionary power'.[85] But whereas individual 'understanding', 'experience', 'imagination' and 'insight' tend to be products of centripetal forces, 'intellectual humility' ensures that judges see 'decisive force' in precedent, dissents and persuasive authority in the voices of others. [86] Intellectual humility is a respect for the Other; the Other remains another consciousness rather than merely an 'object of consciousness'.

Intellectual humility is necessary because all human knowledge is fallible.[87] Rawls makes a similar point when describing the 'duty of civility'; he insists that the 'ideal of citizenship' obliges us to explain to fellow citizens why, when faced with 'fundamental questions', we make the decisions we do.[88] We must explain how our position can be 'supported by the political values of public reason.'[89] Rawls goes on to state that the duty 'also involves a willingness to listen to others and a fairmindedness in deciding when accommodations to their views should reasonably be made.'[90] Judges are sometimes accused of conservatism when they 'cautiously' develop the law, but while judges are admittedly apprehensive about 'unintended consequences',[91] we should bear in mind that they are also being intellectually humble, they are revealing a preparedness to engage in dialogue. Incrementalism is thus a willingness to accept that 'I might be wrong.'[92] Within this context, judges are indeed conservative, but, as Cass

[85] R.M. Unger, *What Should Legal Analysis Become?* (London: Verso, 1996), p 67.

[86] Intellectual humility is also a feature of the system of majority decision-making. Alder explains that '[t]he justification for majority decision-making is as a device to achieve certainty of outcome in the particular case which, unlike a requirement of unanimity, is conducive to equality of respect for all participants.' See J. Alder, 'Dissents in Courts of Last Resort: Tragic Choices?', (2000) 20 *Oxford Journal of Legal Studies* 221, 222.

[87] See K. Popper, *Conjectures and Refutations* (2nd edn., London: Routledge, 2002). It is for these reasons that Sunstein advocates the dialogic 'incompletely theorized agreements' as 'a crucial part of the lawyer's distinctive solution to social pluralism' rather than the monologic 'general theories.' According to Sunstein, the latter are an 'unlikely foundation for judge-made law' and he advises that 'caution and humility about general theory are appropriate for courts, at least when multiple theories can lead in the same direction.' In attempting to achieve a 'multeity in unity', incremental decisions are thus often incompletely theorized agreements. See C.R. Sunstein, *Legal Reasoning and Political Conflict* (New York: Oxford University Press, 2000), p 59.

[88] J. Rawls, *Political Liberalism*, above n 68 p 217.

[89] *Ibid.*

[90] *Ibid.*

[91] C.R. Sunstein, *Designing Democracy* (New York: Oxford University Press, 2001) p 64.

[92] C.R. Sunstein, *Radicals in Robes: Why Extreme Right-Wing Courts are Bad for America* (New York: Basic Books, 2005), p 35.

Sunstein argues, 'sensibly so.'[93] Related manifestations of this conservatism include the ongoing commitment to refining a general duty of care test in England and the efforts of the Canadian courts to ensure that the *Anns* test reflects Canadian cultural particularity.[94] Understood in these terms, courts are charged with the task of giving expression to the *Sitten* (mores)[95] of the community, to which we now turn.

(ii) Community and the Common Law

In classical common law theory, the common law was understood to be the 'accumulated wisdom of the ages',[96] giving expression to the mores of the community. According to this view, the 'community' was *Gemeinschaftlich*, it was the source or 'bank' of collective knowledge and wisdom,[97] the sum of multiple voices and thus achieved a type of 'multeity in unity'. The notion of 'community' has retained significance in the common law and nowadays finds expression in the 'reasonable person' and notions of 'what is fit and proper.' A similar argument has been advanced by Robert Post who argues that the common law regards the individual as both independent and socially dependent.[98] Interests attached to the human personality such as reputation and privacy, for example, are socially contingent, i.e. the individual might experience wounded feelings in the event of injury to these interests but their worth and the success of any civil action is also dependent on the views and assessments of others.[99] Consider the traditional tests used to ascertain whether a statement was defamatory:

---

93 C.R. Sunstein, *Designing Democracy*, above n 91, p 64.

94 On English law, see, in particular *Donoghue* v *Stevenson* [1932] AC 562; *Anns* v *Merton London Borough* [1978] AC 728; *CBS Songs Ltd* v *Amstrad Consumer Electronics plc* [1988] 2 ALL ER 484; *Murphy* v *Brentwood District Council* [1990] 2 ALL ER 908; *Caparo Industries plc* v *Dickman* [1990] 1 ALL ER 568 (HL); *Spring v Guardian Assurance plc* [1994] 3 ALL ER 129; *Marc Rich & Co and others* v *Bishop Rock Marine Co Ltd & others* [1995] 3 ALL ER 307; *Stovin* v *Wise (Norfolk County Council, Third Party)* [1996] 3 WLR 388; See further K. Stanton, 'Professional Negligence: Duty of care Methodology in the Twenty-First Century' (2006) 22 *Professional Negligence* 134. On Canadian law, see *Kamloops* v *Neilson* [1984] 5 WWR. 1; *Cooper* v *Hobart* (2001) 206 DLR (4th) 193; *Edwards* v *Law Society of Upper Canada* (2001) 206 DLR (4th) 211; *Hill* v *Hamilton-Wentworth Regional Police Services Board* (2007) 285 DLR (4th) 620. See further N. Rafferty, 'The Canadian Supreme Court's Approach to the Duty of Question and the Tort of Negligent Investigation' (2008) 24 *Professional Negligence* 78.

95 See G.J. Postema, *Bentham and the Common Law Tradition* (Oxford: Clarendon Press, 1986).

96 *Ibid*, p 63, quoting Blackstone (1 Comm. 442).

97 *Ibid*, p 66.

98 R. Post, 'The Social Foundations of Defamation Law: Reputation and the Constitution', (1986) 74 *California Law Review* 691.

99 See T. Gibbons, 'Defamation Reconsidered', (1996) 16 *Oxford Journal of Legal Studies* 587, 592.

whether the statement subjected the individual to ridicule or contempt, whether it lowered the individual in the eyes of right-thinking members of society or whether it caused the individual to be shunned or avoided.[100] Each test is dependent on the moral judgement and core values of the community and it is for this reason that Post suggests defamation law 'presupposes an image of how people are tied together, or should be tied together in a social setting.'[101]

On this account, defamation law concerns itself not only with corrective justice but also with distributive justice, as both reputation and free speech are 'social primary goods' in the Rawlsian sense.[102] We also find reference, albeit implicitly, to both corrective and distributive justice in recent privacy case law, particularly in the construct of the 'reasonable expectation of privacy' test.[103] In the event of an unauthorised disclosure of private facts, courts first consider whether, on a subjective level, the aggrieved individual felt she had a reasonable expectation of privacy in the case at hand. But even if she insists that this expectation was present, it does not follow that she will be entitled to a remedy. For the court must also consider, on a more general and objective level, whether the community agrees with her. And so we return to the issue of distributive justice. Among other things, this ideal maintains that the law should not compensate trivial claims because, as Pound noted, a reciprocal sharing of the benefits and burdens of society or 'give and take' is the unavoidable consequence of the way in which we choose to live. When weighing competing interests, the 'oversensitive must give way.'[104]

The emerging law of privacy is thus illustrative of the enduring influence the notion of 'community' has had on the common law. But we can find further evidence in private law. The determination of causation in individual cases is another example. Writing in the *Law Quarterly Review* in 2005, Lord Hoffmann referred to the 'great achievement of Hart and Honoré', who were able to 'unpack the concept of causation' and 'showed that when judges say that it is a matter of common sense, they usually mean that it accords with ordinary moral notions of when someone should be regarded

[100] See L. McNamara, *Reputation and Defamation* (Oxford: Oxford University Press, 2007).
[101] Post, above n 98, 693.
[102] See J. Rawls, *A Theory of Justice* (Revised edn, Cambridge: Harvard University Press, 1999), pp 90-95.
[103] See *Campbell* v. *MGN* [2004] 2 AC 457. See also N. Moreham, 'Privacy in the Common Law: A Doctrinal and Theoretical Analysis' (2005) 121 *Law Quarterly Review* 628.
[104] R. Pound, 'Interests of Personality' (1914) 28 *Harvard Law Review* 343, 354.

as responsible for something which has happened.'[105] Hart and Honoré use 'ordinary language philosophy'[106] to elucidate the concept of causation and, in doing so, they show that the 'ordinary moral notions' which inform it stem from the community. Thus 'common sense' and community mores are firmly interlinked. Postema explains that in classical common law theory, judges drew on 'common reason' or the mores of the community in a novel case. According to these theorists, 'common reason' is, 'we might say, juridical common sense.'[107]

If the communitarian 'embeddedness' thesis is correct,[108] then the community, although it does not feature in modern discourse as prominently as it did in classical law theory, will always inform judicial decision-making. In determining what is 'fit and proper', courts have regard to the *Sitten* of the community and, like incrementalism, the use of dissents and persuasive authority, this exercise is necessarily dialogic. Thus, those who insist that common law judgments are no more than monologues have (perhaps intentionally, or through ignorance or a lack of charity) overlooked the importance of these features of our legal system. In attempting to achieve a 'multeity in unity', we see a strong commitment to dialogism rather than monologism in the common law. However, like other institutions, the legal system does not remain impervious to the effects of monologue creep, which we now consider.

5. Monologue-Creep

As we noted earlier, individuals tend to gravitate towards monologue. This is often the consequence of anthropological and psychological centripetal forces, the pursuit of an ideal or simply an attempt to preserve and maintain self-identity. Polyphony or heteroglossia unnerves us; we are intimidated by the prospect of an overwhelming chaos of multiple voices and instead seek to base ourselves in the familiarity of our internal monologues. Moreover, given that we are prone to acting in this way, we are prey to the monologue 'out there' in society: e.g. the 'visions' of the party-hack or ideologue.

Yet no matter how much we seek to resist the impulse to engage in monologue, we are forever vulnerable to a process which we might term monologue-creep. In our formative years, when faced with multiple voices,

105 Hoffmann, The Rt Hon Lord, 'Causation' (2005) 121 *Law Quarterly Review* 592, 593. See further H.L.A. Hart and T. Honoré, *Causation in the Law* (2nd edn, Oxford: Oxford University Press, 1985).
106 F. Schauer, '(Re)Taking Hart', (2006) 119 *Harvard Law Review* 852, 852-853.
107 G.J. Postema, above n 95, p 71.
108 S. Caney, above n 77.

we latch onto those that are 'authoritatively persuasive'. Over time, perhaps tentatively, we begin to accept those that are also 'internally persuasive'. Emerson explains that in Bakhtinian theory the '[i]ndividuation of the personality is the process of a consciousness working over the "ideological themes" that penetrate it "and there take on the semblance of individual accents".'[109] Thus, these voices begin to exert a stronger hold on us; not only do they become our *Weltanschauung*, they also become intertwined with our *Persönlichkeit*, our sense of who we are. Hence, we resort to monologue, or at least tend towards it, in order to preserve self-identity. Some even go so far as to identify an age at which voices become 'internally persuasive'. Lord Hoffmann, writing extra-judicially in 2005, refers to Maynard Keynes' observation that 'there are not many who are influenced by new theories after they are 25 or 30 years of age.' For Lord Hoffmann, '[if] therefore, you are looking for the intellectual influences on the older judicial members of the House of Lords, the best way is to ask what was new and exciting in legal philosophy 50 years ago.'[110]

Monologue-creep can impact on individuals, groups or even nation states and the examples are plentiful – consider teenagers who define themselves as 'goths' or the emerging 'Tea Party' movement in the United States. Monologue creep may also assume less obvious forms such as the 'soft-power' influence of US culture globally following World War II.[111] Once an idea is embraced by a group, the phenomenon of group dynamics[112] ensures that the thought ingrains itself on those who embrace it and thus we see in this process the existence of memes, in Dawkin's terminology.[113] Monologue-creep is particularly common in academia, where many feel the need to align themselves to a particular 'school of thought', and it is at this point that we examine the views of a group of lawyers we might label Strasbourg enthusiasts. They exhibit a high degree of optimism concerning the ECHR and the jurisprudence of the ECtHR. But this enthusiasm seems to tend in a utopian direction, which means, in the words of Berlin, that their enterprise 'is likely to lead to…disillusionment and failure.'[114]

6. The Strasbourg-Enthusiasts - Monologism in Action?

[109] C. Emerson, above n. 62, p 127.
[110] Hoffmann, above n105, 594.
[111] See J.S. Nye, *Soft Power: The Means to Success in World Politics* (New York: Public Affairs, 2004)
[112] On group dynamics, see O. Pedersen, above n 31.
[113] R. Dawkins, *The Selfish Gene* (Oxford: Oxford University Press, 1989), ch. 11.
[114] Berlin, above n 6, p 48.

The Strasbourg-enthusiast believes that the application of Strasbourg principles and case law will automatically lead to an improved state of affairs. Among other things, they are concerned with 'tidiness' in the law,[115] i.e. the notion that one can design a friction-free and distributively just scheme of allocating burdens and entitlements. Speaking in 1997, Lord Irvine, for instance, insisted that judges were 'pen-poised' to develop a right of privacy in the common law.[116] He explained that the new privacy law would be a 'better law' as judges would have to balance Arts. 8 and 10 ECHR.[117] Strasbourg-enthusiasm is even more common in academia. Bennett, for instance, in this issue, proposes an action based on Art. 8 ECHR that would encompass dignitary interests generally.[118]

The ECtHR itself has spurred these enthusiasts on. As a result of its 'assertive jurisprudence'[119] over the past twenty years, the Strasbourg Court has expanded the remit of ECHR rights to private law relationships. According to the Court, a state has, in some circumstances,[120] a positive obligation to take active measures to ensure that an individual's rights under the ECHR are not infringed by another private party.[121]

---

115 In *Canadian National Railway Co* v. *Norsk Pacific Steamship Co Ltd* (1992) 91 DLR (4th) 289, 365, McLachlin J 'refus[es] to accept injustice merely for the sake of doctrinal tidiness' quoted by R. Mullender in 'The Reasonable Person, The Pursuit of Justice, and Negligence Law' (2005) 68 *Modern Law Review* 681, 690.

116 House of Lords, Debates (24 November 1997) C 784.

117 *Ibid.*

118 See T. Bennett's essay in this issue, 'Corrective Justice and Horizontal Privacy'.

119 R.S. Kay, 'The European Convention on Human Rights and the Control of Private Law' (2005) 5 *European Human Rights Law Review* 466, 466.

120 Those situations in which positive obligations can arise were set out by the ECtHR in *Özgür Gündem* v. *Turkey* (2001) 31 EHRR 49, at para 42: 'Although the essential object of many provisions of the Convention is to protect the individual against arbitrary interference by public authorities, there may in addition be positive obligations inherent in an effective respect of the rights concerned. The Court has found that such obligations may arise under Article 8. Obligations to take steps to undertake effective investigations have also been found to accrue in the context of Articles 2 and 3, while a positive obligation to take steps to protect life may also exist under Article 2.'

121 See *X and Y* v. *Netherlands* (1985) 8 EHRR 235, in which the Court stated that the obligations on the State involved 'the adoption of measures designed to secure respect for private life even in the sphere of the relations of individuals between themselves.' See also the decisions of the ECtHR in *A* v. *United Kingdom* (1998) 27 EHRR 611, *Refah Partisi and Others v. Turkey* (2003) 37 EHRR 1; *MC* v. *Bulgaria* (2005) 40 EHRR 20, *Pla and Puncernau* v. *Andorra* (2006) 42 ECHR 25; *von Hannover* v. *Germany* (2005) 40 EHRR 1. See also A. Clapham, *Human Rights Obligations of Non-State Actors* (Oxford: OUP, 2006) at 349-352.

While this obligation has been recognised by the UK courts in privacy cases,[122] these positive obligations affect a wide range of private law relationships. The ECtHR, for instance, has held that a state has a positive obligation to protect immigrant tenants who wish to receive satellite television from their home country, even in cases where the private tenancy agreement expressly prohibits the installation of satellite dishes for reasons of safety or aesthetics.[123] On the ECtHR's account, a human right to receive satellite television stems from Art. 10 ECHR.

For this reason, the Strasbourg court insists that we must be ever-vigilant about human rights and considers that Art. 8 ECHR, for example, pervades all human relationships. Unlike the UK courts, the European Court of Human Rights (ECtHR) presumes that victimhood, or the potential for it, is ubiquitous. According to the Court, Art. 8 protects:

'...a person's physical and psychological integrity; the guarantee afforded by Art. 8 of the Convention is primarily intended to ensure the development, without outside interference, of the personality of each individual in his relations with other human beings. There is therefore a zone of interaction of a person with others, even in a public context, which may fall within the scope of "private life".'[124]

As Kay emphasises, there are 'few grievances that cannot be accommodated to a claim of interference with this kind of interest.'[125] He argues that if we were to apply this in private law, 'we could, effectively have a situation where the Convention obliges every person to respect every other person's "physical and psychological integrity" – except when, all things considered, it is better not to do so.'[126] On the ECtHR's account, Art. 8 stretches across public and private law; it becomes a general monologue.

As in every instance of Bakhtinian 'pure' monologism or dramatic monologue in the literary sense, the Strasbourg enthusiasts also have their 'main heros', those individuals who know 'how to drive the human

[122] '[T]he ECtHR has recognized an obligation on member states to protect one individual from an unjustified invasion of private life by another individual and an obligation on the courts of a member State to interpret legislation in a way which will achieve that result.' (*per* Lord Phillips MR) in *Douglas* v. *Hello* [2006] QB 125, at 149.

[123] See *Autronic AG* v. *Switzerland* (1990) 12 EHRR 485; *Khurshid Mustafa and Tarzibachi* v. *Sweden* (2009)

[124] *von Hannover*, above n 121, [50].

[125] R.S. Kay, above n 119, 477.

[126] *Ibid.*

caravan.'[127] One such hero is the Vice-President of the European Human Rights Commission, Mr Sperduti, who has highlighted the 'precarious position' of individuals and has argued that it is 'necessary to expand the interpretation of the European Convention in order to find therein means of protecting the individual against his fellow-men.'[128]

Heroes, such as Mr Sperduti, are perhaps well-intentioned and there are indeed some compelling arguments as to why human rights should be applied in private law.[129] First, since the 1950s, private companies and organisations have enlarged to the point that their financial income now dwarfs that of many small nation states.[130] In such circumstances, the individual is equally vulnerable when dealing with either a large corporation or state authorities. Second, with increasing privatisation it is 'difficult to see how a function ceases to be a public function simply because of a change in who carries it out.'[131] Third, critics question why a small municipality with a limited budget is obligated to comply fully with all constitutional human rights provisions, while large corporations are rarely subjected to the same level of scrutiny.[132]

The human rights monologist seeks to protect and empower the vulnerable individual. At the same time, human rights are deontological constructs and, quite understandably as such, are assessed from the 'victim-perspective'.[133] Vulnerability can be a feature of private law as well as public law relationships, and the argument that judges should apply a general human rights monologue in private law is compelling if one agrees that corrective justice and the protection of weaker individuals are important ideals in a democratic society. But we should remember that private law is dialogic. Classical private law is concerned with complex relationships between

---

127 I. Berlin p 15

128 'Oral Interventions', Fourth International Colloquy (n 56) 111, 113 quoted by A.I.L Campbell, 'Positive Obligations under the ECHR: deprivation of liberty by private actors' (2006) 10 *Edinburgh Law Review* 399, 408.

129 See G. Brüggemeier, A. Colombi Ciacchi and G. Comandé (eds.), *Fundamental Rights and Private Law in the European Union: Volume 1* (Cambridge: Cambridge University Press, 2010).

130 See, for example, the news story from 2007, 'Tesco: Richer than Peru' http://www.guardian.co.uk/business/2007/apr/15/supermarkets.uknews

131 The Rt. Hon. Lord Justice Sedley, *Freedom, Law and Justice* (London: Sweet & Maxwell, 1999), p 28. Campbell, above n 128, 403, provides the example of *Storck* v. *Germany* (2006) 43 EHRR 6, in which the ECtHR found that the applicant's right to liberty under Art. 5 (1) ECHR had been infringed. The applicant had been admitted and confined to a private psychiatric institution without a court order.

132 See A. Barak, 'Constitutional Human Rights and Private Law', in D. Friedmann and D. Barak-Erez (eds.) *Human Rights in Private Law* (Oxford: Hart, 2001), p 20.

133 A. Freeman, 'Legitimizing Racial Discrimination with Anti-Discrimination Law: A Critical Review of Supreme Court Doctrine', (1978) 62 *Minnesota Law Review* 1049, 1051.

actors in society and the economy; relationships founded on principles of freedom of choice, contract, autonomy and action. Sometimes they may prove mutually beneficial but these relationships are not always harmonious or devoid of friction. Such is the reality of life. For, under the Bakhtinian 'law of placement', each of us is situated differently.[134] We may occupy the same space but our cognition of this space is unique to us; there are, as Holloway and Kneale explain, 'differences in simultaneity'.[135] While there are limits such as public policy, the starting point in classical private law is that sellers may discriminate against buyers, just as testators may discriminate against potential heirs.[136] It may even be the case that the seller or testator has acted in a manner which not only offends the other party but also offends other members of the community. The human rights monologist, concerned as he is with tidiness in the law, might regard this as an unsatisfactory state of affairs, a clear instance in which the right to equal treatment has been infringed.[137] The monologist may even wish to step in and settle disputes where the actions of a private party, although not unlawful on the basis of the present private law, nonetheless offend 'civil mores'.

While possibly well-intentioned, there are at least three objections to applying a general human rights monologue in private law. We will examine each of these objections in turn:

i) First, we cannot simply assume that human rights discourse can provide 'reasonable answers' to all complex private law disputes.
ii) Second, on an operational level, how do we decide who is vulnerable? Is there a standard against which we can measure degrees of vulnerability?
iii) Third, like Lefft J in 'The Canengusian Connection', the monologist assumes that private law is unwilling or simply unable to protect vulnerable parties and, as we shall see, this is a rather bold assumption.

(i) *Can Human Rights Discourse Provide 'Reasonable Answers'?*

Civilians often refer to the notion of 'solving cases' (*Lösen von Fällen*). In the English language, at least, the word 'solution' is not an altogether satisfactory way of describing how judges, bearing the 'burden of

---

[134] J. Holloway and J. Kneale, 'Mikhail Bakhtin: Dialogics of Space' in M. Crang and N.J. Thrift (eds.) *Thinking Space* (London: Routledge, 2000) p. 74.
[135] *Ibid.* Bakhtin speaks of 'simultaneous coexistence'. See M. Bakhtin, above n 5, p. 29.
[136] See P. Atiyah, *The Rise and Fall of Freedom of Contract* (Oxford: Clarendon Press, 1979).
[137] *Cf. Pla and Puncernau* v. *Andorra* (2006) 42 ECHR 25.

judgment',[138] decide cases. In developing the Kantian idea of 'Public Reason',[139] Rawls argues that we must come to a 'reasonable answer' in 'all, or nearly all,' cases 'involving constitutional essentials or basic questions of justice.'[140] The 'reasonable answer' attempts to 'balance', 'combine' or 'otherwise unite' the values of a pluralistic society. But importantly, unlike the judges in 'The Canengusian Connection', he believes that this cannot be achieved by resorting to 'philosophical doctrines – to what we as individuals or members of associations see as the whole truth.'[141]

We arrive at 'reasonable answers' by overcoming the 'burdens of judgment.' As 'rational' and 'reasonable' individuals we are faced with choices, often conflicting and sometimes equally compelling. Rawls lists six sources of 'reasonable disagreement':[142] cases where there is 'conflicting and complex' evidence, where there is disagreement about the weight that should be attached to various considerations, where we have to interpret 'vague' and 'indeterminate' concepts, where our 'total experiences are disparate enough for [our] judgments to diverge', where we have to make an 'overall assessment' about 'normative considerations of different force', and finally, where we must select between competing values because of 'limited social space.'

Judges encounter these burdens in every case where there is a 'basic question of justice' and, as Rawls puts it, '[m]any hard decisions may seem to have no clear answer.'[143] But does rephrasing the detail of private law disputes in human rights language makes things any easier?

This essay argues that it does not. For almost every legally protected interest can be classified as, or stretched to be, a human right in one way or the other. This also includes the basic operating of principles of classical private law: freedom of contract and action can be classified as human rights in

---

138 J. Rawls, above n 68, pp 54-58.

139 For Rawls, *Ibid*, pp 212-213, 'public reason' affords a political society a 'way [to] formulat[e] its plans, to [put] its ends in an order of priority and to [make] its decisions accordingly.' The capacity to achieve this is 'rooted' in the 'human members' of the society. On questions of 'constitutional essentials' and 'basic justice', p 224, the 'principle of political legitimacy' requires that the 'basic structure and its public policies are to be justifiable to all citizens.' But in making these justifications, we draw on a limited number of sources, namely 'presently accepted general beliefs and forms of reasoning found in common sense, and the methods and conclusions of science when these are not controversial.'

140 *Ibid*, p 225.

141 *Ibid*.

142 *Ibid*, pp 56- 57.

143 *Ibid*, p 57.

themselves.[144] On a Nietzschen view, the proponent of slave morality assumes that we are *all* vulnerable *all* of the time; the result is that *jedermann* becomes the hopeless victim.[145] But to what extent does this constitute a 'reasonable answer'? The difficulty with this approach is that we find not only compatible but also incommensurable voices in real life.[146] Those who carry the 'burden of judgment' on their shoulders must continue to make what Berlin terms 'tragic choices'.[147] Relying on Strasbourg principles will not make these decisions any easier because '[w]e are doomed to choose, and every choice may entail an irreparable loss'[148] and for each problem we 'solve', another predicament arises. If anything, a judge who chooses to apply Strasbourg principles *without* engaging in dialogue with precedent and the community will appear to be deciding the case arbitrarily, thus accentuating any feeling of loss. Talk of 'balancing' or 'weighing' competing interests will not help either. As Alder points out, this metaphor is 'inappropriate because there is no common scale against which the different components can be compared.'[149]

Strasbourg enthusiasts, like Mr Sperduti, earnestly pursue an ideal, but in doing so they are locked in monologue, however one which pursues a utopian ideal, the 'notion of the perfect whole, the ultimate solution, in which all good things coexist.' But such lofty plans are always doomed to fail.[150] Utopianism can only be a product of monologue, whether on the part of the individual thinker or as a result of group dynamics. Moreover, utopias are designed on the premises of 'correct' answers and can never reflect the reality of multiple voices in the 'world symposium'. According to Berlin, those who pursue an ideal in this monologic way 'rest on … comfortable beds of dogma' and 'are victims of forms of self-induced myopia, blinkers that may make for contentment, but not for understanding of what it is to be human.'[151]

---

144 See R. Brownsword, 'Freedom of Contract, Human Rights and Human Dignity' in D. Friedmann and D. Barak-Erez, above n 132.

145 According to Nietzsche this is a 'pessimistic distrust of the whole human condition' ('ein pessimistischer Argwohn gegen die ganze Lage des Menschen'). See sec. 260 of *Jenseits von Gut und Böse* (1886) in G. Colli and M. Montinari (eds) *Nietzsche Werke* (Berlin: de Gruyter, 1968).

146 On incommensurability, see I. Berlin, above n 6, p 55; J. Raz, The Morality of Freedom (Oxford: Oxford University Press, 1986), ch 13; R. Chang (ed.) *Incommensurability, Incomparability and Practical Reason* (Cambridge: Harvard University Press, 1997).

147 Alder makes this point, above n 86, 224.

148 I. Berlin, above n 6, p 13.

149 J. Alder, above n 86, 224.

150 I. Berlin, above n 6, p 13.

151 *Ibid*, p 14. In relation to the contentment point, see Pedersen, above n 31, on the avoidance of cognitive dissonance.

We find several examples of this myopia in English law. Consider the use of Art. 8 ECHR by the UK courts in developing a new privacy action. Art. 8 has given new 'strength and breadth'[152] to the doctrine of breach of confidence, and the new action affords a remedy to individuals in cases where private information has been unlawfully disclosed to third parties. But while Strasbourg enthusiasts may celebrate the arrival of a 'privacy tort', this new action does not actually fill the privacy vacuum in English law; far from it – importing a right of privacy into English private law raises more questions than answers. Are claimants in *Wainwright*-type situations (where there is an invasion of physical space rather than informational privacy) protected by the new tort?[153] What occurs when there is a misappropriation of personality? Does a post-mortem right of privacy/publicity exist in English law? Focused on importing Art. 8 into a limited number of disputes involving high-profile celebrities, UK courts have not even begun contemplating such important questions. These questions will only be meaningfully addressed when courts engage in dialogue with precedent, the community, persuasive authority and work, as the common law does, from the bottom-up, rather than deducting from the Strasbourg provisions. For, as Mullender argues, the Strasbourg principles are not only 'powerful reasons for action' but are also 'invitations to more work'.[154]

(ii) *Assessing Vulnerability*

The second objection against the application of a general human rights monologue in private law is that it would cause significant operational problems. As argued above, human rights are assessed from the 'victim-perspective'[155] and the protection of the vulnerable individual is thus central to human rights law. But in private law, this raises some difficult questions. How do we decide who is vulnerable? Should we measure degrees of vulnerability in order to ensure that the truly vulnerable are protected? As we will see, problems of this kind are pervasive in the recent privacy case law.

Privacy has long been a neglected interest in English law and the lack of a distinct remedy has led to distinctly awkward decisions in the past, in which courts acknowledged that a significant interest had been infringed but were

152 *A* v *B* [2003] QB 195, 202 (*per* Lord Woolf CJ).
153 See below for a description of the *Wainwright* case and the problems which result from it.
154 R. Mullender, 'Tort, Human Rights and Common Law Culture' (2003) 23 *Oxford Journal of Legal Studies* 301, 316.
155 A. Freeman, above n 133.

forced to conclude that a remedy was unavailable. *Kaye v. Robertson*[156] concerned a prominent actor who had suffered severe injuries in a car accident. While in hospital, reporters for a tabloid newspaper, *The Sunday Sport*, gained access to his private room, interviewed and photographed him, before being ejected by the hospital security staff. Medical evidence indicated that Mr Kaye's condition was such that he was unable to give informed consent and the judges of the Court of Appeal highlighted his particularly vulnerable position. Bingham LJ, for example, was sympathetic:

'If ever a person has a right to be let alone by strangers with no public interest to pursue, it must surely be when he lies in hospital recovering from brain surgery and in no more than partial command of his faculties.' [157]

But English law, as it stood at that time, could offer little protection to the claimant. He (just about) succeeded in bringing an action in malicious falsehood but that, in itself, was unsatisfactory as the claimant was forced to jump through the proverbial hoops and prove special damage under the action.[158] The potential for judicial paralysis in such cases was highlighted by Bingham LJ who warned that had the claimant failed to establish a cause of action the court would have been 'powerless to act, however great [the] sympathy for the plaintiff and however strong [the] distaste for the defendant's conduct.'[159]

Similarly, in *Wainwright v. Home Office*,[160] a mother and her mentally impaired son were subjected to a strip search by prison officers on their visit to a prison. It emerged in court that the officers failed to conduct the search in accordance with the Prison Rules 1964 and the claimants asserted that they had been humiliated and that their right to privacy had been invaded as a result. However, Lord Hoffmann emphasised that the common law was 'unwilling' if not 'unable' to 'formulate any such high-level principle.'[161]

One would think that a finding of vulnerability would be uncontroversial in cases where there has been a physical intrusion into a private space,

---

[156] [1991] FSR 62.
[157] *Ibid*, at 70 (*per* LJ Bingham).
[158] Glidewell LJ, *Ibid* at 68, reasoned that Mr. Kaye had 'a potentially valuable right to sell the story of his accident and his recovery'. If the defendants were allowed to publish the article in the way they proposed, the 'value of this right would…be seriously lessened, and Mr. Kaye's story thereafter would be worth much less to him.' At a stretch, therefore, the Court was able to identify special damage and award an interlocutory injunction.
[159] *Ibid*, at 70.
[160] [2004] 2 A.C. 406.
[161] *Ibid*, at 419.

particularly where the claimant is interacting with state authorities, as in *Wainwright,* or is seriously ill, as in *Kaye.* But courts remain opposed to 'a judicial power'[162] declaring a general right of privacy because a general wrong would result in 'an unacceptable degree of uncertainty.'[163] While decisions such as *Wainwright* and *Kaye* were widely criticised, many commentators insisted that this anomaly would be rectified by the coming into force of the Human Rights Act 1998. We need only remind ourselves of Lord Irvine's insistence that judges were 'pen-poised' to develop a right of privacy in the common law.[164] The Human Rights Act has certainly given courts the impetus to develop a new privacy action, but while some commentators regard these developments as evidence of progress in the protection of human rights in the UK, a closer examination of the case law reveals that the new tort has a very narrow remit.[165] The new action can best be described as a disclosure of private information tort and, as such, does not extend to the other forms of invasion of privacy.

This new tort caters for a particular type of claimant, generally a public figure or celebrity who complains that a media outlet has published or is about to publish information concerning his private life. Although non-public persons can avail of this action, the case law of other countries shows that such claims are uncommon.[166] There are, of course, cases where the public spotlight has fallen on non-public figures who have, for example, become victims of high profile crimes. But, generally, complaints from non-public persons concerning informational privacy relate to questions of data protection and will fall under relevant domestic and EU legislation in this area.[167] By contrast, the bulk of the disclosure cases involve individuals whose 'trade' is publicity,[168] celebrities who cannot be conveniently described as 'vulnerable'. Rather these cases are often characterised by celebrities attempting to preserve, control or manage their public persona and/or image for commercial gain.[169] In the recent case of *Terry v. Persons Unknown*, for example, Tugendhat J thought it 'likely' that the 'real concern of the applicant in this case [was] the effect of publication upon the

162 *Ibid*, at 421 (*per* Lord Hoffmann).

163 *Ibid*, at 422.

164 House of Lords, Debates (24 November 1997) C 784.

165 See P. O'Callaghan, 'Privacy in Pursuit of a Purpose', (2009) 17 *Tort Law Review* 100.

166 See J. Krzeminska-Vamvaka and P. O'Callaghan, 'Mapping out a Right of Privacy in Tort Law' in G. Brüggemeier, A. Colombi Ciacchi and G. Comandé (eds) *Fundamental Rights and Private Law in the European Union: Volume II* (Cambridge: Cambridge University Press, 2010).

167 Directive 95/46/EC and Directive 2002/58/EC.

168 *Campbell*, above n 103, at 470 (*per* Lord Hoffmann)

169 See *Douglas v. Hello (No. 3)* [2006] QB 125.

sponsorship business'.[170] Similarly in *Campbell*, Lord Hoffmann described the claimant as:

'a prima donna celebrity against a celebrity-exploiting tabloid newspaper. Each [party] in their time has profited from the other. Both are assumed to be grown-ups who *know the score*.'[171] [Emphasis added]

For Strasbourg enthusiasts, *Douglas* and *Campbell* are cases involving circumstances where important human rights have been infringed. But using human rights language in this context has the effect of masking the real dispute, which is often nothing more than an old-fashioned civil action between two parties 'who know the score'.[172] Thus the Strasbourg enthusiast demonstrates – like the Canengusian judges – that his views are narrowly focused and this suggests that Strasbourg enthusiasts apprehend a distorted reality through a prism that filters out much of what is relevant.[173]

(iii) *Protecting the Vulnerable Individual in Dialogic Private Law*

Presumptions that both parties 'know the score' are not uncommon in civil actions. Contract law operates on the presumption of capacity to contract; in tort, 'knowing the score' is expressed through the principle of personal responsibility:[174] damages, for example, can be apportioned where contributory negligence is present.

But while private law often presumes that private parties 'know the score', it does not ignore the plight of the vulnerable individual: the presumption can be rebutted in cases where an individual has been exploited or otherwise wronged. Consider the case of an individual standing surety for the business debts of his/her spouse, but when the lender attempts to implement the agreement, the individual claims that his/her spouse forced him/her to sign

---

170 [2010] EWHC 119 (QB), at [131] (*per* Tugendhat J).

171 *Campbell,* above n 103, at 498 (*per* Lord Hoffmann).

172 Sometimes there are significant personal interests at stake e.g. where an individual is being harassed or 'hounded' by the press (see *von Hannover*, above n 121) or where children are the subjects of the news reports (see *Murray* v *Express Newspapers* [2009] Ch 481.

173 On the 'theory of aspects', see E. Mickiewicz's essay in this issue, 'An Exploratory theory of Legal Coherence in Canengus and Beyond'.

174 'Personal responsibility' is used in a general way here, not just focusing on the behaviour of the wrongdoer but also on the conduct of the injured party or the party alleging injury. On responsibility generally, see T. Honoré, *Responsibility and Fault* (Oxford: Hart, 1999); on the behaviour of the plaintiff see, in particular, pp 89-90. See also A. Beever, 'Corrective Justice and Personal Responsibility in Tort Law' (2008) 28 *Oxford Journal of Legal Studies* 475.

the agreement in the first place.[175] One could perhaps argue that there are significant human rights at stake here, but judges have developed a means to protect the legitimate interests of the vulnerable party in this case without the need to apply a general human rights monologue. The equitable doctrine of undue influence arises in cases where one party is in a more powerful position than the other and coerces the weaker party into a transaction, which is disadvantageous to that weaker party.[176] Equitable principles and doctrines such as these provide relief in cases where a strict application of the law would otherwise lead to injustice or unfairness. Through the doctrine of undue influence, fashioned by incremental development, courts have managed to find a way to accommodate the security interests of the claimant, as well as those of the defendant, in freedom of action.[177]

To describe this as a 'balance' might be too optimistic, but in accommodating the conflicting interests in this way, the doctrine arrives at a 'reasonable answer' for it also gives expression to the principle of personal responsibility. While equity will intervene to protect a vulnerable individual from being wronged by another party in a more powerful position, it will not protect individuals from their own foolishness. In the seminal case of *Allcard v. Skinner* (1887),[178] Lindley J questioned whether 'it is right and expedient to save persons from the consequences of their own folly' or whether it 'is right and expedient to save them from being victimised by other people?' He decided that undue influence sought to achieve the latter. He went on to state that:

'It would obviously be to encourage folly, recklessness, extravagance and vice if persons could get back property which they foolishly made away with, whether by giving it to charitable institutions or by bestowing it on less worthy objects. On the other hand, to protect people from being forced, tricked or misled in any way by others into parting with their property is one of the most legitimate objects of all laws; and the equitable doctrine of undue influence has grown out of and been developed by the

---

175 On these classic 'unfair suretyships' cases see A. Colombi Ciacchi and S. Weatherill (eds) *Unfair Banking Practices in Europe: The Case of Personal Suretyships* (Oxford: Oxford University Press, 2010). See also M. Kenny, 'Standing Surety in Europe: Common Core or Tower of Babel?', (2007) 70 *Modern Law Review* 175.

176 See *Royal Bank of Scotland* v. *Etridge* (No 2) [2002] 2 AC 773, at 794 – 800 (*per* Lord Nicholls).

177 This argument is open to criticism. Unger argues that principles associated with the market and the 'pitiless world of deals' triumph over those associated with community. See R.M. Unger, 'The Critical Legal Studies Movement', (1983) 96 *Harvard Law Review* 561, 625.

178 (1887) L.R. 36 Ch. D. 145.

necessity of grappling with insidious forms of spiritual tyranny and with the infinite varieties of fraud.'[179]

Equity protects vulnerable individuals when they have been wronged, but this protection is curbed by the principle of personal responsibility. Equity acts to secure the interests of the vulnerable, but if judges advert to the principle of personal responsibility as a salient concern, it may check their urge to act in inappropriate cases and thereby throw light on genuine instances of vulnerability. By contrast, a human rights monologue with deontological impulses, focused on victimhood and oppression, does not measure the victim's personal responsibility. Naturally, it would be absurd to view a victim's foolishness as some sort of mitigating factor where human rights are infringed; it would be absolutely abhorrent to argue that victims of genocide were somehow contributorily negligent. But this point highlights the very real difference between human rights discourse and private law. Within human rights discourse, the status of victim is such that the victim's actions are usually considered inconsequential, but in a classic private law dispute where both parties are deemed to 'know the score' the question of personal responsibility or even foolishness on the part of the claimant is often pivotal. Two examples from recent privacy case law are illustrative here.

In *Campbell*, the claimant had publicly denied ever taking drugs and thus the Law Lords unanimously agreed that the press had the right to correct this misdescription.[180] The question of personal responsibility on the part of the claimant also rears its head in *Mosley v. News Group Newspapers Ltd.*[181] Details of the claimant's liaison with prostitutes appeared in a published newspaper article, which accused him of being involved in a 'sick nazi orgy.'[182] It emerged in court that the claimant had received warnings from friends that he was being 'watched by some unidentified group of people hostile to him' but he continued to arrange his parties.[183] For this reason, Eady J remarked that to 'a casual observer… it might seem that the claimant's behaviour was reckless and almost self-destructive.'[184] He went on to explain that while this

---

179 *Ibid*, at 183.

180 In this case, the defendant conceded that the *Mirror* was 'entitled to publish the fact of her drug dependency and the fact that she was seeking treatment [because] she had specifically given publicity to the very question of whether she took drugs and had falsely said that she did not.' Lord Hoffmann accepted that 'this create[d] a sufficient public interest in the correction of the impression she had previously given'. See *Campbell*, above n 103, at 474.

181 [2008] EMLR 20.

182 *Ibid*, at [1].

183 *Ibid*, at [225].

184 *Ibid*, at [226].

did 'not excuse the intrusion into his privacy' it '*might* be a relevant factor to take into account when assessing [causation]'.[185] Was the claimant therefore 'the author of his own misfortune?'[186] Eady J mused that a public figure who regularly meets prostitutes, for example, risks public exposure or blackmail. But in this particular case, the judge found no evidence to suggest that the 'surveillance [the claimant] was warned against had any connection with [the defendant]' and thus presumably the claimant's actions were not considered to be a relevant factor in assessing causation.[187] Nonetheless, the judge's remarks on causation deserve close attention because he underscores the importance of dialogue with the community. But we are not concerned here with the ideal of a Kantian ethical community; rather, this is a dialogue among the law's addressees that is relevant to the law's operations. The judge reaches out into practical life or 'public reason' and finds support for his approach in it – he engages in a type of empirical dialogue. Unlike the Strasbourg enthusiast who knows how to 'go on' in a world full of victims, the judge in this case assumes that he does not have all the answers.

But more significantly still, *Campbell* and *Mosley* demonstrate that judges are willing to regard the actions of the claimant as consequential in privacy cases. Among other things, therefore, these cases highlight that private law is unsuited to the application of a general human rights monologue. For this reason, presumably, academics and judges have favoured indirect horizontal effect over direct effect in fashioning the new privacy action.[188] And so the question arises: does indirect effect fare any better in providing 'reasonable answers'?

7. Human Rights and Private Law: 'Multeity in Unity'?

Under the indirect effect model, human rights are but one of a number of voices that inform private law, albeit they are part of a 'higher-order' public law.[189] Treating human rights as higher order rights may look like monologue-creep but while we should avoid monologic utopianism at all

185 *Ibid.*

186 *Ibid*, at [225].

187 *Ibid*, at [226].

188 See M. Hunt, 'The "Horizontal Effect" of the Human Rights Act' [1998] *Public Law* 423; G. Phillipson 'The Human Rights Act, "Horizontal Effect" and the Common Law: a Bang or a Whimper?' (1999) 62 *Modern Law Review* 824; W. Wade, 'Horizons of Horizontality' (2000) 116 *Law Quarterly Review* 217; A.L. Young, 'Horizontality and the Human Rights Act 1998' in K.S. Ziegler (ed) *Human Rights and Private Law: Privacy as Autonomy* (Oxford: Hart, 2007); I. Leigh and R. Masterman, *Making Rights Real: The Human Rights Act in its First Decade* (Oxford: Hart, 2008).

189 J. Laws 'Law and Democracy' [1995] *Public Law* 72, 84.

costs, on Berlin's account '[p]riorities, never final and absolute, must be established' so that a plural society can function.[190] Indirect effect is thus the closest we come to reconciling incommensurable values and to achieving a 'multeity in unity'. In privacy law, for example, courts have developed the equitable doctrine of breach of confidence into a *de facto* tort of misuse of private information. In doing so, they have given effect to Arts. 8 and 10 ECHR while simultaneously taking account of the complexity of private relationships.

Before courts balance Arts. 8 and 10 ECHR, they must first establish whether the claimant had a reasonable expectation of privacy. This first step is crucial as it prevents taking into account 'considerations which should more properly be considered at the later stage of proportionality.'[191] Rather than assuming that human rights are at stake and that a balancing of conflicting rights is therefore warranted, the claimant must first show that Art 8 may be at stake: that there has been a *prima facie* infringement of her right. Thus, at an operational level, a presumption of victimhood is avoided. Moreover, as Moreham argues, the reasonable expectation test goes 'some way towards striking an appropriate balance between objective and subjective measures: "reasonableness" acts as an objective check without removing the subjective focus of the action'.[192] The test, assessed from the claimant's perspective, is subjectively sensitive. Did the individual have an expectation of privacy? However, the use of the term 'reasonable' acts as an 'objective check'[193] and thus ensures that the risk of viewing this solely from the 'victim perspective' is reduced.

The net result is that courts are provided a means to categorise claimants, as is common in other legal systems.[194] Thus, we find a number of distinctions in the law between voluntary and involuntary public figures, between individuals who actively seek publicity and those who avoid it. For instance, in disclosure cases courts have afforded a higher level of protection to children or relatives of public figures than to publicity-seeking celebrities themselves.[195] The reasonable expectation test also allows courts to take

---

190 I. Berlin, above n 6, p 17.

191 *Campbell*, above n 103, at 466 (*per* Lord Nicholls).

192 N. Moreham, above n 103, 645.

193 N. Moreham, *Ibid*, maintains that the test enables 'a court to distinguish between X, an outspoken, "out" campaigner for gay rights, and Z, who has never discussed his homosexuality, and between Y, who voluntarily appeared on a 24-hour surveillance "reality TV" show, and Z, who has never sought publicity'.

194 German courts distinguish between absolute and relative persons of contemporary history (*Personen der Zeitgeschichte*). See O'Callaghan, above n 165.

195 *Cf. Murray* above n 172 and *Campbell* above n 103.

account of the nature of the information in question. While the significance attached to the 'nature' of the information will invariably depend on the standpoint from which one views it, the test itself affords judges space to engage in dialogue in order to tease out the significance they should attach to it in the individual case. Thus the judge has to pay attention to the world around him – not something we see all that much of in the egotistic Canengusian judges. Such attention to fine-grained detail is evident in *Campbell.* In this case, there were two types of information at play: first, the information that the appellant had been using drugs, a charge which she vehemently denied in the past. Noting that the claimant was a voluntary public figure, the Court unanimously found that the press had the right to correct this information. The second type of information, the photographs of the appellant taken outside a Narcotics Anonymous meeting, related to her medical treatment, information of an intimate nature, and the majority of their Lordships held that Ms Campbell was entitled to damages for the publication of these photographs, recognising that a celebrity who actively seeks publicity has the right to keep certain intimate information private.

The reasonable expectation of privacy test is a product of indirect horizontal effect; it is a product of a private law informed by multiple voices, including human rights discourse. Of course much work remains to be done, but the test constitutes a more suitable construct for private law actions than the general human rights monologue espoused by the ECtHR obliging each individual to respect each other's 'personal and psychological integrity.' Indirect effect is the closest we come to 'multeity in unity' when attempting to accommodate human rights discourse in private law. But in developing this doctrine, UK judges have been more respectful of others and more attentive to factual complexity than the judges of 'The Canengusian Connection.' While the Canengusian judges note the facts in the case before them and describe social problems as they see them, they are so preoccupied with their own 'speechifying' that they fail to engage in dialogue in any meaningful way. Not only does this mean that the judges miss an opportunity to engage with one another and find a way to accommodate their competing interests in the case before them, it also means that their own individual philosophies suffer as a result. To paraphrase Arvind, for all the room the judges devote to refuting the arguments of their fellow judges, they do not question the fundamental assumptions of their own philosophies.[196] Buber and Bakhtin would find conduct of this sort contemptible and an affront to the very nature of what it means to be human.

---

196 See T.T. Arvind, above n 67.

8. Conclusions

Human rights discourse and adjudication is a necessary component of every modern and democratic society. But in taking account of these rights, we should not simply cast aside the classical operating principles of private law. For the fundamental principles of autonomy, freedom of contract and certainty, and the presumption that parties 'know the score' serve important purposes. While protecting and empowering the vulnerable individual is a function of human rights law, vulnerability is not always clear-cut in private law relationships. Of course, it does not follow that the vulnerable individual should be neglected by the existing private law regime and, although some will regard them as imperfect, we find many examples of 'reasonable answers' in private law. We see, for instance, in the doctrine of undue influence that judges have found a means to protect vulnerable individuals while also preserving the basic operating principles of private law. Likewise, in tort law, the 'reasonable expectation of privacy' test demonstrates that we can accommodate competing interests, even in those cases where an ECHR right is the impetus behind the action. The test does not presume that vulnerability is present; rather the onus is on the claimant to show that his vulnerable position has been exploited by the defendant. Moreover, the court enjoys space to engage in dialogue and to take account of a wide range of salient features.

Of course we must not forget that ECHR rights are important values in themselves and the Human Rights Act has imposed new duties and responsibilities on courts to ensure that existing law is compatible with the ECHR.[197] But, in doing so, courts should continue to work from the bottom-up, to engage in dialogue with past decisions and the community rather than resort to applying a general human rights monologue. For the Strasbourg enthusiast becomes the classic *Ich-Erzähler*, a narrator with a limited perspective, when he assumes that complex private law disputes can be solved by applying Strasbourg principles alone. He becomes the victim of 'self-induced myopia'. Rather than concern ourselves with 'tidiness' in the law and the pursuit of a utopian 'perfect whole', we should pay close attention to Rawls' conception of a 'realistic utopia', the idea of a 'social world [which] allows a reasonably just constitutional democracy existing as a member of a reasonably just Society of Peoples', accommodating, among other things, 'reasonable pluralism'.[198] Mullender argues that 'utopia' in this

[197] See sec. 2(1), sec 3 and sec. 6(1) , (2) and (3) HRA 1998. But this does not mean that they must follow ECtHR in every instance. On this point, see G. Robertson and A. Nicol, Media Law (5th edn., London: Sweet & Maxwell, 2007), pp 69-70. See also J. Wright, *Tort Law and Human Rights* (Oxford: Hart, 2001).

[198] J. Rawls, *The Laws of Peoples* (Cambridge: Harvard University Press, 1999, pp 11 -12.

sense has 'some plausibility in the British context' as it probes 'the bounds of political possibility'.[199] He provides the examples of the extension of the franchise and the development of the welfare state.[200] But Rawls' conception of a 'realistic utopia' is appealing for another reason. For unlike utopianism in Berlin's sense, which is characterised by monologue and nothing else, the 'realistic utopia' is fundamentally dialogic. Rawls elucidates that '[b]y showing how the social world may realize the features of a realistic utopia, political philosophy provides a long-term goal of political endeavor, and in working toward it gives meaning to what we can do today'.[201] For a 'realistic utopia' is essentially about 'endeavor' rather than the declaration of a perfect end-state; we are not in possession of all the answers and hard cases will continue to arise. But if we refrain from 'speechifying' and monologue, we can, collectively through dialogue, work towards 'reasonable answers' and a 'realistic utopia'. As Rawls puts it, this idea 'describes what is possible and can be, yet may never be, though no less fundamental for that.'[202]

---

199 R. Mullender, 'Human Rights, responsibilities, and the pursuit of a realistic Utopia' above n 34, 50.
200 *Ibid*, 51.
201 J. Rawls, *The Laws of Peoples*, above n 198 p 128.
202 J. Rawls, *Political Liberalism*, above n 68, p 213.

CONNECTING CANENGUS TO THE UNIVERSITY CURRICULUM

Gemma Turton*

The article 'The Canengusian Connection: a Kaleidoscope of Tort Theory' was published over twenty-five years ago, yet it retains a place on the reading list of many tort modules.[1] This essay seeks to explore why, after this lengthy period of time, the article remains relevant and stimulating, and to consider how it can be incorporated into the delivery of a modern tort law module. 'The Canengusian Connection' is a sort of 'Case of the Speluncean Explorers' for tort law.[2] It is a fictional decision set in the imagined island of Canengus which is a common law jurisdiction operating a mix of Canadian, English and American law. It contains a simple factual scenario and the opinions of five fictitious judges, each aligned with a particular theoretical viewpoint. Each judge is almost a caricature of the theory he or she represents, seeing the positive in their view and the negative in all other views. This gives the article a number of uses as a teaching tool. 'The Canengusian Connection' can serve as an introduction to various theories of tort law. Its value, however, goes far beyond this. Incorporating the article into the delivery of a tort module provides a more stimulating, holistic experience of law by ensuring that theoretical concerns are not isolated from practical decision-making. This is particularly helpful in aiding students to develop coherently reasoned opinions about tort law.

The first section of this essay describes and analyses the judgments in 'The Canengusian Connection" before pointing up its usefulness in the context of a course on tort law. As we will see, Hutchinson and Morgan encourage understanding of the criticisms that students (and other critics) might level at any single theory in its pure form. They also give an insight into judicial reasoning that may assist students to develop their own arguments in a more coherently reasoned manner. As well as developing these points, this essay dwells on a trend towards corrective justice-based systems of liability that has grown in the years since Hutchinson and Morgan published their essay.

*Lecturer, University of Leicester, England. I am grateful to John Hartshorne, James Lee, and Richard Mullender for their valuable comments on earlier drafts of this article.

[1] A.C. Hutchinson and D. Morgan, 'The Canengusian Connection: a Kaleidoscope of Tort Theory' (1984) 22 *Osgoode Hall Law Journal* 69.

[2] L Fuller, 'The Case of the Speluncean Explorers' (1949) 62 *Harvard LR* 616.

Canengus: an introduction to Tort Theories

The facts of the scenario are relatively uncomplicated. The victim, Derek, was driving along an unlit road and saw a single headlight coming towards him which he assumed to be a motorcycle but was in fact a car driven by Allan. Upon realising that it was a car, Derek applied the brakes but they were not functioning properly so he swerved and was injured when his car landed in a ditch. A neighbour, Martin, heard and saw the accident but did nothing to check whether anyone was injured, nor did he call the emergency services. Finally, Derek's same-sex partner was later informed about the accident over the telephone by hospital staff and was told that Derek was still in intensive care which led to him suffering psychiatric illness.

These facts enable the article to address not only basic negligence but a spectrum of issues including contributory negligence, omissions liability, and liability for psychiatric illness from different theoretical foundations. This provides the opportunity not merely to explain what the various theories are, but to apply them to concrete challenges such as how to apportion liability between a careless defendant and a careless claimant, and understand how each theory tackles particular issues. Besides what the article says about judicial decision-making, it also provides a clear exposition of the different theoretical approaches to negligence. Since each judgment is focused on the same set of facts, it is easy for readers to compare different approaches to the various issues raised by Hutchinson and Morgan. However, the article goes beyond identifying examples of applications of the different theories in real case law and presents an ideal solution to the problem from each perspective.

The authors' fictional format enables them to present their readers with a collection of unconventional judgments in the law of negligence. Hutchinson and Morgan are able to present particular theories (*e.g.*, the economic analysis of Mill J) in their pure form. Thus the reader is not confronted by judges who are constrained by the normal language of tort law, such as duty, breach and remoteness. Nor are these judges bound by fears of 'opening the floodgates' or creating new areas of liability. This allows them to make a complete paradigm shift and suggest how the problem should be resolved without recourse to tort law (*e.g.*, Lefft and Prudential JJ).

The first of the judges, Doctrin C.J., adopts a formalist approach to resolving the case. She begins by stating that although the case appears to raise some moral issues her sole concern is the legal aspect of the case.[3] To this end, her task is to apply 'the law as it is, and not as some think it ought to be'.[4] By breaking down Doctrin's judgment and some of the criticisms levelled at it by the other judges, the weakness of this approach becomes apparent. Doctrin adheres to a strict model of the separation of powers and aspires to 'the formal and neutral application of the rules'.[5] The 'rules' that she applies are obviously derived from case law that was up-to-date twenty-five years ago, so some of this has been superseded by later decisions, although it is perhaps surprising how little has changed.

Doctrin begins by addressing the relative responsibility of the victim of the accident, a driver who had not maintained his brakes in working order, and the defendant, another driver of a car with only one functioning headlight. Doctrin notes that both drivers owed a duty of care as road users, both were negligent because both failed to maintain their cars in a roadworthy condition, and concludes that a fifty percent reduction in damages is appropriate. She does not explain whether this reduction is based on each party's relative causal potency or relative blameworthiness or any other basis. Doctrin next turns to the question of the (possible) omissions liability of the nearby resident who saw and heard the accident but did nothing to assist. This she answers by holding that there is no legal duty to rescue outside of those special relationships, statutorily specified, that establish such a duty. The expansion of these categories of relationship, in her opinion, is the role of the legislature, not of the judiciary. Accordingly there is no duty to rescue in this instance. Finally, she turns to the claim for psychiatric illness by the same-sex partner of the victim of the car accident who was informed of the accident via telephone by the hospital staff and was told that his partner was in intensive care and that it would be some time before there was any definite news. After noting that the courts are gradually expanding recovery for psychiatric illness in line with increasing medical understanding, Doctrin declines to continue this expansion. The victim's partner did not see the accident, nor did he come upon its aftermath. Doctrin recognises previous expansions including the abandonment of the rule that the claimant should have witnessed the accident and the adoption of the rule that he or she must have been in the accident's immediate aftermath.[6] This particular development was justified by the 'fundamental nature' of the mother and family relationship. In the absence of a similarly fundamental relationship in

[3] Above n 1, 71.
[4] *Ibid.*
[5] *Ibid.*
[6] *McLoughlin v O'Brian* (1982) 2 WLR 982.

this instance there is, in Doctrin's view, no justification for further expansion.

In taking a formalist approach to this problem, Doctrin does not seek to explain why recovery for psychiatric illness is limited to those who witnessed the immediate aftermath of an accident, nor why the closeness of the family ties matter to the outcome. Her priority is 'to maintain certainty and generality so as to avoid a doctrinal wilderness of single instances'.[7] The existing 'patchwork quilt'[8] of liability for psychiatric illness is perhaps testimony to the failure of such an incremental approach to avoid the 'wilderness' she fears.

In ways reminiscent of Doctrin CJ, students (particularly those new to law) often want to know 'the answer'. Faced with uncertainty and disagreement, they want to know 'what the law is'.[9] This can lead to students making demands for certainty from those teaching them. This demand for certainty seems to be a symptom of the shift from curriculum-based school education to university education. Students are accustomed to being provided with a comprehensive, detailed curriculum which tells them exactly what they will be examined on. In contrast, the 'learning outcomes' provided for university modules are brief and much more vague. Students often express anxiety at this lack of certainty about what they are expected to know because they are accustomed to being tested on their knowledge rather than on their skills.

'The Canengusian Connection' serves as a useful reminder to students that certainty is rare. Moreover, it should reassure them that uncertainty can be tackled by developing a strong grounding in theoretical arguments. McFarland argues that students are thrown into 'the sea of common law' and '[w]hile they think they are drowning and are disoriented, many will stop asking "what is just?" and instead, looking for a plank floating in the water, only ask "what is the rule?"'.[10] By challenging Doctrin's justifications and conclusions, students may see more clearly that it is not enough to know 'the law as it is'. Suppose, for example, that Derek's partner arrived at the hospital just as Derek was being brought in. In such circumstances, his claim would then depend on how widely a judge construes the concept of the 'immediate aftermath'. In order to justify where the line is drawn, one

---

[7] Above n 1, 75.

[8] R. Mulheron, 'The 'Primary Victim' in Psychiatric Illness Claims: Reworking the "Patchwork Quilt"' (2008) 19 *King's Law Journal* 81.

[9] J. Boyle, The Anatomy of a Torts Class (1985) 34 *Am. U. L. Rev.* 1003, 1007-1008.

[10] R. McFarland, 'Teaching the Law of Wrongs without Searching for What is Right' (2009) *J. Juris* 323, 330.

must have an overarching theory of liability in mind and understand where the immediate aftermath rule fits in to it.[11]

While Doctrin recognises that there are rules and exceptions, the problem remains as to where to draw the line. She does not present a clear theoretical foundation for liability, accepting only that judges can shift the line on an incremental basis. The lack of a firm basis for her decision about where to draw the line is criticised by the other judges, one of whom seeks to 'clear away the rhetoric behind which her cloak-and-dagger approach to public policy lurks'.[12] Morgan has observed that judges lack an empirical basis from which to address certain public policy issues such as the fear of police defensive practice, yet he argues that '[i]t would be strange to require the courts to close their eyes to such manifest social consequences of their decisions'.[13] By adopting an unthinking, formalistic approach, Doctrin commits this error of closing her eyes to the social consequences of her decisions.

At the opposite end of the theoretical spectrum to Doctrin, we find Lefft J who represents the Critical Legal Studies Movement. For Lefft, the legal process 'is a major force in creating, sustaining and justifying our social situation' which is characterised by vast inequalities.[14] Attacking the perception that the law is objective and neutral, he argues that 'judges hold in place the deep structure of [a] society that sacrifices people for profits' and set out in their decisions 'rationalizations of our ideological prejudices'.[15] He identifies the two dominant and conflicting ideologies of individualism and welfarism that have exerted influence over tort law, criticising all of the other judgments as presenting accidents as 'an inescapable and natural feature of modern life'.[16]

In this vein, the economic efficiency approach to tort law receives the greatest criticism, but no theory, even the no-fault insurance scheme

[11] Indeed the decision of the High Court of Australia in *Annetts v Australian Stations Pty Ltd* [2002] HCA 35 supports the view that the immediate aftermath requirement is an arbitrary barrier to recovery. See also H. Teff, *Causing Psychiatric and Emotional Harm: Reshaping the Boundaries of Legal Liability* (Oxford, Hart Publishing, 2009), 69 (arguing that '[i]nvidious distinctions are inevitable when the "immediate" aftermath is treated in isolation, as a crude notion of temporal proximity').

[12] Above n 1, 76.

[13] D. Morgan, 'Policy Reasoning in Tort Law: the Courts, the Law Commission and the critics' (2009) 125 *LQR* 215, 221.

[14] Above n 1, 104-105.

[15] *Ibid*, 105.

[16] *Ibid*, 106.

proposed by one of his colleagues (Prudential J), is exempt from criticism. Lefft considers the concept of financial compensation to have the dehumanizing effect of turning people into property. There is a clear danger that an economic analysis of negligence could have this effect. But, arguably, in more moralistic, justice-based approaches, people retain an intrinsic value - it is just that financial compensation is the most appropriate method of repairing the damage inflicted. Lefft's focus is on reduction of risk and ensuring that 'all persons can decide the risks to which they are individually exposed' by undertaking a 'complete restructuring of all aspects of social life'.[17] Noting that currently 'the elite in our society hold a monopoly on knowledge',[18] he advocates the democratization of information and risk. On this basis he declines to pass judgment on the case at hand. Although this is a critique of law generally, it may open students' eyes to the context in which tort law operates and the relationships it maintains.

Situated between these two extremes of formalism and critical legal scholarship, are three judgments based on more familiar concepts of corrective and distributive justice, strict- and fault-based liability, that seek to explain or remodel the negligence system. Due perhaps to the trends in tort theory at the time the article was written, and perhaps to the preferences of Hutchinson and Morgan, 'The Canengusian Connection' does not put forward a coherent corrective-justice based account of negligence liability.[19] The closest approximation to corrective justice in 'The Canengusian Connection' is the judgment of Wright J. Wright rejects the more utilitarian economic efficiency approach as failing to 'take individuals seriously', holding instead that '[w]hen one person harms another, the injured has a moral right to demand and the injurer a moral duty to pay compensation'.[20] Insofar as Wright's view is individualistic and centres around the causation of harm, it is a reflection of corrective justice. It is not, however, an entirely fair portrayal of corrective justice and is more useful as an example of strict liability. Corrective justice is a system of individual responsibility that

---

[17] *Ibid*, 108.

[18] *Ibid.*

[19] The dominant theory today is that we can best explain negligence law and tort more generally by reference to the ideal of corrective justice. See for example E. Weinrib, *The Idea of Private Law* (Cambridge, MA, Harvard University Press, 1995); S. Perry, 'The Moral Foundations of Tort Law' (1992) 77 *Iowa Law Review* 449; J. Coleman, 'The Practice of Corrective Justice' in D. Owen (ed), *Philosophical Foundations of Tort Law* (Oxford, Oxford University Press, 1995). See also the more recent contribution in A. Beever, *Rediscovering the Law of Negligence* (Oxford, Hart Publishing, 2007). On corrective justice, see below n 20 and associated text.

[20] Above n 1, 87.

requires a person who causes wrongful loss to another to correct that loss. In a system of fault-based liability, 'wrongful loss' is loss caused by faulty conduct, that is, by a lack of reasonable care. In contrast, strict liability identifies loss as 'wrongful' if a particular activity causes it (often an activity that involves significant risk of harm) regardless of the level of care taken to try to prevent harm.

Thus both fault-based liability and strict liability are suitable systems of implementing corrective justice. Strict liability is more advantageous for victims because they are not required to prove a lack of care on the part of the defendant, only that the defendant's conduct caused the harm. Because of this, Wright prefers strict liability over fault-based liability. This leads him to focus solely on the causation requirement of corrective justice: 'the focus is rightly placed upon the activity rather than the defendant's conduct: the *what* happened is more important than the *how* or *why*'. Wright states that 'within such a regime, causation becomes not *a* basis for liability but *the* basis'.[21] This, he believes, enables him to do corrective justice more comprehensively because cases will no longer fail because of the absence of fault. He therefore finds that Allan's faulty headlight set a causal chain in motion, and so is the cause of the losses to Derek and his partner. Derek's faulty brakes 'may well have extended the causal chain' but they did not set the chain in motion. This leads Wright to reject the contributory negligence argument. He also considers that the psychiatric illness suffered by Derek's partner is another consequence in the same chain of causation and the fact that the harm is emotional rather than physical does not provide sufficient justification for rejecting his claim.

Wright J presents this strict liability approach as being more coherent than Doctrin's formalism because it pursues an overarching goal (doing corrective justice), but at the same time strict liability is portrayed as being neutral or objective because it depends only on causation and not on a finding of fault. The heavy emphasis on causation in this model provides a good opportunity for discussion of developments in the understanding of causation. The term 'causation' in an objective sense relates only to factual causation: was the defendant's negligence *a* cause of the harm. In their work on causation, Hart and Honoré showed that any event does not have one single cause, but it caused by the convergence of a set of conditions which were together sufficient for its occurrence. This is known as the NESS (Necessary Element of a Sufficient Set) test. An example commonly used to illustrate this is that of a fire. The 'sufficient set' of conditions for the occurrence of a fire is

[21] *Ibid*, 91. See also, P. Cane, *The Anatomy of Tort Law* (Oxford, Hart Publishing, 1997), 47-49 (on 'outcome-based' strict liability).

oxygen, a flammable substance, and a source of ignition. If you take away any one of these three elements there will not be a fire, so the presence of each element is equally necessary in order to start a fire. Each element is therefore equally deserving of being called *a* cause of the fire. Richard Wright, building upon the 'NESS' test elaborated by Hart and Honoré, has shown that each of the conditions that together were sufficient to bring about the harm was *a* cause of the harm.[22] The designation of one particular event, such as the defendant's conduct or the defendant's negligence, as *the* cause, is shorthand for it being the *responsible* cause.[23] This still calls for an attribution of responsibility.[24] Building upon the example of a fire, we might ordinarily say that a person dropping a lighted match is the cause of the fire. The match is just one cause along with oxygen and flammable material, and we designate it as the *responsible* cause when the dropping of a match is out of the ordinary. If the fire occurred during a manufacturing process that required the absence of oxygen, then we would no longer deem the source of ignition to be the responsible cause. Instead, we would call the presence of oxygen the responsible cause.

In the negligence inquiry, the task of labelling something as 'out of the ordinary' is fulfilled by the 'breach of duty' question. There must be a basis on which particular conduct is labelled the *responsible* cause and for Wright J this basis is still, implicitly, faulty conduct. This can be seen in Wright J's statement that Allan's *faulty* headlight set the chain of causation in motion. A system of strict liability could equally decide that any driver, careless or not, is responsible if he is involved in an accident which injures someone else.[25]

By presenting a model of strict liability that claims to be objective, the authors are able to exploit Wright J's judgment to further their argument that judicial decision-making is not neutral. In this sense, Wright J is a straw man, also used by the authors to attack corrective justice. They could have used Wright's judgment to develop a theory of corrective justice using fault-based liability where the moral, social and other concerns surrounding liability would be discussed more openly. Instead they have impliedly

[22] R Wright, 'Causation in Tort Law' (1985) 73 *Cal. L. Rev.* 1735; Richard Wright, 'Causation, Responsibility, Risk, Probability, Naked Statistics, and Proof: Pruning the Bramble Bush by Clarifying the Concepts' (1987) 73 *Iowa L. Rev.* 1001; H.L.A. Hart and T. Honoré, *Causation in the Law*, (2nd ed. Oxford: Oxford University Press, 1985).

[23] Richard Wright, above n 22, 1012.

[24] In *Stapley v Gypsum Mines Ltd* [1953] AC 663 Lord Asquith identified the responsible cause by asking whether the negligence was the 'real' or 'effective' cause. More recently in *South Australia Asset Management Corp. v York Montague Ltd* [1997] AC 191 Lord Hoffmann asked whether the harm was within the scope of the defendant's duty of care.

[25] See, for example, the French loi du 5 juillet 1985 sur les accidents de la circulation.

equated corrective justice with strict liability and their arguments concerning the policy decisions concealed by the strict liability approach could be seen as being valid concerns about corrective justice too. It is therefore important to maintain the distinction between corrective justice and its expression in the form of strict liability in order to make it clear that the authors have only really highlighted some of the fallacies of strict liability. Corrective justice then emerges relatively unscathed from Wright's judgment.

Despite these criticisms of Wright J, his judgment can still be a useful aid in addressing the distinction between factual and legal causation and the idea that 'causation' in the sense of '*the* cause' rather than '*a* cause' involves a choice in the allocation of responsibility. Moreover, it drives home the point that choices of the sort we are considering need to be justified.

The remaining judgments present two differing distributive models for negligence law: economic efficiency and the compensatory imperative. In itself this can reinforce appreciation of the idea that 'distributive justice' concerns the allocation of resources among a wider population, but does not prescribe a single criterion of merit on which the allocation should be based. This may clarify for students the point that 'public policy' is not, of itself, an argument. Public policy may require maximisation of wealth, it may prioritise compensation according to need, or it may pursue some other objective.[26]

Mill J takes the view that the law is primarily a reflection of public policy as decided by the judiciary: 'The common law is a vast and intricate doctrinal edifice, but its chief architect has been policy and not logic'.[27] He calls for the judiciary to discuss openly these issues of public policy and in order to achieve consistency in judicial opinions, he says that they should be 'guided by a systematic theory of civil liability'. For Mill, that theory is economic efficiency, in other words the sole objective is the maximisation of overall wealth. 'Rules of tort law must be designed and implemented so as to facilitate and simulate the operation of a free and competitive market'.[28] This approach treats overall financial gain as desirable and ignores the human cost. He later states that the rule of liability 'will determine whether resources are used in an economically efficient manner' and 'must as closely

[26] On public policy arguments, see J. Bell, *Policy Arguments in Judicial Decisions* (Oxford: Clarendon Press, 1983), 23-24 and ch 3.
[27] Above n 1, 77.
[28] *Ibid*, 80.

as possible approximate the apportionment of risk that would have been arrived at by the litigants *if they had been able to bargain*'.[29]

This economic approach to liability involves an application of the Learned Hand formula.[30] Under this formula, accident precautions are justified so long as their cost (B) is outweighed by the seriousness of the injury (L) multiplied by the probability of the injury occurring (P). In other words, where B < PxL the precautions should have been taken and the defendant will be liable, but where B > PxL the defendant will not be liable. This is a potentially off-putting formula for students to apply. However, 'The Canengusian Connection' addresses it with clarity by assigning costs to the precautions that the parties could have taken and balancing them against the likelihood of harm and seriousness of harm. Mill states that the loss to Derek (L) is approximately $1 million and the probability (P) of this was 0.001 so that accident cost is $1000. The cost to Allan of repairing his headlight (B) was $250 so, in this instance, the cost of the precautions is outweighed by the cost of the accident. Mill also looks at the cost to Derek of preventing the accident by repairing his brakes (B) which is $200 - so also outweighed by the cost of the accident. Mill then asks, as between Derek and Allan, who could have avoided the accident the most cheaply. Derek could have repaired his brakes for $50 less than the cost of replacing Allan's headlight, so Derek is the 'cheaper' cost-avoider of this accident.[31] Consequently, responsibility falls entirely on Derek. Mill also holds that the neighbour should be liable for his failure to rescue because it was an 'easy rescue' with minimal costs.[32] Finally he considers that the only barrier to recovery for psychiatric illness should be proof that the harm is real. If the harm is real and the cost of prevention by the defendant is lower than the expected cost of the harm then the defendant will be liable.

Critics of the economic approach applied by Mill often focus on the extent to which it ignores the human cost of accidents. As Conaghan and Mansell have argued, the Learned Hand formula is 'ideologically objectionable in its shallow and impoverished view of human activity'.[33] In 'The Canengusian Connection', Wright draws on the Ford Pinto case to illustrate the moral

[29] *Ibid.*

[30] *United States v Carroll Towing Co* 159 F 2d 169 (2d Cir 1947).

[31] Above n 1, 84.

[32] Above n 1, 86.

[33] J. Conaghan and W. Mansell, *The Wrongs of Tort* (London, Pluto Press, 1999, 2nd edn), 62.

shortcomings of economic efficiency.[34] Moreover, this approach to judging is broadly comparable to the cost-benefit analysis that English courts currently undertake (which also considers the practicality of the precautions and the potential deterrent effect of liability). A concern with the potential deterrent effect of liability is also apparent in s.1 Compensation Act 2006 which requires courts to have regard to the desirability of the defendant's activity.[35]

A further point for discussion concerning Mill J's efficiency-based approach is the degree to which he individualises the calculation involved. Since the goal is the maximisation of overall wealth in society, his is an aggregative approach to accident compensation.[36] As such, it is concerned with individual costs only in so far as they reduce overall wealth. Mill combines this with the Learned Hand formula to determine who should have avoided the relevant costs. To this end, he makes an *ex post* comparison of the costs of avoiding the accident for the specific individuals involved. However, if the economic efficiency model requires liability to fall on the *cheapest* cost-avoider, then the structure of tort law is an inappropriate mechanism for achieving this. Tort law only looks at the parties involved in the particular dispute now before the court. Hence, the question Mill J addresses is whether the claimant or the defendant could have avoided the accident most cheaply. Yet in so far as the economic efficiency-based approach seeks to maximise wealth in society as a whole, it ought to be open to the court actively to seek out alternative methods of avoiding the accident that may (other things being equal) be cheaper still. For example, in this particular case the accident occurred as the parties were driving around a bend and it may be cheaper for the local authority to place streetlights on dangerous bends.

Another way of approaching the question of economic efficiency is to focus it less on the particular accident that occurred, but to apply the Learned Hand formula to the risk created by the parties. This involves an *ex ante* comparison between the cost to the individual of taking precautions against a risk and the value of that risk. Viewed from this standpoint, Allan's faulty headlight is a source of risk for all other road users, so the expected cost of

---

34 *Grimshaw v Ford Motor Co.* 174 Cal. Rptr. 348 (1981). For further discussion of this case, see Man Chun Siu, 'Conflict in Canengus: the Battle of Consequentialism and Deontology' (2010) 7 *J. Juris*, 539, n 36 (and associated text).

35 Interestingly it has been found that neither English nor American courts tend to apply the Hand formula in such a formulaic and purely financial way: R Wright, 'Hand, Posner and the Myth of the "Hand Formula"' (2003) 4 *Theoretical Inquiries in Law* 145.

36 On aggregation, see J. Rawls, *A Theory of Justice* (Oxford, Oxford University Press, 1971), 36-37. See also 22-24.

harm is the probability of harm multiplied by the average value of loss amongst that population. If Derek's loss is roughly equivalent to the average cost of accidents within the scope of the risk created by Allan, then, as Mill calculated, the cost for Allan to repair his headlight is lower than the value of the risks he has created. Likewise, by driving with faulty brakes Derek has created a risk of accidents to other road-users generally and the cost of mending the brakes, as Mill calculated, is lower than the value of this risk. Prior to the occurrence of this specific accident, economic efficiency would therefore require both Derek and Allan to repair their cars. Using the facts of 'The Canengusian Connection' can therefore provide a concrete focal point for discussion of whether economic efficiency requires an *ex ante* or *ex post* calculation of costs.

The other distributive model proposed in the article, by Prudential J, is the replacement of the tort system with a no-fault compensation scheme. Prudential first finds justification for such an approach in the difficulties faced by claimants in establishing legal causation. For him, the most important goal is compensation and 'proximate causation' remains an indeterminate and uncertain barrier to recovery. Prudential's concerns seem in part to have motivated recent developments in the approach courts take to factual causation, such as the development of the concept of 'material contribution to risk' as the test of causation in cases of evidential uncertainty[37] and the effective circumvention of the rules on causation in *Chester v Afshar*.[38]

Prudential J first notes the frequency with which accidents occur. He also notes the role of technological developments in particular: 'accidents regularly befalling large numbers of…citizens are not so much due to human error as to the complicated and uneasy environment in which we live'.[39] Against this, echoing the figures found by the Pearson Commission,[40] Prudential contrasts the inefficiencies of the tort system: forty-five percent of those injured never recover anything, only one percent reach the courts and many of them still settle, often below value.[41] Of those who settle, the

[37] *Fairchild v Glenhaven Funeral Services* [2002] UKHL 22, [2003] 1 A.C. 32.

[38] [2004] UKHL 41; [2005] 1 A.C. 134.

[39] Above n 1, 102.

[40] Royal Commission on Civil Liability for Compensation for Personal Injury (Cmnd. 7054, 1978).

[41] See P. Cane, *Atiyah's Accidents, Compensation and the Law* (Cambridge: Cambridge University Press, 2006, 7th edn), 464 (noting that: '[m]uch has changed in the past 40 years; but the situation the Pearson Commission uncovered in the 1970s remains, in its essentials, unchanged').

cost of legal representation and administration of the system amounts to over fifty percent of the value of their compensation.
In ways reminiscent of Atiyah, Prudential J concludes that the tort system is a 'litigation lottery'.[42] He claims that society is already heading in the direction of socialised compensation, arguing that the growth of insurance schemes shows that it is considered appropriate to spread the costs of accidents over a whole community. As with the other judgments, the themes addressed here serve as a concise introduction to those ideas addressed more thoroughly elsewhere, such as the inefficiencies of the current 'patchwork of a tort system and private insurance' and the pitfalls of opting for a system of first-party liability insurance.[43] Prudential concludes that 'if loss-distribution is our intended goal, a patchwork of a tort system and private insurance is a less than efficient way to proceed'.[44] The most important word here is 'if'. *If* loss-distribution and compensation are the goals, then the tort system is inefficient; *if*, however, the goal is to vindicate individual responsibility, then as will be argued below, a corrective justice-based tort system is appropriate.[45]

As we have seen, each judgment presents a theory in a nutshell and explains how a concrete problem would be resolved from that perspective. This section has highlighted some limitations and discussion points related to the various theories. It has also noted, in passing, the pedagogical usefulness of the judgments. We will now examine the pedagogic value of 'The Canengusian Connection' in more detail.

A challenge for students: relating Canengus to a corrective justice-based theory

As noted earlier, a number of corrective justice-based accounts of tort law have emerged since the publication of 'The Canengusian Connection' and corrective justice is arguably now the dominant theoretical foundation for negligence.[46] Since there is not a strong corrective justice-based account of negligence in Canengus, a fruitful exercise is to ask students to develop a sixth judgment makes more effective appeal to this ideal. It also provides an

[42] Compare to P. Atiyah, *The Damages Lottery* (Oxford, Hart Publishing, 1997).
[43] Above, n 1, 99. See also J Conaghan and W Mansell, 'From the permissive to the dismissive society: Patrick Atiyah's Accidents, Compensation and the Market' (1998) 25 *Journal of Law and Society* 171.
[44] Above n 1, 99.
[45] On the interpretative consequences of placing emphasis on particular considerations in the field of accident compensation law, see E. Mickiewicz, 'An Exploratory Theory of Legal Coherence in Canengus and Beyond' (2010) 7 *J. Juris*, sections 4-5.
[46] See A. Beever, above n 19, 46-50.

opportunity to consider the interrelationship, if any, of corrective and distributive justice.

This is a task to which Lefft J's judgment is highly relevant. For he observes the conflicting directions in which negligence is pulled, between corrective justice on the one hand, and distributive concerns on the other: 'tort law is generally based on broad individualistic principles .... However, there exist certain counter-principles which ensure that the less fortunate in society are not excluded from relief'.[47] He later notes, for example, that 'in rescue situations, there is a robustly individualistic principle which does not require rescue, but this is being constantly eaten into by a communally-inspired requirement to act in cases of a special relationship'.[48] Whilst Hutchinson and Morgan use this to support Lefft's argument that the whole of tort law is a matter of politically significant choice, it can be used to advocate a mixed corrective- and distributive justice-based approach to negligence. If negligence is conceived as a system of individual responsibility then it should primarily implement corrective justice because this, rather than distributive justice, relates to individual interactions. However, there are certain distributive 'tools' which are required for the practical implementation of a system of corrective justice: insurance enables compensation to be paid, as does the doctrine of vicarious liability. There will also be areas, such as public authority liability, where the distributive impact of the law is clearly relevant. In cases involving public authority liability, individual judgments impact on the distribution of goods within the wider community because the defendant has limited resources provided by the public purse. But, as Jonathan Morgan has argued, negligence will lose coherence if the focus of those who elaborate it shifts away from corrective justice and individual responsibility and towards the availability of insurance.[49] Where this happens, a distributive mechanism affects liability decisions.[50]

Distributive concerns such as delivering compensation to accident victims and spreading losses as widely as possible are collective rather than individual concerns. They therefore require structures for implementation that also involve the whole of society rather than the individualistic structure of a negligence claim. If the focus of the courts shifts away from individual responsibility towards compensation and loss-spreading, as it has done in a number of recent decisions where the availability of insurance to one party has affected the allocation of liability, then negligence will lose coherence as

[47] Above n 1, 106.
[48] *Ibid.*
[49] J Morgan, 'Tort, Insurance and Incoherence' (2004) 67 *MLR* 384.
[50] *Ibid.*

a system of individual responsibility.[51] Furthermore, the individualistic structure of negligence will prevent it from adequately addressing distributive concerns. Insurance is a useful tool that enables negligence law to have practical effect, but for the reasons described above it ought not to become a factor in the attribution of liability. By containing the significance of insurance in assigning liability and refocusing on corrective justice, the courts may also go some way to addressing the perception that there exists a 'blame culture'.[52] Atiyah has expressed concern that aspects of tort law have been 'stretched' in order to pursue a compensatory objective at the expense of the coherence of the law.[53] Clearly refocusing on corrective justice would not solve all the problems of the perception of a blame culture. But if courts are less willing to stretch the law to enable claimants to pin responsibility on a defendant with a 'deep pocket', they may at least begin to address the issue.

Students could discuss and reflect upon the corrective justice-based approach, in the context of Canengus, by defending it against the views of the other judges. In corrective justice causation is not *the* basis of liability but *a* factor in liability along with factors determining wrongfulness. Despite initially appearing to base his decision on corrective justice, Wright J claims that causation is the sole basis of liability and in so doing conceals considerations of wrongfulness within his exposition of causation. Wright's decision is criticised by Mill and Prudential for placing excessive emphasis on causation and for claiming that causation provides an objective basis for liability. However, as argued earlier in this essay, these are valid criticisms of strict liability but not of corrective justice. Unpacking the criticisms of Mill and Prudential in more detail makes this clear.

Mill argues that Wright's strict liability model places excessive emphasis on causation. He argues that proof of causation can often be problematic and as such is a barrier to recovery. In his view the Learned Hand formula avoids the difficulties associated with causation because it is premised not on causation of harm but on risk of harm. If harm occurs then liability will fall on whoever could have reduced the risk of this harm most cheaply. In this way, Mill avoids an *ex post* determination of causation by shifting the entire focus of the negligence inquiry to an *ex ante* consideration of the cheapest cost-avoider. This means that in a case such as *McGhee v National Coal*

[51] See for example *Lamb v Camden LBC* [1981] QB 625, 637-8; *Vowles v Evans* [2003] 1 WLR 1607; *Gwilliam v West Hertfordshire NHS Trust* [2003] QB 443.

[52] On blame culture generally see R Mullender, 'Negligence Law and Blame Culture: A Critical Response to a Possible Problem' (2006) 22 *PN* 2.

[53] P Atiyah, *The Damages Lottery* (Oxford, Hart Publishing, 1997), chapter 2.

Board,[54] where proof of causation would have been a barrier to recovery had the House of Lords not developed the 'material contribution to the risk of harm' approach, the claimant would be able to recover under an economic efficiency system because the defendant could have reduced the risk of harm more cheaply than those at risk. For liability to be imposed it therefore seems to be enough that the defendant was responsible for a source of risk of the particular harm, regardless of whether it can be shown that the specific risk for which the defendant was responsible is the risk that eventuated in harm. Mill's criticism of strict liability is not a criticism of how the causation requirement operates, but a criticism of the fact that there is a causation requirement at all. In effect, then, this is an objection to a system of individual responsibility, and this is natural because Mill's vision is, as we noted earlier, aggregative.

Prudential also criticises Wright's view because of its emphasis on causation which Prudential calls 'a labyrinth for which Wright J. offers no realistic through-route'. Again, these are valid criticisms of Wright's understanding of causation, but not valid criticisms of corrective justice. This is because, as noted earlier, Wright confuses issues of factual and legal causation. Prudential rightly asserts that Wright 'has to smuggle in basic value judgments as formal causal criteria'. Prudential is also right to object that 'within any compensation scheme based on fault, the conundrum of causation represents an insuperable barrier to the achievement of personal or social justice', but this is because he is referring to a 'compensation scheme'.[55] If the objective is compensation of those who have suffered injuries then it is arbitrary for the outcome to depend upon proof that the harm was caused by somebody else's fault. If, however, the scheme is not primarily one of compensation but of individual responsibility, then it is entirely appropriate for recovery to depend on causation.[56] This will result in some injuries going uncompensated in negligence, and some risk-creators going unsanctioned. But just as punishment of conduct has its place in criminal law, and compensation has its place in welfarism, individual responsibility also has a place, and that place is in negligence law. When viewed as calls for additional institutional structures rather than the wholesale replacement of negligence, Mill and Prudential's approaches leave corrective justice untouched. 'The Canengusian Connection', therefore, provides much more than an illustration of how to apply tort to a concrete

---

[54] *McGhee v National Coal Board* [1972] 3 All ER 1008.

[55] Above n 1, 95.

[56] See, for example, Honoré's discussion of 'outcome responsibility': T. Honoré, 'Responsibility and Luck. The Moral Basis of Strict Liability', in T. Honoré, *Responsibility and Fault* (Oxford, Hart Publishing, 1999).

scenario and an examination of alternative approaches to accident compensation. It also provides a context in which students can consider how fault-based liability and corrective justice can be defended against those who argue for alternative means of compensation.

The next section considers the pedagogic value of alerting students to the various discourses examined by Hutchinson and Morgan in their essay.

Canengus and judicial reasoning: Building student competence

Tort theory continues to be an area of debate and, as noted by Lefft J, this can result in tort law being stretched in opposing directions. For a student to be able to understand tort law they need to be able to understand and identify the theoretical assumptions underlying judicial decision-making. 'The Canengusian Connection' is divorced from the reality of case law in the sense that each judgment exclusively pursues one theoretical objective and is able to express the underlying theory explicitly. Mill and Wright JJ do relate their positions to case law, but the fictional format employed by the Hutchinson and Morgan enables them to explore solutions outside the framework of traditional tort concepts. This can still aid students to identify the theoretical assumptions underlying the reasoning of real judgments because they have gained an understanding of how each theory would be reflected in practice.

Building on students' increased capacity to recognise different theoretical approaches, it becomes easier for them regularly to recognize the links between theory and practice (and, likewise, the place of theory *within* practice).[57] We must not, however, assume that a lack of sensitivity to theory is solely the responsibility of students. McFarland has criticised American law schools for neglecting moral and legal philosophy.[58] He argues that students with some grasp of these subjects would be better equipped 'to exercise judgment between that which is good and that which is not'.[59] Whether this is true of English universities or not, legal philosophy and legal reasoning seem to be addressed in discrete modules such as jurisprudence, legal skills, and analysing law. There is a risk that students see the skills learnt

[57] Inability to grasp links between law and relevant theory provides an example of 'aspect blindness' in the (Wittgensteinian) sense specified in E. Mickiewicz, above n 45, section 4. On theory as a feature of practice, S.E. Fish, *Doing What Comes Naturally: Change, Rhetoric, and the Practice of Theory in Literary and Legal Studies* (Oxford, Oxford University Press, 1989), ch 17.

[58] Above n 10, 324.

[59] *Ibid*, 331.

in such modules as being divorced from the skills required in the study of each branch of the law. 'The Canengusian Connection' has the value of taking a range of philosophies relating to tort law and presenting them in concrete rather than abstract terms. Asking students to consider how each theory, or each judge, would approach other cases that they study, or other fictional scenarios, can help incorporate this searching, analytical approach throughout the whole module. Exploring theoretical responses to problem scenarios thus helps avoid the numbing repetition of 'facts', 'held', exemplified by Doctrin CJ.

'The Canengusian Connection' can also help students express their opinions in a reasoned manner. As Hutchinson and Morgan make plain, the law is malleable.[60] When applying doctrine to factual situations, students should be able to present a reasoned argument. This means not only having their own ideas about what the solution ought to be, but being able to explain and argue *why* it ought to be that way, finding support in case law and academic writing. Boyle has said that students ought to make arguments about the law, but these arguments will only be valid if they can 'think like a lawyer'.[61] Duncan Kennedy has argued that students 'learn a list of balanced, formulaic, pro/con policy arguments that lawyers use in arguing that a given rule should apply to a situation despite a gap, conflict or ambiguity, or that a given case should be extended or narrowed. These are arguments like "the need for certainty" and "the need for flexibility", "the need to promote competition" and "the need to encourage production by letting producers keep the rewards of their labor"'.[62]

Incorporating 'The Canengusian Connection' into the teaching of a tort module helps counter this simplistic pro/con model and students learn instead that issues can be approached from a range of perspectives.[63] It also challenges the unthinking repetition of received policy arguments by emphasising the need to situate policy concerns within a wider theoretical framework (embracing, *inter alia*, ideals of justice and relevant political

[60] Above n 1, 76-77 (discussing *Home Office v Dorset Yacht Co Ltd* [1969] 2 QB 412, 426, *per* Lord Denning MR).

[61] Above n 9, 1008. (Among other things, Boyle's point concerns the process of enculturation in a disciplinary community, as described in J. Seeley Brown and P. Duguid, 'Space for the Chattering Classes', *Times Higher Education Supplement*, 10 May 1996 (Multimedia Feature, iv, iv-vi).)

[62] D Kennedy, 'Legal Education as Training for Hierarchy', in D Kairys (ed.) *The Politics of Law: A Progressive Critique* (New York, Basic Books, 1998, 3rd ed.), 59.

[63] See P. O'Callaghan, 'Monologism and Dialogism in Private Law' (2010) 7 *J. Juris*, section 4.

philosophy). 'The Canengusian Connection' can help bridge the gap between a student's instinctive opinion and being able to express it in a doctrinally and theoretically informed manner. By taking a problem scenario and presenting five rather stylised solutions to it, 'The Canengusian Connection' provides a reference point for students who are beginning and perhaps struggling to articulate their own opinions. If their instinct is, for example, that Martin ought not to be liable, they can go beyond the formalism of Doctrin CJ's argument that the law has simply not extended that far yet, and argue that it also ought not to go that far by expressing their ideas in terms of corrective justice, rights, economic efficiency. Thus, Hutchinson and Morgan have given those students who read their essay a valuable reference point. This reference point helps those who read the essay to identify particular viewpoints. Moreover, it may encourage them to combine elements from the judgments and, in so doing, work up their own hybrid approach.

From Canengus to Leicester

This year, law students at the University of Leicester were required to read 'The Canengusian Connection' in preparation for tutorials addressing duty of care and some of the exceptional duty scenarios such as duties for pure economic loss, or public authority duties of care. When responding to problem questions they were asked to consider how each of the five Canengusian judges would approach the solution. One such problem scenario involved police liability to the victim of a serial killer for negligent investigation and failure to prevent her death.[64] Addressing the problem from the perspective of Doctrin CJ allowed students to apply the existing case law such as *Hill v Chief Constable of West Yorkshire Police,*[65] *Osman v Ferguson,*[66] and *Smith v Chief Constable of Sussex.*[67] Students then went on to unpack any ideas they had found in such cases about economic concerns, compensation, and rights-based arguments as well as contributing arguments from further reading. For example, from a rights-based approach, some argued that since there is no general 'right to be rescued', the police ought not to owe a corresponding duty to rescue. Responses of this sort could be linked to relevant wider reading: for example, the Law Commission's recent consultation paper on administrative redress, which considers some of the

[64] For an analysis of the current state of the law relating to duties owed by the police see C. McIvor, 'Getting Defensive about Police Negligence: The *Hill* principles, the Human Rights Act 1998 and the House of Lords' (2010) 69 *CLJ* 133.
[65] [1988] 2 All ER 238.
[66] [1993] 4 All ER 344.
[67] [2008] UKHL 50.

economic arguments specific to public authority defendants.[68] Moreover, the benefits of this approach became apparent when some students built on an argument, advanced by Claire MacIvor, which concerns child-welfare claims against local authorities. On McIvor's analysis, the real problem in cases of this sort is under-funding and under-staffing.[69] In light of this point, the students argued that the same may be true in relation to police forces.

This provided an opportunity to ensure the students had understood 'The Canengusian Connection' and to discuss some of the ideas contained in it. Moreover, because public authority liability is such a policy-laden area of tort law, it was also beneficial to provide the students with a range of clear theoretical starting points from which to discuss the approach taken by the courts. Mullender has said that tutorials provide 'a setting in which knowledge of legal product and its limitations can be supplemented with an understanding of legal process: *i.e.*, the repertoire of argumentative strategies which make it possible to offer plausible (if not unquestionably correct) answers to legal problems'.[70] The main strategies that Mullender highlights are analogical arguments, appeals to the law's purposes and appeals to public policy. 'The Canengusian Connection' introduces students to certain arguments about the purposes of negligence law and the place of public policy within this branch of tort, and incorporating it into tutorials in the way described earlier helps students to articulate these kinds of arguments.

Finally, 'The Canengusian Connection' highlights the idea that many legal terms lack concrete meaning and have been assigned specific legal definitions. As is the case throughout the law, the law of negligence assigns a technical definition to conceptual labels in order to give them meaning. Terms such as 'negligence', 'proximity' and 'assumption of responsibility' have no concrete meaning. In the context of duty of care, some authors have argued that concepts such as foreseeability and proximity 'are not bland but are meaningful terms that do, or at least can, play a justificatory role in deciding cases'.[71] Yet as Lord Bridge recognised in relation to 'proximity' and 'fairness', they 'are not susceptible of any such precise definition as would be necessary to give them utility as practical tests, but amount in

[68] Law Commission, 'Administrative Redress: Public Bodies and the Citizen' (Law Commission Consultation Paper No 187 (2008)).
[69] C McIvor, 'The negligence liability of child welfare professional and policy-based immunities: A critique of recent English developments' (2006) 14 *Torts Law Journal* 205.
[70] R Mullender, 'Law, Undergraduates and the Tutorial' [1997] 3 *WebJCLI*: http://webjcli.ncl.ac.uk/1997/issue3/mullen3.html
[71] A. Beever, above, n 19, 9.

effect to little more than convenient labels to attach to the features of different specific situations which…the law recognises pragmatically as giving rise to a duty of care'.[72]

'The Canengusian Connection' serves to illustrate this point with clarity, taking for example the first question asked by Doctrin: was Allan negligent? The answer, according to Doctrin, is whether, 'in failing to have his car in proper working order, [Allan] breached the standard of care to which a reasonable man would adhere'. Doctrin largely focuses on the fact that there is a statutory duty to have properly functioning headlights, and whilst the statutory provision may not have been intended to set the standard of care in negligence, breach of a statutory duty can be taken as a starting point for finding that the duty in negligence has been breached. In a somewhat confusing statement, Doctrin states that '[a] defendant can rebut the *prima facie* case by showing that the statutory breach occurred without any negligence on his part. I agree with the trial judge that the malfunctioning headlights could reasonably have been discovered'.[73] Doctrin's reasoning is circular because she uses 'negligence' as part of the definition of 'breach of duty', and fails to explain *why* the malfunction could 'reasonably' have been discovered. Students should be able to challenge Doctrin's reasoning, asking, for example, what is it that makes Allan's conduct reasonable or unreasonable? When could he have discovered the fault? If he could only have discovered it whilst on the journey in question, ought he to have stopped his journey until he was able to replace the headlight? Would it have been reasonable for him to continue his journey so long as he took a route that avoided unlit roads, or drove at a slower speed? Doctrin applies a concept of negligence without explaining what that entails. 'The Canengusian Connection' can thus alert students to the need to question what judges mean by their use of particular terminology.

In contrast, Mill provides a definition of 'negligence' which asks whether 'it would have been cheaper for the defendant to have avoided the accident than to make good the expected losses'.[74] This definition is purely economic, weighing up the financial cost of the precautions (repairing the headlight, $250) against the probability of the accident (0.001) multiplied by the cost of the accident ($1million). On this basis, Allan was negligent because he could have avoided an expected loss of $1000 by spending $250. In further contrast, Wright refuses to judge Allan's conduct at all, preferring instead the

[72] *Caparo Industries v Dickman plc* [1990] 2 AC 605, *per* Lord Bridge. See also, J Steele, 'Scepticism and the Law of Negligence' (1993) 52 *CLJ* 437.
[73] Above n 1, 72.
[74] Above, n 1, 83.

definition that 'fault amounts to an interference *per se*'. On this view, somebody is negligent if they cause harm. Wright therefore seems to adhere to a strict-liability model of tort liability. Yet Wright still attaches liability to the failure to repair the headlight, rather than to the mere act of driving, so without acknowledging it he is making the judgment that it is Allan's negligent (undefined concept) conduct that sets in motion the chain of events that leads to Derek's injury. We can contrast this with the French system of motor accident compensation which provides that where the victim is injured in an accident involving a motor vehicle, the driver or guardian of the vehicle is responsible.[75] Indeed where the victim was another driver whose conduct was faulty, as Derek was in this instance, Allan would only escape liability if Derek was the sole cause of the accident. This is obviously a strict liability argument so it is of limited use in understanding the meaning of 'negligence'. However, Wright's argument that Canengus's fault-based liability regime ought to take account of the human as we all as financial costs of accidents provides support for the conclusion that 'negligence is a term that has no inherent meaning.[76]

Conclusions

This essay has argued for a stimulating and rigorous study of tort law and has considered (by reference to practical experience in Leicester) how 'The Canengusian Connection' can assist in accomplishing this goal. Only rarely, will students encounter in the case law frank judicial discussion of the theoretical foundations of negligence law of the sort that we see on display in 'The Canengusian Connection'. In cases where judges speak with the frankness on display in Canengus, their decisions provide, like the essay we have been examining, a valuable pedagogic resource. One such case is *White v Chief Constable of South Yorkshire Police,* where theoretical considerations (concerning, *inter alia*, corrective and distributive justice) divided the court.[77] The understanding of corrective justice and other theories acquired from 'The Canengusian Connection' should assist students to recognise the corrective justice-based concerns of Lord Goff in *White,*[78] critically to assess the validity of the policy arguments surrounding psychiatric illness and

[75] Above n 25.

[76] Above, n 1, 87.

[77] [1999] 2 AC 455. Lords Steyn (at 495) and Hoffmann (at 510) appealed to distributive justice and the injustice that would exist if the police claimants had succeeded while the claims of bereaved relatives had failed; Lord Steyn further noted that negligence is an 'imperfect system of justice' (at 491) where corrective justice would necessarily be limited by the distributive need to treat like cases alike.

[78] *Ibid*, 488.

rescue, and to challenge Lord Hoffmann's reliance on distributive justice and what the ordinary person would think fair between classes of claimants.[79]

The approach to the delivery of a tort module we have examined shows that 'The Canengusian Connection' has a value that goes beyond enhancing students' understanding of, and ability to recognise, the various justificatory theories of tort law. Its incorporation into the teaching of a tort module can help academics to teach process as well as knowledge of legal sources.[80] Where this happens, students will find themselves in an environment where the onus is on relating particular doctrines (on which they tend to focus) to the underlying theories that shape, among other things, fault-based and strict liability regimes.[81] Moreover, the understanding and skills gained from the use of 'The Canengusian Connection' will aid them to develop a coherent overview of negligence law and other branches of tort rather than seeing them as no more than the sum of their doctrinal parts. It is to be hoped that this may also influence students' approach to law and the contexts in which it is embedded: that instead of seeing particular areas of law in isolation they will see the importance and value of understanding law as one entity that is intertwined with, *inter alia*, politics, economics, morality, sociology and history.

[79] *Ibid*, 510.

[80] Above n 70.

[81] The widespread tendency among undergraduates (particularly those new to the study of law) to focus on legal sources may reflect not just a desire for certainty but also the emphasis in Britain's strongly positivist legal culture on the law as 'laid down'. See P.S. Atiyah and R. Summers, *Form and Substance in Anglo-American Law* (Oxford, Clarendon Press, 1987), 258 and 397.

AN EXPLORATORY THEORY OF LEGAL COHERENCE IN CANENGUS AND BEYOND

Emilia Mickiewicz*

1 Introduction

When Allan Hutchinson and Derek Morgan arrived at Newcastle Law School (NLS) for the symposium examining 'The Canengusian Connection'[1], they walked along the same corridors and visited the same rooms in which they had taught and discussed tort law and academic comment with their students in the 1980s. Although familiar with the place and some former colleagues, they saw NLS anew: the decor and equipment had changed; they were greeted by students and members of staff who were new to them. And while 'The Canengusian Connection' remained the same as it was in 1984, it now took on an altered significance; the doctrinal, social, and political background, against which those participating in the symposium read it, had changed.

We might say that the authors of the essay, as well as the participants in the symposium, were discovering new aspects of objects and ideas with which they were already familiar. Accident compensation law, which was the central concern of the symposium, was (as in the 1980s) identified as meaningful in multiple ways – but not quite the same ways since the relevant practices and purposes had altered (*e.g.*, corrective justice had in the intervening years become a more pressing concern for many commentators on tort). But while change was very much in the minds of those who participated in the symposium, we can identify one thing that held constant in the years between 1984 and 2009. Negligence law (like law more generally) reveals distinct meanings when placed in the horizon of altered practices and purposes.

This is a point that Hutchinson and Morgan were mindful of when they composed their essay. They introduced their readers to an imaginary compensation claim in which five fictive judges invoke various principles and policies and, in so doing, breathe life into the legal field under investigation. However, Hutchinson and Morgan do not stake out a

---

*Ph.D. candidate, Newcastle Law School. I would like to thank Richard Mullender, Carol Forrest and Patrick O'Callaghan for the comments on the draft.

[1] A.C. Hutchinson and D. Morgan, 'The Canengusian Connection: The Kaleidoscope of Tort Theory' (1984) 22 *Osgoode Hall Law Review*, 69.

'position' of their own (on the question as to how we should respond to accidents). Hence, we find in their essay a position on positions. They impress upon their readers the fact that the area of legal activity they examine is one in which a variety of sometimes diametrically opposed views have a place. As we read their essay, we have a keen sense of the tension that can arise in accident compensation law and the constantly changing social context in which it is embedded. This prompts a question that is the central concern of this essay: how does law, entangled in a network of often divergent and developing contextual considerations, become intelligible and coherent?

On the analysis offered below, we can unearth the beginnings of an answer to this question in 'The Canengusian Connection'. This is because Hutchinson and Morgan throw light on legal intelligibility and legal coherence as an exploratory activity. They do this by taking their readers on a journey around the legal issues with which they are concerned and making their particular aspects explicit in the interpretations of these fictive judges. But our focus will not be exclusively on the authors of 'The Canengusian Connection'. We will contrast their analysis with that of a prominent legal formalist and tort scholar, Ernest Weinrib. To assess his views on legal coherence critically, we will refer to the hermeneutics of Martin Heidegger and the later philosophy of Ludwig Wittgenstein. But first we must look more closely at 'The Canengusian Connection'.

2 Accidents, Compensation, and Controversy in Canengus

In their essay, Hutchinson and Morgan introduce a negligence dispute following a traffic accident in the fictitious land of Canengus, where the laws are based upon a mixture of Canadian, English and American doctrine. The claim involves, *inter alia*, an action against a driver (Allan) who failed to repair one of the headlights in his car.[2] The claimant (Derek) identifies the defendant's failure to maintain his vehicle as the cause of the accident. Allan also brings third-party proceedings against a witness to this event (Martin), who failed to call an ambulance, thus failing to take on the role of a rescuer and delaying the arrival of medical help to the claimant.[3] The five judges propose different solutions to these claims and invoke a rich variety of reasons for their respective decisions.

[2] *Ibid*, 69-70.

[3] *Ibid*, 69-70.

Doctrin CJ proposes to resolve the case 'in accordance with the law as it is, and not as some think it ought to be'.[4] She draws a sharp distinction between legal and moral statements, observing that 'arguments of law and morality are … mutually exclusive'.[5] Accordingly, in her opinion, she does not rely on any sources external to law and proposes a solution that is based solely on existing doctrine. She argues for 'the formal and neutral application of the [existing] rules',[6] for she believes that this will preserve 'certainty and generality so as to avoid a doctrinal wilderness of single instances'.[7]

Mill J's judgment is very different. He argues that 'the law should seek to simulate an outcome that would be produced by market forces in a world which generates no transaction costs'.[8] According to Mill J, judicial choices should be made so as to support 'economic efficiency'.[9] He thus concentrates on the economic consequences that specific decisions are likely to generate in the future. He argues that it is policy and not logic that shapes common law doctrine.[10] Moreover, he urges the judiciary to acknowledge that the main purpose of law is the maximisation of overall wealth.[11]

Mill J's views contrast sharply with the arguments advanced by Wright J, who advocates a deontological interpretation of tort law. On Wright's J account, Mill's forward-looking or consequentialist approach fails to 'take individuals seriously.'[12] Mill J is insensitive to the separateness of persons, summing their interests in an aggregate.[13] He fails to recognise that individuals are intrinsically valuable and their rights cannot be 'overridden by appeals to general utility'.[14] According to Wright J, the compensation which defendants are obliged to pay to claimants stems from their status as moral persons. Moreover, he argues that 'when one person harms another, the injured has a moral right to demand and the injurer a moral duty to pay compensation'.[15]

---

[4] *Ibid,* 70-71.
[5] *Ibid,* 71.
[6] *Ibid,* 75.
[7] *Ibid.*
[8] *Ibid,* 80.
[9] *Ibid,* 81.
[10] *Ibid,* 77.
[11] *Ibid,* 80.
[12] *Ibid,* 87.
[13] See Man Chun Siu, 'Conflict in Canengus: the Battle of Consequentialism and Deontology' (2010) 7 *The Journal Jurisprudence*, section 3 (applying the political philosophy of John Rawls to Mill J's thinking).
[14] See n 1, above, 90.
[15] *Ibid,* 87.

The next judgment is that of Prudential J. He proposes an approach to the case that can be described as socio-legal. He describes tort law as a 'litigation lottery', in which large numbers of deserving accident victims 'never recover anything' and in which the administrative costs of delivering compensation are 'astronomical'.[16] Instead of concentrating on tort-based liability, he proposes a no-fault, insurance-based compensation scheme allowing for the costs of accidents – which are an 'endemic feature of modern life' – to be borne by society as a whole.[17] He sees this approach as socially just since society as a whole benefits when people undertake risky but desirable activities such as driving.[18] He argues that judges 'should add a touch of concern and compassion for our fellow human beings to the tort system'[19] and should, therefore, concentrate on the harm suffered by the victims of accidents instead of focusing their attention on the fault of the defendant.

The last judgment is delivered by Lefft J. His contribution gives expression to views associated with the Critical Legal Studies Movement. According to Lefft J, judicial decisions are 'rationalisations of our ideological prejudices'.[20] Judicial activity is, on this view, informed by individual purposes and (class-based) biases, rendering law a mere tool in the hands of a skilled judge. He observes that 'the elite in our society hold a monopoly on knowledge'.[21] He thus presents a Marxist analysis, according to which the ideology of a ruling class dictates the outcome of judicial decisions. Pointing to the impossibility of an objective and fair trial in a society where choices are made by a privileged and self-interested group, Lefft J dismisses all the justificatory frameworks introduced by his colleagues and observes that the 'vast paraphernalia of legal rights and entitlements amounts to nothing more than a sugar coating on a bitter pill'.[22]

By introducing their readers to the spectrum of views we have surveyed, Hutchinson and Morgan demonstrate that multiple and often contradictory purposes shape tort law and that it, consequently, has the appearance of a

---

[16] *Ibid,* 97.

[17] *Ibid.*

[18] *Ibid,* 95-100. See also G. C. Keating, 'A Social Contract Conception of the Tort Law of Accident' in G.J. Postema (ed.) *Philosophy and the Law of Torts* (Cambridge: Cambridge University Press, 2001), where the author invokes the Kantian theory of social contract and argues for a no-fault liability scheme as the regime that most effectively accommodates burdens and benefits following from the pursuit of desirable activities by members of a community.

[19] See n 1, above, 96.

[20] *Ibid,* 105.

[21] *Ibid,* 108.

[22] *Ibid,* 105.

patchwork quilt. For this reason, their analysis contrasts sharply with that of Ernest Weinrib.

3 Weinrib's Formalist Account of Legal Coherence

According to Weinrib, the various doctrines that lend negligence law its distinct character give expression to a single idea, namely corrective justice.[23] This prompts Weinrib to argue that it is quite wrong to construe this body of private law as serving multiple purposes that (to use his term) are external to the law itself (*e.g.*, forward-looking policy goals such as accident-prevention and the ideal of distributive justice). Corrective justice is concerned with righting wrongs between the two parties to a claim, who are connected as the doer and the sufferer of the same harm.[24]

Because corrective justice, according to Weinrib, discloses what he terms an unmediated juridical relation between two parties, it abstracts from their social status and welfare, considering them as equal at the outset of the transaction.[25] Weinrib associates the equality of the parties to a negligence action with their status as moral persons. Moreover, this view of the parties to a claim conveys a Kantian, deontological, view of people which asserts that individuals are ends in themselves and their rights cannot be sacrificed for the sake of achieving external goals of the kind mentioned earlier.[26] A 'legal wrong' is understood as a disturbance of this equality which *must*, according to the standards of corrective justice, be restored by the party who inflicted harm, notwithstanding external circumstances.

In assuming that negligence law is exclusively concerned with corrective justice, Weinrib offers a vision of this branch of tort and legal coherence, in general, that is radically different from the one that we might draw from 'The Canegusian Connection'.[27] Weinrib seeks to justify his position in an

---

[23] E. J. Weinrib, 'On the Immanent Rationality of Law' (1988) 97 *The Yale Law Journal* 949.

[24] *Ibid,* 984.

[25] *Ibid,* 980.

[26] While, according to Weinrib, corrective justice 'represents the structure of the relationship between parties in private law', it does not provide a normative foundation justifying this relationship. Weinrib finds such a foundation in the Kantian notion of right. On Weinrib's view, both corrective justice and Kantian right are implicit in the discourse of private law 'as a coherent justificatory enterprise' providing respectively 'its unifying structure and its normative idea'. See E. J. Weinrib *The Idea of Private Law* (Cambridge, Massachusetts: Harvard University Press, 1995), 19-20.

[27] Hutchison and Morgan are not, themselves, proponents of coherence. See A.C. Hutchinson and D. Morgan, 'Shock Therapy: Policy, Principle and Tort' (1982) 45 *Modern LR* 693, 693 (describing tort law as a 'battleground').

essay entitled 'Legal Formalism: on the Immanent Rationality of Law'.[28] He argues that perceiving law as being informed by multiple, external purposes will necessarily undermine its coherence. This leads him to seek to explain tort law by offering a formalist account of its nature. Formalism, says Weinrib, 'embodies a profound and inescapable truth' about law's inner coherence.'[29] The law is coherent and intelligible when a number of concepts that it consists of, as well as their application in judicial decisions, could be conceived as expressions of a single, unifying form. 'One achieves a complete understanding', Weinrib claims, 'when the form is exhibited and the content is seen as adequate to it.'[30] On Weinrib's account, the form of corrective justice shapes private law and is exhibited in all its doctrines such as duty of care, remoteness or damage, as well as in particular judgments.

Weinrib uses the example of a table to develop this point. He explains that the form of a table can only be plausibly conceived of by reference to its content, and, conversely, the content of a table can only be made intelligible by reference to its form. Form and content are, according to Weinrib, correlative and interpenetrating.[31] Because one is unimaginable without the other, 'form … is content and content form, with the distinction between them being notional, not ontological'.[32] The form of a given matter is not a new, separate attribute of a given phenomenon, but is a principle disclosing the thing's intelligibility. This, Weinrib argues, is as true of tort as it is of a humble table.

Form determines what a given phenomenon is in two ways: positively, by highlighting its essential characteristics and negatively, by distinguishing it from all other phenomena. 'Form', says Weinrib, 'is the ensemble of characteristics that constitute the matter in question as a unity identical to that of other matters of the same kind and distinguishable from matters of a different kind.'[33] Thus, form distinguishes the thing (be it a body of legal doctrine or a table) as something determinate; and without the form there would be 'an indeterminate something or other that is nothing in particular'.[34] This means that form allows us to apprehend the thing as meaningful: it is either something that the form discloses or nothing at all. If there is no form, we are left with mere unintelligibility. When we seek to

---

[28] See n 23, above.
[29] *Ibid,* 950.
[30] *Ibid,* 974.
[31] *Ibid,* 959.
[32] *Ibid.*
[33] *Ibid,* 958.
[34] *Ibid*, 957.

disclose the meaning of a given thing, we are asking what the thing *is*, and, according to Weinrib, the form provides an unambiguous answer to this question.[35] These points lead Weinrib to declare that 'tort law has the only purpose it can coherently have: to be tort law'.[36]

In making this rather gnomic sounding declaration, Weinrib is simply applying his account of 'form' to the area of private law concerned with wrongdoing, outside of contractual relations and the law of restitution. For Weinrib, as we have already noted, takes the view that form discloses the intelligibility of a given phenomenon. And form, on his account, distinguishes tort from all other phenomena. Moreover, he takes the view that, in order to be coherent, the phenomenon under scrutiny cannot exhibit more than one form.[37] To demonstrate this point, Weinrib explains why private law, once identified as exhibiting the form of corrective justice, cannot be coherently thought of as disclosing, for example, the form of distributive justice. Unlike corrective justice, which is concerned with restoring the notional antecedent equality between two parties, distributive justice is concerned with a proportionate allocation of resources among an unrestricted number of individuals.[38] Weinrib defines distributive justice as encompassing three elements: 'the benefit or burden that is the subject of the distribution, the recipients among whom the benefit or burden is to be distributed, and the criterion according to which the distribution is to take place'.[39]

On this view of distributive justice, the amount that each party receives or the burden that s/he will be bound to bear depends on criteria that are set for each particular distribution. This means that the forms of distributive and corrective justice represent two different functions of equality: proportional (in the case of distributive justice) and quantitative (in that of corrective justice). This, in turn, imposes two separate standards of coherence. As Weinrib puts it: in the case of distributive justice, 'coherence ... is a harmony of criterion, benefit (or burden), and beneficiaries (or

[35] *Ibid,* 958.

[36] E.J. Weinrib 'Understanding Tort Law' (1989) 23 Val.U.L.Rev 485, 525-526. See also n 23, above, 958 and A.C. Hutchinson, 'The Importance of Not Being Ernest' (1988) 34 *McGill Law Journal* 234, 240.

[37] See T.T. Arvind 'The tortological question and the public-private relationship in tort law'(2010) *7 The Journal Jurisprudence*, section 3.

[38] See n 23, above, 981.

[39] *Ibid.*

burden-bearers)', while in that of corrective justice, 'coherence …lies in the singleness of the relationship of doing and suffering'.[40]

In accordance with the conception of form, described above, which holds that form unequivocally determines its content, Weinrib argues that both forms could not satisfactorily explain the same juridical relation simultaneously. 'They [corrective justice and distributive justice] constitute the most abstractly comprehensive structures of justification and thus cannot be combined into a single overarching justificatory structure. Each form is its own distinctive and self-contained unity. They both pertain to the ordering of external relations among persons, but they order these relations in different ways. Because the forms of justice represent mutually irreducible conceptions of coherence, no single relationship can coherently combine the two forms.[41] If a corrective element is mixed with a distributive one, each necessarily undermines the justificatory force of the other, and the relationship cannot manifest either unifying structure.[42]

If we accept that Weinrib's account of tort is correct, then only one of the five judgments in 'The Canengusian Connection' is defensible: that of Wright J. Like Weinrib, Wright J identifies the compensation that the defendant pays to the claimant as being required by corrective justice. Moreover, he regards this ideal of justice as underwriting the status of the parties as moral persons. To this we can imagine Weinrib adding the further observation that the other four judgments fail a test of coherence since they do not give adequate expression to corrective justice and, in some cases, seek (quite misguidedly) to meld it with distributive justice. Plainly, Weinrib's account of coherence can be put to a wide range of critical uses. But should we accept his account of coherence? Before trying to answer this question, we must examine the writings of Wittgenstein and Heidegger and the notion of 'aspect perception'.

4 Wittgenstein and Heidegger on Coherence and Aspect Perception

While Weinrib's theory of private law may seem appealing, putting a powerful critical tool in the hands of those who use it, it can hardly be reconciled with negligence law as it exists in common law jurisdictions. When deciding cases in tort, judges do not refer exclusively to the ideal of

[40] *Ibid,* 983.

[41] While Weinrib does not talk in terms of 'uncombinability', he alerts his readers to the problem. On uncombinability, see J. Gray *Post-Liberalism. Studies in Political Thought* (London: Routledge, 1993), 301.

[42] See n 23, above, 949.

corrective justice and the associated principle of personal responsibility. On the contrary, as Lord Edmund-Davies observed in *McLaughlin v O'Brian*, judges regularly base their decisions on public policy grounds when deciding negligence law claims.[43] For instance, in cases concerning the liability of public bodies, even where the claimant is able to show that s/he has indeed suffered harm as a result of the defendant's careless conduct or omission, the court may nevertheless refuse to impose liability on public policy grounds.[44] This follows from, among other things, judicial application of the third requirement of the *Caparo* duty of care test which concerns the question of whether the imposition of liability would be just, fair, and reasonable.[45] This component of the *Caparo* test invites judges to consider this question in the light of the consequences that their decisions may bring about for society as a whole.

On a Weinribian view, this concern with society as a whole (rather than the parties to a claim) is a betrayal of corrective justice and a source of incoherence. Weinrib regards this approach as completely misconceived. Among other things, we might describe his critique as driven by an 'elevated' theory of private law.[46] He identifies an ideal central to negligence law (corrective justice) as a basis on which to explain it to us. And this ideal becomes a 'measuring rod' of legal coherence. Moreover, interpretations of negligence law that are not founded exclusively on this ideal are, according to Weinrib, incoherent and unsustainable.

While Weinrib's view offers a neat solution to the matter of the normative foundations of negligence law (and tort more generally), it seems that this area of law is more complex than he recognises. Moreover, to describe it (as Weinrib does) as informed solely by the ideal of corrective justice is to offer an unduly narrow and dogmatic account; for corrective justice is only one aspect of the vast legal field we are surveying. So, before accepting Weinrib's analysis, it is surely worth considering whether it is possible to develop an alternative view that fits better with the tort law we have, while being coherent at the same time. To this end, we will have to return to the concept of form, on which Weinrib's theory of legal coherence rests.

---

[43] *McLaughlin v O'Brian* [1983] 1 AC 410, 424-428.

[44] See, for example, *Mitchell & Anr v Glasgow City Council* [2009] 1 AC 874.

[45] *Caparo Industries plc v Dickman* 2 AC 605, 617-618, *per* Lord Bridge.

[46] On 'elevated' analysis of the sort described in the text, see R. Mullender, 'Introduction: A Dance to the Music of Tort' (2010) 7 *The Journal Jurisprudence*, n 22 (on Andrew Halpin's account of 'elevated' philosophy).

As we noted earlier, Weinrib's account of form serves as an ultimate measuring rod of legal coherence that unambiguously identifies particular phenomena as distinct from all other things. However, it is questionable (for reasons explained below) whether a given phenomenon is inextricably bound to and determined by a single form. We can find support for this argument in Wittgenstein's *Philosophical Investigations* and other components of his later philosophy.[47] Wittgenstein demonstrates that one and the same content can intelligibly exhibit many alternative forms, which are themselves contingent and, therefore, cannot serve as ultimate bedrocks of intelligibility and coherence.

To illustrate this point Wittgenstein refers to Jastrow's duck-rabbit puzzle picture:[48]

By confronting readers with a paradoxical experience of seeing two objects (a rabbit or a duck) expressed in one and the same content, Wittgenstein provided an insight into the nature of our perception and the way we construct meanings in general. What we conceive to be a form allowing us to see a phenomenon as a whole, distinct from all other things (for example a rabbit), is not inextricably bound to its content, but is a conceptual scheme that we create by identifying similarities and differences between the investigated phenomenon and phenomena that we are already familiar with. To see an aspect, states Wittgenstein, is to 'bring a concept to what we see'.[49] If we had never seen a rabbit or a duck in our life, we would probably be unable to envisage the above figure as a picture of a rabbit or a duck. The fact that we perceive a given phenomenon as a genus of a certain kind does not exclude the possibility of conceiving it in alternative terms.[50] This is because form is not something inherent in phenomena. Rather, it is a concept brought by us (as interpreters).

[47] L. Wittgenstein *Philosophical Investigations* (Oxford: Wiley-Blackwell, 2009), trans. G.E.M. Anscombe, P.M.S. Hacker and Joachim Schulte.

[48] *Ibid*, 400.

[49] *Ibid.*

[50] In the light of this point, we have a basis to suppose that we can resist 'monologue creep' as described in P. O'Callaghan, 'Monologism and Dialogism in Private Law' (2010) 7 *The Journal Jurisprudence*, section 5 ('Monologue-Creep').

According to Wittgenstein, to see an image 'as something' is to perceive only one of its multiple aspects. As he puts it, to recognise Jastrow's figure as a picture of a duck (or a rabbit), is to 'light up an aspect' of this image.[51] Wittgenstein explains his 'aspect lighting' theory by reference to another example.[52] When I look at the picture of a face I can study its expressions and features. But when I suddenly recognise it as a picture of my friend I have lit up a new aspect of the figure, seeing it as something different from what I saw before. What is peculiar to this experience is that, even though I am aware that the content of the picture has not changed, I still see it anew; and I see it anew because I have assessed it in the light of my previous experiences. And just as we can see particular aspects of a face or situation, so too may we miss them. For example, we can look at Jastrow's duck-rabbit puzzle and continuously see a rabbit, while being unable to comprehend it as an image of a duck. When this happens, we are (to use Wittgenstein's phrase) 'aspect-blind'.[53]

Connecting these insights with Weinrib's theory, one may suspect that in conceiving of form as determinative and bound to its content, Weinrib faces the problem of 'aspect-blindness'. On Weinrib's account, form determines content in accordance with the principle of *tertium non datur*: either the thing is what the form discloses, or it is something unintelligible. As Weinrib puts it, a phenomenon that does not disclose a single form is 'an indeterminate something or other that is nothing in particular'.[54] Because an investigated phenomenon can, on this view, only be coherently conceived of as an expression of a single form, Weinrib identifies the form as an ultimate 'measuring rod' of coherence. Yet, as Wittgenstein's analysis shows, form is contingent and may assume a variety of shapes. This means that a single form (e.g., the ideal of corrective justice) may not provide the only applicable and ultimate standard to which one may refer when assessing the intelligibility of a practice, institution, or other object under scrutiny.

Form (in Wittgenstein's view) is a concept that we bring to phenomena. We should not think of it as inherent in the objects that we seek to interpret. For those who engage in the interpretation of, *inter alia*, a practice or institution, actively construct form by identifying how the object under examination relates to other phenomena. Among other things, this involves the identification of the relationships in which the object under examination

[51] See n 47, 400.

[52] *Ibid.*

[53] *Ibid,* 432. See also L. Sterne, *The Life and Opinions of Tristram Shandy, Gentleman* (Oxford: Oxford University Press, 1983), 174 and 329 (on 'hobby-horses').

[54] See n 23, above, 957.

stands alongside other items in the same field and with the wider context. Wittgenstein's account of the aspects of particular objects is relevant to interpretation on the model contemplated here. He states that '[an] aspect is not a property of an object, but an internal relation between it and other objects'.[55] He also argues that this 'relatedness' to other objects allows us to pick out or 'light up' new aspects of the things we scrutinise.

As well as throwing light on the way in which we can pick out new aspects of an object, or practice, or institution under scrutiny, Wittgenstein is also elucidates the way in which our understanding of a particular object may remain fixed over time. He talks of 'continuous aspect perception'.[56] By this, he means the way in which we, as interpreters, have an immediate experience of an object as already saturated with a (comparatively stable) meaning.[57] When we apprehend things in this way, it reflects the extent to which we feel familiar with them. To see objects around us in this way is practically important. It is our ability to continuously recognise ourselves, other people, and objects as entities of a certain kind that constitutes our identity as free agents and allows us to operate effectively within the world. It is only because I can conceive of myself as one and the same person everyday that am I able to make decisions that I consider to be my own, stemming from my own projects, desires and experiences. Moreover, I can skilfully deal with items within the world because I expect them to exhibit similar features every day. This is because the meaning they bear emerges from the multiple relations in which they are entangled and from the context in which they are embedded. Therefore, although one can distinguish different aspects of phenomena and conceive of them in alternative terms, the ascription of significance is far from chaotic. Rather, it is organised by the way in which particular items are connected to the wider background that determines, as Wittgenstein puts it, their situatedness in 'the whole tapestry of life'.[58]

Wittgenstein terms the context against which we apprehend a 'form of life'. He describes a form of life as 'the given'.[59] By this he implies that it is the world as we find it. With the multiplicity of contingent interactions that persist within it, it serves as the only available and, hence, ultimate bedrock of coherence. It is the context (or 'the surroundings'), says Wittgenstein, that

[55] See n 47, above, 212.
[56] *Ibid,* 201.
[57] S. Mulhall, *On Being in the World: Wittgenstein and Heidegger on Seeing Aspects* (London: Routledge, 1990), 124.
[58] See n 47, above, 279.
[59] *Ibid,* 468.

lends 'importance to things' and makes it possible to make judgments of coherence.[60] Moreover, 'the given' is the 'inherited background against which I distinguish true and false'.[61] Wittgenstein also considers this background as 'a system, a structure of taken-for-granted convictions that makes identifications and discrimination possible'.[62] As every validation takes place within this system, the background itself 'belongs to the very essence of what we call an argument'.[63]

While the background described by Wittgenstein is ultimate, this is only in a historical, factual sense.[64] This is because forms of life vary across time and cultures. They are shaped by intersubjective human ways of acting (*Handlungsweise*).[65] Consider, for example, a bow taken by someone from Japan.[66] As a traditional form of behaviour, it bears distinct meanings for participants in this culture. In other parts of the world, the same physical action bears different meanings. This is because our activities are always 'nested in the wider context of a historical culture, for the most part we are not so much unique individuals as we are participants and place-holders'.[67] Human actions and practices (accident compensation procedures included) are, therefore, not meaningful in themselves. Rather, they become intelligible and coherent when placed against the wider backdrop of human practices and other shared ways of acting. As Wittgenstein puts it, 'what determines our judgement, our concepts and reactions, is not what one man is doing now, an individual action, but the whole hurly-burly of human actions, the background against which we see an action'.[68]

Years before Wittgenstein pursued the theme of a coherent experience of the world, the German philosopher, Martin Heidegger, dwelt on the same subject. But there are real differences between these two thinkers. Heidegger upholds the Continental philosophical tradition, while Wittgenstein's later

---

60 L. Wittgenstein *On Certainty* (Oxford: Blackwell, 1975), 94-95.

61 *Ibid,* 94-95.

62 *Ibid,* 102.

63 See n 47, 'Aphorism', 105.

64 K.O. Apel 'Wittgenstein and Heidegger: Language Games and Life-forms' in C.E. Macann (ed.) *Critical Heidegger* (London: Routledge, 2004), 269.

65 See n 47, above, 165, 167, and 206.

66 C. Guignon 'Philosophy after Wittgenstein and Heidegger' (1990) 50 *Philosophy and Phenomenological Research* 649; see also H.L.A. Hart *The Concept of Law* (Oxford: Oxford University Press, 1994), 55-58 (where Hart provides the broadly similar example of a rule specifying that men must remove their hats in church (which is intelligible to the members of a particular society who accept it as their own reason for action and as having specific cultural significance for them)).

67 See C. Guignon, n 66, above, 655.

68 L.Wittgenstein *Zettel,* (Oxford: Basil Blackwell, 1967), (trans. G.A.M. Anscombe), 98.

writings make plain the very considerable influence that Anglo-Saxon analytic philosophy continued to have on him as he developed the arguments that appear in *Philosophical Investigations* and associated works. However, a 'surprising affinity' exists between these two thinkers.[69] Like Wittgenstein, Heidegger takes as his starting point the fact that our experience of phenomena in the world is organised into an intelligible whole, rather than existing as 'a blooming, buzzing confusion'.[70] And, like Wittgenstein, Heidegger connects this fact to the holistic nature of human understanding. According to Heidegger, 'something is encountered as something in a pragmatically relational totality'.[71] On his view, our understanding of phenomena presupposes a form of Being-in-the-World.[72] By 'Being-in-the-world', Heidegger indicates that phenomena are only meaningful to us if we know what place they occupy in our world, what purposes they serve, and what relationships they have with us and with other phenomena.

Heidegger explains this approach to human understanding in his much discussed workshop example. In this example, he introduces a distinction between things 'present-at-hand' and things 'ready-to-hand'.[73] A hammer achieves its significance not 'as' a hammer from within, but from the place it occupies within the entire field in which it is involved. It becomes meaningful only if we are able to answer the question 'what is it for?' Only when we are able to answer this question, can we begin to use a hammer. Among other things, we might use a hammer in order to drive nails into a board. We might do this when building a house. Thus, a hammer becomes meaningful as 'ready-to-hand': *i.e.*, as a tool that we are able to handle skilfully and that is entangled in the 'equipmental context of means/ends relations by our projects'.[74] In other words, it is only intelligible 'within-the-world' of which it is a part.[75] As Heidegger puts it, 'the ready-to-hand is always understood in terms of a totality of involvements'.[76] When detached

[69] See n 64, above, 241.

[70] See n 57, above, 126.

[71] See n 64, above, 250.

[72] M. Heidegger, *Being and Time* (Oxford: Blackwell, 2005), 79: 'What is meant by "Being-in"? Our proximal reaction is to round out this expression to "Being-in 'in the world'", and we are inclined to understand this Being-in as 'Being in something' This latter term designates the kind of Being which an entity has when it is 'in' another one, as the water is 'in' the glass, or the garment is 'in' the cupboard. By this 'in' we mean the relationship of Being which two entities extended 'in' space have to each other with regard to their location in that space.'

[73] *Ibid*, 98.

[74] See C. Guignon, n 66, above, 654.

[75] See n 72, above, 122.

[76] *Ibid,* 118.

from this context, it becomes 'de-worlded' – an unintelligible object that is merely 'present-to-hand' and that cannot be 'seen as something'.[77] We can only 'stare' at it, but 'when we … stare at something [that lacks a place in 'a totality of involvements'], our just-having-it-before-us lies before us as a failure to understand it any more'.[78]

'Seeing as', which is only possible in a holistic field of involvements, is identified by Heidegger as a constitutive state of understanding. According to Heidegger, '[t]he "as" makes up the structure of the explicitness of something that is understood. It constitutes the interpretation. In dealing with what is environmentally ready-to-hand and interpreting it with reference to its context, we "see" it as a table, a door, a carriage, or a bridge'.[79] Therefore, every understanding is an interpretation and every interpretation is circumspective.[80] This means that interpretation cannot abstract from the circumstances in which it takes place, *i.e.*, from the entire field of its involvements.

As there are multiple circumstances or involvements in which a given thing is entangled, it is possible to interpret it in a variety of ways and to envisage its multiple aspects – a hammer is meaningful as a tool that could be used to drive nails into boards, as a tool that could be used to build a house, and so on. Engaging in interpretation, we make a thing stand out from the field of its involvements as an 'aphopatic as'*: i.e.*, we only bring one of its aspects to light. This does not mean that we can freely throw any 'signification'[81] over the interpreted phenomenon; 'the thing in question already has an involvement which is disclosed in our understanding of the world, and this involvement is one, which gets laid down by the interpretation'.[82] Understanding, for Heidegger (as for Wittgenstein), already takes place within a system. Heidegger terms this system a 'fore-structure' or a 'background'.[83] Moreover, he explains that it is everything that we have, see, and grasp in advance.[84] It is the world as we find it, in which every

[77] *Ibid,* 79. See also S. Fish on 'interpretative communities in S. Fish, *Is There A Text in This Class*, (Harvard: Harvard University Press, 1980), 147–174.

[78] See n 72, above, 190.

[79] *Ibid,* 190.

[80] *Ibid,* 191 and 200.

[81] *Ibid,* 190.

[82] *Ibid,* 190-191.

[83] *Ibid,* 192-195.

[84] *Ibid,* 191. The three elements of the fore-structure are fore-having, fore-sight and fore-conception,

understanding is grounded and which allows us to approach things as coherent.[85]

Having now looked in some detail at both Heidegger and Wittgenstein, it is abundantly clear that their respective approaches to coherence are radically different from Weinrib's 'measuring rod' approach. On Weinrib's view, we can only identify something (*e.g.*, an institution or a practice) as coherent by embracing the form that shapes it and that invests it with significance. Wittgenstein and Heidegger take quite a different view. They tell us that when we seek to assess the coherence of something, we are engaged in an exploratory process within the entire field of involvements. They also stake out the position that form is not enclosed within a particular object under examination. Instead, a particular object is rendered intelligible by the life-world of which it is a part. This point has an important corollary. It is, as Apel observes, the very life-world that, with Heidegger and Wittgenstein, 'assumes the role of the ultimate bedrock'.[86]

The picture of interpretation that emerges from the analyses of Wittgenstein and Heidegger is one in which those seeking to make sense of an object, or a practice, or an institution do not make perfunctory use of a measuring rod but engage instead in an exploratory activity. They identify and dwell on the objects within the field they scrutinize and seek to bring them into a relationship in which they hang together as elements in a harmonious whole.[87] This Wittgensteinian-Heideggerian view is similar to that of a prominent legal philosopher who argues that the pursuit of coherence is an activity that involves the 'attempt to make things "hang together"'.[88]

The pursuit of coherence, on the Wittgensteinian-Heideggerian view contemplated here, is a very different undertaking from discovering a single and ever-valid form bound to a phenomenon. It is analogous to a journey. We (so to speak) walk around the object, or practice, or institution under scrutiny with the aim of describing its different features or aspects. Moreover, we seek to grasp the ways in which it relates to other things. In this latter regard, our aim is to pinpoint the relations between the object we are examining and the relations of mutual interdependence in which it stands

[85] On the 'pre-interpretive' stage of interpretation in R. Dworkin, *Law's Empire* (London: Fontana Press, 1986), 65.

[86] See n 64, above, 257.

[87] Just as Wittgenstein and Heidegger are relevant to the view of coherence offered here, so too is N. Simmonds, *The Decline of Juridical Reason* (Manchester: Manchester University Press, 1984), 7.

[88] *Ibid.*

in the wider context. Thus, we come to see the object we are surveying as part of a 'pragmatically relational totality' (to use Heidegger's phrase).

This approach to the pursuit of coherence is clearly a more complex undertaking than that described by Weinrib. And we must add a further consideration to this already complex activity. Based on the concepts that we bring to the field we are scrutinising, we each make sense of it in a variety of ways – each of which we have grounds for describing as coherent (rather than as chaotic or as an indeterminate mess). Therefore, the process of understanding unfolds in a fashion characterised by Heidegger as circular.[89] In our efforts to make sense of the objects, *etc.*, that we scrutinise, 'we are going [*wandern*] in a hermeneutic circle'.[90] Although the German expression '*wandern*' used in this passage of Heidegger's work is usually translated as 'going', the word '*wandern*' could also be (and perhaps more accurately) translated as 'walking'. 'wandering' or 'rambling'. In the German language, the expression '*wandern*' describes, among other things, embarking on a long trip (in the mountains or a forest, for example). Those who set out on such a journey seek to make sense of a whole that is (because it is composed of a multiplicity of parts) complex. Such an undertaking is broadly similar to that with which we are concerned, namely, making sense of a body of law that is composed of a multiplicity of parts that stand in a variety of relations with the wider society of which tort and law more generally are parts.

Heidegger throws further light on interpretative processes of the sort we are concerned with when he observes that 'when something is understood but is still veiled, it becomes unveiled by an act of appropriation, and this is always done under the guidance of a point of view, which fixes that with regard to which what is understood is to be interpreted.'[91] The meanings of a phenomenon become unveiled by the observer from different perspectives, against different backgrounds. To put the same point another way, we walk around the object we are investigating and, with each step, we develop a deeper, more complex understanding of it and the field within which it is situated.

If we adopt the approach outlined here, then we have a realistic prospect of 'com[ing] into [the object under scrutiny] in the right way' (to use Heidegger's phrase).[92] Moreover, we will not – unlike those who apply a (Weinribian-style) measuring rod – 'de-world' it. In light of these points, we

[89] See n 72, above, 92 and 362-363.
[90] *Ibid,* 27.
[91] *Ibid,* 191.
[92] *Ibid,* 195.

should view the process of walking in circles as an enabling condition of interpretative adequacy and, ultimately, coherence.[93] If we wish to see things accurately, there is simply no way of avoiding all the hard work that this entails. For we cannot detach the objects we scrutinise from the fields in which they are situated and in which they form components of our practices and projects. Moreover, interpretative activity of the sort we are contemplating has no obvious endpoint. For, as Guignon has observed, 'there is no final explanation for our forms of life that would put an end to inquiry and consequently … attempts to understand ourselves and our world are an open-ended, ongoing project'.[94]

Having looked in some detail at Wittgenstein and Heidegger, we must now consider the ways in which their thinking illuminates the process of pursuing coherence in the law of tort.

5 Using Wittgenstein and Heidegger to Pursue Coherence in Tort

The heads of tort liability concerned with accident compensation (most obviously negligence law) are (like accident compensation law, more generally) informed by multiple purposes. To make sense of negligence law, for example, is a tough task. And to establish coherence in this branch of tort is an even tougher one. Indeed, it is an undertaking that requires just the sort of time-consuming, complicated, exploratory effort that Wittgenstein and Heidegger help us to understand. This might prompt the objection that judges and lawyers, more generally, are not really capable of this sort of thing. After all, few of them pore over the pages of Wittgenstein and Heidegger.

While this may be true, passages of Lord Steyn's speech in *McFarlane v Tayside Heath Board* suggest that judges and lawyers are quite capable of rising to the sort of interpretative challenge that we have been contemplating.[95] In *McFarlane*, the pursuers (a married couple with four children) sued for the costs of raising a fifth child (which was born after the defendant had negligently performed a sterilisation procedure on the husband). Following the operation, the couple had been told by the defendant that they did not need to use contraceptive measures since the husband's sperm count was negative.[96]

---

[93] See C Guignon, n 66, above, 669.

[94] *Ibid,* 669.

[95] *McFarlane v Tayside Health Board* [2000] 2 AC 59, 76-84.

[96] For detailed discussion of the case, see J. Steele, *Tort Law: Text Cases, and Materials* (2nd edn, Oxford: Oxford University Press, 2010), 456-460. See also D. Morgan and B. White,

By a majority, the House of Lords held that the mother could recover compensation for pain, suffering, and the inconvenience of pregnancy and childbirth. The majority of their Lordships also identified medical and other expenses and loss of earnings associated with the birth as recoverable. However, the House unanimously decided that the costs of raising the 'unwanted' child were irrecoverable.[97]

As well as wrestling with the facts of this particular claim, Lord Steyn reflected on the relevance of corrective justice and distributive justice to the law of negligence. Thus, we find him identifying tort law as 'a mosaic in which the principles of corrective justice and distributive justice are interwoven'.[98] Moreover, he notes that 'in situations of difficulty and uncertainty a choice sometimes has to be made between the two [ideals]'.[99] He concludes that *McFarlane* is such a case. He finds support for this conclusion in the views of 'the traveller on the underground' or ordinary person).[100] For such a person 'would consider that the law of tort has no business to provide legal remedies consequent on the birth of a healthy child, which all of us regard as a valuable or good thing' (rather than a burden within a distributive justice scheme).[101]

Lord Steyn finds support for his distributive justice-based analysis not just in the views of ordinary people, but also in other cases in which judges have made recourse to the ideal of distributive justice.[102] Moreover (and significantly for the purposes of this discussion), he advances 'an argument of coherence'.[103] He notes that '[t]here is no support in Scotland or England for a claim by a disadvantaged child for damage to him arising from his birth'.[104] He adds that '[c]oherence and rationality demand that the claim by

'Everyday Life And The Edges Of Existence: Wrongs With No Name Or The Wromg Name' (2006) 29 *UNSWLJ* 239, section II.

97 *McFarlane v Tayside Health Board*, n 95, above, 113-114.

98 *Ibid,* 83.

99 *Ibid.*

100 *Ibid,* 82.

101 *Ibid. Cf Cattanach v Melchior* [2003] HCA 38 (where the High Court of Australia responded to a claim much like that in *McFarlane* by applying a 'corrective justice approach, without recourse to subjective judicial notions of community conscience' (D. Morgan and B. White, n 96, above, section II)). In *Cattanach*, the plaintiff sought compensation for the costs of bringing up a healthy child. By a majority, the Australian High Court held that she could recover. See J. Steele, n 96, above, 459.

102 *McFarlane v Tayside Health Board*, n 95, above, 83 (finding support for his decision in *Frost v Chief Constable of South Yorkshire Police* [1998] 3 WLR 1509).

103 *Ibid,* 83.

104 *Ibid,* 83 (finding support for his 'argument of coherence' in *McKay v Essex Area Health Authority* [1982] 1 QB 1166).

the parents [in *McFarlane*] should [like the claims brought by disadvantaged children] be rejected'.[105]

The features of Lord Steyn's speech that we have noted make it most apparent that he is not making use of the sort of measuring rod that, according to Weinrib, judges should employ when deciding negligence claims. It seems more accurate to state that Lord Steyn surveys a field in which, *inter alia*, relevant case law, corrective justice, and distributive justice (along with the views of ordinary people) each have a place. We can explain the significance he attaches to corrective justice by reference to Wittgenstein's account of 'continuous aspect perception'.[106] For this ideal of justice occupies a central place in the law of negligence and demands attention from all those who reflect on this branch of private law. However, Lord Steyn, as we have noted, treats distributive justice as the controlling consideration in this case. For this reason, we can (drawing on Wittgenstein once again) describe him as 'lighting up' an aspect of the field he surveys on which judges and lawyers usually place much less attention.[107]

Lord Steyn includes these considerations as he (so to speak) walks around the law. We might see, in this procedure, a commitment on his Lordship's part to avoiding the problem of aspect blindness. Moreover, he seeks to pursue coherence by placing emphasis on, *inter alia*, existing case law and the views of 'the traveller on the underground'. Here, his Lordship treats the law of negligence as being situated within what Wittgenstein has termed 'the whole tapestry of life' of a particular society.[108]

When we reflect on these features of Lord Steyn's approach to the claim in *McFarlane*, it is clearly not the neat procedure described by Weinrib. But it is an approach that faces up to the demands of a case that gives rise to 'difficulty and uncertainty'.[109]

6 Conclusions

The Wittgensteinian-Heideggerian account of interpretation and the pursuit of coherence enables us to understand why 'The Canengusian Connection' is

---

105 *Ibid,* 83.

106 See ns 56-57, above, and associated text.

107 See n 51, above, and associated text.

108 On the Wittgensteinian notion of situatedness in 'the whole tapestry of life.' see n, 58, above and associated text. (We might also describe negligence law as being placed by Lord Steyn within what Heidegger calls a 'totality of involvements'. See n. 76, above and associated text.)

109 See n 99, above, and associated text.

such an influential essay. Hutchinson and Morgan take us on a tour of accident compensation law. We survey this field from five distinct standpoints and, while doing so, build up an illuminating picture of the whole. The assemblage of institutions and practices on which we gaze is far from harmonious. On occasion, we have to make tough choices. And this is true not just of accident compensation law as a whole, but also of negligence law. We can see this in *McFarlane*. Lord Steyn recognises that corrective justice and distributive justice are relevant to his decision and that, while each is a part of the 'mosaic' he is examining, he has to make a choice between them. This leads him to consider not just these ideals of justice but also other aspects of the law – including the influence that the views of ordinary people have over its development, and claims by disadvantaged children arising from their entry into the world. Thus, having walked around this branch of tort, Lord Steyn makes an all-things-considered judgment. Moreover, he is determined to ensure that the judgment he makes fits into the existing body of negligence doctrine. Hence, we find him advancing 'an argument of coherence'.

'Coherence', as Lord Steyn understands that term, does not mean the application of a measuring rod (on the model described by Ernest Weinrib). Instead, it involves a journey around negligence law. Likewise, it involves a tough choice; a decision that makes recourse to distributive justice rather than corrective justice. Wittgenstein and Heidegger clarify this process and, for that reason, those who want to make sense of tort law should pay close attention to their writings.

GATHERING THE WATER: ABUSE OF RIGHTS AFTER THE RECOGNITION OF GOVERNMENT FAILURE

David Campbell, Durham Law School, Durham University UK[1]

One of the many achievements of the late Professor Mike Taggart of the Faculty of Law of the University of Auckland is the most thorough analysis ever made of the leading English case on 'abuse of rights', *Bradford v Pickles*.[2] Published in 2002, Taggart's *Private Property and Abuse of Rights in Victorian England*[3] was the first of the books in the distinguished Oxford Studies in Modern Legal History Series edited by Professor Brian Simpson. Taggart's book is an exercise in what has come to be called the 'legal archaeology' pioneered by Simpson,[4] and he (Taggart) tells us that those to whom he described his research whilst it was in progress typically responded: 'Oh, you are doing a Simpson' (xi). If that were not daunting enough, after he had begun his research, Taggart learned of Simpson's substantial discussion of *BvP* in his 1994 Selden Society lecture on *Victorian Law and the Industrial Spirit*

---

[1] I am grateful to Gary Armitage, Richard Mullender, Colin Murray, Brian Simpson, Warren Swain and Gary Wickham for their comments. This is the second time Brian Simpson has shown great generosity by assisting me to formulate criticisms of his own work, and on this occasion he has asked me to emphasise that he is not, of course, responsible for the views expressed in my paper, and to explain that his Selden Society Lecture, given at a late afternoon meeting of the society, was not an occasion at which it would not have been appropriate to raise the refinements and qualifications which might well have been made to the arguments advanced in it

[2] *The Mayor, Alderman and Burgesses of the Borough of Bradford* [1894] 3 Ch 53 (ChD); [1895] 1 Ch 145 (CA); [1895] AC 587 (HL). Hereinafter this case will be referred to as *BvP*.

[3] M Taggart, *Private Property and Abuse of Rights in Victorian England: The Story of Edward Pickles and the Bradford Water Supply*, Oxford, Oxford University Press, 2002. Hereinafter this book will be referred to as *PPARVE* and references to it will be made, unattributed, in parentheses in the text.

[4] Though the first important example probably was Danzig's 1978 *The Capability Problem in Contract Law*, what Taggart follows Nyquist in calling 'single case scholarship' is, as Taggart rightly says (195 n 1), 'known around the world as "doing a Simpson"', in proper acknowledgement of Simpson's mastery of the form. In the US particularly, this approach has come to be known as 'legal archaeology': D Threedy, 'Legal Archaeology: Excavating Cases, Reconstructing Context' (2005-6) 80 *Tulane Law Review* 1197. With respect, Professor Threedy *ibid*, 1198 is wrong to say that Simpson 'coined' this phrase. Simpson tells us (AWB Simpson, *Leading Cases in the Common Law*, Oxford, Oxford University Press, 1995, 12) that it was suggested to him by Professor Peter Fitzpatrick, who has personally confirmed to me that he did indeed himself invent this term.

(xi).[5] We may be thankful that Taggart did not abandon his research as he understandably says he considered doing, not only because of the intrinsic value of his book, which discusses the case at much greater length than did Simpson,[6] but because the attitude to the case which evolves in Taggart's book can be very interestingly contrasted to that taken in Simpson's lecture. The disapproval of *BvP* that dominates commentary on the case is powerfully expressed in Simpson's lecture, but this disapproval significantly is much more equivocal in Taggart's book.

The main reason for this, I will argue, is that the dominant attitude to *BvP* rests on an assumption that intervention in the public interest generally is beneficent which Taggart himself stated with pronounced conviction in other work, but which does not survive his very close study of the case. This study shows that the contrast between Pickles' selfishness and the beneficence of the Corporation of Bradford, on which the criticism of *BvP* as an obstacle to a doctrine of abuse of rights rests, is implausible, largely because the Corporation actually went about securing its water supply in a highly objectionable manner. I will explore the implications of this for the attitude we should currently take towards intervention in the public interest, and this will take us on to a consideration of the role of abuse of rights in an area in which Professor Taggart made a first rank contribution: modern administrative law.

The absolutist interpretation of **BvP**

The facts of *BvP*[7] arose from the nineteenth century growth of Bradford, from a market town of some 6,000 inhabitants in 1801, into 'Worstedopolis', the 'worsted' or 'wool capital of the world', which, in 1901, was the ninth largest city in Britain, with a population of over 400,000. This growth of course placed enormous demands on Bradford's water supply and, amazing to say, for a considerable period from 1846 onwards this was substantially met from a single source, the incredibly productive 'Many Wells Spring', which rose some seven miles to the west of Bradford in what was then the

5 AWB Simpson, *Victorian Law and the Industrial Spirit*, London, Selden Society, 1995. Hereinafter this lecture will be referred to as *VLIS*.

6 Simpson is very generous in his comparison of Taggart's and his work in his General Editor's Preface to Taggart's book (vii).

7 This account is based principally on Taggart's book, supplemented by reference to the reported cases, Simpson's paper, some of the accounts of the Bradford water supply to which one is led by Taggart, and my own local knowledge supported by reference to the Ordnance Survey mapping. Taggart's account differs from Simpson's in ways which are sometimes very significant but which, with one exception, I shall pass over silently.

hamlet of Hewenden. By the time of the litigation, it was estimated that the enormous sum of £200,000 had been spent in order to add this spring to the Bradford supply (42). After the municipalisation of the supply in 1854, the Corporation of Bradford undertook extensive works which reduced its dependency on Many Wells, to the point where, in the early 1890s when the facts of *BvP* arose, it was providing less than 4% of the Bradford supply, and by the beginning of the twentieth century, Bradford had a superabundance of supply which made it immune to shortage (21).

The Many Wells Spring was fed by water which gathered under the land of East Many Wells Farm.[8] With one exception, at no time did the Corporation or the private Company which preceded it pay the Pickles family which had owned East Many Wells Farm since the 1790s (12 n 31, 13 n 37) anything for the water extracted from the spring (2). The exception is that, in the 1860s, the Corporation paid the defendant's father £400 to desist from coal mining which it was feared would interfere with the spring. This payment (and a payment of £600 to a third party coal merchant also involved) would appear to reflect the lost value of the coal as the statutory procedure for making this payment would have provided, but unarguably it was indirectly a payment for the water (39 n 56). In the 1890s, the defendant, Edward Pickles, then owner of East Many Wells Farm, devised a similar plan to mine a seam of flagstone under his land. This plan would involve drainage of the water which fed the spring in a way which certainly would seriously interfere with and perhaps extinguish the spring. The litigation was conducted in the two circumstances that Pickles' works certainly threatened the Many Wells supply, but that critical, or even really important, dependency on that supply had ended prior to that litigation.

From the outset, Mr WT McGowen, the long-serving, very highly respected Town Clerk of Bradford, a solicitor by training and clearly a formidable holder of his office (28-32), whose influence on the Corporation's conduct throughout this episode Taggart shows to be great, took the view that Pickles had no real interest in mining and that the threat to the spring was an

[8] A substantial part of the land of East Many Wells Farm was to the west of the mouth of the spring used for the Bradford water supply, and Taggart expresses puzzlement at the Farm's name (12 n 30). Unless my reading of his book is faulty, he seems to be unaware that there is a West Many Wells Farm half a mile to the west of East Many Wells Farm, and, most understandably, he does not fully appreciate (8 n 19) what I know from personal experience to be the case, that in wet weather this area is peppered over more than a mile with welling, in some cases spouting, springs. If, as I presume, this is the reason for the name Many Wells, this would seem to reconcile the name and the site of the Farm. The information about the name of the spring provided by *VLIS*, 9 n 15 does not support my speculation.

attempt to, in a lay sense,[9] blackmail the Corporation into paying for the water (36-8).[10] Mr McGowen's 'intransigent' attitude (72) seems to date back to the defendant's father's success against the Corporation (30, 25). Mr McGowen pressed his view on the Corporation, which Taggart concludes was always minded or even resolved to 'have no truck with Edward Pickles' (72). As for Pickles, by thorough analysis of the proposed works which builds on *dicta* particularly of North J[11] and on clear suggestions in Simpson,[12] Taggart puts it beyond argument that Pickles was, at the very most, only tangentially interested in the stone prior to the litigation (44-7, 72). Negotiations which Taggart describes as desultory (39, 72) understandably therefore having failed, the Corporation refused to pay anything at all, and instead obtained an injunction to prevent Pickles carrying out his plan, which Pickles challenged.

BvP is a classic case because, on what I will call the absolutist interpretation of it, Pickles' motive was deemed irrelevant as he had (as close as it is possible to conceive) an absolute right to do with his land as he wished, and the injunction was lifted by the Court of Appeal, which was affirmed by the House of Lords, because Pickles' motive was irrelevant. The absolutist interpretation cannot be stated more forcefully than it was by Simpson in a paper on *Keeble v Hickeringill* and the common law attitude to the malicious exercise of rights:

> The House Lords, with what can only be called glee, ruled that [Pickles'] motive was quite irrelevant to the legality of his action. Just as the owner of a box of matches can while away the time by striking them to watch them burn simply to irritate a passing boy scout who has urgent need of two to pass his fire-lighting test, so could Mr Pickles abstract the water just to annoy the Mayor of Bradford.[13]

Now, it has long been observed that the absolutist interpretation of *BvP* is wrong,[14] and, especially as Taggart teases out the nuances of Pickles'

---

9 Taggart formed such a view of Mr McGowen's character that he (Taggart) believed that McGowen would not have baulked at pursuing criminal proceedings against Pickles if blackmail in the legal sense could have been argued, but, so far as he (Taggart) could say, he thought that, on the contemporaneous law, this could not be argued (43-4).

10 *VLIS*, 12 notes Mr McGowen's attitude.

11 *BvP* (Ch D), 60, 63.

12 *VLIS*, 10-2.

13 AWB Simpson, 'The Timeless Principles of Common Law: *Keeble v Hickeringill* (1707)', in Simpson above n 4, 45, 74.

14 In work going back to 1940, Lawson raised doubts about whether the facts of *BvP* showed malice: FH Lawson, 'Notes on the History of Tort in the Civil Law' (1940) 22

supposedly absolute right more thoroughly than anyone else has ever done (chs 5-6, Epilogue), I want to put consideration of the absolutist interpretation as precedent to one side. As we will see, Simpson himself focuses on something much more interesting. I do not wish to deny that much of the *dicta* in the Appeal Court judgments supports the absolutist interpretation, but much of it does not, and, for what it is worth, I myself believe that those Courts, had they not thought Pickles actions had some colour, would have found it entirely possible to distinguish *BvP* from previous authority interpreted as setting up an absolute disregard of motive.[15] Let us also ignore the tedious paradox whether any sane person, even the bad character in Simpson's example of the match burner, can ever act out of pure, disinterested[16] malice, for even the match burner presumably found some gratification in irritating the boy scout, and recognise that Pickles did not do as he did 'just to annoy the Mayor of Bradford' (73). He did what he did to force payment for the water, that is to say, out of self-interest, and what the case was about is whether this form of exercise of self-interest was legitimate.

Prior to the publication of his essay on *Keeble v Hickeringill* in *Leading Cases in the Common Law*, Simpson had already, in his Selden Society lecture, levelled the accusation that the Lords' opinions, particularly the famous speech of Lord Macnaghten, evidence 'a hint of what can only be called glee at the grasping, greedy behaviour of Edward Pickles',[17] and his own opinion of the case is that it is:

> a most striking illustration of the persistence, in the common law tradition, of the individualistic conception of property rights celebrated, over a century earlier, in the passages of Blackstone which I have quoted. The claims of public interest surely favoured the Corporation against Edward Pickles. But Pickles' despotic dominion triumphed in spite of the obvious awareness

(3rd ser) *Journal of Comparative Legislation and International Law* 136, 162, 165 and FH Lawson, The *Rational Strength of English Law*, London, Stevens, 1951, 117. Lawson himself was clearly of the opinion that Pickles was not acting maliciously in the sense of fruitless spite but with the purpose of forcing the corporation to buy him out: FH Lawson, *Negligence in the Civil Law*, Oxford, Clarendon Press, 1950, 17.

[15] Taggart cites Lawson to the effect that '[i]t is arguable that Bradford Corporation failed merely because it could find not appropriate form of action' (191), with the strong implication that this was a merely technical argument (152-5), 'worthless', Lawson tells us, in Scots law. But the 1940 paper in which Lawson said this concludes with the observation that the then House of Lords might well have built on the Scots position over abuse of rights, '[t]hough not, perhaps, on the actual facts of the Pickles case': Lawson, 'Notes' above n 14, 165 n 3.

[16] Simpson above n 13, 73.

[17] *VLIS*, 15.

> of the judges of the potential consequences of their decision. Let there be sanctity of property even if the heavens fall, or even if the City of Bradford is converted into a howling desert.[18]

What really interests Simpson about *BvP* is not the absolutist interpretation but rather the 'clash between private property rights and the public interest' which he believes the case articulates.[19] He is in particular anxious to argue against Blackstone's definition of the right of property as 'that sole and despotic dominion which one man … exercises … in total exclusion of the right of any other individual in the universe',[20] and Blackstone's drawing the following implication of that definition:

> So great … is the regard of the law for private property that it will not authorise the least violation of it; no, not even for the general good of the whole community. If a new road, for instance, were to be made through the grounds of a private person, it might perhaps be extensively beneficial to the public; but the law permits no man, or set of men, without consent of the owner of the land. In vain may it be urged that the good of the individual ought to yield to that of the community.[21]

What Simpson fundamentally finds objectionable about Pickles' actions is not that he could do anything he liked, which he couldn't, but that, as a 'greedy Yorkshireman' motivated by the Victorian industrial spirit, he was the *homo economicus* of his day when, for reasons of his own self-interest, he opposed the public interest in economic development represented by the Corporation of Bradford.[22]

Simpson has been highly critical of the law and economics of the Second Chicago School, and, in particular, has enjoyed considerable success in challenging the treatment of property rights in the work of Ronald Coase. The dismissive reference in his Selden Society lecture to 'some ideal theoretical world' in which, as 'everyone behaves with economic rationality', 'it may well be that absolute rights of private property are perfectly compatible with rapid economic development',[23] is a criticism of Coase's 'The Problem of Social Cost'[24] as an exercise in mere theory. Simpson made

18 *ibid*, 16-7.

19 *ibid*, 5, 7.

20 *ibid*, 6-7, quoting *Comm* II, 2. In my opinion, Simpson overstates the extent to which Blackstone actually treated property rights as absolute, but reasons of space prevent further discussion of this. Taggart raises the relevant issues (109-10).

21 *VLIS*, 7; quoting *Comm* I, 139-40.

22 *ibid*, 9, 3, 8.

23 *ibid*, 6-7.

24 RH Coase, 'The Problem of Social Cost' (1960) 3 *Journal of Law and Economics* 1.

a similar criticism of Coase in the course of other of his legal archaeological studies,[25] and has made a direct attack upon Coase[26] of the first importance which should be a focal point of any discussion of the 'liberal economic' and the 'public interest' attitudes towards intervention. I believe that Simpson's argument against Coase is misdirected in large part because he (Simpson) fails to see that Coase is at least as great a critic of the 'ideal theoretical world' in which 'everyone behaves with economic rationality' as Simpson himself.[27] But Coase is also to the forefront of those who have argued against the public interest case for intervention by showing that it is much more difficult, but not impossible, to identify the action required by the public interest than typically is appreciated, and I believe that Taggart's book provides more than sufficient evidence that this was the case in *BvP*.

Though his explicit writings on law economics are entirely *en passant*, Taggart certainly shared Simpson's views about them, and he particularly focused his obvious wrath on the 'public choice' economics which have been to the forefront of pointing out the problems of the concept of the public interest. Taggart's explicit comments on these economics are not, in truth, especially penetrating, and I do not wish to argue against them directly, but I do wish to argue against at least part of Taggart's important views on administrative law from which his views on law and economics arise. Taggart did not come to *BvP* as a tort lawyer. His principal strengths were in public law, and, in particular, he was amongst the first rank of those engaged in the most recent attempt to develop a distinct administrative law appropriate to the Commonwealth jurisdictions still haunted, to varying but always significant degrees, by the ghost of AV Dicey.[28] Taggart was interested in 'the reasons why the common law rejected [an abuse of rights doctrine] and in the light this sheds on the different starting points of private and public law' (166). The rejection of a doctrine of abuse of rights in *BvP* is a 'symbol' of all that Taggart thought wrong about the division between public and private law (201), and in an important 1997 paper on 'The Province of Administrative Law Determined?' he attacked the case as he then understood it:

> The marked difference in public law and private law approaches ... is underpinned by the absence of an abuse of rights doctrine

---

25 AWB Simpson, 'Victorian Judges and the Problem of Social Cost', in Simpson above n 4, 163, 195.

26 AWB Simpson, 'Coase v Pigou Reexamined', in G Korngold and AP Morriss, eds, *Property Stories*, New York, Foundation Press, 2004, 9.

27 I do not wish to enter into discussion of the wider issues here, but I will mention that Coase has accepted some of the specific problems with bargaining solutions that are raised by *BvP* in RH Coase, 'Blackmail' (1988) 74 *Virginia Law Review* 655, 671.

28 M Taggart, 'The Province of Administrative Law Determined?', in M Taggart, ed, *The Province of Administrative Law*, Oxford, Hart, 2007, 1, 20.

> in the common law. This French-inspired doctrine is widely accepted in civil law countries and the Canadian civil law Province of Quebec, and basically prevents a right-holder abusing the right by exercising it for the sole purpose of harming another or for a purpose other than that for which it was granted or in an unreasonably disproportionate fashion. The common law turned its face against such a doctrine at the end of the 19th century,[29] refusing to investigate the motives or reasons for the exercise of lawful powers by private individuals or corporations, no matter how discriminatory or harmful to the public interest. Nothing could be more at odds with the starting point of administrative law, and the absence of such a doctrine – unless and until this position is re-examined – will hinder to some extent the blending or synthesis of public and private law.[30]

By 're-examined', Taggart meant reversed, and he intended *PPARVE* to contribute to the reversal. But Taggart had sufficient openness of mind that, on examining this great Victorian case on the relationship of citizen and state, he began to see things were not as he imagined. I do not say that Taggart changed his mind about abuse of rights. He didn't. But I do think his book on *BvP* gives great weight to the argument that such a change of mind would be justified, and that he to some extent recognised this.

Gathering the Water

Whilst I certainly would have read Taggart's book in any event, I took it up with a particular, personal interest. Hewenden Beck, the (I think) natural water course fed by the spring harnessed to the Bradford supply, is a sub-tributary of one of West Yorkshire's most important rivers, the Aire, and between 1989 and 1999 I had a house 5 miles north of Hewenden on the other side of the Aire Valley. I knew the area that Taggart describes well from walking there, and, for what it is worth, I must say I was surprised and impressed at his grasp (70) of the geography of a landscape complicated by extensive, impressive Victorian civil engineering works which had in part been allowed to collapse into a confusing decay. Since the time of Taggart's researches, considerable restoration of the works has been undertaken, and Hewenden is in fact a tourist destination in a small way, because of the

[29] *BvP* and *Allen v Flood* [1898] AC 1 are cited here.
[30] Taggart above n 28, 17.

works and because, as it descends, Hewenden Beck runs over an attractive waterfall in a particularly nice bluebell wood. However, I cannot say that the upland landscape around Hewenden gives rise to an immediate feeling of affection. It is bleak and in poor weather harsh, and the principal feeling to which it gave rise in me was admiration for those who had made a living in it without benefit of modern amenities. By far the most famous account of the general atmosphere of this landscape is *Wuthering Heights*, although, to be accurate, Catherine Earnshaw's moors and the now ruined house thought by some to be the inspiration for Wuthering Heights itself are four to five miles to the west of Hewenden. So strong is the pathetic fallacy generated by the unfolding of this strange and morbid story in this sometimes grim landscape that one imagines that this atmosphere will never be better captured.

But in 2006, Robert Edric,[31] the distinguished contemporary Yorkshire novelist, added a strikingly original touch to our conception of the Victorian Yorkshire landscape in his *Gathering the Water*.[32] Edric's story is situated in North Yorkshire some 20 miles north of Hewenden,[33] but whilst this is, at least to a Yorkshireman such as myself, in important ways a quite different setting to that of *Wuthering Heights* and *BvP*, in substantial part it shares its bleakness, and Edric conveys this in a way which, one can say without absurdity, may be compared to *Wuthering Heights*. One critic, making the point, albeit striking rather too facetious a tone doing so, headed her review 'Wuthering Depths'. *Gathering the Water* has gothic features akin to *Wuthering Heights*, but much of its power is derived from a quality completely absent from Emily Bronte's on the face of it deranged narrative, for its gothic features are contrasted to a matter of fact plot which will call *BvP* to the mind of any reader who has studied the common law. Its central character, Mr Charles Weightman, is a surveyor charged with overseeing the 'drowning' of an inhabited valley to create a reservoir which will supply *inter*

---

[31] Robert Edric is the pseudonym of Gary Edric Armitage. I am very grateful to Mr Armitage for answering questions about his book.

[32] R Edric, *Gathering the Water*, London, Doubleday, 2006. Edric had discussed this theme in 1994 in *The Earth Made of Glass*. The recently published *Salvage* makes up what Edric himself, though not yet his critics, calls his 'flooding trilogy'.

[33] Edric calls his setting the Forge Valley. There is a Forge Valley in North Yorkshire, but it is not the fictional valley of Edric's imagination, which is situated in or near the Nidderdale sytem of reservoirs which were developed principally to serve Bradford and Leeds and which finally made Many Wells much less important (21). Another reservoir serving Bradford and Leeds just to the south of Nidderdale, Thruscross, was created in 1966 by the drowning of West End, a village already largely abandoned for other reasons. During the 'droughts' of 1989 and 1990, the reservoir's level fell so low as to reveal the village, which, most eerily, one was able to walk through. Peter Robinson's crime novel, *In a Dry Season*, turns on the discovery of a body when the waters recede from his fictionalised version of West End.

alia Bradford and Leeds with water. As the story begins, most of the affected population have left the area, but not all, much to the disappointment of Weightman, who had been given a different impression by the Board which employed him:

> To hear the Board men speak, you might think I had been bound for a wilderness of unmapped moor crying out only for the civilising of their scheme. To hear these men speak, you might think I had been handed the crown and sceptre of a fabulous kingdom, as yet unexplored, and over which I exercised sole and absolute dominion. I see now … why they might have encouraged me in such a belief.[34]

Gathering the Water describes Weightman's trials as he tries to remove the remaining population, for, the point of relevance to us is that, as he does so, he is, of course, roundly hated, and, being a man of sensibility, he to some extent comes to hate himself. Abandoned homes (but 'mistakes were … made')[35] are smashed by gangs of 'wreckers' brought in by railway, and Weightman feels his lot to be worse than theirs:

> I cannot ignore the obvious comparison between the wreckers and myself. These other men are skirmishers, come seemingly out of nowhere, destructive and quickly withdrawn; and, allowing the comparison, I find myself little more than a camp follower, a scavenger, benefitting from this brutality, and trudging with my account book through the aftermath, the mess and loss and suffering of battle.[36]

Of course, there is a benefit. The growth of manufacture in what were becoming great cities is 'yet another weight placed upon the scales of loss and gain', but, to those losing their homes through compulsory purchase followed by wrecking, 'the loss was all here and the gain all elsewhere'.[37]

Edric brings to the foreground what does not emerge at all from Simpson's lecture and emerges only incidentally from Taggart's book. They draw a clear contrast between commendable public interest and selfish individualism, but it cannot have appeared like this to Pickles' contemporaries, and, in an important sense, the attitude Simpson is attacking in the judgments, which we will see Taggart shows was shared by significant elements of public opinion, is evidence of precisely this. To contemporaries, the public interest

34 Edric *loc cit*, 9.
35 *ibid*, 56.
36 *ibid*, 58.
37 *ibid*, 89-90.

must have been, not merely unclear, but contested. Simpson's entire argument rests on the following sentence: '[s]ince economic development was conceived to be broadly in the public interest this conflict could be seen to be between private property and public interest'.[38] But 'broadly' hardly captures the range of things, good and bad, done in the name of economic development in industrialising England, and it will not have been the guide to right action at the time which Simpson retrospectively believes it to have been, even if, a hundred years later, one agrees with it. Was it so clear to contemporaries that the growth of Bradford in this way was in the public interest? If it wasn't, then the badness (71) of Pickles' conduct must be seen in a different light, for the moral quality of that conduct is not entirely defined by itself but by the interest to which it is opposed, and it cannot have been black and white in the way Simpson says and Taggart set out to say (72). Pickles' behaviour is greedy and grasping only if it can be contrasted to the virtue of direct pursuit of the public interest, and this, of course, requires us to know what the public interest was, and to be able to have confidence in the Corporation of Bradford acting in its name.

It is very paradoxical to see Simpson and Taggart so keen to endorse the supply of water to Bradford, and I am at a loss to understand how the Victorian industrial spirit which Simpson so deplores in Pickles and the judges who find for him does not seem to taint the growth of Bradford, one of *laissez faire* capitalism's greatest successes. I have made almost no inquiry into the facts, but, whilst I doubt neither the influence of the public interest nor the overall wisdom of public acquisition of the supply, as a reader of Engels and JB Priestley, I surmise that in Worstedopolis the public interest will have been given concrete form by a powerful class of men who, to use Marx's word (*Träger*), were bearers of the industrial spirit to a far higher degree than the rather pathetic self proclaimed 'Quarry Owner' Edward Pickles (35), and that their concern for the water supply of industrial Bradford will have been informed by that spirit.[39] I do not want to hold Simpson and Taggart at all responsible for, in the end, an incoherence that is

[38] *VLIS*, 6.

[39] Taggart cites WA Robson in order to pass an excoriating verdict on the performance of the Company in supplying water (18 n 53), but he makes no investigation of the performance of the Corporation, pointing only to a noted local historian's bare statement of a belief that the public acquisition was a great achievement (20). My vestigial research into the matter does lead me to think that Taggart's account of municipalisation has some of the quality of a public interest variant of Whiggism; shall we call it 'Webbism'? I repeat, however, that I do not doubt that public acquisition of the supply was overall a good thing. The best account of the municipalisation of the supply I have been led to by Taggart to A Elliott, 'Municipal Government in Bradford in the Mid-nineteenth Century', in D Fraser, ed, *Municipal Reform and the Industrial City*, Leicester, Leicester University Press, 1982, 111, 118-22 and the PhD on which it is based.

characteristic of all theories of the capitalist state, but to portray Pickles as representing the industrial spirit against the capitalists which used the state to provide a water supply to Worstedopolis is implausible.

The significance of statute

Though the overwhelming preponderance of commentary on *BvP* is solely concerned with the common law position on abuse of rights, the rights of the parties were mainly determined by statute and it is impossible to understand the case without appreciation of the statutory position. The common law argument was a residuum of the statutory argument. The Corporation, in order to distinguish its buying out of the defendant's father's mine from its refusal to buy out the defendant's, had to stress that the defendant's behaviour was illegitimate in a way his father's had not been (50).[40] Though the wording of the relevant provision, which is quoted below, makes no reference to this whatsoever, establishing it would no doubt have helped secure the interpretation of the statute the Corporation required. North J alone of those who heard the case found for the Corporation on the statute. This finding rendered his statement that the nature of Pickles' conduct was irrelevant *obiter*, but, alerted to the possibility of an appeal, he felt obliged to discuss that conduct, of which he manifestly disapproved, even going so far as to use the word 'blackmail'.[41] Once the Corporation lost on the statute, it became essential to mount an argument about the defendant's state of mind in interfering with the supply, for the interference arose from the exercise of rights the Corporation was then obliged to acknowledge him to have. Let us, then, turn to the statute.

Obviously, major works such as taking Many Wells water to Bradford would involve interference with the property of others, and s 233 (supported by other sections) of the Bradford Waterworks Act 1842,[42] the Local Act which incorporated the private Company that first brought the Many Wells Spring into the service of the Bradford supply, gave the Company the right to take the Many Wells water by consensual or compulsory purchase as the

---

40 The defendant's grandfather also mined coal prior to the connection of Many Wells to the Bradford supply (23).

41 *BvP* (Ch D), 68. I repeat that I do not want to enter into the discussion of the absolutist interpretation as precedent, but the reader may be interested to note that, shortly before *BvP*, North J had found no difficulty in issuing an injunction against a householder who banged trays together to annoy his music playing neighbour in *Christie v Davey* [1893] 1 Ch 316. This nuisance case was not cited to him in *BvP*. The issues are discussed by Taggart (179-80).

42 5 and 6 Vict ch vi.

legitimate means of effecting such interference, under a procedure which included identification of possibly affected land prior to Parliamentary approval (16). But, although the Company bought the land on which the spring actually rose for £2,000 (11); incurred very substantial expense in dealing with affected downstream landowners (14), including building the £6,500, 16 acre Hewenden Reservoir at the boundary of the Pickles' land and in view of their farmhouse (38) to preserve the water supply to others (11, 14); and had every opportunity to purchase sufficient of the Pickles family's interest as to protect the spring (16, 79, 118), it did not do so. The Pickles family were not even formally notified or given a chance to object to the proposed use of Many Wells under the 1842 Act (14).

s 234 (supported by other sections) of the 1842 Act sought to prevent anyone interfering with the Many Wells spring after the Company had purchased it. s 234 was reenacted as s 49 of The Bradford Waterworks Act 1854,[43] one of the Acts which municipalised the private Company, and all the judgments in all the litigation accepted that the two sections were in legal effect identical. s 49 provided:

> It shall not be lawful for any person other than the said Company to divert, alter, or appropriate in any other manner than by law they may be legally entitled, any of the waters supplying or flowing from steams and springs called "Many Wells" … the same, or to sink any well or pit, or do any act, matter, or thing whereby the waters of the said springs may be drawn off or diminished in quantity.

The litigation was required because s 49, which was excoriated in the litigation for its ambiguity, was not drafted in a way which clearly gave the Corporation power to stop Pickles' mining plans.

The parallel I have drawn between Edric's *Gathering the Water* and *BvP* is weak in at least one way. *BvP* could never have arisen if the Many Wells works necessitated physical invasion of East Many Wells Farm (14, 20). The typical circumstance envisaged by Edric is compulsory purchase of a dwelling and Edward Pickles was concerned only with an underground flow of water which it was not clear prior to *BvP* was his property in such a way as to exclude the Corporation's use. Taggart tells us that '[a] constant refrain of Edward Pickles … was that all he wanted to do was … "exercise ordinary

[43] 17 and 18 Vict ch cxxiv. The copy of this Act I have used is in a publication prepared by the Bradford Corporation setting out the Local and General legislation relevant to the municipalisation of the supply: *The Acts Relating to the Transfer of the Bradford Waterworks to the Bradford Corporation*, Bradford, Firth and Field, 1856. This publication is available via Google Books. s 49 is at 173.

landowners' rights'" (35, 35 n 48), but Taggart essentially concludes that Simpson was right to say that *BvP* was a case of first impression about what these rights were.[44] But, after it was found that Pickles had the necessary property in the water, then we must say that, not having bought out the Pickles family, the Corporation wished to use s 49 to curtail their property rights without paying to do so.

Taggart argues that, unless s 49 did just this, it had no purpose whatsoever. This makes the 'clash between private property rights and the public interest' Simpson identifies stark, and is the ground of Taggart's brilliant but, in my opinion, wrong argument that *BvP* is not a case of statutory ambiguity at all but of outright 'disobedience of the legislature' (94). The choice, Taggart would have it, is between an interpretation of s 49 which benefits Pickles by reducing s 49 to nothing, or an interpretation which gives it the effect sought by the Corporation which reduces Pickles' property right to nothing. I myself do not agree with this, for s 49 seems to me to be directed at those without a proprietary interest who interfere with the supply. I can see a value in this even in the circumstances of the case, and the principal ambiguity that arose did so because s 49 was to be used against a defendant whose proprietary interest had not previously been made clear.

This is not a sufficient argument against Taggart, but there is no need to persist with it because, in respect of understanding abuse of rights, I am afraid I see no point to Taggart's interpretation, other than setting up Simpson's stark 'clash', for it runs against the surely unarguable fact that ambiguity *was* perceived by the parties, by contemporary commentators, and by all those who heard the case (88-92), including, as Taggart is obliged to admit, North J himself (87-8). Fundamentally, this is the ambiguity of it being necessary, in order to give s 49 effect, to believe that Parliament had intended to expropriate without compensation, and had not made this *prima facie* implausible construction stick by use of as close as possible to crystal clear language to that effect (91). In my opinion, it didn't use such language because it would not have had such an intention.[45]

There was, I submit, no a 'clash between private property rights and the public interest'. That the public interest could be exercised through compulsory purchase was never at issue in *BvP*. The possibility that 'Blackstone's despotic dominion [might] reign uncontrolled', as Simpson put

---

[44] *VLIS*, 14.

[45] B Rudden, 'Comparative Law in England', in WE Butler and VN Kudriatsev, eds, *Comparative Law and Legal System*, New York, Oceana, 1985, 75, 83.

it elsewhere,[46] never existed. This was not a case about whether the public interest could be exercised but in what manner it should be exercised. And it seems a point of general agreement that the overwhelming contemporaneous opinion was that the legitimate form of expropriation of private property was compulsory purchase (104-5). The question, then, is why compulsory purchase was not made. Taggart's principal contribution seems to me to show that the failure to buy out the Pickles family was the result of a negligent mistake, or of two negligent mistakes.[47]

I have mentioned that the Company did purchase the land on which rose the particular spring from which it took the water, Trooper's or Many Wells Farm (81), and it would appear that it must have thought it had secured the supply by doing so. However, not only is the eastern boundary of East Many Wells Farm only 20 yards from the mouth of the spring, but the property is largely situate upland of Trooper's Farm (12, 94), and, as Taggart puts it, '[i]t would have been plain as a pikestaff (to anyone who had inspected the property) that the water gushing from the Spring came from underneath the upland farm' (93). Even North J found essentially this as fact.[48] *BvP* may have been a case of first impression over rights to water such as Pickles claimed, but, allowing this, Taggart rightly goes on to say, in serious criticism of the Company, that the unclear legal situation prior to 1842 therefore 'would have alerted even the dimmest of investors and their advisers to the need to ascertain the legal position and make provision accordingly' (108). On the basis of materials available to him (Appendix n 3), Taggart is unable to explain why the Company took the line it did, though he does argue that the actual drafters of the 1842 Act (31) would not have visited the site (93 n 79). However this is, the failure to buy out the Pickles family created a situation in which the Company was exposed to threats to a spring in which it proceeded to make an enormously costly investment and on which it proceeded to place a simply immense reliance. Looking back on this having seen North J reversed by the Court of Appeal, the Corporation's own Water Engineer, Mr James Watson, wrote to Mr McGowen to say that the Company 'must have been little short of simpletons' to put themselves at this risk (61).

---

[46] In his General Editor's Preface to J Getzler, *A History of Water Rights at Common Law*, Oxford, Oxford University Press, 2004, vi.

[47] In my opinion, there was a third mistake, for the terms on which the Corporation later settled with the defendant's father left them open to the defendant's later actions, and I should have thought it arguable that the Corporation should have done more at that time to secure its interests.

[48] *BvP* (ChD), 56-7.

Simpson quotes Mr Watson's letter to back up his conclusion that '[w]hether the outcome of the case made much sense can well be doubted'.[49] The argument is that, as the Company must have been simpletons to do what they did in 1842, and as s 49 (ie s 234) 'could be interpreted as covering Pickles' scheme',[50] as of course it could, then, in the public interest, it should have been interpreted as covering Pickles' scheme. With some further argument about the Corporation's actions in 1854, this essentially was the position of Mr McGowen (68, Appendix n 3). But it is here that Taggart substantially departs from Simpson and advances the fundamental criticism of the Corporation. For, although Taggart cannot explain the Company's mistake, the conclusion he draws from showing that they made it is that '[i]t is difficult to acquit the actual legal advisers and Parliamentary agents of the promoters of the Bradford Waterworks Company of the charge of negligence in this respect' (118-9). The risk to the spring existing, there is no doubt that everyone except North J who heard this case read s 49 *contra preferentum* against the expropriating authority, and their reward has been to be regarded with contempt or outright animosity. But should statutes be 'benevolently' interpreted to give a green light to public undertakers by covering up the consequences of their negligence to their benefit (98-102, 198-201)? Should common law sweeping up doctrines be invented so that they can be used to do this?

I have spoken somewhat loosely of the Corporation and the Company because, though the Corporation's agents such as Mr Watson might well have said nasty things about the Company, whatever problem the Company caused, the Corporation of course reproduced it in 1854 by adopting s 234 as s 49 and not doing anything else (61). As again contemporary newspaper opinion put it, the Corporation had 'managed to get into a somewhat serious fix' by reproducing the risk to the spring (42),[51] and sympathy with the failure of the s 49 argument was sparse:

[49] *VLIS*, 16. Simpson also conveys Mr Watson's belief, which Taggart shows was doing the rounds in the Corporation, that the Pickles family had lain low by not objecting to their not being included in the register of interests under the 1842 Act in order to be able later to blackmail the company. Taggart shows this to be completely implausible, not least because objecting to the provisions of a Local Act would have been impossibly expensive (13, 27, 94). On the other hand, Taggart also shows that the accusation (noted by Simpson *loc cit*) that the company was attempting to avoid expense by not buying out the Pickles family was equally implausible (94-6). It seems we are just dealing with a mistake which, even with the benefit of Simpson's and Taggart's research, cannot be satisfactorily explained..

[50] *VLIS*, 12.

[51] Mr McGowen thought Pickles was behind the newspaper commentary (43), and, for reasons on which I will not expand, this seems plausible, but it does not substantially diminish the point made.

> The Corporation had no rights over [Pickles'] land – for the absurd clause on which it relied did not in any way give them more than their common law rights. Bradford had made a mistake in the way in which its waterworks were acquired; and it is nothing but right that Bradford should pay for the mistake (69).

Taggart tells us the author of this newspaper opinion 'put his finger exactly on the crucial point' (68). Taggart does much to show that the Corporation, not being nearly so dependent on Many Wells as it had been when it settled with the defendant's father (25), took the line it did towards Pickles because it could not find it in itself to acknowledge its mistake. As I have noted, Mr McGowen certainly was aware of Pickles father's success against the Corporation despite s 49, and, as Taggart says, '[i]t is not clear why McGowen and the Corporation in 1890 thought that "this time" Edward Pickles was in the wrong as a matter of law' (27). Given the very unclear law about water rights (ch 5), general defects in statutory protection of the type offered by s 49 about which the Corporation had been anxious when giving Select Committee evidence (26), the general solicitude about ensuring private property could be expropriated only with compensation (16), behind which lay a settled rule that interpretation of Local Acts should be *contra preferentum* (96-7), the Corporation's decision to litigate, and to continue to the point where the in the end the litigation fruitlessly cost the ratepayer the very large sum of £4,000 (71), was wholly questionable: 'it is at best puzzling and at worst suggests that there may be some truth to Pickles's claim that the deep-pocketed Corporation had threatened "to swamp" him with the litigation' (27).

I believe the impression to which this gives rise, of, as newspaper comment had it, a 'powerful corporation' acting in an 'undignified and unfair', 'high-handed, overbearing and unreasonable' manner (68), is confirmed in what Taggart rightly calls an 'extraordinary' (59) episode during the litigation, about which he does great service in uncovering important information (59-61). After the Court of Appeal had decided to reverse North J but before its judgment was published, Lord Herschell LC, a member of that Court, told the plaintiff's leading counsel, Cozens-Hardy QC, that, if the plaintiff would apply to Parliament for the power to compulsorily purchase the water, the Court of Appeal would not publish its judgment until after Parliament had passed the necessary Local Act. Despite Mr Cozens-Hardy being of the opinion that his client should do as Lord Herschell suggested, it did not do so, and appealed the case to the Lords. Whatever sympathy one has for the Corporation when it became aware of Pickles' mining plan, I submit one can have none for it in respect of this refusal to accede to a compromise offered in what must have been most awkward circumstances by the Lord Chancellor,[52] which Taggart can only attribute to the Corporation continuing to not being able to admit to its mistake in 1854 (61).[53]

Simpson puts Lord Herschell's offer down to the Court of Appeal being 'not a little nervous of the possibly appalling practical consequences of their decision [which] appeared to enable Edward Pickles to hold the City to ransom'.[54] But, with respect, there never was a threat of ransom. Bradford always had the possibility of obtaining the power to compulsorily purchase Pickles' interest, and Lord Herschell was, I submit, merely trying to bring it to its senses about this. Taggart puts forward, albeit in a footnote (59 n 57), the far more plausible 'competing explanation' of Lord Herschell's offer 'that the Court thought that the Corporation should pay for the water rights'. Simpson then puts forward the Corporation's refusal to reluctance to pay the expense of sponsoring the necessary Bill. I leave this to the reader to evaluate.[55] But Simpson does make it clear that, had the Corporation sought compulsory purchase powers, the price would not have been any extravagant sum Pickles asked but the 'fair price' the compulsory purchase procedure determined. Mr Cozens-Hardy told his client this. Taggart very valuably adds from unreported notes of the proceedings that Mr Cozens-Hardy would have been aware that the Court of Appeal disapproved of the size of Pickles' demands (60 n 58), and that Lord Herschell had predicted that 'the compensation to Pickles probably would not be a very big sum' (60). The Corporation still ignored his advice.

To this picture of deplorable official obduracy I will only add mention of one point where Taggart's account of the facts differs from Simpson's. Pickles 'was not a rich man' (70), and, although he will in the end have been able to recover costs, this episode must have been tantamount to ruinous for him (71), for though he may have won the battle, he lost the war (69). After

52 It is mere speculation on my part, which is not directly backed up by anything in Taggart, but I should have thought the Corporation's stupidity really was enormous because its refusal of this compromise effectively ensured it would lose in the House of Lords. It may be significant in this regard that their Lordships did not find it necessary to call upon Pickles' counsel (62).

53 Taggart exactly says that '[t]he Corporation could not admit to being duped in 1854'. On what Taggart shows us, I am most unsure that any party 'duped' the Corporation save itself, but, if it was duped, it was by the Company, not Edward Pickles. I think Taggart is using 'duped' in an unusual way.

54 *VLIS*, 14-5.

55 It is inconsistent of Simpson to have the Corporation wishing to avoid this expense and yet give weight to the far fetched possibility of Pickles, a private person of limited means, opposing the Bill were it introduced.

the litigation he continued with his stone works and made repeated offers to sell his land to the Corporation, but the Corporation continued to refuse to deal with him, and he emigrated to Canada in, Simpson no doubt is right to conclude, defeat.[56] For Simpson, this is a tale of evil getting its due reward: Pickles' 'greed … caused his downfall', for his 'very success doomed his plan; it is in the nature of blackmail that the threat must never be carried out. He had so successfully disrupted the underground supply that [he] made the land useless as a source of water'.[57] But Taggart tells us this was not the case (69), and this improving story is unfounded. In June 1897, the Corporation undertook works to tap Many Wells by alternative means, and used the supply, although of greatly diminished relative importance, for a further half century (70). It 'had had in mind this contingency plan' throughout the litigation (69).

In sum, I can only quote Taggart's own principal explanation of the actions of the Corporation, and his evaluation of those actions. The first is that 'the Corporation never did pay for its mistake of 1854, and therefore never publicly admitted to making one' (69). The second is that:

> The Corporation did not take any of the opportunities offered to buy the land or the water rights, neither did it go to Parliament to acquire such rights compulsorily. Instead, it pursued expensive litigation so far as it could go. And when the legality of the matter had been definitively sorted out, the Corporation refused to negotiate (72).

I believe that the material Taggart uncovers shows that the public interest which Simpson and he identify with the actions of the Bradford Waterworks Corporation to be a very slippery concept indeed, and *BvP* is in fact the result of government failure. The Corporation made at least one extremely serious negligent mistake about its business, and obstinately persisted in a course of action consequent upon that mistake to the prejudice of an affected private party, rather than admit that mistake.

Criticism of *BvP* on the basis of the absolutist interpretation, when it is not just wrong, involves, in my opinion, saying the following: a landowner should, at common law, utilise his land in a way which is consistent with the public good as identified by a public body. He should not be able to insist upon being compensated for this. If, as should be the case, a statutory procedure for compensation exists but has negligently and then obstinately not been exercised by the relevant body, this is of no relevance to the common law position, which requires the private party to fill in the gaps left

---

[56] *VLIS*, 17.
[57] *ibid*, 18.

by the state by surrender of that part of his ownership which is causing a problem for the body which cites the public interest in support of its activities. I do not find this an attractive position. It amounts to a servility I find worrying. The particular thought which led me to write this paper was that I could not see how to distinguish *BvP* understood in this way from the *Congreve* case,[58] surely one of the foundations of modern administrative law, and a number of the common like cases. It is important to question how this servile position could become so dominant that it seems quite unproblematic to the great majority of those who have considered *BvP*, including, in Simpson, one of law's greatest commentators and, in Taggart, a highly distinguished one.

Taggart's engagement with the case led him into ambivalence over this, and, as a result, I think it fair to say his book reads unevenly and, in particular, the paragraph headed 'Time for Reconsideration?' at the end of the last chapter proper reads a little strangely. Taggart gives a list of distinguished commentators who over the course of the 20th century attacked the absolutist *ratio* of *BvP* just as he intended to do, and concludes with the question '[i]s it time to heed these persistent calls for a reconsideration of the common law position' (193). But Taggart's book has shown that these commentators have not understood *BvP* as it can now be understood on the basis of Simpson's and his legal archaeological research, and so the answer to this question to which his book leads is 'I am not sure', which I think was Taggart's position, or 'no', which is mine.

I think that those who understand *BvP* in terms of the absolutist ratio will read this question as merely rhetorical, but in the even more curious 'Epilogue' which follows his last chapter proper, Taggart says that this question was 'deliberately left hanging'. This Epilogue also leaves the question hanging. It really is as if Taggart did not know how to finish his book after his research had disrupted his own original understanding of *BvP*. Looking at this frankly, he says *PPARVE* does not answer this question because this:

> would require another book, and a different kind of book, than this one has become. This is a different book than the one I set out to write. I first became interested in *Pickles* for the light it would shed on the public/private law divide, and the implications of (re)privatisation of public utilities, such as water companies. But I soon got drawn into the fascinating story, and realised the importance of understanding the case in the context of its own time and place. It dawned on me that by projecting

58 *Congreve v Home Office* [1976] QB 629.

> contemporary concerns back into the past and looking for future guidance, I was misusing historical method in the cause of advocacy (196).

This is very well said. In work published shortly after (the writing of which perhaps overlapped with) his book, Taggart maintained that '[i]t is no doubt time to heed … persistent calls for a reconsideration of [*BvP*]', but writing his book seems to have given him a greater appreciation that the 'the difficulty of doing so … should not be underestimated', in essence because the absolutist interpretation was 'far too simplistic', but more because he was no longer clear about where he stood on the 'tussle between individual autonomy and the public interest'. [59] I have been unable to piece together from Taggart's subsequent writings what, in the end, he thought could be done about *BvP* in terms of concrete law reform. He maintained his general position, but entered into no detail, perhaps because the difficulties of reform, especially reform based on importations from the civilian tradition, were given greater weight (165) than they would have been were Taggart still of the mind with which he began his research. But, in the end, it had all became rather more abstract: 'a clash of values'.[60] I can, however, confidently say that someone whose last work evidenced a commitment to the wide use of *quantum meruit* in determination of utility pricing by courts[61] would not agree with the view of the case that, in essence, I had formed prior to reading Taggart's book, but which I think his book confirms: that development of a doctrine of abuse of rights would be a serious mistake. It is a mistake which follows from a view of the relationship between citizen and government that has been dominant but which we should now abandon, the key to which, in Taggart's case, is to be found in public law. Public law discussion of this issue must, of course, begin with Dicey.

Taggart and Dicey on administrative law

Reflecting on Emerson's maxim that 'to be great is to be misunderstood', I have long thought that Dicey must be a truly great figure because he is in a league with Karl Marx and Adam Smith when it comes to being subject to

---

[59] M Taggart, 'The Peculiarities of the English: Resisting the Public/Private Law Distinction', in P Craig and R Rawlings, eds, *Law and Administration in Europe*, Oxford, Oxford University Press, 2003, 107, 114.

[60] *ibid*.

[61] M Taggart, 'Common Law Price Control. State-owned Enterprises and the Level Playing Field', in L Pearson *et al*, eds, *Administrative Law in a Changing State*, Oxford, Hart, 2008, 185.

criticisms which are based on a complete lack of sympathy with his work. I am afraid I simply cannot see the justice of an attack, even when mounted by one of our most distinguished administrative lawyers, on 'the denial of the subject [of administrative law] expressed in Dicey's insular individualism',[62] when this denial made good sense in Dicey's own time, even if one doesn't agree with it, and, I will argue, makes even better sense now, even if one doesn't agree with it.

The key to understanding Dicey is the apparent truism that, born in 1835 and dying in 1922, he was, as one of his biographers has put it, a 'Victorian jurist', whose views were, it appears, essentially settled by the 1860s.[63] As an 'old Liberal' extremely concerned about the extension of the franchise, it is inevitable that some of what he said now seems antediluvian, and either silly or unsavoury or both as a result. In his 1942 essay in defence of Kipling, Orwell began by saying that '[i]t is no use pretending that Kipling's view of life, as a whole, can be accepted or even forgiven by any civilised person',[64] and surely something milder but essentially like this must be said of Dicey's view of democracy. But just as Orwell recovered the profound good sense in Kipling, I believe we must now see the similar but much greater sense in Dicey. Writing of a 'popular faith in the English Constitution' 'which in 1905 has become almost incomprehensible', Dicey asked '[w]here shall we now find the ardent believers in the Constitution of England? If they exist at all, they belong in spirit to the past'.[65] Dicey has lacked for readers who can penetrate the period veneer of passages like this to see the importance of what he says, and, in particular, that, '[f]or all its conservatism, much of Dicey's constitutional writing *also* reflects a salutary concern with the need to impose effective inhibitions on power and the defence of the citizen from power's all-inclusive claims'.[66] Though he celebrated classical liberal values with an enthusiasm which causes embarrassment to almost any legal academic who reads what now seem to be purple passages indeed, Dicey was not remotely foolish enough to end his life as a triumphalist liberal, and the preponderant tone of his work in the twentieth century (putting his entanglement with Home Rule aside) is a melancholic if not pessimistic

---

62 R Rawlings, 'Distinction and Diversity: Law and the LSE', in R Rawlings, ed, *Law, Society and Economy*, Oxford, Clarendon Press, 1997, 1, 7.

63 RA Cosgrove, *The Rule of Law: Albert Venn Dicey, Victorian Jurist*, London, Macmillan, 1980, 22.

64 G Orwell, 'Rudyard Kipling', in *All Propaganda is Lies, Complete Works*, vol 13, London, Secker and Warburg, 150, 151.

65 AV Dicey, *Lectures on the Relation Between Law and Public Opinion in England During the Nineteenth Century*, Indianapolis, Liberty Fund, 2008, 312-3.

66 D Sugarman, 'The Legal Boundaries of Liberty: Dicey, Liberalism and Legal Science' (1983) 46 *Modern Law Review* 102, 110.

recognition of an 'ominous' growth of 'collectivism'. It is remarkable that one of the most acute analysts of the shift in English political culture and government that has produced the maximalist[67] welfare state is preponderantly now thought in public law circles to have been something of a fool about just this.[68]

Jennings acutely observed that, from 'the Whig point of view', Dicey saw the constitution as 'an instrument for protecting the fundamental rights of the citizen, and not as an instrument for enabling the community to provide services for the benefit of its citizens,'[69] though, to complete one's understanding of Dicey's position, one should add that Dicey, for reasons he thought good, wanted to keep it the way he saw it. Dicey extolled sovereignty of Parliament and the nineteenth century law and institutions that embodied it; insisted that sovereignty of Parliament as a wonderfully valuable understanding and practice of government rested on the nineteenth century liberal political culture which it was uniquely fit to institutionalise; and foretold the consequences for the practice of government of the replacement of that political culture with a collectivist one, a process I have said that he believed was ominously gathering force towards the end of this life, the main constitutional sign of this being the initial development of an administrative law akin to *droit administratif*. So far as one can tell, Dicey did not even toward the end of his life, overall believe the game was up,[70] but he did believe things were 'vehemently' going in the wrong direction.[71] I am sufficiently misanthropic to be able to imagine him at this time, in his late seventies, saying to himself: go ahead continuing to do what I am counselling you not to do and see where you end up. And, in the welfare state in the maximalist form it has taken as we survey it 88 years after Dicey died, we have done it, and we have ended up somewhere like where he said we would.

Dicey's principal objections to collectivism were that it would promote extensive, ill-advised improving projects that are 'likely to cause huge loss, and it may be ruin, to England',[72] and will necessarily involve a 'marked

---

[67] I take the terminology from N Barry, *Welfare*, Milton Keynes, Open University, 1990, 105.

[68] WH Greenleaf, *A Much Governed Nation*, *The British Political Tradition*, vol 3, London, Methuen, 1987, ch 7. There are extremely valuable references to Dicey in *The British Political Tradition passim*.

[69] WI Jennings, 'In Praise of Dicey' (1935) 13 *Public Administration* 123, 132.

[70] Dicey above n 65, 387.

[71] *ibid*, 377.

[72] *ibid*, 397.

decline' in 'reverence for [the] rule of law.[73] These quotations are taken from the updating 'Introductions' he supplied in 1914 and 1915 to the last editions he saw in print of his two great works on the constitution. I want to quote at length one of these passages in the belief that it will not be familiar to all readers:

> [I]t is more than possible that English legislation may … combine disastrously the defects of socialism with the defects of democratic government. Any grand scheme of social reform, based on the real or supposed truths of socialism, ought to be carried out by slow and well-considered steps taken under the guidance of the best and the most impartial of experts. But the democratic idea that the people, or any large number of the people, ought to have whatever they desire simply because they desire it, and ought to have it quickly, is absolutely fatal to that slow and sure kind of progress which alone has the remotest chance of producing fundamental and beneficial social changes. Democratic legislation, on the other hand, ought to have the advantage of harmonising with, or at any rate not going much beyond, the public opinion of a given time. But this harmony between law and sentiment is easily contemned [*sic*] by socialists, who feel that they know better than do the electors of England what is really good for the English people. Hence it is all but certain that great changes planned by enthusiasts will, if they seem to be popular, be carried out with haste and without due consideration as to the choice of means proper to a given end, and, on the other hand, that on some occasions a party of self-called reformers will force on the electors changes which, whether good or bad, are opposed to the genuine convictions of the people.[74]

As we now live under a system of government which has authoritatively been described as having a 'chronic tendency to hyper-innovation' which has led to 'an age of fiasco',[75] who, other than a very staunch collectivist indeed, can now maintain that Dicey was entirely wrong about the changes to the constitution that makes possible these grand schemes? But, if one wished to describe the development of modern public law in a phrase, one would say it has been based on maintaining precisely this. As a matter of intellectual history, the twentieth century growth of collectivism in the advanced

73 AV Dicey, *An Introduction to the Study of the Law of the Constitution*, 8th edn, London, Macmillan, 1915, xxxviii.

74 Dicey above n 65, 397

75 M Moran, *The British Regulatory State*, Oxford, Oxford University Press, 2003, 171.

capitalist countries no doubt is based on the development of welfare economics, put into modern shape by AC Pigou in 1912,[76] which gave a fundamental theoretical justification to piecemeal but extensive state intervention by means of transfers backed by coercion. Such extensive intervention has required a public law which normalises coercion in the public interest. The process by which this has been brought about in respect of administrative law has been felicitously described by Harlow and Rawlings as giving the 'green light' to state action, as opposed to the 'red light' observed by Dicey,[77] and it has involved ridiculing Dicey and those broadly taking his position in the twentieth century, of whom Allen[78] and Hewart[79] have been the most common Aunt Sallies.[80]

Whilst a sense of proportion must be maintained about this, the green light has involved unacceptable arbitrariness underpinned by an even more unacceptable authoritarianism, to the point where the late Professor Griffith argued, to my mind convincingly, that what were called the liberal democracies can no longer be properly described as such at all.[81] It is to Taggart's great credit that he draws attention to an important aspect of this not typically noted in the leading works of the new constitutional and administrative law but revealed in detailed accounts of specific parts of the welfare system:[82] the 'Kafka-like'[83] aspect of normal life for many intended beneficiaries of the welfare state which undermines their conception of their own selves.[84]

---

[76] AC Pigou, *Wealth and Welfare*, London, Macmillan, 1912. In 1920, Pigou expanded this book in 1920 to produce what remains the foundational work of welfare economics: AC Pigou, *The Economics of Welfare*, 1952 reprint, New Brunswick, Transaction Books, 2002.

[77] C Harlow and R Rawlings, *Law and Administration*, 3rd edn, Cambridge, Cambridge University Press, 2009, ch 1.

[78] CK Allen, *Bureaucracy Triumphant*, Oxford, Oxford University Press, 1931.

[79] Lord Hewart of Bury, *The New Despotism*, London, Benn, 1929.

[80] M Taggart, 'From "Parliamentary Powers" to Privatisation: The Chequered History of Delegated Legislation in the Twentieth Century' (2005) 55 *University of Toronto Law Journal* 575. In this paper, Allen and particularly Hewart are contrasted, much to their disadvantage, with John Willis, whom Taggart greatly admired: M Taggart, 'Prolegomenon to an Intellectual History of Administrative Law in the Twentieth Century: The Case of John Willis and Canadian Administrative Law' (2005) 43 *Osgoode Hall Law Journal* 223.

[81] JAG Griffith, 'The Political Constitution' (1979) 42 *Modern Law Review* 4-5.

[82] Taggart, 'From "Parliamentary Powers"' above n 80, 612-3.

[83] Lord Plowden, 'Foreword', in J Simkins and V Tickner, *Whose Benefit?* London, Economist Intelligence Unit, 1978, 11.

[84] '[F]reedom in the management of a personal income' was one of the 'essential liberties' Beveridge sought to preserve in his conception of the welfare state: WH Beveridge, *Full Employment in a Free Society*, London, George Allen and Unwin, 1944, 21. For but the latest authoritative description of the consequences of the arbitrariness of welfare support which, concerned with myriad improving goals, pays little regard to this freedom see Economic Dependency Unit, *Dynamic Benefits*, Centre for Social Justice, London, 2009, pt

In my opinion, Dicey has been anathema to modern administrative lawyers because they have not placed the same value on liberty that he did. There is a good reason and a bad reason for this. The good reason is that modern public law works with a superior idea of freedom than did Dicey. Dicey's views belong to what TH Marshall called the 'civil' stage of the development of a full sense of citizenship, and the welfare state is our attempt to institutionalise the 'social' stage. One way of understanding the relationship between the stages which may be found in Marshall[85] is to say that social citizenship is needed to make formal civil (and 'political') rights, and therefore freedom, actual. I myself think it is a strong criticism of Dicey[86] to argue that his belief in the efficacy of the remedies of ordinary law turns on an equation of civil citizenship with actual citizenship which is wrong, leading him to think that tortuous liability for personal wrongdoing[87] could be 'the *primary* means of calling officials to account', which rightly has been called a 'deterrent theory of liability ... in which the deterrence is symbolic'.[88] The facile way he does this draws the plausibility it has from the, to contemporary eyes, incredible smallness of the size and scope of the government he had in mind, but, nevertheless, it is a rather puzzling attitude as, legal developments proper aside, his views must have been formed in a cultural atmosphere of which the Chancery of *Bleak House* and the Circumlocution Department of *Little Dorrit* were important constituents.[89]

1. On the admittedly bad, indeed in my opinion unacceptable, example of the social fund, written from as sympathetic a viewpoint as it is possible to take when one knows the facts, see T Buck and R Smith, eds, *Poor Relief or Poor Deal?* Aldershot, Ashage, 2003, pt 2. The law, if such it can be called, is updated in T Buck, *The Social Fund*, 3rd edn, London, Sweet and Maxwell, 2009.

85 eg TH Marshall, 'Citizenship and Social Class', in TH Marshall and T Bottomore, *Citizenship and Social Class*, London, Pluto, 1992, 1, 16: 'The right to education is a genuine social right of citizenship [a]nd there is no conflict with individual rights as interpreted in the age of individualism [f]or civil rights are designed for use by reasonable and intelligent persons, who have learned to read and write. Education is a necessary prerequisite of civil freedom'. For Dicey's view of state provision of education see Dicey above n 65, 195-8.

86 It is a criticism that can readily be restated and applied to modern administrative law: A Hutchinson, 'The Rise and Ruse of Administrative Law and Scholarship' (1985) 48 *Modern Law Review* 293.

87 C Harlow, *Compensation and Government Torts*, London, Sweet and Maxwell, 1982, 18.

88 C Harlow, *State Liability*, Oxford, Oxford University Press, 2004, 23-4. Professor Harlow has been anxious not to throw out the baby with the bathwater, and has sought to find a defensible role for tort in the control of government in the works just cited and elsewhere.

89 Dicey above n 65, 300 n 32 said that, in the Circumlocution Office, Dickens 'attacked the action of the State as compared with that of individuals'! This is one of the few actually outright silly things I have read in Dicey.

But, turning to the bad reason, and if the anachronism may be excused, Dicey had a clarity of view about what would be involved in the pursuit of actual citizenship which modern public law has quite wrongly failed to appreciate. In the last edition of de Smith on which Professor Street worked, the basic point that is urged against Dicey's insistence that the executive be 'governed by the same principles applied to ordinary citizens in private disputes' is that this 'is impossible':

> Once government vests wider discretionary powers in public authorities and creates special tribunals outside the ordinary court system there are no private law principles which can be applied when the powers or proceedings of an authority or tribunal are called into question. Like it or not, the common law courts were forced to develop a system of principles of administrative law.[90]

I submit this is a *petitito principii.* What Dicey urged is impossible only if we like the state we get with administrative law, but, of course, modern public law *does* '[l]ike it'. In the heroic mode which they adopt when they consider their actions, as it were, constitutionally, administrative lawyers see themselves as opposed to executive power, ensuring, as Lord Denning put it in 1949, that the 'welfare state' does not become a 'totalitarian state' by ensuring that 'the new powers of the executive' are '[p]roperly exercised'.[91] But the heroic mode involves a blindness about the workaday involvement of administrative lawyers in the extension of the new, arbitrary powers,[92] the proper control of which somehow seems never to be able adequately to be established, and so we are brought to where we are. The creation of modern administrative law has, as Professor Street tells us, been a process by which it has become 'an accepted phenomenon in normal times' that 'our activities are interfered with or controlled by government in the public interest', and if there has been a distinct lack of interest in principle about this until relatively recently, this has been because a 'yearning for certainty' based on the application of 'strict legal rules' has not been uppermost in the minds of 'administrators' who 'maintain that they cannot run the modern state like that' and want 'flexible' 'standards'.[93] This has yielded a law which 'has been

---

[90] SA de Smith, *Constitutional and Administrative Law*, 5th edn, Harmondsworth, Penguin, 1985, 534. Professor Brazier retained the passage in 8th edn, 1998, 504.

[91] Lord Denning, *Freedom Under the Law*, London, Stevens, 1949, 126.

[92] The spirit of this involvement is captured in WA Robson, *Justice and Administrative Law*, 3rd edn, London, Stevens, 1951. I cannot hope to improve on Professor Rawlings description of this work as 'the classic "greenlighter's" handbook': R Rawlings, 'Poetic Justice: The Case of the London Tube', in D Dyzenhaus *at al*, eds, *A Simple Common Lawyer*, Oxford, Hart, 2009, 223, 224 n 5.

[93] H Street, *Justice in the Welfare State*, London, Stevens, 1968, 69, 8-9.

pragmatic, empirical, even adventitious',[94] but this is acceptable because '[w]e look to the state to provide us with security and assistance in so many forms'.[95]

From Dicey's perspective, all this has the look of inevitability. Nevertheless, Dicey has been roundly criticised for just not seeing the issue, with his apparently acerbic conversational retort to a French legal academic that 'in England, we know nothing of administrative law, and wish to know nothing of it' doing signal service in exposing him to ridicule in way one feels was intended by WA Robson, a public lawyer of diametrically opposed inclination to Dicey, who brought it to wide attention.[96] But I think some feeling of guilt must motivate this criticism, which is not merely exaggerated but egregious. Putting Dicey's great contribution to the founding of comparative law in the UK in general, and in relationship to constitutional law in particular,[97] to one side, his views about various components of the *omnium gatherum* of what is now called administrative law were nuanced[98] in a way which will be found surprising by many of his critics, his approval in principle of 'executive legislation' on a French model being a marked case in point.[99] In relationship to the issues that specifically concern us here,[100] Dicey himself, despite what is often said,[101] was perfectly well aware that 'there had been built up since 1832 a whole scheme of administrative machinery',[102] in part because even 'sincere believers in *laissez faire* [had] found that for the attainment of their ends the improvement and the strengthening of governmental machinery was an absolute necessity',[103] and

94 de Smith above n 90, 5th edn, 545; 8th edn, 515.

95 Street above n 93, 1.

96 WA Robson, 'The Report of the Committee on Ministers' Powers' (1932) 3 *Political Quarterly* 346. For Robson's criticism of the attitude he thought this anecdote illustrated, see Robson, above n 92, 28, 423. Robson, it must be recalled, wanted a *droit administratif* in exactly the sense Dicey did not. The contemporary attention paid to this anecdote is no doubt due to its being found in the frontispiece of Harlow and Rawlings above n 77, xii.

97 AV Dicey, *An Introduction to the Study of the Law of the Constitution*, 10th edn, London, Macmillan, 1959, 205.

98 I do not mean only that they changed in the way to which attention was drawn by FH Lawson, 'Dicey Revisited', pt 2 (1959) 7 *Political Studies* 207. Wade's outstanding introduction to the 10th edn of *An Introduction to the Study of the Law of the Constitution*, *loc cit*, drew heavily on this paper, which he saw in proof.

99 *ibid*, 52.

100 Our focus is on the rule of law, but in relationship to sovereignty, how much criticism has rained down on Dicey in ignorance of his many statements to the effect that 'Parliamentary sovereignty… was a an instrument well adapted for the establishment of democratic despotism.' Dicey above n 65, 217.

101 Taggart notes the criticism of 'Dicey's periodisation' (159).

102 Dicey above n 65, 217 n 6.

103 *ibid*, 217.

in part because of the 'obviously and admittedly true' fact of the growth of collectivist government functions:

> During the last fifty years [prior to 1915], and notably since the beginning of the twentieth century, the nation as represented in Parliament has undertaken to perform a large number of duties with which before the Reform Act 1832 no English Government had any concern whatsoever.[104]

Dicey believed that it would be 'conceivable', up to a point, that 'in a country such as England, where the strict rule of law had been for generations accepted by the people, a great number of administrative questions might, in the nineteenth or even the twentieth century, have been wholly left for their determination to the law courts'.[105] This is to say, even a considerable growth of the state might be deplorable but tolerable. But this could be so only up to a point. Dicey not merely saw the 'distinct merits' of, in essence, efficiency to be gained by extending powers to the executive which were not subject to ordinary law,[106] but he believed it was *impossible* to extend the range of powers sought by collectivism without isolating their exercise from ordinary law, and thereby creating the arbitrary rule of administrative law in his pejorative sense. :

> when the state undertakes the management of business properly so-called, and business which hitherto has been carried on by each individual citizen simply with a view to his own interest, the Government … will be found to need that freedom of action necessarily possessed by every private person in the management of his own personal concerns.[107]

Such freedom of action, backed by the state's power of coercion, is bound to create arbitrary authoritarianism (as well as have good effects).

There is really nothing much that distinguishes Dicey's position from the position stated by the learned editors of de Smith in criticism of him, except the conclusion that is drawn. For Dicey insisted that, as a technical matter if it may be put this way, a growth of arbitrary power and a loss of liberty were inevitable costs of the improving policies of collectivism - this was one reason for his loathing of collectivism – but, unlike those editors, he was not prepared to meet these costs. It was in the twentieth century, in laws such as the National Insurance Act 1911[108] and *Local Government Board v Arlidge* of

[104] AV Dicey, 'The Development of Administrative Law in England' (1915) 31 *Law Quarterly Review* 148, 149.
[105] *ibid*, 149-50.
[106] Dicey above n 65, 371.
[107] Dicey above n 104, 150.
[108] Dicey above n 65, 367.

1915 as he interpreted them, that Dicey came to believe that there was being created 'in England a system bearing a marked resemblance to the administrative law of France'[109] which 'saps the foundation of that rule of law which has been for generations a leading feature of the English constitution'.[110] But, as I have said, he believed that the issue was undecided, and his last position seems to have been that *ultra vires*, impeachment and enforcement by the ordinary courts ('in some means or other' to be developed) of what 'the spirit of judicial fairness and equity [and] the rules of fair dealing' would require of a government department's conduct would perhaps suffice. So long as 'the ordinary law courts can deal with any actual and provable breach of the law committed by any servant of the Crown', this would still preserve 'that rule of law which is fatal to the existence of true *droit administratif*.'[111]

In setting himself against administrative law as law other than ordinary law, Dicey, then, sought to prevent the growth of collectivism in a precise way it is important to appreciate. He not only saw administrative law in the pejorative sense he gave it as a necessary consequence, but also, if I may put it this way, as a necessary condition of collectivism, and so, by working against the development of such administrative law, he believed he could work against the development of collectivism. Logically, he was right, but practically one might think this a rather forlorn effort, the stance of a constitutional law Canute against the tide of economic forces which, standing on our copies of *Das Kapital* volume one and *The Great Transformation*, we now can clearly see. But Dicey was well aware that it was a background collapse of faith in *laissez faire* that was driving matters,[112] and we have seen that he cannot be accused of excess of confidence in the success of his attempt to make the limited and in a sense tangential contribution a constitutional lawyer might hope to make. It seems to me the height of cheek to blame Dicey for prejudicing 'whole generations against administrative law in any form'[113] when, once his readers understand the 'sense' in which he meant administrative law, the 'paradox' of his denial of administrative law 'disappears'.[114] Robson's anecdote relates to a conversation which must have taken place in the earliest years of the twentieth century, and, at that time, Dicey could say that the English knew nothing of administrative law because, as he understood it, they didn't. If his

---

109 *ibid*, 371.

110 Dicey above n 104, 150.

111 *ibid*, 151-3.

112 Dicey above n 65, 363-4.

113 de Smith above n 90, 5th edn, 534; 8th edn, 515.

114 HVR Wade and CWF Forsyth, *Administrative Law*, 10th edn, Oxford, Oxford University Press, 2009, 20. Professor Forsyth puts the point as a criticism of Dicey.

tone was acerbic, this can be put down to his fear that in the near future they would.

In sum, Dicey could hardly have more strongly insisted that the government should be confined within the framework of the 'administrative law' he believed to be a very effective check on arbitrary power, the ordinary law of the nineteenth century constitution.[115] Those blaming Dicey for this have not clearly seen his meaning because, being on the whole happy enough with a growth of government functions in the public interest, they have been so preoccupied with this interest that they have almost sublimated the fact that departure from the ordinary law *does* involve the extension of arbitrary power. Their own thinking ultimately involves a denial of the Austinian analytical connection between law and coercion in the general climate of tergiversation about this established by Hart, for it would appear that the public interest acts as a sort of moral whitewash for arbitrary power.

Professor Loughlin adds to the stock of superior criticism of Dicey in his essay in Taggart's *Festschrift* when he acknowledges that 'Dicey may have been correct in his assumption that administrative law eroded the foundations of the post-1688 settlement'. But he goes on to say that this 'simply pushes back discussion to … more basic questions', the first of which is '[h]ow does a historic, evolutionary constitution acquire normative status? Can such immanent normativity retain its authority in the light of social, economic and cultural change'.[116] This may be a criticism of public law at some fundamental philosophical level, but how can it be a criticism of Dicey, who had no doubt about, and gave good reasons for, the normative status of the nineteenth century British constitution, and clear indications about what would be the result of collectivist social, economic and cultural change?

I do not doubt that Dicey was wrong about this in ways which undermine his view of the constitution. It is a rare fair criticism of Dicey from the

[115] I think some understanding of this lies behind Taggart's criticism of 'Dicey's persistent denial of any useful distinction between public and private law' (Taggart above n 61, 204), which represents one of the regrettable 'peculiarities of the English' (Taggart above n 59). But this is rather strangely put as Taggart generally denies this distinction himself, and I am not entirely sure what he means. If he means, as the fact that he makes this point in the course of a strong criticism of Harlow leads one to suspect, that he actually wants a really separate administrative law, then, for what it is worth, I am at complete odds with him, for, like Harlow above n 88, 22, I believe that Dicey's principle of equality within unitary government is overwhelmingly attractive. I do not, however, think he really means this.

[116] M Loughlin, 'Why the History of English Administrative Law is Not Written', in Dyzenhaus *et al*, eds above 92, 151, 175.

perspective of modern administrative law, which Loughlin forcefully restated in the paper I have just mentioned, that he (Dicey) seriously underestimated the role of 'administrative law', of a type of which he could not have approved, in the nineteenth century constitution he celebrated. We have seen that Dicey was not ignorant of the growth of administrative law involving a great expansion of state functions. 'Nor', he observed, 'is the importance of this extension of the activity of the State lessened by the consideration that its powers are in many cases exercised by local bodies, such, for example, as County Councils',[117] because '[i]t should never be forgotten that powers given to local authorities are, no less than powers possessed by the central government, in reality powers exercised by the state'.[118] This growth was part of a process I have said that Dicey found deplorable but was ultimately prepared to tolerate because it did not involve the creation of an explicit *droit administratif*.[119] It seems that Dicey was so preoccupied with this mark of the erosion of the rule of law that he did not place sufficient weight on the way that the growth, and, more important, centralisation[120] of local functions meant that, even in its absence, those functions could not plausibly be said to be under the control of the ordinary courts. As even now the great works of administrative law wisely follow de Smith's counsel and do not attempt to 'achieve a full mastery of the subject' because this 'requires an encyclopaedic range of knowledge which is hardly worth acquiring',[121] one has to be careful about what exactly one thinks it reasonable to ask Dicey to say about the range of local authority functions in the first modern attempt to describe the detailed law of the British constitution before one can pronounce oneself dissatisfied with what he did. Nevertheless, Dicey's views on local authority functions do seem to underestimate the significance of what was seen as an 'organised oligarchism'[122] by contemporaries writing from Dicey's perspective.

---

117 Dicey above n 97, 389. See also Dicey above n 65, 197-8, 201-4, 206-11.

118 *ibid*, 206 n 65.

119 Dicey above n 97, 389.

120 I use this term because it was the term in contemporaneous use (it was the subject of one of John Austin's few works in addition to his lectures), but a modern must take care to see the differences between what the term connotes now, when we have a very powerful central state and an emaciated local tradition, and what it connoted then, when the opposite obtained: RM Gutchen, 'Local Improvements and Centralisation in Nineteenth Century England' (1961) 4 *Historical Journal* 85, 86.

121 de Smith above n 90, 545.

122 J Toulmin Smith, *The Metropolis and Its Municipal Administration*, London, T Saunders, 1852, 25. Loughlin above n 116, 174 n 91 draws attention to other works of this important defender of traditional forms of responsibility and accountability in 'local government' against centralisation. On Toulmin Smith see WH Greenleaf, 'Toulmin Smith and the British Political Tradition' (1975) 53 *Public Administration* 25.

Far more telling against Dicey, in my opinion, is his failure to take account of what he surely should consistently have criticised as the arbitrariness inherent in the prerogative powers, for, as Harlow and Rawlings justly put it, '[t]he state does not need to possess special powers "in its own name" if those powers are held by government ministers acting in the name of the Crown'.[123] One might go so far as to say that modern administrative law has been an attempt to fill this 'gaping hole'[124] in Dicey's constitutional architecture, but even if this is so, the way it has been done paradoxically has enormously expanded 'the capacity for executive action to regulate the economy free from effective Parliamentary control',[125] and, the point I am arguing, Dicey should play in an important role in our attempt to remedy this.

It is, of course, only by public lawyers that these matters are principally discussed through reflection on Dicey. By far the most generally influential warning that the growth of collectivism will be harmful is that of the neo-liberal movement in economics and politics, and its principal expression ('[t]he classic *cri de coeur* Taggart has it (163 n 114)) remains Hayek's 1944 *The Road to Serfdom*. This is a book avowedly in the Diceyan tradition, bringing Dicey's lamentation of the decline of the English liberal tradition into the era of the established welfare state.[126] Just like Dicey's great books, *The Road to Serfdom* has, of course, been immensely successful in one sense, but a complete failure in another, for the growth of collectivism which it was intended to counter proceeded apace, and, writing of *The Road to Serfdom* in 1946, Orwell told us why this would be so in the peculiarly direct way so characteristic of him:

> Hayek's able defence of capitalism ... is wasted labour, since hardly anyone wishes for the return of old-style capitalism. Faced with a choice between serfdom and economic insecurity

[123] Harlow and Rawlings above n 77, 9. The nature of Dicey's theoretical mistake is set out in well known works by Sir William Wade and Professor Harris to which they refer *ibid*, n 31. An understanding of this mistake in the context of a theoretical tradition of analysis of 'the state in the common law tradition' is begun in J Allison, 'Theoretical and Institutional Underpinnings of a Separate Administrative Law', in Taggart, ed above n 28, 71, 74-9.

[124] Harlow and Rawlings above n 77, 9.

[125] P Craig, 'Preorgative, Precedent and Power', in C Forsyth and I Hare, eds, *The Golden Metwand and the Crooked Cord*, Oxford, Clarendon Press, 1998, 65, 89. Hewart, of course, saw this in a way, and hence the title of his book.

[126] FA Hayek, *The Road to Serfdom*, *Collected Works* vol 2, Chicago, University of Chicago Press, 2007, 194.

> the masses everywhere would probably choose outright serfdom, at least if it were called by some other name.[127]

As it happens, Orwell's own depiction of the consequences of choosing serfdom in *1984* is, in my opinion, undermined by a failure sufficiently to link serfdom to the affluence serfdom bought,[128] which leads to a sort of excess of tyranny, more appropriate to the totalitarian countries, in Orwell's account of Winston Smith's subjugation. Nevertheless, I do not know of any other advocate of the welfare state who has put the trade-off between welfare and liberty in quite this clear a way, which rather illustrates his 'power of facing unpleasant facts'.[129] Richard Crossman's outstandingly brave but utterly unfailing 1956 attempt to persuade socialists to take Hewart seriously,[130] commendably cited by Harlow and Rawlings,[131] is the closest statement by a figure of real influence of which I am aware.[132] Socialists could say that the advantages of social citizenship are so great that we should pay the cost of the growth of arbitrary power to obtain them, and perhaps putting it this clear way might have helped in achieving the necessary balance between affluence and serfdom.[133] But we should not be surprised if frankness over this was rare and that there normally was equivocation over the necessary cost. This has been expressed in what Hegel surely would have called the 'monotonous formalism' of the interminable number of attempts by Labour Party theorists and theorists *manqué* to strike

---

127 G Orwell, 'The Intellectual Revolt', in *Smothered Under Journalism, Complete Works* vol 18, rev edn, London, Secker and Warburg, 2001, 56, 59.

128 This is rather better done in the concentration on serfdom of the privileged elite in *Brave New World*, but Orwell was generally critical of what he saw as the 'hedonistic principle' in left-wing thought: G Orwell, 'Review of [*inter alia*] *Brave New World*', in *A Patriot After All, Complete Works*, vol 12, London, Secker and Warburg, 2001, 210, 211.

129 G Orwell, 'Why I Write', in *Smothered Under Journalism* above n 127, 316.

130 RHS Crossman, *Socialism and the New Despotism*, Fabian Tract 298, 1956. Hewart is not himself even mentioned in this Tract.

131 Harlow and Rawlings above n 77, 45-6.

132 Drawing on 1980 *dicta* of Lord Hailsham which he valuably brought to wider attention, Lord Cooke has given a contemporary statement: 'The [administrative law] jurisdiction is inherently discretionary. This is not always convenient for either practitioners or academics, but it is the simple truth': Lord Cooke of Thorndon, 'The Discretionary Heart of Administrative Law', in Forsyth and Hare, eds above n 125, 203, 220. But I for one cannot place any real weight on this. However it may have been for others, I doubt that Lord Cooke, in his confidence in his ability to identify the public interest, ever found this truth particularly inconvenient.

133 As Hewart above n 79, 152-3 argued, in my opinion compellingly.

a middle ground,[134] with 'middle' doing miraculous work, which reached their nadir in Mr Blair's[135] and Lord Giddens' 'third way'.[136]

One ground on which this equivocation could be based is of great importance to us. In his 1945 response to *The Road to Serfdom*, EFM Durbin, one of the most distinguished and influential economists of the nascent welfare state, rather disparaged Hayek for insufficiently appreciating the strength of the British tradition of liberty, which meant that:

> in this country we have no need to fear the development of a centralised administration. We have a long tradition of increasing democracy combined with the growing activity of the State ... it would be a thousand pities if [Hayek's argument] should lead any of us to doubt our power to combine freedom with [social] security and science with flexibility in the conduct of our economic affairs. If we have "economic planning" it will ... fulfil the wishes of our people. It will be the servant of our freedom and will bring another part of our common life within the control of our social wisdom.[137]

Now, this is a rather ill-directed charge to level at Hayek, whose entire political thought was, as I have said, an attempt to restate nineteenth century liberalism for the twentieth century, and whose fundamental lament in *The Road to Serfdom* was that the British were no longer being true to their strengths. But, even if we allow that Durbin's confidence had some purchase at the time it was made, at the time of the creation of Beveridge's welfare state, what Durbin was wrong and Hayek right about is that the strengths of the British political tradition on which Durbin relies are strengths which collectivism inevitably works against. Though I will not argue it here, leaving the reader to take it for what it is worth, it is my view that the experience of the maximalist welfare state has shown that positive and negative liberty, civil and social rights, and freedom and social justice are, choosing my word carefully, inimical, and this places a persistent tension at the heart of the

134 P Diamond, ed, *New Labour's Old Roots*, Exeter, Imprint Academic, 2004.

135 P Mandelson and R Liddle, *The Blair Revolution*, London, Faber, 1996 and P Mandelson, *The Blair Revolution Revisited*, London, Politico's, 2002. For administrative law, the formal middle ground is captured in the title of Hancher and Reute's review of Harlow and Rawlings: L Hancher and M Reute, 'Forever Amber' (1985) 48 *Modern Law Review* 243.

136 T Giddens, *The Third Way*, Cambridge, Polity Press, 1998.

137 EFM Durbin, 'Professor Hayek on Economic Planning', in, *Problems of Economic Planning*, London, Routledge and Kegan Paul, 1949, 91, 106.

institutions of the welfare state and our thinking about them, including administrative law and our thinking about it.[138]

This tension has been relieved in the case of administrative law because, until recently, the sacrifice of legality for effectiveness has not been sufficiently regretted during a period in which, as the student of regulatory theory has so far seen perhaps more clearly than the public lawyer,[139] the advance of the public interest by means of soft law 'draws gasps of admiration for the efficiency of what is in effect lawlessness'.[140] To the extent this is so, Durbin could not consistently say that the British political tradition will protect one and then go on to undermine that tradition, or, at least, it has turned out that he would not have been able to do so over the middle and long terms. It is as if Durbin were sawing away the branch on which he sat, whilst not realising he had a saw in his hand. The link that Hayek stressed between executive contempt for the rule of law and irrationality in policy formulation has been graphically illustrated by the normalisation of government failure in the hyper-innovative state. But, although developed by Hayek and others in economic and philosophical ways which are of a sophistication which rather starkly contrasts with the period artlessness of Dicey's views on *laissez faire*, the fundamental issues are stated by Dicey.

The constitutional significance of abuse of rights

In a sense, the mischief at which Simpson's lecture and Taggart's book are directed may not be a great one for it must be questioned whether the mischief which a private law doctrine of abuse of rights is to remedy exists at all.[141] Taggart tells us that *BvP* is 'seldom cited' (195), and, when he reviews the common law (chs 6-7), he draws on some fine scholarship to show that common law and equity are replete with conditions for the exercise of rights that amount to specific limits on abuse of rights or, to put it the other way around, amount to requirements of good faith. It seems strange but characteristic that Taggart spent a great deal of time adopting

138 T Poole, 'The Reformation of English Administrative Law' [2009] *Cambridge Law Journal* 142, 164-5.

139 R Creyke and J McMillan, 'Soft Law v Hard Law', in L Pearson *et al*, eds, *Administrative Law in a Changing State*, Oxford, Hart, 2008, 377.

140 P Goodrich, 'Law's Labour's Lost' (2009) 72 *Modern Law Review* 296, 310.

141 In 1940, Lawson described *BvP* as surrounded by contrary authority, in tort and elsewhere, and easily confined to 'its own little island of fact': Lawson, 'Notes' above n 14, 161. In 1951, he described *Allen v Flood* and *BvP* as 'exceptional': Lawson, *Rational Strength* above n 14, 117.

Haar and Fessler's use of certain private law good faith requirements to the regulation of public bodies[142] without asking how it was possible for the private law to do this for those bodies and not for itself. In the law of contract and tort with which I am familiar, there is, in my opinion, no such thing as the 'unlovely *Pickles* doctrine'.[143] In respect of the use of land, I myself believe that the law of nuisance, based as it is on a balancing of opposed legitimate interests, can readily do the work done by abuse of rights, indeed can hardly avoid doing so, although Taggart does not seem to think this (188-91) and Simpson certainly does not,[144] which is something that gives me great pause. There do, however, seem to be particular problems arising from the physical nature of underground water flows,[145] which I will ignore, though, in a most interesting fashion, they may make these flows of *water* refractory to regulation by a law of *land.*

For our purposes here, all this is by the by. Having noted in his essay on 'The Province of Administrative Law Determined?' that 'there are many doctrines in the common law (quite a few of which have an equitable origin) which place limits on private law's instinctive privileging of self-regarding behaviour', Taggart went on to say that 'legislative interventions are even more numerous and invasive'.[146] And surely the most important issue is that we must evaluate abuse of rights knowing that since, *BvP*, '[s]uccesive waves of regulatory legislation have left little room for [self-interested] behaviour' (193).

BvP really speaks not to direct reform of the law of abuse of rights but to an attitude to the relationship of citizen and state which informs our conception of the relationship of private and public law. In particular, one now has to ask whether it is now wise to seek further to add to the extensive powers of government under primary and secondary legislation by having a background sweeping up doctrine of abuse of rights. Recognition of the problems of doing so may be traced back at least to Blackstone,[147] but they were set out for moderns by FH Lawson in 1950:

---

[142] CM Haar and DW Fessler, *The Wrong Side of the Tracks*, New York, Simon and Schuster, 1986.

[143] Getzler above n 46, 316.

[144] Simpson above n 25; *VLIS*, 18-28 and Simpson above 26.

[145] The principal modern discussion of which is Getzler's volume in the Oxford Studies in Modern Legal History Series: Getzler above n 46, reviewed by Taggart in (2005) 25 *Legal Studies* 337. Getzler's account of the absolutist interpretation is standard: *loc cit*, 315-6.

[146] Taggart above n 28, 5.

[147] *Comm* I, 139: 'it would be dangerous to allow any private man, or even any public tribunal, to be the judge of the common good, and to decide whether it be expedient or no'; quoted in *VLIS*, 7.

> it is clear that as soon as the theory of abuse of rights passes the stage where subjective malice is the sole test, it is really a socialist doctrine. It implies that a man's right is no longer, as it were, a sphere within which he is sovereign, over which he may dispose according to his own view of his interests and his ideas of right and wrong; it is to be subject to the control of society in the person of the judge, who exercises his a veto over his decisions in accordance with what he considers to be the purpose for which society has conferred the right.[148]

Taggart (158) cites this passage, and his scholarship allows him to identify another to similar effect but expressed in more florid language by HC Gutteridge,[149] Reader and then Professor of Comparative Law in the University of Cambridge between 1930-41, whom Bernard Rudden described as 'undoubtedly' 'the most influential academic comparatist' of the period between the wars.[150] Apart from some slighting language, Taggart engages with these passages only by making reference to a 'more balanced' treatment of social limits upon private rights in a 1934 commentary by VE Greaves, a Russian émigré lawyer, upon the Soviet Civil Code! One cannot doubt that this Code made the social ontology of private rights in land more clear than did the nineteenth century common law, but we should not allow ourselves to be made dizzy with the success of this argument against 'insular individualism'. For surely this clarity was bought at a cost, one insisted upon by Greaves.

Having noted that the frankly political dominance of the courts by the Soviet government 'deprives the administration of justice by the Soviet courts of the stability which is a typical attribute of justice in all non-communist countries', Greaves fatefully predicted that it was 'not impossible to surmise that the Soviet government will suddenly adopt a new social or economic policy materially differing from the present social-economic aims of the Soviets, and as a result, all rights lawfully acquired under the now existing policy may be left without protection, if their exercise should no

148 Lawson, *Negligence* above n 14, 18-9. This passage reworks views Lawson had advanced 10 years previously: Lawson, 'Notes' above n 14, 164.

149 HC Gutteridge, 'Abuse of Rights' (1933-5) 5 *Cambridge Law Journal* 22, 43-4. I myself find this an exemplary paper, one which sees the problems with *BvP* as known through the absolutist interpretation, and weighs up the pros and cons of reform carefully and with what seems to be useful comparative analysis, though I am in no position to maintain an opinion of the accuracy of that analysis.

150 Rudden above n 45, 85.

more correspond to the new social or economic purposes of the state'.[151] After the chaos of the initial attempted revolutionary restructuring of the Russian economy, the Bolsheviks were obliged to retreat to a period of substantial acceptance of capitalist economics under the 'New Economic Plan'. This period of relative quiet and success involved limited interference with the ownership of agricultural holdings. It is this period that Greaves reviewed in his paper. His predictions of the future were to be borne out by the forced collectivisation of agriculture, to which, of course, rights in land recognised only in so far as they served the public interest, were no obstacle at all. In the first sentence of the paragraph Taggart otherwise quotes, Lawson had referred to, precisely, the Soviet Code as 'probably' 'the most famous statement' of the principle of abuse of rights, which, Lawson had said in an earlier version of this discussion, 'has its natural affinities with public rather than private law'.[152]

I am not making the ridiculous and distasteful accusation that Taggart, or the strain of administrative law he represents, would endorse anything like collectivisation, but I am asking where the stopping point in the trumping of the individual interest by the public interest is? Just consider Simpson's attitude to the irritation of the boy scout. What sort of 'communitarian'[153] regulatory regime does Simpson have in mind that would actually ground realistic legal prevention of this bad behaviour?[154] Sadly, we have examples of the answer, and not merely in the fiction of Orwell. Taggart came to *BvP* with the intention of throwing it down and with it the distinction between the public and private law as he understood it, and though, to his credit, he did not carry this through, he does not supply this stopping point in a theoretically defensible manner. It is to this that I now turn.

The public interest and the feint of the state

Taggart's writings on public law, which can be traced back to a prize winning paper on administrative tribunal procedure published in 1981, are very markedly the product of their time because almost all of them are dominated by a concern to oppose the privatisation and marketisation of

[151] VE Greaves, 'The Social-Economic Purpose of Private Rights', pt 2 (1934-5) 12 *New York University Law Quarterly Review*, 441, 465-6.
[152] Lawson, 'Notes' above n 14, 164.
[153] Simpson above n 46, vii.
[154] I am trying to make a wider point than the narrower point that, however, is of the greatest importance, which is that it is inconceivable that such a doctrine will not interfere, in ways which we simply cannot see how to control, with legitimate economic competition.

much of the service provision which the maximalist welfare state had taken to itself. Perhaps the most striking instance of this is that, when called on to write a chapter on 'The Nature and Functions of the State' for a work of reference, he did not seek to provide the *Rechtstheorie* for want of which Dicey has been so often castigated, but a prolonged criticism of the new public management![155] This intensity of focus might be explained by the fact that the New Zealand experiment with 'Rogernomics' arguably was the most jarring, if this is a strong enough word, experience of new public management in the advanced capitalist countries, as Taggart's colleague in the Faculty of Law at Auckland, Professor Jane Kelsey, has made clear in an internationally influential body of work.[156] Concluding that the argument against the new public management had been in an important sense lost, Taggart argued for continued governance of privatised services, such as the water supply, by public law principles, and he was hardly alone in believing this made it urgent to attack the distinction between private and public law in the way we have seen in his essay on 'The Province of Administrative Law Determined?' His attack on *BvP* was given particular impetus by the way he thought it might well sanction the removal of the particular obligations of public law from privatised services: '[o]n the hoarding around the level playing field … one can imagine the great graffiti artist's deviant scrawl "*Pickles* Rules Okay"' (200).

In a paper on 'British Socialists and the British Constitution' which has greatly influenced my thinking on these matters, Anthony Wright has shown just how happy were the leading theorists in and around the Labour Party with the latitude the elective dictatorship allowed them to pursue the public interest as they defined it.[157] They 'had a crash constitutional education' in the 1980s as they witnessed 'Mrs Thatcher's march through the constitution'.[158] If one substitutes David Lange for Margaret Thatcher and Roger Douglas for, say, Keith Joseph, one can say that Taggart got his own constitutional education in this way, and his central concern has been to get lawyers, who '[a]s a group … were rather slow to appreciate the impact of these changes [and] the threat to their subject posed by "the contracting

155 M Taggart, 'The Nature and Functions of the State', in P Cane and M Tushnett, eds, *The Oxford Handbook of Legal Studies*, Oxford, Oxford University Press, 2003, 101.

156 Taggart cites J Kelsey, *The New Zealand Experiment: A World Model for Structural Adjustment?*, Auckland, Auckland University Press and Bridget Williams Books, 1995 in Taggart above n 61, 203 n 96.

157 For a most influential celebration of power the elective dictatorship gave to the pursuit of the socialist definition of the public interest not mentioned by Wright, see A Bevan, *In Place of Fear*, London, Heinemann, 1952, 100.

158 A Wright, 'British Socialists and the British Constitution' (1990) 43 *Parliamentary Affairs* 322, 337. 322.

state'",[159] to face up to that threat. This is so in a way which it is uncomfortable but essential to note.

Taggart's very strong criticism of the new public management of course implies that the old public management based on extensive direct provision was better, and, indeed, he very much believed this was so. I do not doubt he was right, but I must depart from the way he saw the issues. Having embarked on the reinvention of administrative law, Taggart has said disparaging things about *Wednesbury*,[160] *ultra vires*,[161] etc,[162] but, except in relationship to its becoming clear how little the old ways offered the left-wing administrative lawyer opposed to the new public management, these were persuasively measured criticisms which led to Taggart insisting on the need for a concept of judicial deference appropriate for the era of social rights[163] which appeals even to one like myself who sees this era as a bout of self-indulgence by those enamoured of the administrative law of human rights which will either create a lot of mischief or be seen to be a reinvention of the wheel. Taggart does not, in fact, seem much disturbed by what went on under the old public management. His reviews of the subject are basically paeans to the likes of Robson,[164] who, if he was subjected to the same standard of criticism as Dicey has been, would widely be called an *apparatchik*, and, in a paper in the *Festschrift* for Sir William Wade which I read with some amazement, Taggart reviews the UK and Commonwealth law of compulsory purchase prior to Thatcher and finds nothing much to complain about! We are told that the 'administrative law doctrine of *ultra vires* has been a potent weapon in ensuring private property is only taken for authorised public purposes',[165] and, in sum, that the 'leitmotifs in Sir William

159 Taggart above n 28, 2. The hortation was extended to the international level in M Taggart, 'The Tub of Public Law', in D Dyzenhaus, ed, *The Unity of Public Law*, Oxford, Hart, 2004, 455, 479.

160 M Taggart, 'Reinventing Administrative Law', in N Bamforth and P Leyland, eds, *Public Law in a Multi-layered Constitution*, Oxford, Hart, 2003, 311 and M Taggart, '*Associated Provincial Picture Houses Ltd v Wednesbury Corporation*' (1948)', in P Cane and J Conaghan, eds, *The New Oxford Companion to Law*, Oxford, Oxford University Press, 2008, 55.

161 M Taggart, '*Ultra Vires* as Distraction', in C Forsyth, ed, *Judicial Review and the Constitution*, Oxford, Hart, 2000, 427.

162 M Taggart, 'Rival Theories of Invalidity in Administrative Law', in M Taggart, ed, *Judicial Review of Administrative Action in the 1980s: Problems and Prospects*, Auckland, Oxford University Press, 1986, 70.

163 M Taggart, 'Proportionality, Deference, Wednesdbury' [2008] *New Zealand Law Review* 423.

164 Taggart, 'From "Parliamentary Powers"' above n 80.

165 M Taggart, 'Expropriation, Public Purpose and the Constitution', in Forsyth and Hare, eds above n 125, 91, 105.

Wade's work – resisting arbitrariness and preserving individual liberty – can be seen at play in this area'.[166]

There is a passage in Wade's *Administrative Law* which Taggart quotes repeatedly throughout his work, including in *PPARVE* (199-200), which is too long and too familiar to quote here in full but which has *BvP* in mind when it contrasts the 'unfettered discretion' of the private actor with the restraints on a public authority, to which 'unfettered discretion is inappropriate' because such an authority 'possesses powers solely in order that it may use them for the public good'.[167] Taggart finds this so congenial a passage because he has a naïve belief in the self-certifying worth of things done, not in the pursuit of self-interest, but in the public interest. This reaches a point which brought a wry smile to my face at least in Taggart's well known 'list of public law values' which 'includes openness, fairness, participation, impartiality, accountability, honesty and rationality'.[168] His omission of the core value of administrative law – the extension of government power without too punctilious a regard for any or all of the preceding values when they are believed to hamper pursuit of the public interest – is unaccountable unless one sees just how great was his belief in that interest. His entire work is motivated by the belief that 'more is expected of the state' than of private action, but, whilst one hopes that this is so, Taggart does not seem to be aware that, though the criticism of government failure does not fail to point out instances of want of virtue on the part of those holding power,[169] the fundamental criticism is of virtue itself, for that an effort to act in the public interest is made with virtuous intent is a necessary but not remotely a sufficient condition of success in doing so. When Hegel told us that, with Robespierre, virtue was a serious matter, he (Hegel) was not pointing to a viable form of politics.

In his work on expropriation, Taggart is happy if the working of administrative law has ensured that taking took place only when it was in 'the public interest', as if this was the end, rather than the start, of the problems. I believe *BvP* is an illustration of these problems. Nevertheless, in the 'Epilogue' to *PPARVE*, Taggart suggests that the Appeal Courts in *BvP*, perhaps influenced by a notion of 'the equality of state and citizen … so admired by AV Dicey (97), were wrong to construe s 49 *contra preferentum* against the Corporation, because the Corporation was not the Company:

---

166 *ibid*, 112. See also Taggart above n 159, 468.

167 Wade and Forsyth above n 114, 296-7.

168 Taggart above n 28, 3.

169 He minimises incidences of these episodes in a striking passage in *PPARVE* (200), which contains an even more striking reference to a tort as an adequate remedy for them.

> The fact that the original adventurers (who had established the [C]ompany for personal gain) had sold out to the local municipality, which was a creature of statute and guardian of the welfare of its inhabitants, was not treated as relevant … Any public interest in the continued supply of water to Bradford was trumped by Pickles' absolute property right (198).

That Taggart can maintain this after what he has shown of the conduct of the Corporation of Bradford is worthy of discussion only because his influential views are what Louis Althusser would have called 'symptomatic' of a most important attitude towards the public interest which I hope to criticise here, in essence, a bias towards believing that 'public' equals 'good'. The problems of virtuous action backed by coercive powers, identified by Dicey, are that it may lead to a vanguard, authoritarian lack of respect for the opposed views of others in the belief that this disregard is in their (via the collectivity's) interest, and that, in this disregard, avoidable policy mistakes can and will be made. The twentieth century has far, far worse cases of this than the growth of the arbitrary and foolish exercise of executive power in the welfare state made possible by administrative law, but the maximalist welfare state is a case of it.

And, entirely contrary to Taggart's view, this has got worse over the last thirty years. Taggart's concern to somehow preserve governance in the public interest over privatised or marketised provision can now be seen to misunderstand what the new public management has actually meant. In my opinion, the undoubtedly extensive reengineering of the technique of public management never called into question the role of the national state, and the development of quasi-markets as a response to the initially successful neo-liberal critique of government failure has meant that the national state has not 'contracted',[170] been 'hollowed out',[171] 'retreated',[172] or 'shrunk'[173] since the 1970s, much less come to an 'end'.[174] After a period of initial retrenchment, the share of gdp under state management in the advanced capitalist countries had actually increased (prior to the immense deficits

[170] I Harden, *The Contracting State* (Buckingham: Open University Press, 1992).

[171] R Rhodes, 'The Hollowing Out of the State: The Changing Nature of Public Service in Britain' (1994) 65 *Political Quarterly* 138.

[172] S Strange, *The Retreat of the State* (Cambridge: Cambridge University Press, 1996).

[173] HB Feingenbaum *et al*, *Shrinking the State* (Cambridge: Cambridge University Press, 1999).

[174] K Ohmae, *The End of the Nation State* (New York: Free Press, 1995). The corollary point that the common understanding of globalisation is mistaken is made in L Weiss, *The Myth of the Powerless State* (New York: Cornell University Press, 1999) and PQ Hirst *et al*, *Globalisation in Question*, 3rd edn (Cambridge: Polity Press, 2009).

incurred in response to the credit crunch),[175] but much of that management is now of a quasi-market form, the change of technique having proven to be a most effective way of (to adapt a felicitous phrase) 'bringing the state back in'.[176] The state has, very successfully, not retreated in the face of the neo-liberal critique, but feinted away from it, and resumed growth. I have argued this point in terms of regulatory theory elsewhere,[177] and I am happy to abandon the argument I had drafted in terms of administrative law for this paper because in an, in my opinion, pathbreaking essay in Taggart's *Festschrift* that must provoke a fundamental shift in administrative law theory, Professor Harlow has shown 'that colonisation of the private by the public is the true characteristic of contemporary government and that the state, far from ceding power to the public sector, was everywhere active behind the scenes'.[178]

I will give only one brief illustration here. Rawlings has recently examined the attempt to introduce a partial but very substantial privatised element into the running of the London Underground. He rightly describes this, 'the UK's flagship scheme' of public/private partnership, as a 'spectacular failure' and hopes that 'lessons are learned about the functional limitations of contractual ordering and the importance of vindicating public law values like transparency and accountability'.[179] But, of course, the 'contractual' verdict on running the Tube in its modern form is that one shouldn't do it. What is meant by saying the Tube is an instance of the public good variant of market failure is that the market would not do it, and this is why the Tube since 1933 has effectively been a public concern. And when the pressures on the public running of the Tube, manifested in familiar deferred 'long-term maintenance and renewal' and 'worst-case instances of conventional procurement'[180] that left the late twentieth century Tube with the 'ageing (commonly Victorian) infrastructure',[181] the deficiencies of which were brought to general attention by the Kings Cross fire, there seemed to be no way of getting the requisite finance together for an adequate response on the basis of continuing to run the Tube as a purely public concern, the

175 FG Castles, 'Testing the Retrenchment Hypothesis: An Aggregate Overview', in FG Castles, ed, *The Disappearing State* (Cheltenham: Edward Elgar, 2007) ch 2.

176 PB Evans *et al*, eds, *Bringing the State Back In*, Cambridge, Cambridge University Press, 1985. The summary of what has happened in S Vogel, *Freer Markets, More Rules* (Ithaca: Cornell University Press, 1996) 269 is exemplary.

177 D Campbell, 'Relational Contract and the Nature of Private Ordering: A Comment on Vincent-Jones' (2007) 14 *Indiana Journal of Global Legal Issues* 279.

178 C Harlow, 'The "Hidden Paw" of the State and the Publicisation of Private Law', in Dyzenhaus *et al*, eds above n 92, 75, 77-8.

179 Rawlings above n 92, 246.

180 *ibid*, 233.

181 *ibid*, 225.

public/private partnership was devised. It just is not accurate to regard this as a private matter. The entire thing was driven by a public authority in defiance of the market verdict on the Tube, with a non-market outcome sought and the conduct of the project stipulated in detail by that authority. It is, in my opinion, the principal shortcoming of regulatory theory, and of both the new public management and its public interest critics, including those in administrative law, that it just is not understood that that one cannot create a 'market' to realise a social goal postulated by the state, for the essence of a market is that it produces order in the absence of such a goal, and the imposition of such a goal destroys the market.[182]

What annoys Rawlings is that a new form of management was adopted despite it being able to be predicted that it would be worse than the old, but that this form departed from what the market would have done and what would have been done on old public administration principles and practices does not stop this being a new form of *public* management. Financial sense, accountability, etc are casualties in this episode, but they were casualties of the public sector trying to expand its activities, not merely beyond the limits of the market but beyond its own previous limits, and I am at a loss to understand how administrative lawyers, and their fellows in the other theoretical enterprises of the maximalist welfare state, fail to see this. Administrative law has been[183] based on breaking down the Diceyan limits to executive power. In the new public management, it has perceived its own self as a limit, and has pretty successfully broke itself down. That this is regarded as a criticism of the private sphere just shows the extent of the theoretical problem that has beset regulatory theory in general and administrative law in particular, which, if the unfairness to certain distinguished, honourable contributors who are exceptions be allowed, has typically failed to look its essential role in the great extension of arbitrary power in the face.

---

[182] D Campbell, 'The Hybrid Contract and the Merging of the Public and Private Law of the Allocation of Economic Goods', in D Campbell and ND Lewis, eds, *Promoting Participation*, London, Cavendish, 1999, 45. Reasons of space preclude me from applying the argument of this paper to Dicey's conception of the division between private and public, of the nineteenth century collapse of which under Mill's influence he gave an acute analysis summarised in Dicey above n 65, 378.

[183] I have tried to avoid direct citation of what I regard as very poor criticisms of Dicey, but I am impelled to mention Lord Sedley's recent throwaway reference to Dicey's 'xenophobic and counterfactual insistence that Britain, unlike France, had no body of administrative law': S Sedley, 'On the Move' (8 October 2009) 31(19) *London Review of Books* 3-5. It is not that Lord Sedley is no better than others in coming to terms with Robson's story, it is that he calls one of Britain's greatest comparative lawyers a xenophobe when writing for a readership almost all of whom will not be able to know any different.

Conclusion: Socialism, citizenship and the crisis of the welfare state

I believe Taggart started on his researches into *BvP* with the intention of showing it was wrong, for he came to the case wishing to further tip the balance for the claimed public interest against the private interest. In the course of his researches, he began to see that this was unwise, and, whilst he never sorted out his thoughts on this, leaving his book something of a tangle at the end, and not developing the reform of *BvP* in his subsequent public law works, he rightly and commendably all but abandoned his initial intention. He concentrated instead on the nature and scope of administrative law, which was, as it were, to look at things from the opposite direction, which was more congenial to him. But his lack of enthusiasm for actual reform of the law of abuse of rights after writing his book was not really carried through to his theoretical position on the clash of values involved in the distinction between public and private law, for the appeal of a doctrine of abuse of rights in the abstract at least never waned for one who retained his naïve belief in the public interest.

As it has been developed in its maximalist form, the welfare state has not known, continues not to know, and cannot know, any principled bounds. When Dicey wrote the first edition of *An Introduction to the Study of the Law of the Constitution*, the state consumed 9% of gdp. When Pigou wrote the first edition of *The Economics of Welfare* it consumed 13%. When Marshall wrote *Citizenship and Social Class* it consumed 32%. Prior to the response to the credit crunch, it consumed almost 50%. That response will take it well in excess of 50%. This has to stop, but one cannot see how as the welfare state has failed to confine itself to the minimalist provision of welfare floors and is beset by a maximalist clamour for the satisfaction of social rights which knows no theoretical limit. The results of this have been pretty much as Beveridge said they would be: 'to give by compulsory insurance more than is needed for subsistence is an unnecessary interference with individual responsibilities. More can be given only by taking more in contributions or taxation. That means departing from a principle of a national minimum, above which citizens shall spend their money freely, and adopting instead the principle of regulating the lives of individuals by law'.[184] All one would add is that Beveridge did not make explicit here what he certainly knew,[185]

184 *Social Insurance and Allied Services*, Cmd 6404, 1942, para 294.
185 WH Beveridge, *Why I am a Liberal*, London, Herbert Jenkins, 1945.

that the law which would develop would principally be the administrative law of the maximalist welfare state.

Now, Beveridge's welfare state has been in one crisis or another for longer than I have been alive – Marshall gave 1952 as the date of its first.[186] But, recognising the possibility of crying wolf, I do still wish to state that, if they wish the welfare state to survive, its citizens must now appreciate that social citizenship has costs as well as benefits, and is a matter of duties, especially the duty of restraint, as well as of rights. In particular, they must reassert the primacy of the private in the allocation of economic goods. Whilst, even before the current acute worsening of the situation, the fundamental problem is the fiscal burden of a system that knows no limit, another grave problem is a loss of liberty. This is inevitable because the welfare state rests on coercion, and, whilst it would be wholly wrong to say that the coercion has not been subject to control, it is essential that those on the left now develop a principled opposition to 'the growth of a powerful and uncontrolled surveillance state'[187] which they have played the main part in fostering.

I am aware that I have allowed a personal note to intrude upon this paper in a way not normally thought proper in academic writing. I must beg the reader's further indulgence because I am afraid I am now going to conclude by deepening this personal note. I write as a socialist whose views are a, I hope not unmediated but certainly clear enough, reflection of his having been born in 1958 into a working class, mining community in the North East of England. My family, most of the friends of my childhood and adolescence, and myself have been greatly enriched by the welfare state. A necessary condition of my now being an academic writing this paper was my being provided with a very heavily subsidised grammar school, undergraduate and postgraduate education by the welfare state. I write this paper because I wish to defend the welfare state. But the way now to defend it is to shrink it. We will not do this whilst we maintain the approvingly naïve attitude towards yet further, indeed unlimited, extension of the state which would be embodied in the adoption of a doctrine of abuse of rights. Lawson was right to criticise this attitude as socialist when socialism was identified with statism. Socialism now requires the revival of a Diceyan recognition of the cost to liberty of collectivism which will allow us to look the problem of virtuous authoritarianism and government failure in the face and shrink the state in response to it. But I find this congenial as, in my opinion, the only possible justification for socialism has ever been that it is necessary, as

[186] TH Marshall, *Social Policy*, 1st edn, London, Heinemann, 1952, 92.
[187] Harlow above n 178, 79.

Orwell said in 1940, to 'preserve and even enlarge the atmosphere of liberalism'.[188]

188 G Orwell, 'Inside the Whale', in *A Patriot After All* above n 128, 86, 110. It is an issue whether, even at this early time, Orwell had already rather given up on this under the influence of a belief in a coming general totalitarianism.

CONFLICT IN CANENGUS: THE BATTLE OF CONSEQUENTIALISM AND DEONOTOLOGY

Man Chun Siu*

1 INTRODUCTION

This essay makes extensive use of a work of political philosophy that appears in the bibliography that draws 'The Canengusian Connection: the Kaleidoscope of Tort Theory' to a close. [1] In his *A Theory of Justice*, John Rawls advances an array of arguments for justice as fairness that prompt us to think hard about impartiality and the difficulties people have in acting as this ideal demands.[2] Moreover, he presents his readers with arguments that will, he believes, assist them in their efforts to fashion institutions that are socially just. However, he recognises that it is part of human nature that individuals are selfish rather than altruistic. This means that they are ready to sacrifice other people's welfare rather than their own. This leads to his construction of a device called the 'veil of ignorance' to secure an impartial perspective. He argues that, when people adopt this perspective, they can identify principles of justice that satisfy the demands of impartiality.

This essay explores the possibility of using Rawls's 'veil of ignorance' to assess three of the judgments in Hutchinson and Morgan's essay, namely, the judgments of Mill, Wright and Prudential JJ.[3] Among other things, their respective views on the law of negligence provide an example of the disorderly discourse that is a prominent feature of common law culture.[4] But out of this disorder, we may be able to find clues as to how we might do justice as fairness. Whilst Mill and Wright JJ give expression to moral philosophies that stand at the extreme ends of a deontological-consequentialist spectrum, Prudential J's advocacy of a no-fault compensation scheme exhibits assumptions associated with a mixed

* Newcastle Law School graduate 2010.

I owe particular thanks to Richard Mullender from whose clear-minded criticisms of earlier drafts I have learned much. I am also grateful to David Campbell, Emilia Mickiewicz, Patrick O'Callaghan, Ole Pedersen, Aron Ping D'Souza, and Ashley Wilton for their comments on earlier drafts of this essay.

[1] A.C. Hutchinson and D. Morgan, 'The Canengusian Connection: the Kaleidoscope of Tort Theory' (1984) 22 *Osgoode Hall Law Journal* 69, 111-113.

[2] J. Rawls, *A Theory of Justice* (Oxford: Oxford University Press, 1971).

[3] A.C. Hutchinson and D. Morgan, n 1, above, 76-86 (Mill J), 87-94 (Wright J), and 94-104 (Prudential J).

[4] G. Keating, 'A Social Contract Conception of the Tort Law of Accidents' in G. Postema, ed, *Philosophy and the Law of Tort* (New York: Cambridge University Press, 2001), ch.2

conception of accident compensation law. Moreover, Prudential J's position deals (as we will see) with a weakness in Hutchinson and Morgan's essay. For they fail to indicate which of the views in 'The Canengusian Connection' works best. But before explaining how we can use Rawls to address this deficiency, we must look at his account of the veil of ignorance.

2 The Original Position and the Veil of Ignorance

Rawls imagines 'a purely hypothetical situation' which he calls 'the original position'.[5] This is a situation in which 'no one knows his place in society, his class position or social status'.[6] Thus those in the situation described by Rawls find themselves behind a 'veil of ignorance'.[7] Rawls introduces the veil of ignorance and the original position with the aim of identifying 'principles of justice'.[8] He regards them as necessary because he recognises that our views of justice are often distorted by the characteristics of human nature, such as selfishness, resentment, alienation and false consciousness.[9] Moreover, he recognises that biased laws and policies are generated as a result of, *inter alia*, selfishness.[10] This prompts him to regard impartiality as a necessary condition of a moral point of view.[11] With the aim of securing a condition of impartiality (or 'mutual disinterest'), he creates the hypothetical device of the veil of ignorance.[12] It is aimed at countering selfishness and, more importantly, securing an impartial, bias-free viewpoint.

Rawls is not merely concerned about individual bias and selfishness. He is also critical of utilitarianism (a form of consequentialism). For this body of thought tells us to organize society in ways that maximize aggregate utility or expected well-being (*i.e.*, the greatest good of greatest number). This inevitably sacrifices individual interests to the aggregate welfare of the whole community. Rawls's criticism of this weakness of utilitarianism is telling. He complains that it merely adopts for society as a whole 'the principle of choice for one man' - thus fusing many people into one.[13] It fails to 'take seriously the distinction between persons'.[14] As someone much influenced

---

[5] J. Rawls, n 2, above, 12.
[6] *Ibid.*
[7] *Ibid.*
[8] *Ibid.*
[9] J. Rawls, 'Justice as Fairness', *Journal of Philosophy (*1958) Vol. LXVII, 163-4
[10] J. Rawls, n.2, above, 24.
[11] For a helpful account of 'impartiality' in adjudication, see W. Lucy, 'The Possibility of Impartiality' (2005) Vol. 25, Issue 1 *Oxford Journal of Legal Studies* 3.
[12] J. Rawls, n 2, above, 17-22 and 189 (on 'mutual disinterest').
[13] *Ibid*, 24 and 27.
[14] *Ibid*, 27.

by the moral philosophy of Immanuel Kant, this is something that Rawls is not prepared to accept.[15]

The influence of Kant is also apparent in the emphasis Rawls places on the respect due to individuals.[16] On Kant's account, 'humanity' has intrinsic value.[17] Unlike things, people (on account of their humanity) merit respect and ought not to be used as mere means.[18] This leads Rawls to embrace the Kantian account of social contract.[19] His aim in doing so is to ensure that lawmakers promulgate only those law's to which all members of society could give their consent.[20] Moreover, Rawls takes the view that emphasis ought to be placed on individuals so as to reduce the chances of sacrificing their welfare and neglecting the separateness of persons.[21] Given that Rawls embraces the Kantian approach to justice, it comes as no surprise to find his emphasis on impartiality in reaching universal agreement on principles of justice.[22]

In order to secure impartiality, Rawls, as we have seen, places people in the original position and behind the veil of ignorance. The limited knowledge they possess makes it impossible for them to think in the selfish way to which people are prone.[23] For the people in the original position do not know their class position or social status.[24] However, they are aware of 'general facts'.[25] While Rawls says little about these facts in his account of the original position, it seems reasonable to think that they include some awareness of risks in society. This is important because Rawls describes society as 'a cooperative venture for mutual advantage'.[26] He also says that it is concerned with 'the proper distribution of the benefits and burdens of social cooperation'.[27] So it seems natural to imagine the people behind the

[15] For an account of the influence exerted on Rawls by Kant, see S. Freeman, *Rawls* (New York: Routledge, 2007), 21-22 (noting that Kant is the philosopher who 'most profoundly influenced' Rawls).

[16] *Ibid*, 21. See also J. Rawls, n 2, above, 586.

[17] R.J. Sullivan, *Immanuel Kant's Moral Theory* (Cambridge: Cambridge University Press, 1989), 358, n 6.

[18] *Ibid*, 195.

[19] T. Pogge, *John Rawls: His Life and Theory of Justice* (Oxford: Oxford University Press, 2007), 60-61.

[20] See S. Freeman, n 15, above, 142-144.

[21] J. Rawls, n 2, above, 27.

[22] *Ibid,* 60-1

[23] *Ibid,* 136-142.

[24] *Ibid*, 12.

[25] *Ibid,* 142

[26] *Ibid,* 4.

[27] *Ibid.*

veil of ignorance thinking about the sort of risk-regulation with which accident compensation law is concerned.[28] Moreover, they would do so with the aim of 'adopt[ing] the alternative the worst outcome of which is superior to the worst outcome of … other[ ] [possible arrangements]'.[29]

As well as presenting us with the original position and the veil of ignorance, Rawls also draws a distinction between 'rationality' and 'reasonableness'.[30] On his account, those who act rationally intend to further their own interests, whilst those who act reasonably take into account of the interests of others.[31] Since the limitation on knowledge imposed by the veil of ignorance erases any conception of an individual's particular situation, this forces those in the original position to think of all members of society. By contrast, those who do not find themselves behind the veil of ignorance would be likely to have a very different view of practical questions. For they would be unwilling to sacrifice their own interests for the interests of others. Hence, the original position works to promote impartiality. Thus Rawls concludes that, when placed behind the veil of ignorance, people will take account of all members of society. For when the veil is lifted, they could be any one of the individuals within the relevant group - from the best placed to the least advantaged.

Rawls' veil of ignorance helps us to understand how people would behave impartially. However, he does more than this. This is because the veil of ignorance provides us with the means with which to analyse the views of the three judges mentioned earlier. As we have noted, Mill and Wright JJ are each positioned at the opposite ends of a deontological-consequentialist spectrum, while Prudential J occupies a position that lies between these two extremes. Moreover, Prudential J's views on accident compensation law have, as we will see, much to recommend them – not least because they place emphasis on the notion of community responsibility.

---

28 Concern with risk-regulation seems highly likely since Rawls's political philosophy focuses on what he calls 'the basic structure': *i.e.*, 'the basic social and political institutions that structure daily life and individuals' decisions and actions, and which distribute fundamental rights and duties and determine the division of advantages of social cooperation'. See S. Freeman, n 15, above, 464.

29 *Ibid*, 153. (In making choices between alternative sets of arrangements in the way described in the text, the people in the original position apply a 'maximin' rule, according to which they should seek to maximize their minimum payoff. See S. Freeman, n 15, above, 474-475.)

30 *Ibid,* 550 for a helpful account of the Rawlsian distinction between 'the rational' and 'the reasonable'.

31 *Ibid*, 296-297.

3 *Quot Homines, Tot Sententiae*[32]

In 'The Canengusian Connection', Mill J places emphasis exclusively on economic efficiency. On his account, promoting the efficient allocation of resources is the 'central purpose' of negligence law.[33] To this end, he endorses the Hand Formula (which states that judges can impose liability when doing so satisfies a test of cost-justified accident prevention).[34] But this approach gives rise to a problem. Mill J is prepared to sacrifice the interests of individuals in the course of maximising utility. For this reason, we can see that his approach to negligence claims is utilitarian and gives expression to the maximum happiness principle - according to which we should seek to pursue the greatest good of the greatest number.[35]

There are many difficulties with this approach. People in countries like Britain, Canada, and the USA expect the law to be attentive to them as individuals. Rawls's account of the veil of ignorance reflects this. No one wants to discover that he or she is to be sacrificed or used for the purposes of maximizing utility. The sense of horror that comes with such a discovery is something that Hutchinson and Morgan convey in 'The Canengusian Connection' in their discussion of *Grimshaw v Ford Motor Co* (the Ford Pinto case)[36]. This is the case in which the Ford Motor Company decided (on the basis of a cost-benefit analysis) that it would be more efficient (cheaper) to pay compensation rather than spend money making its Pinto cars safer.[37] This approach, like that of Mill J, abandons the idea that people are inviolable. The emphasis is not on individuals and their interests. And an understandable reaction on the part of individuals is for them to say: 'I wouldn't want to be sacrificed by Mill J, the Ford Motor Co, or anyone else'.

As with Mill J, we can use Rawls to find fault with Wright J. Like Lord Browne-Wilkinson in *X v Bedfordshire CC*, Wright J clearly thinks that the goal of 'remedying every wrong' lies at the heart of negligence law (and tort more generally).[38] Moreover, Wright J seems to assume that people are intrinsically valuable.[39] If this is the case, then he is a deontologist. And this

[32] There are as many opinions as there are men.

[33] A.C. Hutchinson and D. Morgan, n.1, above, 76-7.

[34] *United States v. Carroll Towing* (2d. Cir. 1947) 159 F.2d 169, *per* Learned Hand J.

[35] On the maximum happiness principle, see W. Kymlicka, *Contemporary Political Philosophy: An Introduction* (Oxford: Oxford University Press, 2002, 2nd edn), 10-12 and 50, n 1.

[36] *Grimshaw v Ford Motor Co* (1981) 174 Cal Report 348. See also A.C. Hutchinson and D. Morgan, n.1, above, p. 87-88.

[37] *Ibid*, 87-88.

[38] *X v Bedfordshire CC* [1993] 2 AC 633, 749

[39] A.C. Hutchinson and D. Morgan, n.1, above, 90-4.

opens the way to a line of criticism where we can make use of Rawls and his paraphernalia of the veil of ignorance and the original position. For Wright J's unwillingness to consider consequences fits awkwardly with the notion of distributive justice.[40]

In our pursuit of distributive justice, there are circumstances where sacrifices must be made in order to bring overall benefit to society as a whole.[41] This gives rise to a dilemma that we can illustrate by using a case drawn not from tort but from the field of administrative law, *R v Cambridge Health Authority, ex p B*.[42] In *ex p B*, Sir Thomas Bingham MR was forced to choose between two approaches to the provision of health care – one deontological and the other consequentialist. The first of these approches involved delivering treatment to a gravely ill child (B) whose life could not, in all probability, be preserved. Laws J applied this approach in the Queen's Bench – taking the view that not to treat B would be to violate her fundamental right to life.[43] The Master of the Rolls reluctantly applied the second approach, which had to do with providing health care for a large number of people whose chances of survival would (in most cases) be very much better than those of B. In light of the limited budget available to Cambridge Health Authority, Bingham MR decided that B's interests should be sacrificed in pursuit of overall benefit to many other health-care recipients. This decision and others like it give us grounds for thinking that Wright J's exclusive focus on deontology is unsatisfactory. While, in cases like *ex p B*, it concentrates the mind of a judge on someone whose interests may be overridden, we need to think about the pursuit of socially advantageous outcomes that benefit large numbers of people. Not to do so would hardly be reasonable in Rawls's sense.[44]

Whilst the original position provides us with the means to identify deficient or unattractive positions, it can also be used to rank possible responses to practical problems (where considerations of social justice arise). This becomes clear when we examine the judgments of Mill J. Wright J, and

---

[40] Distributive justice is a normative idea. It regards allocation of benefits and burdens of economic activity as a guide to socially just outcomes. For more on distributive justice, see, D. Miller, *Political Philosophy: A Very Short Introduction* (Oxford: Oxford University Press, 2003) 74.

[41] On the costs involved in pursuing socially beneficial outcomes, see G. Calabresi, 'The Decision For Accidents: An Approach To Non-Fault Allocation Of Costs' (1965) 78 *Harvard Law Review* 713, 716-721 (on 'the nature of the decision for accidents'). See also G. Calabresi, "Some Thoughts on Risk Distribution and the Law of Torts" (1961) 70 *Yale LJ.* 499, 517-9.

[42] *R v Cambridge Health Authority, ex p B* [1995] 1 WLR 898 (CA).

[43] *R v Cambridge Health Authority, ex p B* (1995) TLR 159.

[44] See n 31, above, and associated text.

Prudential J. We can (as we noted earlier) locate Prudential J in a position between his two colleagues on the deontology-consequentialism spectrum. From this position, he is able to level criticisms at both Mill and Wright JJ. He says that he is filled with 'despondency and horror' at the thought of Mill J's 'indifference to the fate of individuals'.[45] He then turns to Wright J, whose views he recognises have 'intuitive appeal'.[46] While this may be the case, Prudential J finds Wright J's approach to accident compensation to be impractical – being 'thoroughly unequal to the massive task he sets it'.[47] He finds support for this conclusion in, for example, the difficulties judges have in resolving causal questions.[48]

Having rejected his colleagues' views, Prudential J stakes out a position of his own. He tells us that Canengus can only respond adequately to the 'plight' of accident victims by pursing the ideal of 'social justice'.[49] He recognizes that this cannot be achieved unless people engage in risky 'community activities' that are 'done for the benefit of all'.[50] However, these activities lead to 'predictable and almost inevitable accidents'.[51] This leads Prudential J to say that '[i]t is the plight of the injured plaintiff ... that deserves our attention'.[52] He also argues for the abandonment of tort law. His reason for doing so is that it is a 'litigation lottery'.[53] Certainly a scheme of no-fault compensation will have greater appeal than a litigation lottery to those behind the veil of ignorance. For they, as we noted earlier, aim to 'adopt the alternative the worst outcome of which is superior to the worst outcome of the other[ ] [possible arrangements]'.[54] In light of these points, it is unsurprising to find Prudential J concluding that tort should be replaced by 'a thoroughgoing and comprehensive scheme of [no-fault] accident compensation.[55]

---

[45] A.C. Hutchinson and D. Morgan, n.1, above, 94.
[46] *Ibid.*
[47] *Ibid*, 95.
[48] *Ibid.* (In taking account of the consequentialist and deontological dimensions of negligence law, Prudential J embarks an interpretative exercise of the sort described in E. Mickiewicz, 'An Exploratory Theory of Legal Coherence in Canengus and Beyond' (2010) 7 *The Journal Jurisprudence*, section 4.
[49] A.C. Hutchinson and D. Morgan, n.1, above, 95 and 100.
[50] *Ibid*, 101.
[51] *Ibid.*
[52] *Ibid*, 94.
[53] *Ibid*, 97.
[54] See n 29, above, and accompanying text.
[55] A.C. Hutchinson and D. Morgan, n 1,above, 98.

Like the architects of the comprehensive no-fault accident compensation system in New Zealand,[56] Prudential J argues that his approach demonstrates a commitment to 'community responsibility'.[57] For the community benefits from risk-taking and, for this reason, should respond justly to the plight of 'the statistically necessary victims' of accidents.[58] This makes sense – not least from the standpoint of distributive justice.[59] But Prudential J could have added that his approach to accident compensation is a mixture of consequentialism and deontology. He focuses on socially valuable outcomes (consequentialism): 'community activities' that are 'done for the benefit of all'.[60] But he is also determined to make sure that accident victims receive just treatment through a no-fault scheme (deontology). In thinking along these lines, Prudential J might be classified as a qualified consequentialist.[61] He gives priority to valuable outcomes because they are necessary to the pursuit of justice (activities that 'benefit … all').[62] But he wants to treat all accident victims justly (deontology).[63]

4 Back Behind the Veil of Ignorance

Let us now imagine those behind the veil of ignorance contemplating a choice between the views of Mill J, Wright J, and Prudential J. Mill J's approach to accident compensation means that some of them will be sacrificed. Wright J may be committed to corrective justice, but he ignores the benefits to all members of society that come from the 'community activities' that Prudential J describes. For this reason, his commitment to 'reasonableness' in Rawls's sense is worryingly narrow in focus.[64] Prudential J's approach (which draws on the other two positions) is free from these glaring deficiencies (see Diagram 1 below). For this reason, it seems likelier to win the support of those behind the veil of ignorance. If this is right, then

56 Report of the Royal Commission of Inquiry *Compensation for Personal Injury in New Zealand* (Government Printer, Wellington 1967) [Woodhouse Report].

57 A.C. Hutchinson and D. Morgan, n.1, above, 101.

58 *Ibid.*

59 See G. Calabresi, "The decision for accidents: an approach to nonfault allocation of costs" (1965) 78(4) *Harvard LR.* 713. at 714 on the logic of 'loss spreading', and P.S. Atiyah, *Accidents, Compensation and the Law* (Cambridge: Cambridge University Press, 2006, 7th edn) (on community responsibility). 8-10 and 415-421 (on, *inter alia*, 'society's responsibility').

60 A.C. Hutchinson and D. Morgan, n.1, above, 101.

61 On qualified consequentialism, see R. Mullender, 'Thorizing the Third Way: Qualified Consequentialism, the Proportionality Principle, and the New Social Democracy' (2000) 27 *Journal of Law and Society* 493, 500-501.

62 See n. 60, above.

63 See n.s 60-61, above.

64 See ns 32-33, above and accompanying text..

Hutchinson and Morgan should perhaps have identified it as preferable to the approaches of Mill and Wright JJ.

But while Prudential J's approach may be preferable to that of Mill and Wright JJ, this does not mean that conflict in Canengus will come to an end.[65] Qualified consequentialism is a very general idea.[66] Judgments will have to be made as to how consequentialist and deontological considerations should be combined so as to do justice. And this is problematic. It is not obvious how we might rank these considerations. They may, in fact, be incommensurable. But even if this is the case, Prudential J's approach has the attraction of being 'reasonable' in Rawls's sense. This is because it is aimed at accommodating the interests of all Canengusians justly. Moreover, the form of justice that leads Prudential J to adopt this approach is (like that of Rawls) distributive. For these reasons, we could imagine not just the people behind the veil of ignorance but, also Rawls himself identifying Prudential J's approach as preferable to that of Mill and Wright JJ. This is because Rawls staked out the position that '[a] social order is to be accepted as *just* if and only if it could be the object of a fair agreement – of an agreement that takes account of all the individuals who are to live under this social order'.[67]

5 Conclusions

While Hutchinson and Morgan do not rank the positions staked out by Mill, Wright, and Prudential JJ, Rawls's device of the veil of ignorance gives us a way of doing this in a way that satisfies a test of impartiality (see Diagram 1 below). As we saw earlier, the approaches of Mill and Wright JJ (the first consequentialist and the second deontological) have real weaknesses. Mill J's pursuit of the greatest good of the greatest number means that he is insensitive to the separateness of persons. Wright J's deontological approach blinds him to the importance of outcomes that have general benefit. By contrast with these judges, Prudential J offers a preferable alternative. He recognises that society benefits from activities that necessarily lead to accidents. However, he also wants to ensure that accident victims receive compensation. In advocating a New Zealand-style no-fault compensation scheme, he reveals himself to be a qualified consequentialist. He places emphasis on the pursuit of outcomes. However, he also thinks that society should do the intrinsically right thing – which, in this case, means paying compensation to accident victims.

---

[65] R. Mullender, see n. 61, above, 514-5

[66] *Ibid*

[67] T. Pogge, n 19, above, 66.

We should not assume, though, that Prudential J's approach to accident compensation provides a neat solution to the problem with which he deals. This is because it seems to be impossible to rank consequentialist and deontological arguments. The best we can do is to accommodate them in an approach that gives priority to one of the two (consequentialism). But those who place emphasis on deontological considerations will be unhappy about this. For this reason, we can expect the battle of consquentialism and deontology to go on.

Diagram 1

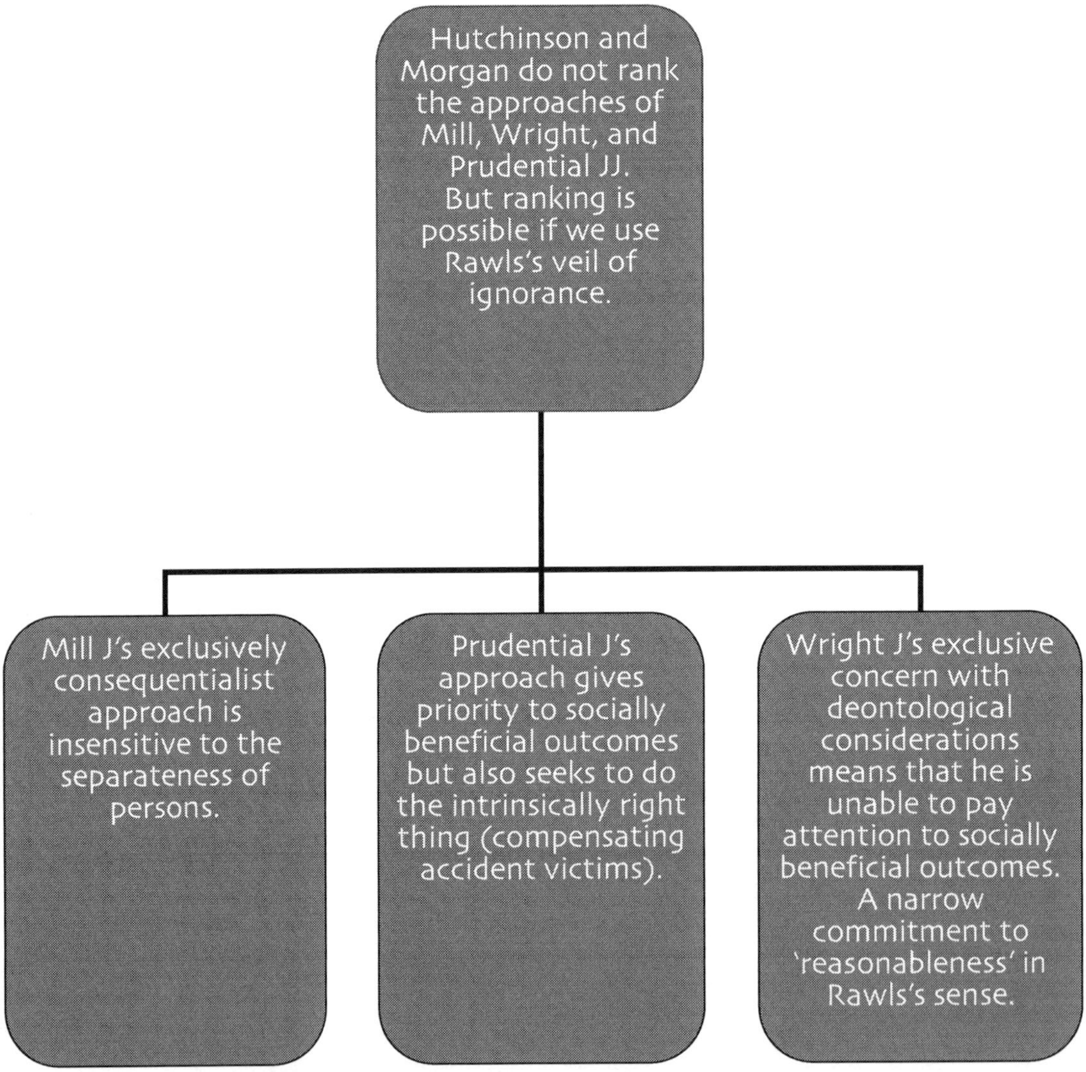

CORRECTIVE JUSTICE AND HORIZONTAL PRIVACY: A LEAF OUT OF WRIGHT J'S BOOK

THOMAS D. C. BENNETT*

Introduction

In Hutchinson and Morgan's 'The Canengusian Connection: The Kaleidoscope of Tort Theory', Wright J (one of their five fictive judges) is a committed defender of corrective justice.[1] In his 'judgment', he examines two ways in which tort can give effect to this ideal: negligence liability and strict liability. Wright J's readiness to engage with a matter of institutional design is highly relevant to the concern that occupies a central place in this essay: how to secure protection for the right to privacy? Central to this essay is the claim that the body of law it focuses on (Article 8 of the European Convention on Human Rights and lower-order (municipal) private law) affords means by which to protect privacy in ways that reflect (a Wright J-like) commitment to corrective justice.[2]

* Barrister; Lecturer, BPP Law School, and Associate Lecturer, The Open University. I am particularly grateful to Richard Mullender for his insightful and encouraging comments on a draft of this piece, and to Patrick O'Callaghan both for his comments and for engaging me in an enlightening discussion of the essay's subject matter during the drafting process. I also owe thanks to Alexander Murray for helping me to structure my thoughts on the appropriateness of traditional classifications of public and private law in an age of human rights, and to Marie FitzPatrick for sharing with me her encyclopaedic knowledge of Tolkien as I searched for some literary analogies.

1 A.C. Hutchinson and D. Morgan, 'The Canengusian Connection: The Kaleidoscope of Tort Theory' (1984) 22 *Osgoode Hall Law Review* 69

2 Reference is made in this introduction to 'lower-order private law', and in this context it means the body of law built up by the municipal courts which is shaped by the 'higher-order public law' of the ECHR. (This is a model that is similar to the model termed 'subordination' in O. Cherednychenko, 'Fundamental rights and private law: A relationship of subordination or complementarity' (2007) 3(2) *Utrecht Law Review* 1. In that essay, Cherednychenko discusses various types of horizontal effect, taking examples from German, Dutch and English constitutional orders. That essay argues that the various models of horizontal effect (that is, the relationship between 'public' and 'private' law) are best described by use of the terms 'subordination' and 'complementarity'.) This (my) essay does not accommodate a discussion of whether the term 'private' within 'lower-order private law' is appropriate, though the author recognises that it may well not be. For a body of law that is shaped and moulded by public law principles may lose some of its private nature, in which case it might be thought of as a form of public-private 'hybrid', though such a classification is also not without its problems. (For a useful discussion of these see B. Markesinis, 'Privacy, freedom of expression, and the horizontal effect of the Human Rights Bill: lessons from Germany', (1999) 115 *LQR* 47.) Alternatively, it may be (though it is also not discussed in the space available in the essay) that the traditional classificatory terms 'public law' and 'private law' are no longer particularly helpful in an age where the shaping of the latter by the former inevitably leaves traces of 'public law'

This essay also stakes out positions on four more particular points concerning the relationship between privacy protection in England and Wales and the concept of corrective justice. It takes as its starting point the new, post-*Campbell* privacy action, commonly labelled 'misuse of private information'.[3] The essay's first aim is to demonstrate how and why this new cause of action fundamentally differs from torts in the traditional mould, giving it an awkward and uncomfortable position in English tort law. In proceeding in this way, the essay lays the foundations for an explanation of how, despite obvious differences between the new action and more traditional torts, principles of corrective justice can still be located within it. The essay then goes on to make use of 'The Canengusian Connection' more directly, by comparing the methodology of the hypothetical Wright J with that of the English High Court judge, Eady J, who has found himself at the forefront of privacy law in England and Wales in recent years, and locating common ground between them.

The essay now moves to consider each of the four positions in turn, before drawing some general conclusions.

1. 'Misuse of private information': the child of direct horizontal effect

> [The] new balancing approach [in 'misuse of private information'] is a fundamental shift in the way we do things. I think that as yet we may not have fully realised quite how fundamental ... The truth may be [simple], namely that the law of privacy is a new creature deriving from the Strasbourg way of doing things, thus requiring language and terminology of its own.[4]

Traditionally, English law has protected privacy interests indirectly through a rather bewildering assortment of legal mechanisms.[5] In terms of protecting private information, however, the mechanism most obviously related to the new action is

---

principles within the newly 'shaped' causes of action. This is an issue that is tentatively returned to in more depth at n 98, below.

3 *Campbell v MGN Ltd* [2004] 2 AC 457

4 Eady J, 'Protecting Freedom of Expression in the Context of the European Convention of Human Rights', a public lecture given at City University, London, 10th March 2010. The transcript is available at: www.judiciary.gov.uk/docs/speeches/eady-j-city-university-10032010.pdf

5 Including, *inter alia*: data protection legislation, protection from harassment legislation, common law actions for trespass to the person and property, nuisance and the equitable doctrine protecting confidences.

the old equitable doctrine designed to protect confidences.[6] That it could be used to protect private, as opposed to merely confidential, information was for many years the subject of heated debate, and there was some fierce opposition to any expansion of the law of confidence.[7] The Human Rights Act 1998 (HRA), however, introduced a new element into English law. By 'bringing home' the rights of the European Convention on Human Rights, and giving Convention rights further effect on the plane of municipal law, the HRA required English law to provide protection for individuals' Article 8 (ECHR) right to private life.[8] The House of Lords' decision in *Campbell* laid the foundations for a new cause of action which has come to be known by the name given to it by Lord Nicholls: 'misuse of private information'.[9] This cause of action has subsequently been used on several high-profile occasions, notably in the cases of *Murray v Big Pictures*[10] and *Mosley v NGN*.[11] Just why the courts created the new cause of action remains the subject of some debate. There are those who argue that 'misuse of private information' is no more than an expansion of the traditional doctrine of confidence.[12] Typically, these arguments come from analysts of the law who reject the view that the HRA has (or is capable of having) 'direct horizontal effect'.[13] This author has previously argued

[6] N. Richards and D. Solove, 'Privacy's Other Path: Recovering the Law of Confidentiality,' (2007) 96 *Georgetown Law Journal* 123

[7] See R. Wacks, 'The Poverty of Privacy' (1980) 96 *LQR* 73

[8] *Rights Brought Home*: The Human Rights Bill, CM 3882 (1997). For some useful background, see J. Wright, *Tort Law and Human Rights* (Oxford: Hart Publishing, 2001).

[9] n 3, above, [14]. In *Campbell*, the supermodel, Naomi Campbell, successfully claimed damages for 'misuse of private information' regarding the publication of photographs taken of her on a public street as she left a Narcotics Anonymous meeting, and an accompanying article detailing the treatment she was receiving for a drug addiction.

[10] [2008] EWCA Civ 446. In *Murray*, the claimant, the three year-old son of author J.K. Rowling, successfully appealed against a decision at first instance to strike out his claim for 'misuse of private information' in respect of the surreptitious taking (by a freelance photographer with a long-lens camera), retaining and publication of photographs taken of him in public with his parents. The Court of Appeal unanimously held that the claimant had a reasonable expectation of privacy in the circumstances, and moreover went so far as to remark that if the claim were brought in the ECtHR, it would likely succeed.

[11] [2008] EWHC 1777 (QB). In *Mosley*, the then Formula 1 racing chief, Max Mosley, brought a successful claim for 'misuse of private information' in respect of material published in a national tabloid newspaper. The material published included pictures (and a link to a website containing a video) of Mosley engaging in sado-masochistic sexual activity with several women (who were alleged by the defendants to be prostitutes), along with some graphic descriptions of the contents of both the pictures and the video.

[12] See B. Pillans, 'Thus far and no further: are we saying it loudly enough?' (2007) 12(6) *Communications Law* 213.

[13] See R. Buxton's outright rejection of Wade's model for direct horizontal effect of the HRA in R. Buxton, 'The Human Rights Act and private law', (2000) 116 *LQR* 48. For a more nuanced rejection of direct horizontality, and an argument in favour of a form of indirect horizontal effect, see G. Phillipson, 'Clarity postponed: Horizontal Effect after

that such arguments are not attuned to the true state of affairs – that the HRA is not only capable of being directly horizontally effective, but that the creation of the new privacy action is a hallmark of such horizontality.[14]

'Direct horizontality' is being used in this essay as a term of art to describe the relationship between the higher-order public law of the ECHR and the HRA, and the lower-order private law of the domestic common law. With higher-order public law providing the impetus for the courts to fashion new causes of action and exerting a shaping force over the form they take, and with these new causes of action providing scope for horizontal actions (that is, actions between private parties) to protect Convention rights, the relationship can be said to be one of 'direct horizontal effect'.[15]

It appears to be common ground that if the HRA were merely 'indirectly' horizontally effective, such indirect effect could not result in the creation by the courts of new causes of action, but only in the expansion of existing ones.[16] By contrast, 'direct horizontal effect' has the potential to "threaten whole swathes of the common law with replacement by private HRA actions."[17] Putting it in such a manner, as Phillipson does, direct horizontality comes under attack from common law traditionalists, who have an instinctive aversion to it.[18] A 'common law

Campbell and Re. S', in Fenwick, Masterman and Phillipson (Eds.) *Judicial Reasoning under the UK Human Rights Act*, (Cambridge: Cambridge University Press, 2007), and also G. Phillipson, 'Judicial reasoning in breach of confidence cases under the Human Rights Act: not taking privacy seriously?' (2003) *European Human Rights LR* 54. By 2009, Buxton had modified his position, accepting that there is some indirect horizontal effect of the HRA, but maintaining his view that the new privacy action is merely an extension of the old equitable doctrine of confidence: see R. Buxton, 'Private Life and the English Judges', (2009) *Oxford Journal of Legal Studies* 413.

14 See T. Bennett, 'Horizontality's New Horizons – Re-Examining Horizontal Effect: Privacy, Defamation and the Human Rights Act – Part 1' (2010) 21(3) *Entertainment LR* 96 and T. Bennett, 'Horizontality's New Horizons –Part 2' (2010) 21(4) *Entertainment LR* 145, both of which build upon the argument that the HRA would have direct horizontal effect advanced in W. Wade, 'Horizons of Horizontality', (2000) 116 *LQR* 217.

15 This echoes closely Wade's model of direct horizontal effect. See W. Wade, n 14, above.

16 M. Du Plessis and J. Ford, 'Developing the common law progressively - horizontality, the Human Rights Act and the South African experience', (2004) *European Human Rights LR* 286; N. Bamforth, 'The true "horizontal effect" of the Human Rights Act 1998', (2001) 117 *LQR* 34; see also G. Phillipson, n 13, above.

17 G. Phillipson, n 13, above, 152. For another alternative view favouring a 'direct horizontal effect' view of the HRA, and making reference to the *sui generis* nature of causes of action that result from direct horizontality, see D. Beyleveld and S. Pattinson, 'Horizontal Applicability and Horizontal Effect' (2002) 118 *LQR* 623.

18 Just where this 'instinctive' aversion comes from may be open to debate. It is used in this essay since the author has in mind the notion that common law traditionalists are,

traditionalist' locates substantial value in the wealth of experience and knowledge inherent in the several hundred years' worth of reasoning in the common law.[19] He sees the common law as a valuable decision-making and certainty-ensuring legal tool which derives value from its longevity, and places trust in it; he is reluctant to see it subverted, altered or replaced by any alternative. By contrast, a 'Strasbourg-enthusiast' sees direct horizontality as a positive step forward.[20] The potential of direct horizontality might thus equally be described by a Strasbourg-enthusiast in terms of its ability to secure the fundamental rights of individuals without getting 'bogged-down' in the complexities of the elements within traditional common law torts. It is difficult to resist the attractive simplicity of stating that a common law traditionalist asks: 'why?', whilst a Strasbourg-enthusiast asks: 'why not?' Perhaps it is more useful, though, to put the sides of the argument the way Eady J has: "[d]epending which way you look at it, we now have the advantage of flexibility, or we have to struggle with ... uncertainty."[21]

Taking the apparent consensus that 'indirect horizontal effect' cannot produce new judge-made causes of action, whilst 'direct horizontal effect' does have the potential for the creation of new heads of liability (desirable or otherwise), we can ask what precisely the new 'misuse of private information' action is. Is it a brand new cause of action? Whilst there is still a tendency amongst some members of the judiciary to talk about it in terms of it being an expansion of the equitable doctrine of confidence, such talk does not properly reflect the breadth of the new action's reach – either its already-evidenced or its potential breadth.[22] Nor, more straightforwardly, does it recognise that the new action is "... new in formulation, new in terms of its applicability, new in its particular reliance upon guidance from the ECtHR, new in terms of the relief it can provide, and new in terms of the

amongst other things, proponents of historical reason, and that much of what a common law traditionalist values comes from a personal embedding in common law culture. Whether a common law traditionalist's aversion to direct horizontality is the result of a conscious decision to demure it, or is a subtler, sub-conscious reaction, is a question worth considering (though there is insufficient space to do so here), given the context of the collection in which this essay appears.

[19] See J.G. Postema, *Bentham and the Common Law Tradition* (Oxford: Clarendon Press, 1986) Ch.1

[20] See P. O'Callaghan, 'Monologism and Dialogism in Private Law' (2010) 7 *The Journal Jurisprudence* 405: ('The Strasbourg Enthusiasts: Monologism in Action?'). It is worth noting that although this essay has very briefly placed Phillipson's work into a category outside that of Strasbourg-enthusiasm, O'Callaghan regards Phillipson as a Strasbourg-enthusiast.

[21] Eady J, n 4, above, p.11

[22] R. Buxton, 'The Human Rights Act and private law', (2000) 116 *LQR* 48

defence it is subject to."[23] As such, we can, and should, view the existence of the new action as evidence of direct horizontality.

This is a view from which Patrick O'Callaghan would dissent. For, writing in this issue, he takes the view that the new privacy action is the result of 'indirect horizontal effect'.[24] It is suggested here that the difference between O'Callaghan and myself in our description of the new action's effect is actually less great than it may at first seem. O'Callaghan recognises the existence of 'elements' within the new privacy action that resemble the elements of more traditional torts, at least at first glance. In contrast to a more openly acknowledged type of constitutional (or *sui generis*) tort – for example, of the kind that exists in Ireland – the new privacy action has a traditional tortious look to it.[25] It does not look like a mechanism by which a claimant may simply arrive at court alleging a violation of a Convention right and successfully demand a remedy. O'Callaghan also considers the new cause of action to be severely limited both in terms of the nature of the information that can form the basis of an actionable claim, and in terms of the types of claimants who are practically able to avail themselves of a remedy under it.[26] This (O'Callaghan's) analysis supports the view that the new action is not expansive enough, nor sufficiently overtly labelled in *sui generis* language to be properly described as being the result of 'direct horizontal effect.' On such a view, 'direct horizontal effect' as a phrase should be reserved for newly created causes of action that provide a simple forum for claimants to directly litigate alleged violations of the Convention without reference to traditional-style tortious elements.

This view can, however, be challenged. In terms of the types of information that the new action protects, O'Callaghan rightly points out that the range of such information has been of a limited nature in cases that have come before the courts since *Campbell*. It may not, however, be quite as limited as he suggests. In *Applause Store Productions Ltd v Raphael*,[27] the court accepted that a person's date of birth and

23 See T. Bennett, n 14, above. In that two-part essay, the argument that the new privacy action is the result of direct horizontal effect is made in greater depth than the space in this essay allows for.

24 P. O'Callaghan, n 20, above, section 7: ('Human Rights and Private Law: 'Multeity in Unity'?')

25 See *Meskell v. Coras lompair Eireann* [1973] IR 121, 133 where it was stated that: "... if a person has suffered damage by virtue of a breach of a constitutional right or the infringement of a constitutional right, that person is entitled to seek redress against the person or persons who infringed that right ...", per Walsh J. For a discussion of constitutional tort models in general, including the Irish model, see S. Gardbaum, 'The "Horizontal Effect" of Constitutional Rights', (2003) 102 *Michigan Law Review* 387.

26 *Ibid* p.27

27 [2008] EWHC 1781 (QB)

religious views are matters over which he would have a reasonable expectation of privacy. This ruling is the most expansive assessment in England of the range of material capable of engaging Article 8 rights thus far, and goes far beyond that which was envisaged in *Campbell*. This is much more than mere incremental elaboration on the old confidence doctrine. Equally relevant in *Applause Store* is the fact that the claimant was neither a celebrity nor a public figure but rather a lay businessman. Clearly then, the new action – whilst most famously (or infamously) used by celebrities – is open to a much broader range of potential claimants. This is precisely what we would expect from a *sui generis* 'constitutional tort'.

As for the label attached to, and the existence of *prima facie* traditional-looking 'elements' within, the new action, these may be described as something of a disguise.[28] Let us hypothesise for a moment that, in a novel claim where a Convention right is alleged to have been unlawfully interfered with, a judge comes to the conclusion that he is both empowered and required to create a new cause of action, horizontally, under the HRA.[29] He is also acutely aware that the case before him has quite easily definable factual parameters (as in *Campbell*) and of the

[28] Or perhaps even the judicial equivalent of Frodo Baggins' Elven cloak from J.R.R. Tolkien's *The Lord of the Rings*. Frodo is given the cloak by the Elf Queen, Galadriel, in Lothlórien. In the movie version of the second part (*The Two Towers*, Dir. Peter Jackson. Perf. Elijah Wood, Viggo Mortensen, Ian McKellan. New Line Cinema, 2002) – though not explicitly in the original novel – Frodo uses the cloak as a disguise which masks his true form; when agents of the dark lord, Sauron, see Frodo in the cloak, they mistake him for a rock. Tolkien purists (who may object to the use of the film version as canon) might feel happier using a comparison with the wolf's disguise from the Grimm Brothers' fairy tale, *Little Red Riding Hood*. In the story, the wolf dresses up as 'Grandma', (the heroine's grandmother) and thereby appears unthreatening. The 'magic cloak', which has appeared in various forms throughout literary history (recently in J.K. Rowling's *Harry Potter* series), has its roots in ancient Norse mythology as the *Tarnhelm*. It features in Richard Wagner's *Ring Cycle* (*Der Ring des Nibelungen*) in the first of the four operas that comprise the work, *Das Rheingold*, where it is used by Alberich as a cloak of invisibility. The most pertinent of these analogies remains, perhaps, Frodo's cloak, since it is in that incarnation that the *Tarnhelm* acts as a form of camouflage, making that which it covers appear both unthreatening and innocuous, and – importantly – utterly different from its true nature.

[29] See T. Bennett, n 14, above, for a lengthier discussion of the root of the courts' authority to create new causes of action directly horizontally. See also W. Wade, n 14, above, which arguably heralded the beginning of the 'horizontal effect debate' and which sets out an argument for a statutory basis for direct horizontality. The language of direct horizontal effect has its roots in the ECJ ruling in *Van Gend en Loos v Neder-Landse Tariefcommissie* (Case 26/62); [1963] ECR 1, and there has since been something of a (linguistic) 'spill-over' effect into municipal law, making use of 'horizontal effect' and 'vertical effect' as terms of art to describe the relationship between higher-order public law and both private individuals and the state respectively.

potential backlash against him if he is seen to be acting in an 'activist' fashion.[30] What is he to do? He does not want to set a precedent that looks like a brand new, alien type of action with seemingly boundless breadth, so he rejects an absolutely direct application of Strasbourg methodology; that is, he decides against overtly following the method of considering: (a) the engagement of; (b) interference with; and, (c), proportionality of any interference with the Convention right. Instead, in a flash of inspiration, he disguises the Strasbourg methodology inside more traditional-looking 'elements', giving the new action the appearance of a more traditional tort.[31] So, to use 'misuse of private information' as an example: 'engagement of Article 8 rights' becomes 'reasonable expectation of privacy'; 'interference' becomes 'misuse' and the 'proportionality' question becomes a defence of 'publication in the public interest'. These 'elements' are less frightening to the common law traditionalist than their Strasbourg equivalents. They look narrower, seemingly limiting the range of circumstances in which the new action can be utilised. As such, they are effective, if superficial, guards against accusations of activism which have the added bonus of appeasing common law traditionalists.[32]

But as seen in *Applause Store*, the judges will protect a wide range of information beyond that envisaged in *Campbell.* As shown by *Murray*, the judges will extend the

---

30 See D. Eady, 'A statutory right to privacy', (1996) *European Human Rights LR* 243 at 247; also see Eady J's remarks concerning 'activist judges' in *Mosley*, n 11, above. The attacks on the 'activism' of judges by the press have been vehement in recent years. In particular, in the context of privacy rights, Eady J has been singled out for stringent criticism. Speaking at the Society of Editors Conference in Bristol on November 10, 2008, and referring to Eady J and his judgment in *Mosley*, Paul Dacre, Editor of the *Daily Mail*, stated: "The freedom of the press, I would argue, is far too important to be left to the somewhat desiccated values of a single judge who clearly has an animus against the popular press and the right of people to freedom of expression."

31 This may be something that O'Callaghan would identify as 'monologue-creep', see P. O'Callaghan, n 20, above, section 5: ('Monologue-Creep').

32 Recognising that the 'elements' within 'misuse of private information' may in reality be no more than 'labels' that disguise the true potential reach of the action echoes remarks made by Lord Roskill in *Caparo Industries Plc v Dickman* [1990] 2 AC 605 at 628, where, in the context of establishing a duty of care test for novel situations in the tort of negligence, he stated: "[p]hrases such as 'foreseeability,' 'proximity,' 'neighbourhood,' 'just and reasonable,' 'fairness,' 'voluntary acceptance of risk,' or 'voluntary assumption of responsibility' will be found used from time to time in ... different cases. But ... such phrases are not precise definitions. At best they are but labels or phrases descriptive of the very different factual situations which can exist in particular cases and which must be carefully examined in each case ... ." The need for 'careful examination' in each case, which Lord Roskill referred to in *Caparo*, is equally applicable to the action for 'misuse of private information', and the 'careful examination' itself might be thought to mirror the 'new methodology' expounded by Eady J (discussed below). It also (as noted at n 72, below) bears some resemblance to the 'salient features' test adopted by the Australian High Court as an alternative means of establishing novel duties of care in negligence.

protection of a 'reasonable expectation of privacy' to claimants (in that case, a young child) that have no *actual* expectation of privacy.[33] O'Callaghan argues that the case of *Wainwright v Home Office*[34] demonstrates that the new privacy action does not extend to physical interferences with Article 8 rights.[35] But on the model outlined above, where the 'elements' are little more than names given to aspects of the ECtHR's methodology in order to disguise their application within the domestic jurisdiction, claimants in a case along *Wainwright* lines may now have an actionable claim. Further, considering that in the subsequent Strasbourg case of *Wainwright v UK*, a violation of Article 8 was found to have occurred, and that it has been made clear that "... Arts 8 and [where relevant] 10 of the Convention are now the very content of the domestic tort that the English court[s] must enforce," it may be unsustainable to argue that the domestic courts could now rule on a *Wainwright*-style case in any way other than that which follows the Convention jurisprudence.[36] The well-known principle that the law looks to substance rather than to form springs to mind: what is important is not how the new action is described, but what it is actually capable of doing.[37]

Of course, what the directly horizontally effective new action, cloaked in traditional-looking tortious elements, has done is introduce substantial confusion to both judicial application of, and academic commentary on, the branch of law we are examining.[38] This essay suggests that the confusion comes from two main sources: the disguised direct horizontality described above, and the problems that then become inherent in trying to understand the new action by analysing it as if it were a tort in the traditional mould. While there is much that remains murky in this area of law, we have at least established that the process of development we have scrutinized cannot be captured in the hoary old language favoured by common law traditionalists. This leads us on to our next topic.

---

[33] n 10, above

[34] [2004] 2 AC 406

[35] P. O'Callaghan, n 20, above, section 6(ii): ('Assessing Vulnerability'). This is an argument O'Callaghan also alludes to in P. O'Callaghan, 'Privacy in Pursuit of a Purpose', (2009) 17 *Tort Law Review* 100 at 113.

[36] n 10, above, [27]

[37] See *Re Montagu's Settlements* [1987] Ch 264 at 278, per Megarry V-C: "...[T]here is something of a tendency in equity to put less emphasis on detailed rules that have emerged from the cases and more weight on the underlying principles that engendered those rules, treating the rules less as rules requiring complete compliance, and more as guidelines to assist the court in applying the principles."

[38] It may be said that the disguising of a Strasbourg methodology within the 'elements' of the new cause of action is in reality an example of some fancy (a Strasbourg-enthusiast might prefer 'ingenious') judicial footwork.

2. Trying to understand the elements of the new action as if it were a tort in the traditional mould is problematic

The new cause of action is not a tort in the traditional common law mould. So much is obvious simply by its elements, even without recourse to a discussion of direct horizontality. For rather than being concerned primarily with providing a remedy, the main aim of the new action is to protect a substantive right. Eady J himself outlined the problems which academics have had trying to classify the new action, stating that:

> The leading text book editors cannot agree about this. The new edition of *McGregor* on Damages, at para. 42.47, thinks it is a tort, whereas *Clerk & Lindsell* on Tort, at para. 28.03, thinks it is an extension from equity – but they cover it in their text book anyway, just in case.[39]

English tort law has traditionally been based around remedies, rather than rights; "[e]very law student used to learn that English [tort] law was not about rights but about remedies."[40] According to corrective justice theory, tort law aims to put right harm done to one person by another by way of compensation. The harm done in many torts is obvious on its face: in trespass or negligence it is the interference with the individual or the individual's property. If damage is caused then, absent a valid defence, the tortfeasor must compensate the victim. Corrective justice theory ascribes intrinsic value to the individual.[41] In pursuing a methodology that allows for the compensation of the victim to correct the harm done, the law recognises his or her intrinsic value.[42] This sets corrective justice theory squarely apart from utilitarian theories of tort law.[43]

'Misuse of private information', however, is neither a trespass nor a negligence-based action. Even assuming, *arguendo*, that it could be classified roughly as a tort at

---

[39] Eady J, n 4, above, p.8

[40] Eady J, n 4, above, p.6 For an alternative view, see A. Ripstein, 'Tort Law in a Liberal State' (2007) 1(2) *Journal of Tort Law* Art.3, (where it is argued that underlying the traditional view of 'wrongs' at the heart of tort law are identifiable, substantive rights).

[41] See n 1, above, p.90. See also E. Weinrib, 'Legal Formalism: On the Immanent Rationality of Law', (1988) 97 *Yale Law Journal* 949, section V(D), ('The Normative Force of the Forms of Justice').

[42] A.C. Hutchinson and D. Morgan, n 1, above, p.90

[43] It should be noted that this paper uses the term 'utilitarian' in much the same way as Kent Greenawalt in K. Greenawalt, *Conflicts of Law and Morality* (Oxford: OUP, 1987) at 98. Such use refers to any theory that makes the consequences of an act the determining factor of that act's morality and disregards, for simplicity, the many variations between different discreet utilitarian and consequentialist theories.

all, it is one that is unique. Its elements are unlike those of any other cause of action. There must be information about which the claimant has a 'reasonable expectation of privacy'; and some sort of 'misuse' of that information by the defendant must be proven (typically publication or dissemination). Once those elements are made out, then the only applicable defence is one of 'public interest' based on a test of proportionality. No moral culpability need be shown on the part of the defendant, nor need the tort be intentional.[44] In that sense, it is a 'tort' of strict liability. Whilst its closest relative in tort law is arguably defamation, there remains a fundamental difference between the two that again harks back to the traditional concern of tort law with remedies rather than rights.[45] Defamation law can be seen as a classic example of corrective justice in action. Rather than having a 'right' to one's reputation, tort law ascribes intrinsic value to the individual and springs to his or her aid when reputational damage occurs. (The key assumption being made here is that reputation is a significant interest since it is part of the whole that makes an individual.[46]) The ability of defamation law to vindicate reputation is a major part of its value as a tort.[47] Certainly, this is reflected in the ECtHR's treatment of reputation as an aspect of the individual's private life.[48] There have been signs in recent ECtHR decisions that the Strasbourg Court is inclined to locate a substantive right to reputation within the ambit of the Convention.[49] If that is so, however, then it exists as part of the right to private life under Article 8, and can be explained by reference to the ECtHR's concern to

---

[44] This mirrors the approach taken in recent years in UK defamation cases involving publication of defamatory material on internet websites, particularly in regard to 'user generated content'. The current position is that an internet service provider who fails to remove within a reasonable time defamatory material from a website that they host, after they have been informed of its presence, will be held liable as a publisher of the material, in spite of not having actually generated it, (see *Godfrey v Demon Internet Ltd* [2001] QB 201; *Bunt v Tilley & Ors* [2006] EWHC 407 (QB)).

[45] See D. Eady, n 30, above.

[46] See R. Post, 'The Social Foundations of Defamation Law: Reputation and the Constitution' (1986) 74 *California Law Review* 691. Also see the deontological impulses present in the work of Immanuel Kant, who uses the term *persönlichkeit* to identify the aspect of an individual in which his/her 'dignity' can be located (see n 59, below).

[47] J. Coad, 'Reynolds and public interest - what about truth and human rights?' (2007) 18(3) *Entertainment LR* 75

[48] See *Pfeifer v Austria* (2009) 48 EHRR 8 at [35]: 'The Court considers that a person's reputation, even if that person is criticised in the context of a public debate, forms part of his or her personal identity and psychological integrity and therefore also falls within the scope of his or her "private life".'

[49] See as other examples: *Cumpana v Romania* (2005) 41 EHRR 14; *Radio France v France* (2005) 40 EHRR 29; *Chauvy and Others v France* (2005) 41 EHRR 29. As yet, however, there has been no Grand Chamber ruling confirming that reputation comes under the ambit of Art.8.

protect 'human dignity' through Article 8, which has been the subject of extensive comment.[50]

'Misuse of private information', then, is unique because there *is* now in English domestic law a substantive right to privacy.[51] It comes from the Convention. As outlined above, some say it comes indirectly,[52] whilst others (including this author) argue it comes directly.[53] However it has come, though, it is undeniably here. And as this process of development has unfolded the ECtHR has placed great emphasis on 'dignity'.[54]

This concept of 'dignity' contrasts with the altogether simpler American conception of privacy as 'the right to be let alone'.[55] Moreover, it throws up questions of *what* is actually suffering the harm. Without care, the damage element in the new English tort could be construed overly circularly: 'interference with the right not to be interfered with' is about as unhelpfully as it could be put. Is the individual herself being damaged, or just her right? This is what Eady J was engaging with when he stated:

> If you are ordered not to do something, or to pay compensation for having done it, because it is not regarded as necessary or proportionate, that is quite a different concept from the court ruling that a legal "wrong" or "tort" has been committed. At least until the judge has carried out the required balancing exercise, it may be said in a real sense that no "wrong" has been committed.[56]

The various problems noted here are hardly surprising. Judges are now having to deal with, *inter alia*, the question of nomenclature ('misuse of private information'), the relevance of and nature of 'dignity', the danger of circularity, and the precise focus of the law's concern (the claimant or her right). These problems are the result

---

[50] See C. McCrudden, 'Human dignity and judicial interpretation of human rights', (2008) EJIL 655. For an alternative argument, that the ECtHR's use of proportionality as a tool in order to conduct a balancing exercise does not adequately protect 'human dignity', see S. Tsakyrakis, 'Proportionality: an assault on human rights?' (2009) 7(3) *International Journal of Constitutional Law* 468.

[51] n 4, above

[52] See G. Phillipson, n 13, above.

[53] T. Bennett, n 14, above. See also K. Hughes, 'Horizontal Privacy', (2009) 125 *LQR* 244.

[54] For a useful discussion of dignity in, *inter alia*, the jurisprudence of the ECtHR, see D. Feldman, 'Human Dignity as a Legal Value: Part 1', (1999) *Public Law* 682; and D. Feldman, 'Human Dignity as a Legal Value: Part 2', (2000) *Public Law* 62.

[55] Warren and Brandeis, 'The Right to Privacy', (1890) 4 *Harvard Law Review* 193 at 205

[56] n 4, above, p.9

of English judges having studiously avoided dealing with these matters over the years.[57] Only when the HRA required the courts to protect private life was a cause of action capable of so doing fashioned. In essence, the HRA parachuted a new, substantive 'right' to privacy into the middle of the common law. Judges were left with the task of having to protect this 'right', using the common law, without having been given any clear indication of how it should be done. This led to the second of Eady J's 'uncertainties' (discussed further below) – an uncertainty as to which principles and rules of law should be applied, how and when.[58]

So, the courts are now faced with a conceptually tricky task. They must endeavour to fit into an area of the law long understood as giving remedies to individuals (for interferences with their persons or property) a cause of action protecting a 'right' to private life. It can be done, but it is not an easy undertaking. Moreover, it is this conceptual confusion that gives 'misuse of private information' its awkward and uncomfortable position within English tort law. It is perhaps more difficult to conceive of a person's privacy as a measurable aspect of their *persönlichkeit* (personality/personhood) in the way suggested.[59] Impact upon reputation is more measurable. Judges can, in many cases, obtain evidence of actual financial loss resulting from reputational harm. Where this is not possible, a somewhat haphazard approach to the calculation of damages has to suffice. However, the presence in most cases of a jury (whose deliberations go unrecorded) typically obscures the inadequacies of this process/procedure. Interference with privacy is, however, far less easily given a value.[60] We might find some assistance in philosopher and novelist J.M. Coetzee's *Diary of a Bad Year*. He describes the individual's view of his/her own body in terms which initially echo Kant's notion of *person* (the physical aspect of the individual, as distinct from *persönlichkeit*). However, it becomes clear that for Coetzee, the manner in which we talk about aspects of 'our' *person* leads to a uniquely human splitting up of our various constituent parts ("my leg", "my eye",

[57] See D. Eady, n 30, above, (at 248), where Eady advocates the introduction of a statutory privacy tort "... to fill most of the gaps left by the present law, such as the lack of a duty or relationship recognised by equity, or the lack of the necessary 'quality of confidence'...".

[58] See section 3 of this essay, below.

[59] See I. Kant, *Critique of Practical Reason* (Cambridge: Cambridge University Press, 1997). Kant's use of the word *persönlichkeit*, whilst literally translatable into English as 'personality' is perhaps better reflected by the English word 'personhood' when used in this context. Kant draws a distinction between the purely physical aspect of the individual, *person*, and the personhood of the individual, *persönlichkeit*, which is the aspect of the individual in which his/her 'dignity' is located.

[60] In *Applause Store*, n 27, above, the claimant was awarded £15,000 in damages for libel, but only £2,000 for 'misuse of private information', seemingly as the result of some overlap between the harm suffered to his/her reputational and privacy-related interests. Similarly, in *Mosley*, n 11, above, the claimant was awarded £50,000 for 'misuse of private information', well below the notional 'cap' on defamation damages of £200,000.

"my brain" as opposed to simply "me"). Coetzee suggests that the individual "... believe[s] there is some non-material, perhaps fictive, entity that stands in relation of possessor to possessed to the body's "parts" and even to the whole body."[61] Otherwise, he suggests, the existence of such locutions as "my leg", "my eye", "my brain" show us "... that language cannot get purchase, cannot get going, until it has split up the unity of experience."[62] We can perhaps use this to help us understand why it is difficult to separate out constituent aspects of the individual's *persönlichkeit* ("my privacy", as opposed to "my reputation"). The difficulty in separating out these aspects leads to a related difficulty in ascribing them a 'value' for the purpose of calculating an appropriate amount of compensation in monetary terms. Judges are also not aided by the relative scarcity of 'misuse of private information' cases to date, which provides a very limited range of guiding examples of damages awards.

So far, then, we have seen how 'misuse of private information' should be thought of as a *sui generis* constitutional tort – albeit one in disguise – rather than a tort in the traditional mould because of its roots in the HRA's direct horizontality. We have also seen that analysing its elements in the manner of a traditional tort leads to conceptual confusion; attempting to squeeze it into this body of private law encourages this confusion. Notwithstanding these issues, however, which set the new action apart from traditional torts, the essay now demonstrates that principles of corrective justice are nevertheless located within 'misuse of private information'.

3. 'Misuse of private information' may not be a tort, but it is nevertheless informed by principles of corrective justice

Given the substantial differences between traditional torts such as negligence and trespass and the new privacy action, a new methodology is clearly needed if principles of corrective justice are to find expression in privacy cases. That there is both a need for and an existence of a new methodology has been recognised judicially in recent years. For example, Eady J used what he called 'The New Methodology' as a subheading to structure his judgment in *Mosley* (and, in so doing, advanced the cause of corrective justice).[63] This new methodology, as outlined above, consists of flexible elements which, although ostensibly narrow in focus, are capable of mirroring the Strasbourg approach and, in particular, placing new focus on the Strasbourg principle of proportionality.[64]

---

[61] J.M. Coetzee, *Diary of a Bad Year*, (London: Harvill Secker, 2007) Pt. 1: ('Strong Opinions'), Ch.13: ('On the body').
[62] *Ibid*
[63] n 11, above, [7]
[64] See *Von Hannover v Germany* (2005) 40 EHRR 1 at [60]

The methodology associated with 'misuse of private information' typically involves conducting a balancing exercise between competing interests. Unlike torts in the traditional mould, in this cause of action the courts are dealing with competing substantive rights, rather than negative freedoms. This is a demanding task for the judges who undertake it, for two weighty interests are in play.

In 'misuse of private information', then, there is a particular problem presented for the judiciary in that the competing interests in play are (typically) the human right to privacy and the public interest in publication of the information.[65] In England, privacy is recognised as a fundamental right under Article 8 ECHR and has been 'brought home' by the HRA. When we ponder how this fundamental right can be linked to corrective justice, Eady J's methodology is worthy of consideration. For it sheds light on how principles of corrective justice might be translated from traditional torts to the new privacy action.

Eady J has talked, extra-judicially, of the uncertainties that such a balancing act produces.[66] He locates two uncertainties in this process, the first of which is inherent and which "[w]e can do nothing about ... ."[67] Eady J's first uncertainty comes from his recognition "... that individual judges are required to carry out a balancing exercise between competing Convention rights;" this being a feature of the 'new methodology'.[68] Moreover, Eady J states that "different persons may come up with different answers on the same set of facts."[69] The only principled way to deal with uncertainty, Eady J insists, is "by applying an 'intense focus' to the facts of the particular case."[70] This does not remove the uncertainty as to outcome, but does help to solve the second of his uncertainties: "uncertainty as to principles or rules of law."[71]

The 'intense focus' on the facts of the particular case is a key theme in the judgments of Eady J. It appears that for Eady J, 'applying an intense focus' means, quite simply, taking into account the widest possible range of relevant facts and factors when conducting a balancing act between the rights of the claimant and

[65] The impact upon the methodology of competing Article 8 and 10 interests is another issue – one which there is insufficient space in this essay to explore – but which does result in a different structure to the methodology. The requirement on judges to apply an 'intense focus' to the facts of the particular case, however, remains the same.
[66] Eady J, n 4, above, p.5
[67] *Ibid*
[68] *Ibid*
[69] *Ibid*, p.6
[70] *Ibid*
[71] *Ibid* p.5

countervailing public interest in revealing the information.[72] It is key to solving the second of Eady J's uncertainties that judges consistently engage in this 'intense focus'. Litigants have the assurance that judges will apply this fine-grained, situation-sensitive approach to the disputes that come before them.

It is clear that the judiciary, including Eady J, have some very strong views about which kinds of information can attract legitimate public interest, and which cannot. In *Mosley*, the sexual nature of the information (detailing the claimant's consensual sado-masochistic sexual activities with multiple partners) was held by Eady J to be incapable of being in the public interest. Eady J explains quite clearly how the new methodology is to be applied:

> In deciding whether a right has been infringed, and in assessing the relative worth of competing rights, it is not for judges to make individual moral judgments or to be swayed by personal distaste. It is not simply a matter of personal privacy versus the public interest. The modern perception is that there is a public interest in respecting personal privacy. It is thus a question of taking account of conflicting public interest considerations and evaluating them according to increasingly well recognised criteria.[73]

Eady J identifies only one way in which an infringement of a claimant's reasonable expectation of privacy may be legitimised: if the information is in the public interest. There are, he explains, two ways in which this might be the case:

> [Where it was] necessary and proportionate for the intrusion to take place, for example, in order to expose illegal activity or to prevent the public from being significantly misled by public claims hitherto made by the individual concerned ... [or where it was] necessary because the information, in the words of the Strasbourg court in *Von Hannover* at [60]

---

[72] The 'new methodology' in 'misuse of private information' bears considerable resemblance to the Australian High Court's 'salient features' test for establishing novel duties of care in negligence cases. This 'salient features' approach was developed as a tool to ensure incremental development of the Australian common law, and reflected a rejection of the tests in *Anns v Merton LBC* [1977] UKHL 4, and *Caparo Industries Ltd v Dickman* [1990] UKHL 2. The 'salient features' test is designed to be flexible, and involves the court undertaking "... a close analysis of the facts bearing on the relationship between the plaintiff and the ... tortfeasor", *Caltex Refineries (Qld) Pty Limited v Stavar* [2009] NSWCA 258, per Allsop P at [102]. The test has its roots in the case of *Graham Barclay Oysters Pty Ltd v Ryan* [2002] HCA 54, and contains a non-exhaustive list of 'salient features' which the court may take into account. These factors are set out usefully in *Caltex* at [103].

[73] n 11, above, [130]

> and [76], would make a contribution to "a debate of general interest" ... That is, of course, a very high test.[74]

The defendant had argued that a legitimate public interest in the information could be found on several grounds; including the assertion that the claimant was a public figure (and should thus be subject to greater scrutiny than non-public figures), the assertion that there was a Nazi theme to the activities (of which Eady J found no evidence), the assertion that there was some criminality to the activities (some of the claimant's partners apparently being prostitutes) and the assertion that the activities were 'depraved and adulterous'. Eady J rejected each of these arguments in strong terms:

> Obviously, titillation for its own sake could never be justified. Yet it is reasonable to suppose that it was this which led so many thousands of people to accept the *News of the World*'s invitation on 30 March to "See the shocking video at [their website] notw.co.uk". It would be quite unrealistic to think that these visits [to the website] were prompted by a desire to participate in a "debate of general interest" of the kind contemplated in *Von Hannover*.[75]

Extra-judicially, Eady J has repeated his assertion that information pertaining to an individual's sexual activities cannot engage the public interest, remarking that "...most privacy cases concern sexual shenanigans of one sort or another where there is no public interest argument available."[76]

While Eady J has plainly done much to map the legal terrain we are surveying, on one subject much more needs to be said: *viz*, the ideal of justice at work in this branch of the law. Eady J has made a number of observations that suggest that corrective justice is highly relevant to the law's operations. In *Mosley*, Eady J's most telling remark, for the purposes of identifying a commitment to principles of corrective justice may be his assertion that:

---

[74] n 11, above, [131]

[75] n 11, above, [132]. Though, of course, 'titillation for its own sake' has been meat and drink to the media (and in particular the tabloid press) for decades. See R. Wacks, *Privacy and Press Freedom*, (London: Blackstone Press, 1995) ch.1. See also A. McLean and C. Mackey, 'Mosley v News Group Newspapers Ltd: how sadomasochism changed the face of privacy law: a consideration of the Max Mosley case and other recent developments in privacy law in England and Wales', (2010) 32(2) *European Intellectual Property Review* 77.

[76] n 12, above, p.11

> When the courts identify an infringement of a person's Article 8 rights, and in particular in the context of his freedom to conduct his sex life and personal relationships as he wishes, it is right to afford a remedy and to vindicate that right.[77]

This statement makes plain Eady J's belief that the courts should fashion a methodology that enables claimants who have had their privacy infringed to obtain a remedy. Eady J explains that the purpose of the law is now to afford protection for the privacy of individuals, and goes so far as to defend pre-emptively such a stance against potential criticism:

> ... [T]he law is concerned to prevent the violation of a citizen's autonomy, dignity and self-esteem. It is not simply a matter of "unaccountable" judges running amok. Parliament enacted the 1998 statute [the Human Rights Act] which *requires* these values to be acknowledged and enforced by the courts.[78]

This remark also indicates Eady J's explicit acceptance of the fundamentally different type of 'damage' that the new privacy action is concerned to remedy: interferences with human dignity.[79]

The decision in *Mosley* might be contrasted with the decision in the more recent case of *The Author of a Blog v Times Newspapers.*[80] Eady J was asked to consider whether the anonymous author of an internet 'blog' was entitled to an injunction to prevent exposure of his identity. The defendant had, through thorough investigation, discovered the identity of the claimant. Moreover, he wished to expose him, since the material that the claimant had written on his 'blog' concerned the practices of the police and the administration of justice. This material was highly critical both of the police and of incumbent politicians. The claimant was in fact, at the time, a serving police officer.

In his response to this claim, Eady J devoted great attention to the issue of proportionality. However, his discussion was essentially academic, since he had already ruled that the claimant had no reasonable expectation of privacy over his identity, as "... blogging is essentially a public activity."[81] Presumably, if the

---

[77] n 11, above, [131]
[78] *Ibid*, [7]
[79] See P. O'Callaghan, n 35, above, for a discussion of the breadth of the *Von Hannover* ruling. See also D. Feldman, n 54, above.
[80] [2009] EWHC 1358 (QB)
[81] *Ibid* [11]

information is 'public', talk of (privacy-invading) wrongdoing makes no sense.[82] Nevertheless, the focus which Eady J again places on the nature of the information is key to understanding how the decision also fits into the framework of principles informed by corrective justice.

Eady J's view was that the information – the identity of the claimant – contributed to a 'debate of general public interest', such as to render its publication necessary and proportionate. Having stated in *Mosley* that this was a 'very high test', Eady J was clearly of the view that, in this case, it was satisfied. Whilst the claimant argued that all that the public needed to know in order to engage in a debate of general public interest was that he was a police officer, and that his name was therefore irrelevant to such a debate, Eady J rejected this:

> It is very often useful, in assessing the value of an opinion or argument, to know its source. As was pointed out, for example, by Lord Nicholls in *Reynolds v Times Newspapers Ltd* [2001] 2 A.C. 127 5 A–B, one may wish to apply greater caution or scepticism in the case of a person with "an axe to grind". For so long as there is anonymity, it would obviously be difficult to make any such assessment.[83]
>
> It seems to me that the public is entitled to know how police officers behave and the newspaper's readers would be entitled to come to their own conclusions about whether it is desirable for officers to communicate such matters publicly....[84]

Here, we may contrast Eady J's approach with that of a utilitarian. An approach of the latter sort would involve a balancing of socially desirable ends. In this case, a utilitarian approach would likely have seen the revelation of the claimant's identity in order to contribute to a debate of general public interest given automatic precedence over the rights of the individual claimant. Eady J noticeably does not do that. By 'intensely focusing' on the facts of the particular case, he ensures that a flexible mechanism is in place whereby claimants can be protected against violations of their dignity and autonomy. Moreover, he engages predictably in the same exercise of focus as he did in *Mosley*. It appears that his expectation is that through the use of the new methodology, such protection will become commonplace. Only in certain instances, where the countervailing interest in

[82] See generally B. Markesinis, n 2, above.
[83] *Ibid* [21]
[84] *Ibid* [29]

revealing the relevant information passes the 'very high test' of proportionality, will the claimant be unable to obtain redress.

This essay suggests that the 'intense focus' involved in weighing/balancing competing interests in the new privacy action might answer both O'Callaghan's and Alder's misgivings about using a balancing exercise to weigh 'incommensurable interests', which Alder argues (and O'Callaghan emphasises) is "inappropriate because there is no common scale against which the different components can be compared."[85] O'Callaghan emphasises this as part of his argument that human rights language is incapable of providing 'reasonable answers' to private law disputes.[86]

Whilst acknowledging that some uncertainty as to the outcome of any particular balancing act will always be inherent in the new methodology, uncertainty as to the types and number of factors that the courts will take into account when conducting the balancing exercise, and as to the structure that will be followed, ought to be removable.[87] Eady J's pursuance of a consistent methodology has aided in this. Clearly, there is some way still to go – especially given the potential which this essay identified earlier for the new action to be used in circumstances beyond simply the publication of private information. However, the foundations are now in place. Moreover, these foundations, it is suggested, can help to provide the 'reasonable answers' that O'Callaghan seeks. This is plain on a close examination of the judgments on which we have dwelt.

It is not, then, the particular outcome of any given case that is key to the locating of principles of corrective justice within Eady J's judgments (indeed, views on the particular outcomes of cases inevitably differ according to the commentator's own moral standpoint). Rather, it is the existence and ready identification of a principled methodology, capable of reflecting the Strasbourg court's commitment to taking individuals seriously, through according sufficient weight to the claimant's dignity and autonomy, that demonstrates that the new privacy action is indeed informed by principles of corrective justice.

4. Causation has a central place in the new cause of action

---

[85] P. O'Callaghan, n 20, above, citing J. Alder, 'Dissents in Courts of Last Resort: Tragic Choices?', (2000) 20 *Oxford Journal of Legal Studies* 221 at 222.

[86] P. O'Callaghan, n 20, above, section 6: ('The Strasbourg Enthusiasts - Monologism in Action?')

[87] It is worth noting that in the eight years since the inception of the Australian 'salient features' test, the 'uncertainty as to factors' has arguably been largely removed from the equation (see *Caltex Refineries*, n 72, above).

In 'The Canengusian Connection', the element of causation plays a key role in Wright J's methodology. As he states (when dealing with the negligence claim before him):

> The focus is rightly placed upon the activity rather than the defendant's conduct: the *what* happened is more important than the *how* or *why*. Within such a regime, causation becomes not *a* basis for liability but *the* basis. It is the fulcrum of liability.[88]

It is out of this that Wright J later moves on to a "rather breathless argument"[89] that strict liability is to be seen as superior to a scheme of fault-based liability.

Writing in 1996, at the time that he was a member of the Calcutt Committee, David Eady QC (as he then was) advocated the introduction of a statutory tort protecting privacy interests.[90] That, of course, never came about. In 1996, however, he suggested how a statutory tort might be formulated and, particularly notably, he suggested that such a tort should have a public interest defence in the *Reynolds* mould.[91] There should be a defence, he suggested, where the information complained of was published:

> (i) with the consent, general or specific, of the individual whose privacy was infringed; or
> (ii) in circumstances which would give rise to a defence of absolute or qualified privilege if the proceedings had been founded on the tort of defamation; or
> (iii) in circumstances in which the defendant, having exercised all reasonable care, did not know that his act would or might constitute an infringement of the plaintiff's privacy; or
> (iv) at a time when the personal information in question had already come into the public domain through no act or fault of the defendant; or
> (v) under lawful authority.[92]

---

[88] A.C. Hutchinson and D. Morgan, n 1, above, p.91
[89] R. Mullender, 'The Scampering Discourse of Negligence Law' (2010) 7 *J. Juris.* 575 ('Hutchinson and Morgan on Negligence Law').
[90] See D. Eady, n 30, above.
[91] See Lord Nicholls' 10 'factors' for the 'responsible journalism' test in defamation: *Reynolds v Times Newspapers* [2001] 2 AC 127 at 205.
[92] D. Eady, n 30, above, p.251

It is parts (ii) and (iii) that are of particular note. For they indicate that, in 1996, David Eady would have sanctioned the use of fault-based liability in a privacy-protecting action. Subsequently, following the 'elements' of 'misuse of private information' formulated in *Campbell* and later cases, Eady J has been unable to locate space for fault-based liability, though he does still take the opportunity to discuss the possibility of it in *Mosley*. Addressing the question of whether a *Reynolds*-style test could be incorporated into the proportionality aspect of 'misuse of private information', Eady J stated that:

> There may be a case for saying, when "public interest" has to be considered in the field of privacy, that a judge should enquire whether the relevant journalist's decision prior to publication was reached as a result of carrying out enquiries and checks consistent with "responsible journalism".[93]

Recognising, however, that there is a fundamental difference between 'misuse of private information' and defamation, as explored earlier in the essay, Eady J cites Lord Phillips MR in *Campbell* and makes clear that "… the same test of public interest should *not* be applied in the 'two very different torts'."[94] Ultimately, Eady J satisfies himself that the relevant authorities show that the "... public interest is to be determined solely by the court *ex post facto*", leaving no room for deference to the defendant's judgment.[95] Clearly, then, no element of fault can be said to exist within 'misuse of private information'. It may be that Eady J still harbours some misgivings about the new action being one of strict liability through his continued discussion of a *Reynolds*-style defence's appropriateness. It is suggested, however, that such a defence would actually be inconsistent with his otherwise clear commitment to a methodology reliant on causation.

It can thus be said that for Eady J, emphasis in the new privacy action is rightly placed on the cause of the interference with the claimant's right, not on the reasons for it. This restricts the opportunities for the defendant in any given case to avoid liability. Only if a public interest defence can be made-out can liability be avoided. This yields further evidence that corrective justice principles are at work within 'misuse of private information'.

One final, brief point should be made. That is that Eady J does make room in his judgments for the claimant to be found to have contributed to his own harm; that

[93] n 11, above, [141]
[94] *Campbell*, n 3, above, [61], cited in *Mosley* (n 11, above) at [141]
[95] *Mosley*, n 13, above, [171]

is, for him to be contributorily negligent. In *Mosley*, Eady J points out that the conduct of the claimant may impact upon the remedy he can obtain.[96] Similarly, in *The Author of a Blog*, whilst ruling on the 'reasonable expectation of privacy' test, rather than on contribution to the level of damage *per se*, Eady J was also clearly of the opinion that the claimant was the author of his own misfortune.[97] Rejecting any possibility of contributory negligence, as Wright J does, may be seen to be at the extreme end of a deep commitment to strict principles of corrective justice. However, Eady J, like the House of Lords in *Campbell*, clearly takes the view that claimants can be at least partly responsible for their own difficulties. This (like a number of other issues examined in this essay) is a matter on which debate seems set to continue.

Some concluding remarks

This essay has had two broad aims: firstly, to explain how the approach to corrective justice adopted by Hutchinson & Morgan's Wright J is relevant to debate in the UK on privacy; and, secondly, to stake out plausible positions in four areas of live controversy.

'The Canengusian Connection', upon which each of the pieces in this collection is based, gives us, through the judgment of Wright J, an indication of how negligence law can be said to be informed by corrective justice and an example of a methodology reflecting thus. It is hoped that this essay demonstrates how principles of corrective justice can also be said to inform 'misuse of private information', in spite of its awkward and uncomfortable position within English tort law.

It is also hoped that this essay can contribute to a reinvigorated debate on the horizontal effect of the Human Rights Act 1998. It has been ten years now since the HRA came into force. Speculative assertions about how it was *likely* to operate, and what horizontal effect it was *likely* to have, must now give way to detailed examinations of the *actual* results of its first decade in use. It is of vital importance that we find a way to understand the new privacy action properly, and that at some point its true boundaries become known. This essay has argued that the true potential breadth of 'misuse of private information' as a *sui generis* action is currently masked by its tort-like elements.

96 *Ibid* [225]

97 *The Author of a Blog*, n 80, above, [33]

The next stage in solving the second of Eady J's 'uncertainties' is to counter the confusion as to the scope of the new action. This, of course, will take time. It will require continued growth in the body of case law using the new action over the coming years, and it will require the judiciary to keep a sharp eye on developments in Strasbourg. Direct horizontality has come under constant attack since it was first mooted as a possibility for the HRA by the late Sir William Wade. In the context of the new privacy action, it has only existed in our legal system for six years. Rarely has anything so new been so vilified. The truth facing both Strasbourg-enthusiasts and common law traditionalists may be very simple indeed: that there is much about the potential reach of direct horizontality and the causes of action it results in that, as yet, we simply do not know.[98] We have not yet encountered its full

[98] As outlined in the introduction to this collection, and in the introduction to this essay, the argument advanced in this piece regarding the effect of the HRA on private law lends itself to a model whereby higher-order public law (in the form of the HRA) exerts a shaping force over lower-order private law and is, in that sense, directly effective (making lower-order private law 'subordinate' on O. Cherednychenko's model, see n 2, above). However, notwithstanding that the argument works on such a model, this author makes room for the possibility that the HRA might affect the traditional fields of public and private law still directly, but on a different model, which is now set out here by way of a very tentative analogy. The argument advanced in this essay may also be plausibly explained, it is equally tentatively suggested, by this new model.

This is the 'Operating System' model, and is based on trying to understand the use of legal tools by analogising them to a computer operating system (*viz* Windows). (The author has simplified some of the Windows terminology, for ease of reference.) It exists because of a concern that today, "public" and "private" law, as terms of art, are limiting. They do not lend themselves to helping to understand the impact that human rights principles have on the development of our common law.

Pre-HRA, the English legal system was running Windows *XP*. Private law actions are a particular file-type (".doc") which can be opened, created, modified and run by the Word2003 programme. Public law actions are the file-type (".xls"), which can be opened, created, modified and run by Excel2003. These 2003 programmes have certain rules, which make up the 'elements' of the actions. They also have certain features which are unique to each: .doc files have a wider range of fonts, while .xls files can be sorted more easily into a searchable format. Pre-HRA, the operating system only supported the opening and running of files of these types. .doc and .xls files were at that time the most advanced file-types available, and did everything that their users required.

When the HRA came into force, it forcibly upgraded the operating system to Windows *Vista*. New file-types were made available, because the new programme, Office2007, does not create .doc or .xls files. Instead, it creates ".docx" and ".xlsx" files. These resemble the older file types, but have a vastly enhanced range of (human rights) features. Windows *Vista* has opened up a range of new (human rights) features available to the courts. Not only *can* they be utilised, but they *must* be utilised, since the new features are built into the new programme, Office2007. Now, older file types can still be opened, run, and used by the new programme. In that sense, .doc and .xls files are obsolete, but far from useless. They are the remnants of an old system, but since they make up the majority of the files on the computer's hard disk, they cannot simply be erased. Nor can they be replaced one-by-one in a short space of time.

potential. And it may be that until we have, none of us is in a position either to glorify or to vilify it.

Any new files (causes of action) created, however, are in the new format. They are at least HRA-compatible. Some, where insufficient protection for human rights was in place, are designed specifically to take advantage of the new human rights features. 'Misuse of private information.docx' is one such new action. It could only have been created using Windows *Vista*'s Office2007 programme. In creating a new cause of action that features human rights methodology in the Strasbourg vein, enabling individuals to protect their human rights in a *sui generis* fashion, the HRA's impact can still properly be described as 'direct horizontal effect'.

So, with the new operating system in place, there is much more scope for new causes of action. Some of the 'new features' of .docx and .xlsx files are common to both. Describing the newly created causes of action in the old terms "public" and "private" law is both unhelpful and misleading; they are neither, because they are created by a different system where .doc and .xls files are *no longer the only available option*. Insofar as the old files can still be used, they rightfully retain their old classifications. New actions, however, must be called something new.

Now, whether we try to draw a distinction between .docx and .xlsx files is another question. Arguably, they now have such similar features, and are created by the homogenous Office2007 programme, and so should be thought of in the same bracket (".newx"). On the other hand, since they resemble some of the old-style files, perhaps we can continue to think of them as "private law plus" and "public law plus" (in the sense that they are 'plus' some human rights features).

Appendix A: Features of 'misuse of private information'

Figure 1: Original breadth[99]

This figure shows the breadth of the action for 'misuse of private information' as it was when it first appeared in the common law in *Campbell v MGN Ltd* [2004] 2 AC 457.

Elements:

1) Reasonable expectation of privacy:
- Details of treatment, pictures of claimant leaving Narcotics Anonymous.
- No reasonable expectation of privacy regarding the fact of C's addiction.

2) Misuse:
- Publication in the defendant newspaper.

3) Public interest defence:
- No public interest in information outside of issues about which the claimant had previously made inaccurate statements.

[99] It may be said that the tripartite structure in this Figure maps neatly onto the schematic account of 'incrementalism' in R. Mullender, 'Negligence Law as a Human Practice', (2003) *Law and Literature* 21(3) 321.

Figure 2: Subsequently evidenced breadth

This figure shows the breadth of 'misuse of private information' as demonstrated by some of the cases in which it has been used since *Campbell.*

Elements:

1) Reasonable expectation of privacy:
- Photographs of child in public with parents (*Murray v Big Pictures* [2008] EWCA Civ 446);
- Various details as to personal relationships of Canadian folk singer (*McKennitt v Ash* [2006] EWCA Civ 1714);
- Details, pictures and video footage of sexual acts (*Mosley v NGN* [2008] EWHC 1777 (QB));
- Information as to date of birth and religious views (*Applause Store Productions v Raphael* [2008] EWHC 1781 (QB)).

2) Misuse:
- Publication in national newspapers (*Mosley*);
- Publication in book (*McKennitt*);
- Retention by photographer/holding company (*Murray*);
- Publication on social networking website with limited access to page containing material (*Applause Store*).

3) Public interest defence:
- No public interest in sexual matters (*Mosley*);
- No public interest in date of birth/religious views of claimant (*Applause Store*);
- Some public interest in identity of claimant if information contributes to a debate of general public interest (*The Author of a Blog v Times Newspapers* [2009] EWHC 1358 (QB)).

Figure 3: Potential breadth

This figure demonstrates the potential breadth of 'misuse of private information' if, as argued in the essay, the labels attached to its 'elements' are mere disguises. It should be noted that, as demonstrated by a number of ECtHR decisions, there may not always be a clear-cut distinction between the 'engagement' and 'interference' elements, *i.e.* the interference may itself engage Article 8 (thus appearing to 'skip over' the 'engagement' element – highlighting the inadequacy of analysing the new privacy action by reference to traditional 'elements').

Elements:

1) Reasonable expectation of privacy (re-labelled 'engagement of Article 8 rights')
The following may engage Article 8 (non-exhaustive list):

- Private information, including: sexual information, date of birth, religious views (as in Figure 2), pictures of the individual (*Reklos and Davourlis v Greece* [2009] EMLR 16);
- Reputational interests (*Pfeifer v Austria* (2009) 48 EHRR 8);
- Non-defamatory, false information (currently actionable under 'malicious falsehood);
- Emotional distress (identified in *R (on the application of Watkins-Singh) v Aberdare Girls' High School Governors* [2008] EWHC 1865 (Admin) at [137] (an application for judicial review) as potentially lying within the ambit of Article 8);
- Bodily integrity (*Wainwright v UK* [2004] 2 AC 406).

2) Misuse (re-labelled 'interference')

- Publication of information;
- Covert obtaining of information;
- Physical interferences with the individual (*Wainwright v UK*);
- Physical intrusions into the private sphere of the individual, *i.e.* into the home, or the personal space of the individual when outside the home;
- Retention of information (*S and Marper v UK* (2009) 48 EHRR 50; *Murray*);
- Coercing the individual into revealing private information;
- Coercing the individual into doing (or not doing) anything* (*Wainwright v UK*);
- Harming the individual's reputation;
- Causing emotional distress.

3) Public interest defence/defence of proportionality**

- Any interference must be justified either proportionately in the public interest or, if the defendant's own Convention rights are in play, as part of a balancing exercise using the proportionality doctrine

* It may be said that the mere act of coercing a person into doing or not doing something that he/she would normally do/not do may constitute an interference. However, in many of these instances, the interference is likely to be proportionate and thus not unlawful.

** There will be instances where certain of the 'interferences' involve the defendant exercising his/her own Convention right, since publication is (on this model) not the only type of possible 'interference'. In such instances, the proportionality defence becomes a balancing exercise between the competing rights which, at that point, are

THE SCAMPERING DISCOURSE OF NEGLIGENCE LAW

Richard Mullender*

'[W]e must … discover the law operating behind all these diverse statements, and the place from which they come'.[1]

1 Introduction

In 'The Canengusian Connection: the Kaleidoscope of Tort Theory', Allan Hutchinson and Derek Morgan describe a set of facts that provide the basis of a negligence claim on the 'small, little known island' of Canengus.[2] Canengus is a common law jurisdiction in which judges base their decisions on Canadian, English, US, and other (*e.g.*, Australian) authorities. The facts described by Hutchinson and Morgan provide the basis of claims that raise matters of 'sensitive and heated' legal debate.[3] Among other things, they include the scope of liability rules allowing claimants to recover in negligence for psychiatric injury and the question as to whether the law's addressees should be under a duty to rescue others. Hutchinson and Morgan do not respond to these matters directly. Rather, they present their readers with the judgments rendered by the five judges who decided the case in the Canengus Court of Appeal. Each of these responses gives expression to the doctrinal and/or theoretical assumptions that inform the thinking of its (judicial) author.

'The Canengusian Connection' helps us to understand why those seeking to make sense of negligence law run the risk of disorientation. Anyone unfamiliar with this branch of tort may conclude that they are stumbling across a battlefield.[4] For the disputatious, disorderly discourse they find

* Newcastle Law School, University of Newcastle upon Tyne. I owe thanks to John Alder, Sheila Dziobon, Andrew Halpin, Emilia Mickiewicz, Patrick, O'Callaghan, Ole Pedersen, David Raw, Man Chun Siu, and Ashley Wilton for their comments on earlier drafts of this essay.

[1] M. Foucault *The Archaeology of Knowledge* (Abingdon: Routledge, 2002), 55.

[2] A.C. Hutchinson and D. Morgan, 'The Canengusian Connection: The Kaleidoscope of Tort Theory' (1984) 22 *Osgoode Hall Law Review* 69, 74.

[3] *Ibid*, 73. (The fictive presentational strategy used by Hutchinson and Morgan bears obvious similarities to that employed in L. Fuller, 'The Case of the Speluncean Explorers' (1949) 62 *Harvard LR* 616.)

[4] See A.C. Hutchinson and D. Morgan, 'Shock Therapy: Policy, Principle and Tort' (1982) 45 *Modern LR* 693, 693 (describing tort law as 'a battleground of social theory'). *Cf* N.J. McBride and R. Bagshaw, *Tort Law* (Harlow: Pearson, 2008, 3rd edn), xiii-xvii (on '[t]he tort wars'). (Hutchinson has recently stated that 'the common law has and continues to impose a duty on its personnel to respect the [doctrinal-cum- institutional] past … by

themselves contemplating exhibits a murkiness that calls to mind the fog of war. Some judges declare that the ideal of corrective justice is central to negligence law's operations.[5] But others identify broad notions like policy and the public interest as shaping doctrine on, *inter alia*, duty of care and remoteness.[6] Those who confront such divergent opinions may turn to academic commentators for guidance. But when they do so, they find that their difficulties grow. This may be because some academics make particularly strong (or sweeping) claims concerning the law. For example, Ernest Weinrib and others who follow his lead argue that negligence law is exclusively concerned with righting wrongfully inflicted harms and that judges should, on all occasions, be 'agents' of corrective justice.[7] Richard Posner flatly contradicts this account of negligence law by identifying it as a branch of tort informed by a commitment to the pursuit of efficiency.[8]

Talk of a 'battlefield' and 'the fog of war' captures something important about 'The Canengusian Connection' and the body of law on which it dwells. Hutchinson and Morgan identify negligence law as a site of conflict concerning, *inter alia*, the purposes that find expression in existing doctrine. However, they do much more than this. And, in order to press the analysis of their essay, negligence doctrine, and associated comment further, this essay explores the possibility that they have thrown light on a scampering discourse. We owe the idea of a 'scampering' discourse not to a judge or an academic lawyer but to an eighteenth century clergyman and novelist, Laurence Sterne, the author of *Tristram Shandy*. By a scampering discourse he means, among other things, an exchange of views that does not move doggedly in a single direction but that heads one way and then another and at a speed that is at times dizzying. The leap from *Tristram Shandy* to the law of negligence may seem large – not least because Sterne exhibits very limited interest in law. But against this we must set the fact that he has much to say

revolutionizing it in continuing acts of transformation'. See A.C. Hutchinson, *Is Eating People Wrong? Great Legal Cases and How They Changed the World* (New York: Cambridge University Press, 2010), 220. This emphasis on 'duty' points up a constraint on the way in which legal disputes may be conducted that talk of a 'battleground' tends to obscure. However, Hutchinson and Morgan continue to place emphasis on 'conflict' in tort law. See their critique of Cass Sunstein's notion of 'incompletely theorized agreements' in A.C. Hutchinson and D. Morgan, 'A Final Letter' [2007] 7 *The Journal Jurisprudence*.)

5 See, for example, *X v Bedfordshire County Council* 1995] 2 AC 633, 663, *per* Lord Browne-Wilkinson.

6 See *Dorset Yacht Co Ltd v Home Office* [1970] AC 1004, 1039, *per* Lord Diplock. See also J. Bell, *Policy Arguments in Judicial Decisions* (Oxford: Clarendon Press, 1983), 43-46.

7 E.J. Weinrib, *The Idea of Private Law* (Harvard University Press, Cambridge, Massachusetts, 1995), 65 (identifying judges as agents of corrective justice). See also A. Beever, *Rediscovering Negligence Law* (Oxford: Hart Publishing, 2009), 63-66.

8 R.A. Posner, *Economic Analysis of Law* (Austin Texas: Wolters Kluwer, 2007, 7th edn), 67-71.

on the deficiencies of discourse and those who participate in it. Moreover, Sterne's reflections have, as we will see, great relevance to negligence law and tort more generally.

While Sterne will bulk large in this essay, he is not the only thinker on whom we will draw in our efforts to make sense of negligence law and the discourse it has spawned. Sterne's account of a scampering discourse, while suggestive, lacks analytic rigour. The writings of two further thinkers will help us to make good this deficiency. They are the Russian literary theorist Mikhail Bakhtin and the French philosopher Michel Foucault. But before drawing on these sources of guidance, we must look closely at 'The Canungusian Connection'.

2 Hutchinson and Morgan on Negligence Law

The judgments in 'The Canengusian Connection' present us, in each case, with a standpoint or perspective that is ideal-typical.[9] For they exaggerate certain features that we might find in the responses made by common law judges to negligence claims.[10] Thus the first judge to whom Hutchinson and Morgan introduce us, Doctrin CJ, places emphasis on existing doctrine as a source of authoritative and determinate reasons for judicial action. As she unfolds this doctrine-bound account of the law, we catch an echo of formalism (or Legal Science) on the model propounded by Christopher Columbus Langdell at Harvard Law School in the nineteenth century. Langdell identified law as 'consist[ing] of certain principles and doctrines'.[11] He also argued that those with 'mastery' of these materials could 'apply them

[9] On ideal types, see P. Worsley, ed, *Introducing Sociology* (Harmondsworth, Penguin Books, 1977, 2nd edn), 336.

[10] To the extent that the judgments in 'The Canegusian Connection' throw light on their judicial authors, Hutchinson and Morgan adopt an approach to character that is reminiscent of Charles Dickens. This is because Dickens would often seek to convey a sense of character by reference to a limited number of salient features (with the result that his readers would find themselves confronted not by complex many-sided people but, rather, by grotesques). Hutchinson and Morgan go about their business in this way by identifying each of their judges as keen to pursue a limited number of themes. In a further respect, Hutchinson and Morgan adopt a Dickensian approach to their judicial characters. For they (like Dickens) employ the device of aptronymy (the use of names that capture the interests and/or personality (or, at least, disposition) of a character). On Dickens' approach to character, see T. Eagelton, *The English Novel: An Introduction* (Oxford: Blackwell, 2005), 149. On aptronymy, see J.A. Cuddon, *A Dictionary of Literary Terms* (Harmondsworth: Penguin Books, 1979, revd edn), 53.

[11] C.C. Langdell, *A Selection of Cases on the Law of Contracts* (Little Brown & Co, Boston, Massachusetts, 1871), viii.

with *constant facility* and *certainty* to the ever-tangled skein of human affairs'.[12] This is the view that Doctrin CJ appears to take. Certainly, she applies existing law to the case before her. And, by going about her business in this way, she expresses her commitment to the view that 'it is with matters of certainty that ... courts ... deal'.[13]

As well as assuming that judges are able to subsume the facts of meritorious claims under the existing law, Doctrin CJ finds support for her approach in a simplistic account of the separation of powers. She tells us that the legislature has the job of making law while 'the judiciary has the task of interpreting, applying and dispensing this received wisdom'.[14] Doctrin CJ's thinking thus intersects with that Sir Owen Dixon CJ who declared that 'there is no other safe guide to judicial decisions ... than a strict and complete legalism'.[15] Quite how we are supposed to reconcile this account of the judicial role with the judge-made common law is not something Doctrin CJ troubles to explain. But later in her judgment, we find the basis on which she seeks to defend the adoption of this incoherent position. She declares that 'it is incumbent on [judges] to resolve the issues presented [to them] in accordance with the law as it is'.[16] Thus Hutchinson and Morgan present us with a judge who (against all the evidence to the contrary) disavows a law-making role.

These features of Doctrin CJ's judgment lead the judge who follows her, Mill J, to describe her as an 'unthinking formalist' who offers an account of 'thejudicial role' that is 'confused, schizophrenic, and altogether too restricted'.[17] He criticizes Doctrin CJ for, *inter alia*, downplaying the extent to which considerations of policy inform her response to negligence claims.[18] Mill J finds support in a judgment of Lord Denning MR for the proposition that 'policy and not logic' has shaped the 'intricate doctrinal edifice' of

---

12 *Ibid.* (emphasis added). (For further discussion of Langdell's views and their relevance to negligence and tort more generally, see G. Edward White, *Tort Law in America: An Intellectual History* (New York: Oxford University Press, 2003), 26, *et seq.*)

13 A.C. Hutchinson and D. Morgan, n 2, above, , 74.

14 *Ibid*, 71.

15 *Swearing in of Sir Owen Dixon as Chief Justice* (1952) 85 C.L.R. xi, at xiv. See also J. Gava, 'Dixonian Strict Legalism, *Wilson v Darling Island Stevedoring* and Contracting in the Real World' (2010) 30 *OJLS* 519, 543 (arguing that, while 'judges *can* act as strict legalists', this 'does not prove that they *should* decide [cases] in this manner'). *Cf* J.N. Shklar, *Legalism, Law, Morals, and Political Trials* (Cambridge, Massachusetts: Harvard University Press, 1986), (describing 'legalism' as an 'ethical attitude that holds moral conduct to be a matter of rule-following').

16 A.C. Hutchinson and D. Morgan, n 2, above, 71.

17 *Ibid* 76 and 82.

18 *Ibid*, 76-77.

negligence law.[19] For, in *Home Office v Dorset Yacht Co Ltd*, Lord Denning stated that adjudication in negligence law is 'at bottom' not a matter of doctrine, but, rather, one of 'public policy'.[20]

Lord Denning treated 'public policy' as a commodious notion (embracing *inter alia*, loss insurance as a consideration relevant to the law's operations).[21] Mill J's focus is, however, narrower. He states that the 'central' purpose of negligence law is to promote the efficient allocation of resources.[22] This leads him to argue that judges should 'design rules of liability which will provide a sufficient incentive to achieve an efficient level of safety'.[23] Moreover, he identifies 'an algorithm for all negligence law' as providing judges with a means by which to undertake this task.[24] This is the 'formula' set out by Learned Hand J in *US v Carroll Towing*.[25] The formula tells us that three variables provide judges with a basis on which to pursue efficiency when determining duty of care questions. These variables are the burden of adequate precautions, the gravity of the harm suffered by the claimant, and the probability of harm. Hand J argued that where the cost of taking care is less than the gravity of harm multiplied by the probability of harm, we have an efficiency-based ground for the imposition of liability.[26] By endorsing this approach, Mill J makes it plain that consequentialist moral philosophy informs his thinking. This is the view that the value of an action derives from the outcomes (good or ill) that it produces.[27]

While Mill J finds in the language of costs and benefits a basis on which to capture negligence law's 'central' purpose, the judge who follows him uses an altogether different vocabulary. Wright J tells us that '[i]ndividuals deserve and merit respect'.[28] He adds that we show them respect when we

---

[19] *Ibid*, 77.

[20] *Home Office v Dorset Yacht Co Ltd* [1969] 2 QB 412, 426, *per* Lord Denning MR (where he also observed that 'talk of "duty" or "no duty" is simply a way of limiting the range of liability for negligence').

[21] *Lamb v Camden LBC* [1981] 1 QB 625, 637-638, *per* Lord Denning MR.

[22] A.C. Hutchinson and D. Morgan, n 2, above, 81.

[23] *Ibid,* 81.

[24] *Ibid*, 82.

[25] *US v Carroll Towing* 159 F 2d 169 (1947).

[26] *Ibid*, 173-174. (Hand J represented his algorithm (or formula) thus: where $B < PxL$, an efficiency-based ground for imposing liability exists. 'B' stands for the cost of taking care, while 'P' (the probability of harm) x 'L' (the gravity of harm) yields the expected harm.) See also A.C. Hutchinson and D. Morgan, n 2, above, 82-83.

[27] On consequentialism, see S. Blackburn, *The Oxford Dictionary of Philosophy* (Oxford: Oxford University Press, 1994), 77.

[28] A.C. Hutchinson and D. Morgan, n 2, above, 90.

vindicate their rights.[29] Moreover, he states that '[a] deep sense of … rights pervades the common law [including negligence]'.[30] On Wright J's account, this commitment to rights finds expression in the view that '[r]ights are trumps over social utility'.[31] Wright J finds support for this claim in Lord Scarman's speech in *McLoughlin v O'Brian.*[32] In this speech, Lord Scarman staked out a position on negligence law that has much in common with that of the Canadian tort scholar Ernest Weinrib. He stated that 'the objective of the judges is the formulation of principle'.[33] By this he meant that judges should fashion doctrines that focus on the relationship between the parties to a claim and that enable them (and the victims of wrongfully inflicted harm) to pursue corrective justice.[34] Lord Scarman's commitment to corrective justice appears to be (like that of Weinrib) unswerving. For he declares that, if the pursuit of principle yields socially unacceptable results, it is the task of the legislature to 'draw a line or map out a new path'.[35]

The features of Wright J's judgment that we have noted provide a basis on which to pin down the moral philosophy that informs his thinking. When Wright J tells us that people deserve and merit respect, he appears to ascribe intrinsic value to them. And when he declares that judges should always base their decisions on principle regardless of the consequences, he seems to assume that principled decision-making is the intrinsically right thing to do. Those who make ascriptions of intrinsic value and assume that we should always do the intrinsically right thing are deontologists.[36] Deontological moral philosophy stands in an irreducibly conflictual relationship with

---

[29] *Ibid*, 90.

[30] *Ibid.*

[31] *Ibid.* (The inspiration for this strand of Wright J's thinking is the account of rights as trumps over utility in R. Dworkin, 'Rights as Trumps', in J. Waldron, ed, *Theories of Rights* (Oxford: Oxford University Press, 1984), ch 7, and R. Dworkin, *Taking Rights Seriously* (London: Duckworth, 1977), 199-200.)

[32] *McLoughlin v O'Brian* [1983] 1 AC 410.

[33] *Ibid*, 430

[34] See E.J. Weinrib, 'Legal Formalism: On the Immanent Rationality of the Law (1988) 97 *Yale LJ* 949, 969.

[35] A.C. Hutchinson and D. Morgan, n 2, above, 90. *Cf White v Chief Constable of the South Yorkshire Police* [1999] 2 AC 455, 500, *per* Lord Steyn (stating that he could see no 'coherent and morally defensible' basis on which to develop (pure) psychiatric injury-focused negligence doctrine and that the judiciary should bluntly declare 'thus far and no further' – thereby leaving Parliament 'to undertake the task of radical law reform' (if disposed to do so)).

[36] See S. Blackburn, n 27, above, 100, and T. Honderich, ed, *The Oxford Companion to Philosophy* (Oxford University Press, Oxford, 1995), 187-188.

consequentialism.[37] In presenting us with a judge who shows every sign of embracing deontology in this unqualified form and setting him alongside a judge who is committed to consequentialism, Hutchinson and Morgan focus our attention on an acute source of tension in negligence law (and tort more generally).[38]

But while Wright J has firm views on the moral impulses that inform negligence law, it is not his only concern. As his judgment moves towards its conclusion, he mounts a hobby-horse that does not have direct relevance to the claim with which he is dealing. He identifies fault-based liability as inferior to a regime of strict liability and offers a rather breathless argument in support of this view. Strict liability, he tells us, is less costly than negligence law to administer and better protects our liberty and rights.[39] It also recognises that "'*what* happened" [to the plaintiff] is more important than "the *how* or *why*"'.[40]

Like Wright J, the judge who follows him, Prudential J, pursues a clear (and very different) theme. For we find Prudential J declaring, in the first paragraph of his judgment, that '[i]t is the plight of the injured plaintiff and not the conduct of defendants that deserves our attention'.[41] He develops this theme by arguing that Canengus can only respond adequately to the 'plight' of accident victims by pursuing the ideal of 'social justice' rather than corrective justice.[42] To this end, he argues that it is necessary to abandon negligence law and replace it with a scheme of no-fault compensation.[43] He takes this view since Canengusians benefit from the use of modern technology.[44] While this technology serves the end of 'collective progress', a subset of individuals inevitably suffer harm due to the risks it generates.[45]

---

[37] T. Nagel, *Mortal Questions* (New York: Cambridge University Press, 1979), 129. See also J.N. Adams and R. Brownsword, *Understanding Law* (London: Sweet & Maxwell, 2006, 4th edn), 36-37.

[38] The source of tension referred to in the text is present in, for example, general duty of care tests that are receptive to both deontological (corrective justice-related) and consequentialist (policy-based) arguments. See R. Mullender, 'Negligence, The Public Interest and the Proportionality Principle' (1997) 5 *Tort Law Review* 9, 10-11.

[39] A.C. Hutchinson and D. Morgan, n 2, above, 92-93. The emphasis placed on liberty by Wright J means that his argument for strict liability bears some similarity to that in R. Epstein, *A Theory of Strict Liability* (Cato Institute, San Francisco, 1980). However, Wright J's emphasis on rights may mark a point of departure from Epstein's argument. See N.E. Simmonds, 'Epstein's Theory of Strict Tort Liability' (1992) 51 *Cambridge LJ* 113, 131.

[40] A.C. Hutchinson and D. Morgan, n 2, above, 91.

[41] *Ibid*, 94.

[42] *Ibid*, 94-95.

[43] *Ibid*, 98.

[44] *Ibid*, 96-97.

[45] *Ibid*, 96-97.

For this reason, Canegusians should, on Prudential J's analysis, be ready to spread the costs of these accidents across the whole of society.[46] They should most definitely not persist with fault-based accident-compensation. For such a system is a 'litigation lottery' in which deserving claimants sometimes receive nothing from defendants.[47] Instead, they should fashion a no-fault alternative on the comprehensive New Zealand model.[48]

The judge who follows Prudential J, Lefft J, does not make a conventional doctrinal response to the claim before him. Instead, he proposes a departure from existing institutional arrangements. But before outlining his preferred approach, he sounds a dramatic note by declaring that he is rendering the last judgment of his career.[49] This, he adds is because the existing law, [f]ar from being a vehicle for social justice, ... represents a formidable barrier to significant social change'.[50] Thus it comes as no surprise to find Lefft J mounting an extended assault on negligence doctrine. He describes it as 'a major force in creating, sustaining and justifying our social situation'.[51] This is because it forms part of an institutional superstructure that 'persuades us that contemporary life is almost rational and just'.[52] Moreover, Canengus's economic substructure (which serves the interests of a minority rather than all the law's addressees) determines the shape of this superstructure.[53] Having subjected the law to these criticisms, Lefft J goes on to attack the judiciary. He describes them as 'hold[ing] in place the deep structure of society' by offering in their judgments

46 *Ibid*, 98.

47 *Ibid*, 96-97.

48 *Ibid*, 102-103. (The ideal of 'community responsibility' informs the set of recommendations that prompted the New Zealand government to establish a comprehensive no-fault compensation scheme. See New Zealand Royal Commission of Inquiry into Compensation for Personal Injury, *Compensation for Personal Injury in New Zealand: Report of the Royal Commission of Inquiry* (Wellington, New Zealand: Government Printer, 1967) ('The Woodhouse Report'), para 55. See also G. Palmer, *Compensation for Incapacity: A Study of Law and Social Change in New Zealand and Australia* (Wellington, New Zealand: Oxford University Press, 1979), 81 (noting that E.E. Isbey (a Labour MP and former trade union secretary) understood 'community responsibility' to mean 'democratic socialism'), and G. Palmer, 'The Future of Community Responsibility' (2004) 35 *Victoria University of Wellington LR* 41.)

49 A.C. Hutchinson and D. Morgan, n 2 above, 104.

50 *Ibid*, 105.

51 *Ibid*, 104.

52 *Ibid*, 105. (This strand of Lefft J's critique has featured in Hutchinson's later writings. See for example, A.C. Hutchinson, 'Les Misérables Redux: Law and the Poor' (1993) 2 *Southern California Interdisciplinary Law Journal* 199, 243.)

53 A.C. Hutchinson and D. Morgan, n 2, above, 105.

'rationalisations of our ideological prejudices'.[54] In making these points, Lefft J's purpose is to debunk negligence law's claims to be 'neutral' as between those who are affected by its operations.[55]

Having identified negligence law as a site of intense political conflict, Lefft J offers us a 'vision' that he regards as 'substantive and just'.[56] He argues that Canengusians should democratise and equalise the risks that are a necessary feature of life in an industrial society.[57] He finds a basis on which to do this in the existing but 'artificially confined' doctrine of informed consent.[58] On Lefft J's analysis, this doctrine provides guidance on the question as to how Canengusians should respond to the risks that pervade their environment. For informed consent is '[f]ounded on the need to promote individual autonomy and to encourage rational decision-making'.[59] As a springboard for social transformation this is suggestive, but it is hardly a vision.[60]

---

[54] *Ibid*, 104-105. (Lefft J's critique appears to be Marxian in thrust since it focuses on the influence exerted by a ruling elite (or class) whose economic power shapes legal and political institutions in ways that serve their interests. See K. Marx, *The German Ideology* (New York: International Publishers, 1947, R. Pascal, ed), 39 (arguing that '[t]he ideas of the ruling class are in every epoch the ruling ideas'), and H. Collins, *Marxism and Law* (Oxford University Press, Oxford, 1982), chs 3 and 4. See also M. Moran, *Rethinking the Reasonable Person: An Egalitarian Reconstruction of the Reasonable Person* (Oxford University Press, Oxford, 2003), 136-137, 256, and 275 (on judicial rationalizations of negligence law's power-laden 'dark side'). Alternatively, we might interpret Lefft J's judgment as Foucauldian in character. For Foucault identifies law as an ideology (or set of 'false universals') masquerading as a neutral institution. On Michel Foucault's account of 'false universals', see L. Downing, *The Cambridge Introduction to Michel Foucault* (Cambridge: Cambridge University Press, 2008), 13. Informing the views of both Marx and Foucault is a theme pursued by Thrasymachus in Plato's *Republic*: '"right" is always the same, the interest of the stronger party'. See Plato, *The Republic* (Harmondsworth: Penguin Books, 1974, 2nd edn), I, 339a.)

[55] A.C. Hutchinson and D. Morgan, n 2, above, 105.

[56] *Ibid,* 109.

[57] *Ibid*, 108-109.

[58] *Ibid*, 110.

[59] *Ibid.*

[60] We might describe 'vision' as 'the ability to see the invisible'. See R.M. Unger, *False Necessity: Anti-Necessesitarian Social Theory in the Service of Radical Democracy* (New York: Cambridge University Press, 1987), 576. However, the suggestion that we apply an existing doctrine (informed consent) more broadly so as to advance the agenda of egalitarian risk-management does not constitute a detailed blueprint for social transformation. . Hence we have grounds for refusing to accept that it adds up to a 'substantive and just' vision. (Lefft J's enthusiasm for the informed consent doctrine is perhaps surprising in one who prides himself on his understanding of the forces that shape negligence law's development. For American judges integrated this doctrine into this branch of tort with the aim of restricting the liability exposure of physicians (who, previously, had faced a mounting number of battery claims on account of their failure to

While the fictive judges described by Hutchinson and Morgan stake out distinctive positions, there are occasions where some of them think along broadly similar lines. For example, Doctrin CJ and Mill J are, on one point, in agreement with one another. They each think that judges must (as Mill J puts the point) 'be careful not to encourage or facilitate bogus claims'.[61] But while they agree on this point, Hutchinson and Morgan indicate that this subject exercises Doctrin CJ more than her colleague. For she finds support in *Huston v Borough of Fremanburg* for the proposition that claims of the sort that concern her are a 'great danger, if not disaster to the cause of practical justice'.[62] Thus, even where two of their judges agree in broad terms with one another, Hutchinson and Morgan continue to emphasise the diversity of judicial views on display in negligence law. While they clearly have grounds for doing so, there are reasons (explored in section 6, below) for thinking that they could have placed more emphasis on the extent to which judges agree with one another.

Aside from the doctrinal realities of negligence law, we might also explain the emphasis on disagreement in 'The Canegusian Connection' by reference to the body of theoretical (or philosophical) thought that informs the authors' thinking. Hutchinson and Morgan were, at the time they wrote this essay, members of the Critical Legal Studies movement and offer an analysis that gives expression to some of its more prominent themes. Among these themes we may number the indeterminacy of legal language, the presence in the law of contradictions, and the political role played by legal doctrines in sustaining particular models of human association.[63] But alongside these strands of Critical Legal thought, we should set a further theme. This is negligence law's human dimension. Hutchinson and Morgan present us with five judgments that tell us much about their authors. Doctrin CJ finds a role in the existing law (defender of the *status quo*). Mill and Wright JJ find eligible ideals within the case law they survey (the pursuit of efficiency (Mill J) and giving individuals their right-based due (Wright J)). In pursuing these ideals, each judge confers on him- or herself a particular role in the law's operations. Mill J presents himself as a hard-bitten realist, ready to sweep

secure 'informed consent'). Battery, rather than negligence, provided the context in which the doctrine of informed consent made its first appearance in American (Californian) tort law. See I. Englard, *The Philosophy of Tort Law* (Aldershot: Dartmouth Publishing, 1993), 162-163.)

61 A.C. Hutchinson and D. Morgan, n 2, above, 86, *per* Mill J. See also 74, *per* Doctrin CJ.

62 *Ibid* (citing *Huston v Borough of Fremanburg* 61 A 1022, 1023 (1905), *per* Mitchell CJ).

63 See, M. Kelman, *A Guide to the Critical Legal Studies Movement* (Cambridge, Massachusetts, Harvard University Press, 1987), and M. Duxbury, *Patterns of American Jurisprudence* (Clarendon Press, Oxford, 1995), ch 6. See also A.C. Hutchinson and D. Morgan, n 4, above, on 'the implied vision', in 'The Canengusian Connection', 'judges as moral and political activists'.

away the illusions that blind his colleagues to economic reality. Wright J, by contrast, assumes the role of a crusader for justice. Hutchinson and Morgan thus succeed in presenting negligence law as 'a theatre of roles': a context within which those concerned with the law's operations are able to present themselves as having a particular character.[64] While both Prudential J and Lefft JJ argue for the abandonment of negligence law, each emerges as a distinct contributor to the debate in which they are participating (the first a sober reformer, the second a more radical thinker). This emphasis on the human dimension of adjudication certainly seems warranted when we examine the significantly different approaches adopted by the judges who have shaped negligence doctrine. Moreover, the association between individual make-up and the way in which a person thinks and approaches practical questions provides one of many points of intersection between 'The Canegusian Connection' and Laurence Sterne's *Tristram Shandy*.

3 *Tristram Shandy*

At first blush, *Tristram Shandy* might appear to contain little that is relevant to negligence law. The novel is supposed to be Shandy's account of his life-story. But he undercuts his efforts to unfold a narrative by recording in fine-grained detail the circumstances he describes. As a result, the novel takes on the appearance of a practical joke. For it becomes an account of Shandy's efforts to get the novel started.[65] But while Shandy fails to chart his progress through life, he offers a detailed account of those closest to him. Most prominent among them are his father, Walter Shandy, and his uncle Toby. He also introduces us to a number of supporting characters (who engage in dialogue with Walter and Toby in Shandy Hall). They include his uncle's servant, Trim, Doctor Slop (the physician who superintended Shandy's birth), and a clergyman, Yorick. These characters are, for Shandy, a spur to reflection and, while he fails to tell us much about his 'life', he offers us a great many of his (and their) 'opinions'.

In the course of presenting us with these opinions, Sterne pursues two themes that (as we will see later) have relevance to negligence law. He uses his characters to point up the limitations of dialogue. On Sterne's account, dialogue is typically a haphazard process that usually tells us more about the idiosyncrasies of those who participate in it than it does about the topics on which they hold forth. In light of these points he pursues the more general theme that humans are ill-suited to engage in critical (or, more particularly,

---

[64] For an account of (human rights) law as 'a theatre of roles', see D. Kennedy, 'The International Human Rights Movement: Part of the Problem?' (2001) 15 *Harvard Human Rights Law Review* 101, 111 (spelling anglicized).

[65] T. Eagleton, n 10, above, 80.

philosophical) reflection. Sterne develops the first of his themes by presenting us with characters whose contributions to conversation are 'hobby-horsical'.[66] By this he means that they seize the opportunities opened up by dialogue to speak on topics and to pursue themes that have captured their imagination.[67] Thus we find Walter Shandy arguing, with numbing regularity, that a child's Christian name plays a significant part in determining whether its life goes well or badly.[68] This theme excites little interest in those whom Walter harangues. For example, rather than dwelling at length on Walter's claims, his brother, Toby, talks at length on a topic that enthuses him: military fortifications.[69] Moreover, the Shandy brothers and Sterne's other characters exhibit a tendency to take up residence in a world shaped by their own thoughts and the words in which they find expression. This is a feature of their behaviour on which Sterne repeatedly reflects. He tells us that the 'swell of imagination and fancy' may lead us astray.[70] As a result, we may find ourselves in 'a wilderness of conceits'.[71] But those in such a wilderness are apt to remain in the grip of the thoughts that have led them there. Sterne illustrates this point by reference to Walter. Having described him as 'setting up another … hypothesis' Sterne adds that it is the 'nature' of such a thought 'that it assimilates everything to itself'.[72]

The picture of conversation that emerges from *Tristram Shandy* is far from positive. 'Conversation' predicates a process in which participants exhibit a high degree of attentiveness to one another's views. But this degree of

[66] L. Sterne, *The Life and Opinions of Tristram Shandy, Gentleman* (London: Everyman, 1912, G. Saintsbury, introduction), 10, 174 and 329.

[67] *Ibid*, 81 (where Walter says to Toby: 'you would provoke a saint;- here you have got us, I know not how, … souse [*i.e.*, suddenly, without warning] into the middle of the old subject [military fortifications] again'). (The hobby-horsical contributions to conversation that feature in *Tristram Shandy* go some way towards explaining why E.M. Forster described Sterne's novel as alive to 'the muddle of life'. See E.M. Forster, *Aspects of the Novel* (London: Penguin Books, 1976, O. Stallybras, ed), 35.)

[68] L. Sterne, n 66, above, , 38-39 and 80-82. (Christian names are only one of many hobby-horses ridden by Walter Shandy. Sterne tells us that his enthusiasms include door hinges (*ibid*, 146).)

[69] *Ibid*, 63-65.

[70] *Ibid*, 31.

[71] *Ibid*, 254.

[72] *Ibid*, 109-110. (See also S.E. Fish, *Professional Correctness: Literary Studies and Political Change* (Oxford: Clarendon Press, 1995), 80 (describing a disciplinary perspective as a 'mould' that 'does not bring light to an antecedently existing reality' but, rather, '*form* to a reality that fades when it is replaced by another [disciplinary 'angle']'). *Cf* L. Sterne, n 66, above, 281 (describing the way in which Walter Shandy's singular thought processes mould the reality external to himself: 'every object before him presented a face and section of itself to his eye, altogether different from the plan and elevation of it seen by the rest of mankind').)

attentiveness is rarely on display in the exchanges that Sterne records. Sterne's characters fasten infrequently on the thoughts of others and probe them for sources of insight and/or evidence of confusion. Rather, they seize opportunities to carry the 'conversation' in a new (and to them more agreeable) direction. It is for this reason that Sterne describes the exchanges that unfold in Shandy Hall as 'scampering' eternally from one topic to another.[73] But while interaction on this unpromising model is a prominent feature of life in Shandy Hall, there are occasions when Sterne's characters rise to the challenge of dialogue by raising doubts about others' hobby-horsical views. However, Sterne goes on to relate that those who face challenges of this sort rarely respond in an open-minded way. This, he explains, is because 'there is no disputing against HOBBY-HORSES'.[74] Thus even when conversation in Shandy Hall takes a genuinely critical turn, the enthusiasms of those who participate in it soon render it unedifying.

These features of conversation lead Sterne to draw a pessimistic conclusion concerning philosophers and philosophy. He describes philosophers as ready to reason on any topic and as committed to going about their business in a systematic fashion.[75] Sterne also identifies philosophy as a discipline concerned with the pursuit of truth.[76] He illustrates these points by reference to Walter Shandy. Walter's commitment to systematic reflection is apparent in, for example, his declaration that 'every thesis and hypothesis have an offspring of propositions: - and each proposition has its own consequences and conclusions; every one of which leads the mind on again, into fresh tracks of enquiries and doubtings'.[77] But while Walter sounds a modest note with his talk of 'enquiries and doubtings', he is apt to assume that he can offer unassailable answers to the questions that he addressees. This assumption finds expression in a text, the *Tristrapaedia*, that he has

---

73 *Ibid*, 136. (Even Michael Oakeshott, who argues that '[a] conversation does not need a chairman', recognizes that one of its features is 'integration'. See M. Oakeshott, *The Voice of Liberal Learning* (New Haven: Yale University Press, 1989, T. Fuller, ed), 98. David Lodge's fictive academic. Morris Zapp, offers a view of conversation that occupies a position between those of Oakeshott ('integration') and Sterne ('scampering' discourse). For Zapp declares that '[c]onversation is like playing tennis with a ball made of Krazy Putty, that keeps coming back over the net in a different shape'. D. Lodge, *The Practice of Writing: Essays, Lectures, Reviews and a Diary* (London: Penguin Books, 1996), 191.)

74 L. Sterne, n 66, above, , 10. See also 83 (noting that 'a man's HOBBY-HORSE is as tender a part as he has about him').

75 *Ibid*, 41 and 137. See also 136 (where Sterne states that Walter Shandy 'had an itch, in common with all philosophers, of reasoning upon everything which happened, and accounting for it too').

76 *Ibid*, 65 (identifying philosophy as a discipline concerned with 'independent facts'). See also 166 (where Sterne associates 'speculative subtilty [sic] or ambidexterity of argumentation' with the pursuit of truth).

77 *Ibid*, 300.

prepared so as to plot for his son a path through life that will make it possible for him to flourish.[78]

Sterne uses the *Tristrapaedia* to point up the misplaced confidence of Walter and other philosophers who believe that they can systematise the practical life of those around them. While Walter makes strenuous efforts to anticipate and counter the difficulties that his son will face as he journeys through life, his efforts are unavailing. The boy grows so fast that his father is unable to lay down a comprehensive plan for his welfare quickly enough. Life simply outpaces the would-be legislator.[79] And just as life outpaces Walter, so too it outsmarts him – by throwing up complexities and contingencies that he is simply unable to anticipate.

But none of this dampens Walter's philosophical ardour. In common with others who have fallen victim to the same enthusiasm, he regularly assumes himself to be in possession of the truth and concludes that a monologue (delivered by him) is preferable to dialogue. Sterne makes this point when he describes Walter's 'aim' as not being to 'discuss' matters with his brother but, rather, to make him 'comprehend' the content of his 'philosophick lectures'.[80] He adds that those who hold their views enthusiastically and use rhetoric in their defence may be unable to recognise the force of counterarguments.[81] In light of these points, Sterne concludes that, while philosophy's ambitions are large, the capacities of those who seek to engage in it are typically very limited.[82] Likewise, the prospects of progress in this discipline are, on Sterne's account, limited. Sterne does not, however, greet the philosophical failure on which he dwells with despair. He takes the view

---

78 *Ibid*, 273 (describing the *Tristrapaedia* as 'an INSTITUTE for the government of [Tristram's] childhood and adolescence'). See also T. Eagleton, n 10, above, 83.

79 L. Sterne, n 66, above, 276. See also T. Eagelton, n 10, above, 80.

80 L. Sterne, n 66, above, 172. See also 52 (on 'the end of disputation' as being 'more to silence than convince') and 187 (where Sterne draws a distinction between a 'dispute' and a 'decree'). *Cf* D. Bohm, *On Dialogue* (New York: Routledge, 2004), 3 (arguing that a participant in a genuine dialogue does not simply 'attempt to *make common* certain ideas or items of information that are already known to him').

81 L. Sterne, n 66, above, 266 (arguing that those who use 'the *engines* of eloquence' to 'drive' (or influence) others are themselves 'driven like turkeys to market' by the force of their own rhetoric). See also 67 (noting that '[w]hen a man gives himself up to the government of a ruling passion, - or, in other words, when his HOBBY-HORSE grows headstrong, - farewell cool reason and fair discretion!'), and 171 (on 'the warmer paroxysms of [Walter's] zeal').

82 *Ibid*, 202 (where Walter Shandy acknowledges that people are 'totteringly put together'). See also Plato, n 54, above, VI, 301c (arguing that '[r]eadiness to learn and remember, quickness and keenness of mind', are capacities that usually make their possessors 'unpredictable' and, hence, unsuited for philosophy).

that we can seek to pursue truth.[83] But we should, at the same time, be alive to humankind's shortcomings. However, these shortcomings do not inspire in Sterne contempt for human beings. Rather, he is wryly amused at the pretensions of many of those who engage in learned disquisition. Moreover, he is ready to tolerate a wide range of views. Peter Ackroyd has identified these features of Sterne's thinking as giving expression to the English imagination.[84] On Ackroyd's account, this is a practical outlook informed by a strong commitment to moderation and compromise.[85] This is a subject on which Terry Eagleton has dwelt. He reads Sterne as encouraging his readers to cultivate the spirit of Shandeism.[86] If Shandy Hall is anything to go by, this would seem to involve acceptance of human imperfection and the idiosyncrasies in which it often finds expression.[87] Likewise, it appears to require the adoption of practices and institutions able to accommodate the ramshackle character of human interaction.

Sterne's emphasis on conversation (or discourse) and his sensitivity to the human failings that make it such a hit-and-miss process have (as we will see) relevance to the operations of negligence law. In the section below, we will seek to develop these strands of Sterne's thought by drawing on the writings of Bakhtin and Foucault. The aim in doing this is analytic: to fashion a set of tools that will enable us to make more adequate sense of the discourse on which Hutchinson and Morgan throw light in 'The Canegusisan Connection'.

4 Bakhtin and Foucault

Bakhtin and Heteroglossia

Readiness to entertain a wide range of views appears to be central to the spirit of Shandeism. Certainly, this aspect of Sterne's practical outlook finds expression in *Tristram Shandy*. For the novel's most prominent characters are highly distinctive and pursue themes that merit application of the adjective 'hobby-horsical'. Thus we encounter in *Tristram Shandy* a plurality of voices. This is a topic that Bakhtin subjects to extended analysis. Bakhtin argues

---

[83] *Ibid*, 65.

[84] P. Ackroyd, *Albion: The Origins of the English Imagination* (London: Vintage, 2004), 402 and 405-408.

[85] *Ibid*, 402. See also L. Sterne, *A Sentimental Journey Through France and Italy* (London: Penguin Books, 1967, G. Petrie, ed), 15 (where, A. Alvarez, notes in his Introduction, that 'casualness and unprejudiced receptivity become a procedure' in Sterne's writings).

[86] T. Eagleton, n 10, above, 90. (Eagelton's observation reveals Alvarez to be wrong when he declares that there is a 'lack of … moral purpose' in Sterne's fictions. See L. Sterne, n 85, above, 9.)

[87] L. Sterne, n 66, above, 315 (noting that 'all men have their failings').

that we find in the novel, as a literary genre, a paradigmatic example of heteroglossia: a plurality of voices, each of which gives expression to a distinct standpoint.[88] Bakhtin developed his account of heteroglossia by reference to the novels of, *inter alios*, Dickens, Dostoevsky, and Thackeray (which he identified as internally dialogised). By this he meant that novels contain a variety of forms of life that find expression in modes of expression (or idiolects) that compete with one another.[89]

Bakhtin pressed his analysis further by identifying it as having relevance to the world around him – arguing, *inter alia*, that practical life (like the novel) presents us with a 'surplus of seeing' (as those who occupy particular positions in society are able to offer insights available only from their perspective).[90] This led him to identify social contexts as 'congeries of contesting meanings'.[91] This is because they (like the novels of Dostoevsky) contain centrifugal and centripetal forces.[92] The centrifugal forces arise because the values and presuppositions that find expression in a particular voice threaten, on account of their distinctiveness, to undermine the (shared) context in which they exert influence. But Bakhtin sets alongside these forces the readiness of fictive characters and people in practical contexts to respond attentively to the utterances of others and to place emphasis on shared concerns. To the extent that they act in this way, centripetal forces arise and counter those that threaten the common life in which fictive characters or members of actually existing societies participate.[93]

In his account of the novel, Bakhtin finds a basis on which to argue that it provides clues as to how we might organize our practical affairs on a normatively appealing basis. He takes this view because the novel instantiates the idea of 'dialogism' (which bears similarities to the spirit of Shandeism).[94] For it affords a space (or framework) within which no single

---

88 M.M. Bakhtin, *The Dialogic Imagination: Four Essays* (Austin: University of Texas Press, 1981, M. Holquist, ed). See M. Holquist, *Dialogism: Bakhtin and his World* (London: Routledge, 1990), 69-70.

89 S. Dentith, *Bakhtinian Thought: An Introductory Reader* (London: Routledge, 1995), 196, and D. Lodge, *After Bakhtin: Essays on Fiction and Criticism* (London: Routledge, 1990), 92.

90 M.M. Bakhtin, n 88, above, 301-331. See also M. Holquist, n 88, above, 35-37 (on Bakhtin's account of a 'surplus of seeing').

91 *Ibid*, 24.

92 *Ibid*, 70.

93 This aspect of Bakhtin's account of a heteroglossia lends support to the claim that '[f]aithfulness to the shape of common concepts is itself an act of normative significance'. See J. Raz, *The Morality of Freedom* (Oxford: Clarendon Press, 1986), 64.

94 See ns 85-87, above, and associated text.

voice predominates.[95] Rather, a plurality of voices finds expression and elicits attentive responses since 'there is neither a first word nor a last word' on the matters that they address.[96] For these reasons, Bakhtin contrasts dialogism with another approach to practical life that he finds deeply unattractive. This is monologism and it takes the form of an effort on the part of those who take a particular view of practical affairs to inscribe it on all available social space (*e.g.*, a particular institution or the practical life of a nation-state).[97] Bakhtin is repelled by monologism on, *inter alia*, the ground that those who engage in it are utterly unwilling to accommodate the views of others.[98] Unwillingness to accommodate the views of others predicates, on the part of those who exhibit it, a capacity for open-mindedness that they choose not to exercise. For this reason, their outlook is different from those who feature in Michel Foucault's account of heterotopia.

Foucault on Heterotopia

According to Foucault, a heterotopia exists in circumstances where worlds of ideas sit alongside one another but those who inhabit one such world cannot enter into dialogue with those who lie beyond its borders. Thus a heterotopia comprises a group of 'unconnected islets' and is, according to Foucault, 'disturbing'.[99] He adds that this is because it 'destroy[s] "syntax" in advance'.[100] This, it would appear, is because those who inhabit the unconnected islets have worldviews that (for reasons unexplained by Foucault) are quite discontinuous from one another. In circumstances of this sort, the impediment to dialogue (between the inhabitants of particular worlds) is not unwillingness to speak but, rather, inability to do so.[101] The

---

95 M. Holquist, n 88, above, 34 (noting that, on Bakhtin's analysis, 'Dostoevsky … permits his characters to have the status of an 'I' standing against the claims of his own authorial voice').

96 *Ibid*, 39.

97 *Ibid.*

98 *Ibid,* 33.

99 M. Foucault, *The Order of Things: An Archaeology of the Human Sciences* (Abingdon: Routledge, 2002), xx.

100 *Ibid*, xix.

101 *Ibid*, xviii. See also B. McHale, *Postmodern Fiction* (London: Routledge, 1989), 44 (characterizing the sort of 'heterotopian space' described by Foucault as a 'plural 'zone' in which 'worlds coexist'). In his account of a heterotopian space or zone, McHale draws on a number of works of fiction, including: I. Calvino, *Invisible Cities* (London: Vintage, 1997, W. Weaver, trans), and T. Pynchon, *Gravity's Rainbow* (London: Picador, 1973) (*ibid*, 43-45). See also 51 (where McHale associates the idea of a heterotopia (or zone) with '"a series of enormous solipsisms"' (quoting from A. Carter, *The Passion of the New Eve* (London: Victor Gollancz, 1977), 167). See also B. McHale, *Constructing Postmodernism* (London: Routledge, 1992), 137 and 250. *Cf* K.R. Popper, *The Myth of the Framework: In*

upshot, as Foucault, recognizes, is 'disorder' (or, rather, the inability to establish order).[102] While Foucault's account of a heterotopia is underdeveloped, we might see it as alerting us to practical problems much like those captured by the idea of solipsism ('the belief that only oneself and one's experience exists').[103]

If this is broadly correct, Foucault describes a state of affairs on which Laurence Sterne throws light. This is apparent when we look closely at Walter Shandy. Sterne tells us that, due to the 'singularity' of his 'notions', Walter's 'judgment … became the dupe of his wit'.[104] As a result, he would, 'like all systematick reasoners, … move both heaven and earth, and twist and torture everything in nature, to support his hypothesis'.[105] These observations have led Terry Eagleton to describe Walter as 'a crazed rationalist full of elaborately useless learning, for whom the real world must conform to the categories of the mind'.[106] Eagleton develops this point in a way that, as we will see later, has great relevance to the discourse of negligence law. He argues that 'Walter … is an idealist for whom concepts are more real than things, and who lives at a lofty distance from the actual world. By manipulating concepts, he believes in his Enlightenment fashion that he can persuade the world to do his imperious bidding'.[107] This, Eagleton recognises, is an extreme state of affairs in which dialogue (the process through which Walter might hope to persuade others) becomes impossible.[108] In circumstances of the sort contemplated by Eagleton, we see concepts operating in the same way as the Shandean hypotheses

Defence of Science and Rationality (London: Routledge, 1994, M.A. Notturno, ed), ch 2. See esp 34 (describing the 'the myth of the framework' as the view that '[a] rational and fruitful discussion is impossible unless the participants share a basic framework of assumptions or, at least, unless they have agreed on such a framework for the purposes of discussion'). See also 46 (where Popper associates the myth of the framework with unwarranted appeals to incommensurability). *Cf* W.N.R. Lucy, 'The Common Law According to Hegel' (1997)17 *OJLS* 685, 686 (on 'paradigm bumping' (which occurs where those who embrace one 'system' of thought use it to 'measure[ ] … another system' and find the latter 'wanting')).

102 M. Foucault, n 99, above, xix, *et seq.*

103 S. Blackburn, n 27, above, 356.

104 L. Sterne, n 66, above, 41.

105 *Ibid.*

106 T. Eagleton, n 10, above, 83.

107 *Ibid.*

108 *Ibid*, 90 (where Eagleton identifies the problem afflicting Walter as common to the characters in the novel: 'Sterne portrays a world in which … communication [is] collapsing, as men and women gradually retreat to their solipsistic enclaves'). See also M. Foucault, n 99, above, xix (noting that 'heterotopias … stop words in their tracks').

mentioned earlier: in the minds of those who embrace them, they assimilate the world around them.[109]

While Sterne finds in idealism a rich source of comedy, in the hands of another contributor to the English literary canon, it takes on a disturbing appearance (and one, as we will see, highly relevant to Mill J's account of negligence law). In *Hard Times*, Charles Dickens presents us with a character who has, through taking up residence in a narrow world of ideas, lost contact with the social context that surrounds him. The character in question is Thomas Gradgrind and he is an unswerving devotee of a particular form of consequentialist political philosophy: utilitarianism.[110] Dickens describes Grandgrind sitting in a room that looks very much like a world of ideas as described by Foucault:

> Gradgrind's … room was quite a blue chamber in its abundance of blue books.[111] Whatever they could prove (which is usually anything you like), they proved there, in an army constantly strengthening by the arrival of new recruits. In this charmed apartment, the most complicated social questions were cast up, got into exact totals, and finally settled – if those concerned could only have been brought to know it. As if an astronomical observatory should be made without any windows, and the astronomer within should arrange the starry universe solely by pen, ink and paper, so Mr Gradgrind, in *his* Observatory (and there are many like it), had no need to cast an eye upon the teeming myriads of human beings around him, but could settle all their destinies on a slate'.[112]

Dickens shows us how those who inhabit a particular world of ideas may work up (in a manner that smacks of solipsism) a monologue that they see as a solution to life's practical problems.[113] We will return to this point in the

[109] See ns 70-72, above, and associated text.

[110] C. Dickens, *Hard Times* (Harmondsworth: Penguin Books, 1969), 48, 131-132, and 238.

[111] *Ibid*, 327 (noting that the term 'blue books' applies to governmental reports that recorded, *inter alia*, the numbers of those suffering from particular types of misfortune (*e.g.*, living in the worst slums)).

[112] *Ibid*, 131-132.

[113] By using the rather clumsy figure of an 'astronomical observatory … without any windows', Dickens' aim seems to be to impress upon his readers the fact that Gradgrind is the victim of what David Lodge has called 'the real solipsism'. Those in this position do not know that they are in a state of solipsism. See D. Lodge, n 73, above, 189. (Gradgrind's monologic approach to practical matters might also be identified as an example of an enormous solipsism as examined by Brian McHale in his account of heterotopia. See n 101, above (and associated text). Likewise, we might use the notion of 'ideology' to gain analytic purchase on Gradgrind's thinking. See T. Eagleton, *Ideology*

section below (in which we will examine 'The Canengusian Connection' and the discourse of negligence law in light of the insights we have drawn from Sterne, Bakhtin, and Foucault).

5 'The Canengusian Connection' and the Discourse of Negligence Law

Applying Sterne, Bakhtin, and Foucault

The five judgments that feature in 'The Canengusian Connection' present us with a plurality of voices (or heteroglossia). This is something that we can explain not just by reference to the realities of negligence law but also by considering the intentions of Hutchinson and Morgan. Their purpose is to present their readers with an impactful overview of the discourse that unfolds in the field they survey. Moreover, the format they employ – the fictive decision of a multi-member and conflict-wracked appeal court – provides an effective means by which to pursue this purpose. So too does Hutchinson's and Morgan's decision to place in the mouth of each of their judges an account of the law that tends in an ideal-typical direction.

The effectiveness of this expositional strategy becomes apparent when we consider the contrasts between the judges' voices. While Wright J invokes the ideal of corrective justice, Prudential J places emphasis on social justice. The upshot is a jarring collision.[114] The effect is the same when we turn to Doctrin CJ and Lefft J. Doctrin CJ seeks to cleave to the existing law by appealing to the separation of powers. By contrast, Lefft J finds in the doctrine of informed consent an ideal (personal autonomy) that provides a ground on which to conclude that Canengus should abandon tort as a compensation mechanism. From these sources of disagreement, a clear message emerges: negligence law is a site of conflict where each of the five judges argues (more or less self-consciously) for a particular model of human

(London: Verso, 1991), 60 (noting that '[i]deologies are discourses unable to curve back upon themselves, blinded by their own grounds and frontiers').)

114 While Hutchinson and Morgan present us with a jarring collision, there are reasons for thinking that corrective justice and distributive justice are not entirely distinct ideals. If we make the assumption that negligence law protects significant interests (interests in physical, mental, and financial security), the question arises as to where we acquire our understanding of 'significant interests'. If, for example, we regard these interests as 'social primary goods' in the sense specified by John Rawls, our thinking on corrective justice is informed by assumptions associated with the ideal of distributive justice. See J. Rawls, *A Theory of Justice*, (Oxford: Oxford University Press, 1971), 62-63 (defining 'social primary goods' as those 'things that every rational [person] is presumed to want' since they 'normally have a use whatever a person's rational plan of life'). See also R. Mullender and A Speirs, 'Negligence, Psychiatric Injury, and the Altruism Principle' (2000) 20 *OJLS* 645, 664, n 116.

association. But this is far from being the whole story. For Hutchinson and Morgan provide grounds for thinking that the discourse of negligence law is dialogic and highly resistant to contributions that are monologic in orientation.

Hutchinson and Morgan make plain negligence law's resistance to monologue in the judgments of Wright and Mill JJ. As we have noted, each of these judges identifies within negligence law a particular practical impulse that provides a basis on which to explain its operations. In Mill J's case, this impulse is the pursuit of efficiency, while in that of Wright J it is the vindication of individual rights. The result is a collision between consequentialist and deontological moral philosophies. Moreover, it is a collision between two monologues.[115] This becomes clear when we pay close attention to the two judgments, in each of which we find the same hectoring, intolerant tone. Wright J declares that 'individuals w[ill] *cease* to exist morally' under a 'utilitarian regime'.[116] This cuts no ice with Mill J who drives home the point that '[r]ules of tort *must* be designed and implemented' so as to facilitate the pursuit of efficiency.[117] But while each of these voices is monologic, Hutchinson and Morgan identify them as part of a larger whole: the plural discourse of negligence law (which, while fraught with tension, retains an enduring shape).

This is a point we can pursue further by examining two components in Bakhtin's account of a heteroglossia: centrifugal and centripetal forces.[118] Consider Lefft J's judgment. He argues that Canengus should abandon negligence law and embrace a new and strongly democratic social blueprint, according to which Canengusians should (as a collectivity) decide on the nature of and how best to regulate the risk environment in which they live. Moreover, he finds support for this position in the existing (if

---

[115] Mill J's judgment provides a paradigmatic example of a monologue since its author seeks to explain the law, without remainder, by reference to efficiency. While Wright J follows his colleague's lead by pursuing a single theme (the centrality of rights to the law's operations), in one respect his judgment is less emphatic. For he identifies both negligence law and strict liability as means to the end of rights-based protection. On this point, see ns 39-40, above and associated text.

[116] A.C. Hutchinson and D. Morgan, n 2, above, 87 (emphasis added).

[117] *Ibid*, 80 (emphasis added). See also A. Ripstein, 'Tort Law in a Liberal State' (2007) 1 *Journal of Tort Law* 13 (arguing that those who, like Richard Posmer, explain tort's operations by reference to the pursuit of efficiency exhibit an 'inability to conceive of what else [it] could be doing').

[118] For general discussion of '[t]he centripetal-centrifugal force metaphor' as relevant to law's operations, see T. Morawetz, 'Understanding Disagreement, The Root Issue of Jurisprudence: Applying Wittgenstein to Positivism, Critical Theory, and Judging' (1992) 141 *University of Pennsylvania LR* 371, 386.

underdeveloped) doctrine of informed consent.[119] In the first of these features of his judgment we find a strong centrifugal force, while in the second we encounter a weak centripetal counterforce. Matters are broadly similar when we examine Prudential J's judgment. He finds in the existing law a concern with 'the plight of the injured'.[120] But he argues that this commitment provides grounds on which to strike down a new institutional path by establishing a no-fault compensation scheme.[121]

While Bakhtin's account of heteroglossia provides a basis on which to point up the pluralism of, and the centripetal and centrifugal forces within, negligence law, Foucault's notion of heterotopia provides grounds for a more troubling analysis. The judgments of Mill and Wright JJ will serve to bring this out clearly. Insofar as their respective analyses are monologic, the spectre of heterotopia looms. We do not appear to be surveying the outcome of a genuine exchange of ideas in which the current position of each of the two judges was, while the debate unfolded, open to revision. Rather, we receive reports from those who inhabit particular normative universes.[122] In one of these universes, the pursuit of efficiency crowds out all other considerations; in the other, rights-based entitlements (underwritten by the ideal of corrective justice) fill the horizon.[123] To the extent that those who make these reports are incapable of engaging with the views of others, then talk of a heterotopia seems warranted.

Just as we can apply Bakhtin's thinking and that of Foucault to 'The Canengusian Connection', so too we can use it to make sense of judgments and commentary on negligence law. Consider the House of Lords' decision in *McLoughlin v O'Brian*. This is a case in which we encounter sharply contrasting judicial voices. Lord Scarman declares that he and his fellow judges should 'adjudicate according to principle'.[124] He adds that, [i]f principle leads to results which are thought to be socially unacceptable, Parliament can legislate to draw a line or to map out a new path'.[125] His Lordship's unqualified commitment to the pursuit of principle wins the

---

119 A.C. Hutchinson and D. Morgan, n 2, above, 110.

120 *Ibid*, 94.

121 102-104.

122 *Cf* M.J. Sandel, *Justice: What's the Right Thing to Do?* (London: Allen Lane, 2009), 27 (describing processes of argument from which open-mindedness is absent as 'a volley of dogmatic assertions, an ideological food fight').

123 In light of the points made in the text, we can describe Wright and Mill JJ as engaging in very different totalizing discourses. Discourses of this sort 'seek[ ] to occupy *all* the available ground'. See J. Hawthorn, *A Concise Glossary of Contemporary Literary Theory* (London: Edward Arnold, 1994, 2nd edn), 217 (emphasis added).

124 *McLoughlin v O'Brian*, n 32, above, 430, *per* Lord Scarman.

125 *Ibid*, 430.

endorsement of Wright J.[126] This is unsurprising. For unqualified deontological impulses find expression in the positions that Wright J and Lord Scarman stake out. Whether we use 'principle', or 'rights', or 'corrective justice' to capture these impulses, the central theme in both judgments is the same: judges have the job of righting wrongfully inflicted harms.[127] But Lord Scarman (like Wright J) has to endure the criticisms of one of his colleagues. Lord Edmund-Davies describes Lord Scarman's account of negligence law as 'startling'.[128] He explains that judicial commitment to principle is not absolute but qualified. For judges have long identified policy considerations as grounds on which to reject otherwise good claims.[129]

While the sharp exchange of views between Lords Scarman and Edmund-Davies occasioned much comment at the time it occurred, it is not as stark as that between Wight J and Mill J.[130] In *McLoughlin*, we do not witness a collision between unqualified deontology and unqualified consequentialism. Rather, Lord Edmund-Davies argues that negligence law's deontological impulses are and should continue to be qualified by consequentialist ones. But the qualified approach defended by Lord Edmund-Davies does not afford a means by which to avoid a collision between deontological and consequentialist moral impulses in negligence law. For judges still have to identify the point at which deontological impulses should yield to consequentialist ones. This is a question that gives rise to tensions not just between the proponents of particular positions but in the minds of individual judges. This is, for example, true of Lord Browne-Wilkinson in *X v Bedfordhsire County Council*. He declares that the ideal of corrective justice has first claim on the loyalty of judges in the law of negligence.[131] But having done so, he grounds his decision on doctrines that serve to shield public bodies from negligence claims.[132] Thus consequentialism triumphs over deontology. For his Lordships' aim is to ensure that public bodies are

---

[126] See ns 33-36 above, and associated text.

[127] See E.J. Weinrib, n 7, above, 65.

[128] *McLoughlin v O'Brian*, n 32, above, 427 (where Lord Edmund-Davies explains that he finds his colleague's approach 'startling' since it 'runs counter to well-established and wholly acceptable law').

[129] *Ibid*, 427-429 (where Lord Edmund-Davies finds support for his account of policy's role in negligence law in, *inter alia*, P.H. Winfield, 'Public Policy in the English Common Law' (1928) 42 *Harvard LR* 76, 95-97).

[130] A.C. Hutchinson and D. Morgan, n 4, above, 695-696.

[131] *X (Minors)* v *Bedfordshire County Council*, n 5, above, 633.

[132] *Ibid*, 663.

able to focus on their central concern: delivering goods and services that benefit the public.[133]

We might regard Lord Browne-Wilkinson's speech in *X's* case as revealing a stable deontological core within the law of negligence (righting wrongfully inflicted harms) from which judges, on occasion, depart. However, this core (assuming it exists) may be less stable than cases such as *X* suggest. Consider *Chester v Afshar*.[134] The House of Lords imposed liability on a surgeon who failed to alert a patient to a 1-2% risk that crystallized in harm. A majority of their Lordships imposed liability on the ground that the defendant had violated the claimant's right to receive a warning of the risks inherent in the surgery she underwent.[135] Moreover, Lord Steyn identified the majority's decision as ensuring that the law gives 'due respect' to 'the autonomy and dignity of each patient'.[136] This (and other such statements from the majority) prompted sharp dissenting responses from Lords Bingham and Hoffmann. They argued that negligence law is not centrally concerned with vindicating rights but, rather, with wrongful harm-infliction.[137] Thus we find the House of Lords engaged in a disagreement as to how we should understand negligence law's normative core. On this topic, we might see the minority in *Chester* as making an appeal to the paradigm case. One commentator has summed up this argumentative move (which is strongly associated with ordinary language philosophy) thus: 'to do something incompatible with the Paradigm Case is *not to play* [the relevant] *game*'.[138] Certainly, the minority in *Chester* take the view that the majority is not playing the game of negligence law as they and others conventionally conceive it. Moreover, we can make sense of this dispute by reference to our earlier discussion of centripetal and centrifugal forces. Lord Bingham and Lord Hoffmann defend a long accepted position (liability should be imposed for the wrongful infliction of harm in circumstances where the

133 See R. Mullender, 'Negligence, Public Bodies, and Ruthlessness' (2009) 72 *Modern LR* 961, 961-962.

134 *Chester v Afshar* [2005] 1 AC 134.

135 The majority of their Lordships found support for their decision in *Chappel v Hart* (1998) 195 CLR 232 (Australian High Court) and in A.T. Honoré, 'Medical Non-Disclosure, Causation and Risk' (1999) 7 *Torts Law Journal* 1. See also E. Jackson, *Medical Law: Text, Cases, and Materials* (Oxford: Oxford University Press, 2010), 202-203.

136 *Chester v Afshar*, n 134, above, 144.

137 *Ibid*, 141-142, *per* Lord Bingham.

138 E. Gellner, *Words and Things* (Abingdon: Routledge, 2005), 60. *Cf* M. Foucault, n 1, above, 68 (on the 'General Grammar' that 'defines a domain of *validity* … (according to what criteria one may [use to] discuss the truth or falsehood of a proposition')), and M. Oakeshott, 'Man on His Past', ch 20 in L. O'Sullivan, ed, *The Vocabulary of a Modern European State* (Exeter: Imprint-Academic, 2008), 108 (arguing that participants in a practice sustain it by exhibiting a 'disposition' to observe its 'manners').

parties stand in a close relationship). By contrast, the majority appear (as the minority point out) to be bending the branch of tort with which they are dealing in a new direction (where the central focus is on the vindication of a right and the associated ideal of personal autonomy).[139] This has led Jenny Steele to describe the decision in *Chester* as 'poised rather awkwardly between the torts of battery and negligence'.[140]

While disagreement of the sort on display in *Chester* weakens negligence law's already rather shaky claims to be a source of guidance to its addressees, it does at least present us with a dialogue. On occasion, we encounter contributions to the discourse of negligence law that suggest an absence of dialogue. In its third *Restatement* on the Law of Torts (1999), the American Law Institute (ALI) has set out an account of negligence law according to which an unswerving commitment to the pursuit of efficiency informs it.[141] Richard Wright has subjected the ALI's analysis to close historical scrutiny. He notes that, while the ALI's first *Restatement* (1934) adopted a position on duty of care that indicated a commitment to the pursuit of efficiency, it recognised that other moral impulses inform the law.[142] Moreover, he notes that the ALI adopted this qualified approach to the pursuit of efficiency in its second *Restatement* (1965). Wright adds that, when the ALI set out its third *Restatement*, the upshot was not only doctrinal (duty of care doctrine dropped out of the picture) but also moral. A single goal (the pursuit of efficiency) filled the horizon.[143] As a result, the ALI effectively blinded itself to the fact that not one but, rather, an array of moral impulses informs

---

[139] *Chester v Afshar*, n 134, above, 147, *per* Lord Hoffmann. (Since the decision of the majority in *Afshar* extends the bounds of negligence liability by weakening existing doctrinal requirements, we might see it as an example of sympathetic (pro-claimant) adjudication of the sort associated with the emergence of a so-called 'blame culture' (in which claimants and judges fail to take considerations of (corrective) justice sufficiently seriously). But to take such a view of the majority's approach would be uncharitable. For their thinking is informed by a conception of justice (of the sort associated with human rights law) in which considerations of respect and dignity figure prominently. (On blame culture, judicial sympathy, and modification of existing doctrine, see R. Mullender, 'Negligence Law and Blame Culture: A Critical Response to a Possible Problem' (2006) 22 *Journal of Professional Negligence* 2, 7-9 (discussing the respective analyses of Patrick Atiyah and Tony Weir). See also R. Mullender, 'Truth, Bullshit, and Blame Culture' (2009) 11 *Legal Ethics* 272, 281 (on the field of interpretative possibility constituted by negligence doctrine).)

[140] J. Steele, *Tort Law: Text, Cases, and Materials* (Oxford: Oxford University Press, 2010, 2nd edn), 65.

[141] J.C.P. Goldberg and B.C. Zipursky, '*The Restatement (Third)* and the Place of Duty in Negligence Law (2001) 54 *Vanderbilt LR* 657.

[142] R.W. Wright, 'Hand, Posner, and the Myth of the "Hand Formula"' (2003) 4 *Theoretical Inquiries in Law* 145, 148.

[143] *Ibid*, 146-147.

negligence doctrine.[144] Among them, Wright numbers 'dignity', 'respect', and the 'implementation of [corrective] justice' (each of which gives expression to deontological assumptions).[145] On this analysis, the ALI now offers us an account of negligence law that amounts to a consequentialist monologue.[146] Thus we have grounds for identifying its members as having taken up residence in a closed world of ideas. To the extent that this is the case, it calls to mind Foucault's account of a heterotopia.[147]

While we can use Sterne, Bakhtin, and Foucault to press Hutchinson's and Morgan's analysis further, their essay exhibits a strength to which we must devote attention. There are, as we will see, reasons for thinking that 'The Canengusian Connection' throws light not on one but, rather, on three closely related but, nonetheless, distinct discourses. Moreover, it provides examples of the way in which movement from one of these discourses to another may take place.

Accidents, Compensation, and Discursive Diversity

'Discourse' embraces a range of exchanges from an open-ended conversation to the examination, at some length, of a particular subject.[148] As Sterne makes plain in *Tristram Shandy*, rising to the demands of discourse in the first sense is much easier than in the second. Insofar as it is open-

---

144 *Ibid*, 147.

145 *Ibid.* (See also E. Mickiewicz, 'An Exploratory Theory of Coherence in Canengus and Beyond' (2010) 7 *The Journal Jurisprudence*, section 4 (on Wittgenstein's notion of 'aspect-blindness').)

146 The shift in the ALI's view of negligence law that occurs between 1934 and 1999 provides an example of 'monologue creep' in the sense specified in P. O'Callaghan, 'Monologism and Dialogism in Private Law' (2010) 7 *The Journal Jurisprudence*, section 5 ('Monologue-Creep').

147 The journey into a closed world (of ideas) might begin when an actor decides to treat a particular body of thought as a source of exclusionary reasons for action. These are reasons that we regard as providing grounds on which to exclude other relevant matters from consideration. Over time, those acting on exclusionary reasons may decide to treat them (in light of what they take to be their explanatory power) as indefeasible. Where this happens, we appear to encounter an absence of negative capability. According to the poet John Keats, this is the ability to 'be[ ] in uncertainties, mysteries, doubts, without an irritable reaching after fact and reason'. On exclusionary reasons, see J. Raz, *Practical Reason and Norms* (Oxford: Princeton University Press, 1990), 35-48 and 182-186, and on negative capability, see J.A. Cuddon, n 10, above, 419. See also S. Coote, *John Keats: A Life* (Hodder & Stoughton, London, 1996) 115 (describing the statement quoted by Cuddon as 'a plea for ... receptivity and openness').

148 *Oxford English Dictionary*. See also M. Foucault, n 1, above, 90 (on 'the rather fluctuating meaning of the word "discourse"', which relates to 'the general domain of all statements', 'an individualizable group of statements' and 'a regulated practice that accounts for a certain number of statements').

ended, those who participate in, say, a conversation can hardly complain if their fellow participants move it in a new direction.[149] But this is not the case when we turn to the sustained examination of a particular topic. To veer off in a new direction is to scamper away from the topic on which participants are focusing. In such circumstances, Sterne's adjective 'scampering' does critical work.[150] For those responsible for such a change of direction exhibit insensitivity to some of the obligations intrinsic to the examination in which they are supposed to be participating. To sustain such an examination, they have to be attentive to relevant contributions from others. And in order to determine what is relevant and what is not, they have to focus their attention on the considerations that give the topic under discussion its distinct shape (*e.g.*, the purposes it is supposed to serve).[151]

In the discourse of negligence law, these considerations include the concepts of wrongdoing and harm, and the principle of personal responsibility. They also include risk and the costs that may arise from the decision to regulate socially valuable activities. Likewise, they include the ideals of corrective and distributive justice – both of which are egalitarian since they identify the law's addressees as inhabiting a plateau of equality.[152] These considerations

---

149 See M. Oakeshott, n 73, above, 118 (arguing that '[a] conversation ... has no predetermined course, we do not ask what it is "for", and we do not judge its excellence by its conclusion').

150 'Scampering' also does psychological and anthropological work. For Sterne alerts us to the fact people are apt to mount their hobby-horses when an opportunity to do so presents itself and that dislocation (in the wider group) is the typical (and more or less practically significant) result. (Sterne's anthropological point is captured in D. DeLillo, *Underworld* (London: Macmillan, 1997), 371 (emphasis added) (describing a street as 'abound[ing] in idiosyncrasy, in *the human veer*'). See also S.E. Fish, *Doing What Comes Naturally: Change, Rhetoric, and the Practice of Theory in Literary and Legal Studies* (Oxford: Clarendon Press, 1989, 508 (noting 'the variety that is a feature of interpretive performance').)

151 In his account of 'discursive formations', Foucault examines four factors that may work to stabilize them. They are (i) a shared object, (ii) 'a certain style, a certain constant manner of statement', (iii) the presence within them of 'permanent and coherent concepts', and (iv) 'the identity and persistence of themes'. See M. Foucault, n 1, above, ch 2. See also 84 (on the 'systematic ordering' of and 'the play of formal constraints' within discourses). (Foucault's phrase 'a shared object' reveals his thinking to intersect with that of the analytic philosopher John Searle on the subject of collective intentionality (on which see J.R. Searle, *Making the Social World: The Structure of Civilization* (Oxford: Oxford University Press, 2010), 43, *et seq*). The collective intentionality of judges works to sustain, for example, the practice of imposing liability for the careless (and therefore wrongful) infliction of harm. Moreover, a judge makes the practical significance of collective intentionality apparent by, *inter alia*, engaging in an appeal to the paradigm case.)

152 Even those commentators who identify corrective justice and distributive justice as discontinuous nonetheless identify each of these ideals as oriented towards equality. See, for example, E.J. Weinrib, n 34, above, 980-981 (identifying corrective justice and distributive justice as representing two different functions of equality, the former

place limits on the range of contributions that we can make to the discourse of negligence law.[153] This is a point that we can develop by drawing on H.L.A. Hart's account of law's internal point of view. Those who adopt this point of view (for example, judges) grasp that it makes certain demands on them and so has normative significance.[154] But simply to apprehend law's normativity (or 'oughtness') is not to embrace it. This means that we find the internal point of view in its strongest form only among those who treat the law a source of authoritative reasons for action. This is a practical outlook that we find, for example, in a judge who is committed to the incremental development of existing negligence doctrine. Such a judge exhibits what Hart calls a 'critical, reflective attitude'.[155] For he or she ponders the question as to whether the normative impulses that find expression in existing doctrine provide grounds for extending it to a novel set of facts.[156] A judge who thinks in this way identifies these impulses as placing constraints on the contributions that he or she can make to the discourse of negligence law.

While the impulses captured in Hart's account of the internal point of view reveal adjudication to be a conventional process, we nonetheless find ourselves dealing, in the context of negligence law, with a range of

quantitative and the latter proportional). (While we cannot examine views such as Weinrib's in depth in this essay, there are reasons for doubting their plausibility. Corrective justice has to do with securing the (significant) interests of persons. Thus we have to consider how we come by our sense of what a person is and what his or her interests might be. According to some political philosophers (for example, Hegel), our sense of ourselves and our interests arises in a social context (most obviously, the state). This, according to Hegel, is the context in which ideas associated with justice as between the members of a group (*e.g.*, the commonweal and distributive justice) grow up and shape practical thought (more or less self-consciously). If we assume that these ideas invest us with a sense of 'self' and 'interests-relating to-self', then we cannot unscramble corrective justice and distributive justice. On Hegel's political philosophy, see J. Rawls, *Lectures on the History of Moral Philosophy* (Cambridge, Massachusetts: Harvard University Press, 2000), 330 (where Rawls notes that Hegel viewed persons as 'rooted in and fashioned by the system of political institutions under which they live), 339-340 (on Hegel's view that a society's system of institutions 'constitute[s] [its] ethical life'), and 353-354 (on the Hegelian theme that 'society is held together … by a sense of reasonable order, and that it is regulated by … a common-good conception of justice'). See also R. Mullender and A. Speirs, n 114, above, and J. Coleman, n 212, below, and associated text.)

153 See n 138, above, on the notion of an appeal to the paradigm case.

154 H.L.A. Hart, *The Concept of Law* (Oxford: Clarendon Press, 1994, 2nd edn), 57.

155 *Ibid.*

156 R. Mullender, 'English Negligence Law as Human Practice' (2009) 21 *Law & Literature* 321, 333, *et seq*. See also R.E. Keeton, 'Creative Continuity in the Law of Torts' (1962) 75 *Harvard LR* 463.

defensible viewpoints.[157] Faced with the same set of facts, some judges want to elaborate existing doctrine while others urge caution. The House of Lords' decision in *Junior Books v Veitchi* serves to illustrate this point.[158] The majority of their Lordships thought it appropriate to extend existing doctrine relating to pure economic loss to a novel set of facts (the installation of defective but non-dangerous flooring). The majority justified their decision by reference to, among other things, a sufficient relationship of proximity.[159] But Lord Brandon saw matters quite differently. In his dissenting speech, he dwelt on the uncertainty that a finding for the claimant would generate and the adverse impact this would have on commercial activity.[160] While majority and minority thus scamper off in opposite directions, they appeal to considerations that, when viewed from the standpoint internal to negligence law, yield respectable reasons for action.[161]

Even where judges agree on which of the parties should prevail in a particular case, we often find them scampering off in different doctrinal or policy-related directions. Consider the Court of Appeal's decision in *Lamb v Camden LBC.*[162] The claimant argued that, as a result of the defendant's negligence, third parties (squatters) had been able to gain access to and damage her home. The Court unanimously rejected this claim. But each of the Court's three members stakes out a distinctive position. Watkins LJ grounds his decision on the doctrine of remoteness. But while doing so, he renders a distinctly hobby-horsical judgment. He expresses the fear that he will never emerge from 'the maze of authorities on the subject of remoteness into the light of a clear understanding'.[163] Moreover, he likens his uncertainties to those of Winston Churchill on the subject of mathematics, and notes that Churchill made this declaration:

> 'I had a feeling once about mathematics - that I saw it all. Depth beyond depth was revealed to me - the byss and abyss. I saw - as

---

157 C. Kutz 'Just Disagreement: Indeterminacy and Rationality in the Rule of Law '(1994) 103 *Yale LJ* 997, 1021.

158 *Junior Books v Veitchi Co Ltd* [1983] 1 AC 520.

159 *Ibid*, 546, *per* Lord Roskill (who enumerates no less than seven factors that establish proximity between the parties (including the fact that the defendants were 'specialists in flooring' and that the claimants 'relied' on their 'skill and judgment')).

160 *Ibid*, 551-552.

161 *Ibid*, 551 (where Lord Brandon makes a contested appeal to the paradigm case of negligence law by arguing that: 'in *Donoghue v Stevenson* ... and in all the numerous cases in which the principle of that decision has been applied to different but analogous factual situations, it has always been stated either expressly, or taken for granted that an essential ingredient in the cause of action ... was the existence of danger, or the threat of danger, of physical damage to persons or their property').

162 *Lamb v Camden LBC*, n 21, above.

163 *Ibid,* 644.

> one might see the transit of Venus or the Lord Mayor's Show - a quantity passing through an infinity and changing its sign from plus to minus. I saw exactly how it happened and why the tergiversation was inevitable - but it was after dinner and I let it go'.[164]

Having turned in this singular performance, Watkins LJ announces that he 'has the instinctive feeling that the squatters' damage is too remote'.[165] Oliver LJ is, by contrast, matter of fact. Having surveyed the doctrine relating to liability for the voluntary conduct of third parties, he concludes that it would be unjust to fix the defendant with liability.[166] Lord Denning MR takes a quite different tack. He looks hard at existing doctrine on liability for the conduct of third parties.[167] However, he cannot find within it a ground for his decision. This leads him to 'look[ ] at the question as one of policy'.[168] From this standpoint, he concludes that the defendant should not be held liable since homeowners such as the claimant usually insure against loss of the sort at stake in the case.[169] Alive to the fact that his response to the claim is not doctrinal, Lord Denning justifies it by noting that, '[i]t is commonplace nowadays for the courts, when considering policy, to take insurance into account'.[170]

While the judgments in *Lamb* scamper off in a variety of directions, they are, in each case, rooted in the practice of negligence law. For the judges who set them out are not seeking to reshape the body of law they are applying. We now turn to some judgments that, while influenced by impulses that shape negligence law's internal point of view, promise to divert this branch of tort from its settled path. The judgments in a case we have already examined, *Chester v Afshar*, are relevant here. For the minority in the House of Lords adopt a conventional approach to negligence adjudication that contrasts vividly with the position staked out by their colleagues in the majority. As we have noted, Lord Steyn was centrally concerned with underwriting 'the autonomy and dignity of each patient'.[171] For this reason, he and his colleagues in the majority were prepared to make what he called 'a narrow and modest departure from traditional causation principles'.[172] This was a description of the change wrought in the law by the majority that the dissentients in *Chester*, Lords Bingham and Hoffmann, found wholly

164 *Ibid.*
165 *Ibid*, 647.
166 *Ibid*, 639-644.
167 *Ibid*, 634-635.
168 *Ibid*, 637.
169 *Ibid*, 637-638.
170 *Ibid*, 638.
171 *Chester v Afshar*, n 134, above, 144.
172 *Ibid*, 146.

unconvincing. On Lord Bingham's analysis, the majority were not making a 'modest' alteration to 'traditional causation principles'. Instead, they were abandoning them. This, Lord Bingham explained, was because the claimant 'ha[d] not established that but for the failure to warn she would not have undergone the surgery'.[173] While recognising that '[t]he patient's right to be appropriately warned is an important right', Lord Bingham pursued the theme that the central concerns of negligence law lie elsewhere.[174] They have to do with compensating those who can establish that a defendant has wrongfully inflicted harm upon another while in a proximate relationship with him or her.[175] When we turn to Lord Hoffmann's speech, we are presented with a clue as to the path down which the majority are striking. For he describes them as focused on 'vindicat[ing] the patient's right to choose'.[176] This is undeniably the case. Moreover, it lends the position that they stake out an appearance that bears obvious similarities not just to the tort of battery but to human rights law (where 'rights', 'autonomy', and 'vindication' figure prominently).[177]

While the majority in *Afshar* strike down this path, they nonetheless place emphasis on one of negligence law's central concerns (wrongdoing). The same point applies, *mutatis mutandis*, to judges whose emphasis is not upon wrongdoing but rather upon harm. Consider the use made of the doctrine *res ipsa loquitur* (the thing speaks for itself) by judges in *Gordon v Aztec Brewing Co* (a decision of the Californian Supreme Court). This doctrine specifies that a judge may infer that a defendant has harmed the claimant where the thing causing injury was under the defendant's control and would not ordinarily do so in the absence of carelessness.[178] Judges in the Californian Supreme Court have applied this doctrine in ways that led Traynor J – himself a prominent member of this court - to describe them as veering away from a fault-based liability regime. On his analysis, they were moving

---

173 *Ibid*, 141.

174 *Ibid*, 141-142.

175 *Ibid*. See also E. Jackson, n 135, above, 203.

176 *Chester v Afshar*, n 134, above, , 147.

177 C. Foster, 'It Should Be, Therefore It Is' (2004) 154 *New Law Journal* 7151. *Cf* K. Amirthalingham, 'Medical Non-Disclosure, Causation and Autonomy' (2002) 118 *LQR* 540, 542 (identifying the majority decision in *Chester* as concerned with 'accountability'). On human rights, see J. Griffin, *On Human Rights* (Oxford: Oxford University Press, 2008), 3 and 33-37.

178 *Scott v London and St Katherine Docks Co* (1865) 3 H & C 596, 601, *per* Erle CJ. *Cf Bharma v Dubb (Trading As Lucky Caterers)* [2010] EWCA Civ 13, [31], *per* Moore-Bick LJ (on '[t]he concept of a shifting evidential burden of proof').

in the direction of strict liability.[179] To the extent that this is the case, it is a dramatic shift in direction (as would be movement from strict to fault-based liability).[180] But it is at the same time one that places emphasis on concerns (risk-regulation, causation, and harm) that occupy a prominent place in negligence law and shape the point of view internal to this branch of tort. However, Traynor J can identify his colleagues as departing from the paradigm case of negligence (which requires a claimant to prove causation on the balance of probabilities.[181] In such circumstances, it is entirely predictable that a judge will respond to an unconventional doctrinal development in the critical way described by Hart in his account of the internal point of view.[182]

Assuming that the distinction we have drawn between conventional and less conventional judgments is sound, we can use the later philosophy of Ludwig Wittgenstein to sharpen it. Wittgenstein uses the phrase 'going on' to capture the process by which the participants in a practice elaborate it.[183] To indicate what he means by 'going on', he describes someone who extends a series of numbers by 'adding 2' thus: '2, 4, 6, 8 …', etc.[184] We might see the incremental elaboration of negligence law as a broadly similar form of 'going on'.[185] For judges extend the notion of 'wrongful harm infliction' (in the context of a proximate relationship) to new sets of facts.[186] But *Chester* and the Californian Supreme Court's use of the *res ipsa loquitur* doctrine present us with rather different processes of development. The judges responsible for these decisions make appeal to values that shape negligence law's internal point of view. However, they are ascribing increased significance to an

---

179 *Gordon v Aztec Brewing Co*, 33 Cal 2d 514 (1949), 530. See also G.E. White, *Tort Law in America: An Intellectual History* (New York: Oxford University Press, 2003, expanded edn), 200-201.

180 For an example of movement from strict to fault-based liability, see *Burnie Port Authority v General Jones Pty* (1994) 68 ALJR 331.

181 On the (appeal to) the paradigm case, see E. Gellner, n 138, above, and associated text.

182 See n 155, above, and associated text.

183 B. Bix, *Law, Language, and Legal Determinacy* (Oxford: Clarendon Press, 1993), 42 (discussing, *inter alia*, L. Wittgenstein, *Remarks on the Foundations of Mathematics* (Sussex: Harvester Press, 1976, C. Desmond, ed), 392-393).

184 L. Wittgenstein, *Philosophical Investigations* (New York: Macmillan, 1968, 3rd edn, G.E.M. Anscombe, trans), sections 185-187.

185 C. Kutz, n 157, above, 1013.

186 See, for example, *McLoughlin v O'Brian*, n 32, above, 430, *per* Lord Scarman (describing judges as developing negligence doctrine by 'start[ing] from a baseline of existing principle and seek[ing] a solution consistent with or analogous to a principle or principles already recognised'). See also R. Mullender, n 156, above, 326-328 and 342-343. More generally, see S.R. Letwin, *On The History of the Idea of Law* (Cambridge: Cambridge University Press, 2005, N.B. Reynolds, ed), 36 (on Aristotle's account of legal rules as 'signposts' or 'directions').

existing practical concern ('due respect' for autonomy (*Chester*); harm infliction (*Gordon*)) and, as a result, veering away from a settled path of development. This means that we cannot employ the notion of 'going on' (in the sense specified earlier) as a basis on which to capture the doctrinal developments we are considering. We might, however, apply Wiitgenstein's account of 'going on' more broadly – to capture the activity of those who find in an existing practice materials with which to fashion a related but distinct alternative (*e.g.*, a strict (rather than fault-based) liability regime).[187] Alternatively, we could use language with a critical edge to describe the sort of activity we are scrutinizing. We could characterise those who engage in it as destabilizing the law's operations by riding hobby-horses that they find attractive.

While distinct from one another, the conventional and less conventional examples of case law we have examined share a (more or less conventional) commitment to the point of view that has shaped negligence law. For it is by reference to values or other considerations that shape this point of view that the judges whose decisions we have examined justify their respective positions. This provides a basis on which to distinguish their contributions to the discourses of negligence law and tort more generally from those who engage in radical critique of these branches of the law (see Appendix 2, below).[188] Consider Patrick Atiyah's writings on accident compensation law. He argues that negligence law is an expensive and often unjust compensation mechanism.[189] This has led him to point up the attractions of alternative institutions (including a no-fault accident compensation scheme

---

[187] *Cf* R.M. Unger, *What Should Legal Analysis Become?* (New York: Verso, 1996), 129 (on 'kenosis' as the practice of 'work[ing] from the bottom up and the inside out'). (While Unger's use of the locution 'from the bottom up' suggests a progressive trajectory, a process of doctrinal development of the sort contemplated in the text need not necessarily be regarded as progressive. *Cf* R. Dworkin, 'Law's Ambitions for Itself' (1985) 71 *Virginia LR* 173, 173 (on 'changes through adjudication' that judges regard not merely as the 'playing out [of] an internal program or design' but as 'improvements'). See also R. M. Unger, *False Necessity: Anti-Necessitarian Social Theory in the Service of Radical Democracy* (Cambridge: Cambridge University Press, 1987), 313 (arguing that 'a framework may influence its own sequel'), and I. Calvino, n 101, above, 28 (arguing that 'the traveller's past changes according to the route he has taken').

[188] As used in the text, 'radical' denotes a readiness, on the part of one offering a critique to make a decisive break with existing practices. See A. Giddens, *Beyond Left and Right: The Future of Radical Politics* (Cambridge: Polity Press, 1994), 45.

[189] See P.Cane, *Atiyah's Accidents, Compensation and the Law* (Cambridge: Cambridge University Press, 2006, 7th edn), 463 and 487 (contrasting negligence law unfavourably with no-fault alternatives on the ground that the administrative costs of the latter are significantly lower), and 175-177 and 183-185 (identifying fault-based compensation as 'bear[ing] no relation to the degree of fault [in particular cases]' and as 'pay[ing] little attention to the conduct or needs of the victim').

on the New Zealand model and self-protection by means of first-party insurance).[190] While Atiyah has in mind a dramatic departure (in one form or another) from the existing law, he nonetheless has much in common with those who defend negligence law and other forms of tort liability.[191] He seeks to make constructive responses to the facts of harm and other forms of misfortune. To this end, he proposes regulatory mechanisms that, on his analysis, offer attractive alternatives. But, while he does this, his thinking continues to intersect with that of tort's defenders. For we find that he shares with them a commitment to egalitarianism.[192] However, Atiyah's egalitarianism has a very strong (primary) orientation towards distributive justice that distinguishes his thinking from that of tort's defenders.[193] How then should we understand this contribution to debate? We might try to categorize Atiyah's as a critical voice within the discourse of negligence law or that of tort more generally. He is attentive to the views of those who defend or who assume the acceptability of the existing law and aims to respond to them with compelling counter-arguments. However, it makes more sense (in light of his arguments) to describe Atiyah as a participant in a discourse closely related to but broader than that on the topics of negligence law or tort more generally. We might call this the discourse of accident compensation law.[194] As Atiyah makes plain, this discourse intersects with negligence law and tort more generally, but is wider ranging:

> The ultimate questions with which we are concerned are: for what injuries or damage ought the law to provide compensation; what

---

190 *Ibid*, ch 18. See also P.S. Atiyah, *The Damages Lottery* (Oxford: Hart Publishing, 1997), ch 8 (on first-party insurance).

191 The idea of a dramatic (or radical) departure from existing practices is, on the analysis offered by Stanley Fish, unsustainable since they shape our consciousness (even as we contemplate their overhaul or abandonment). See S. Fish, n 150, above, 420 (arguing that 'without a mechanism for determining whether a proposed or imagined revision would constitute a step forward rather than a step backward on the journey to a truly transformed society, the journey can never begin'). *Cf* P. Cane, *Atiyah's Accidents, Compensation and the Law* (London: Butterworths, 1993, 5th edn), v (where William Twining describes Atiyah's first edition as 'a brilliantly designed and executed departure from tradition').

192 P. Cane, n 189, above, 5.

193 P.S. Atiyah, *Accidents, Compensation and the Law* (London: Weidenfeld and Nicolson, 1987, 4th edn), 442-445 (where Atiyah wrestles with the question of 'egalitarianism and the problem of drawing the line': 'as medical science has advanced, and prolonged disease and premature death have ceased to be normal hazards in our society, it has become less easy to maintain the distinction between man-caused and natural disabilities').

194 While we can identify Atiyah as a contributor to the discourse of accident compensation law, he shows signs of being actuated by a broader set of concerns. Among them, we may number his concern with 'misfortune' (in, for example, the form of diseases that do not arise from accidents). See P.S. Atiyah, n 193, above, 3-4, and P. Cane, *Atiyah's Accidents, Compensation and the Law* (London: Butterworths, 1999, 6th edn), ch 16).

> form should compensation take; how should it be assessed; and who should pay it?' Important related issues include how compensation should be administered and how the law seeks to reduce the amount of injury and damage inflicted.[195]

Given that Atiyah participates in a discourse distinct from that of negligence law or tort more generally, we can use Wittgenstein's account of 'language games' to throw light on the relationship between these forms of talk.[196] According to Wittgenstein, we can distinguish one language game from another by noting, among other things, the distinct ways in which those who participate in them use particular words.[197] The relevance of this claim to our concerns is immediately obvious. Consider negligence law. In this context 'wrongdoing' has to do with a lack of reasonable care ('fault'). But when we turn to strict forms of tort liability, the meaning of wrongdoing alters.[198] We should not, however, leap from these points to the conclusion that we are dealing with radically different language games. This is because words like 'harm' and 'risk' seem to bear much the same significance in each of the discourses we are considering.[199] To the extent that this is the case, we should perhaps draw back from the conclusion that we are examining distinct discourses, concerned respectively with negligence law, tort in some other form (or in some more general sense), and accident compensation law. But if we assume that we can talk meaningfully about these three discourses, we have, in light of our earlier analysis, grounds for thinking that Hutchinson and Morgan throw light on each of them. Likewise, they demonstrate how rapidly a participant in one of these discourses may move into one of the others. We see this, when, for example, Lefft J finds in the existing doctrine of informed consent a foundation on which to build an alternative model of human association.

While 'The Canegusian Connection' has these virtues, Hutchinson and Morgan fail to point up a particularly attractive feature of negligence law. This is the way in which we can combine some of the distinct normative impulses within it in morally eligible ways. This is, as we will see, a subject to which the concepts of complementarity, coherence, and consilience are relevant.

---

195 P.S. Atiyah, n 193, above, 4. *Cf* P. Cane, n 189, above, 4 (where the locution 'main questions' replaces 'ultimate questions').

196 A. Kenny, *Wittgenstein* (London: Penguin Books, 1975), ch 9.

197 L. Wittgenstein, n 184, above, section 77.

198 G.P. Fletcher, 'Fairness and Utility in Tort Theory' (1972) 85 *Harvard LR* 537, 543 (on 'strict liability or "liability without fault"').

199 See M. Foucault, n 1, above, 67 (on the 'dispersion' of concepts 'through *oeuvres*').

6 Complementarity, Coherence, and Consilience

The concept of 'complementarity' has to do with, *inter alia*, opposing views that can augment – or complement – one another in practically significant ways. This is a topic to which the physicist Niels Bohr devoted attention. He argued that full understanding in a particular area of inquiry may require the use of mutually exclusive concepts, propositions, or explanatory models.[200] While he emphasised the importance of complementarity in the natural sciences, he also identified it as a concept with wide relevance.[201] This has led a number of commentators on negligence law (and tort more generally) to argue that Bohr's arguments concerning complementarity have relevance to their concerns. Thus we find Englard arguing that Bohr has given us a concept that helps us to gain a high degree of analytic purchase on tort law's operations.[202] Likewise, Englard argues that complementarity yields a basis on which to present tort in an appealing light by presenting, *inter alia*, corrective justice and distributive justice as parts of a 'harmonious totality'.[203]

When we examine 'The Canengusian Connection', we find support for the position staked out by Englard. The respective analyses of Wright and Mill JJ (as we have noted) stand in a highly antagonistic relationship. But each of these judges directs our attention to important practical concerns to which the law is alive: providing redress for wrongfully inflicted harm (Wright J) and relevant costs and benefits (Mill J).[204] We can use Wright J's analysis to point up the prominence given to wrongdoing (or, more particularly, fault) and corrective justice in negligence law. Mill J, by contrast, gives us consequentialist tools with which to pin down the limits of this commitment. The usefulness of the sort of analysis contemplated here becomes apparent when we examine general duty of care tests of the sort fashioned by the House of Lords in *Caparo Industries Plc v Dickman*.[205] These tests give sequential priority to the question as to whether the defendant has

---

200 I. Englard, n 60, above, 85 (noting that 'concepts and propositions … are mutually exclusive in that the application of one such concept to a certain thing at a certain time precludes the application of the other to that thing at the same time'), and D. Murdoch, *Niels Bohr's Philosophy of Physics* (Cambridge: Cambridge University Press, 1987), 54 and 60. (See also n 90, above, on Bakhtin's account of a 'surplus of seeing', and P. O'Callaghan, 'Monologism and Dialogism in Private Law' [2010] 7 *The Journal Jurisprudence*, ns 70-72 (and associated text).)

201 G. Holton, *Thematic Origins of Scientific Thought: Kepler to Einstein* (Cambridge, Massachusetts, London, revd edn, 1988), 133.

202 I. Englard, n 60, above, ch 5.

203 *Ibid*, 88.

204 We might see each of these judges as directing our attention to distinct 'aspects' of the practice in which they participate. See E. Mickiewicz, n 145, above, section 4.

205 *Caparo Industries Plc v Dickman* [1990] 2 AC 605, 617-618, *per* Lord Bridge.

wrongfully inflicted reasonably foreseeable harm on the claimant while standing in a proximate relationship with him or her.[206] However, the *Caparo* test qualifies this commitment to corrective justice by building in a further consequentialist limb. One of the purposes of this limb is to draw judicial attention to the question as to whether the anticipated costs of imposing liability would be unacceptably high.[207]

To analyse negligence law in the way suggested here is to invite criticism from, *inter alios*, Weinrib on the ground of incoherence.[208] Certainly, negligence law, on the account we are contemplating, embraces two types of moral impulse (deontological and consequentialist) that stand in a relationship of ineliminable tension. However, we can resist the charge of incoherence by identifying the two types of impulse we are considering as means to the same (egalitarian) end: defensibly accommodating the interests of all the law's addressees. General duty of care tests lend support to this analysis since they are supposed to mediate fairly between the claimant's interest in security and the defendant's interest in freedom of action. Moreover, they are supposed to accommodate the interests of those who are not directly involved in a particular dispute. For judges, when contemplating the (anticipated) costs and benefits of imposing liability, consider the impact that a new liability rule may have on members of society generally.[209] To the extent that judges are motivated to accommodate the interests of all the law's addressees defensibly, we find within negligence law a moral impulse that invests it with coherence. This is a commitment to egalitarianism that provides a 'bridging notion' between the ideals of corrective and distributive justice.[210]

---

206 *Ibid.*

207 *Ibid.*

208 See E.J. Weinrib, n 34, above, 958 (describing negligence law 'as a *this* [a coherent body of law informed by deontological impulses and a commitment to corrective justice] and not a *that*' (an incoherent body of law in which both deontology (and corrective justice) and consequentialism (in the form of policy considerations that express commitments to the public interest and, on occasion, distributive justice)) each have a place).

209 R. Mullender, '*Prima Facie* Rights, Rationality, and the Law of Negligence', ch 6, in M. Kramer, ed, *Rights, Wrongs, and Responsibilities* (Basingstoke: Palgrave, 2001), 179-181.

210 On the idea of a 'bridging notion', see J. Griffin, n 177, above, 69. See also J. Raz, *Ethics in the Public Domain: Essays in the Morality of Law and Politics* (Oxford: Clarendon Press, 1994, revd edn), 281 (on 'coherence' as 'mean[ing] something like "'mutually reinforcing"'). (The use of a bridging notion as a means by which to bring corrective and distributive justice into a harmonious relationship is not something that Englard (in his account of complementarity) considers. Rather, he asserts that complementarity yields a basis on which to 'create a harmonious totality optimally achieving both values'. He does not, however, explain on what basis we are to make judgments of optimality.)

We might see the egalitarianism at work within negligence law as having encouraged doctrinal developments (*e.g.*, general duty of care tests) that give expression to a distinct moral philosophy. This moral philosophy gives sequential priority to deontological impulses (by allowing claimants to seek redress for wrongfully inflicted harms). But consquentialist considerations (having to do with matters of public concern) qualify this commitment in a limited range of circumstances. Where the costs (or anticipated costs) of doing corrective justice are high, they may provide grounds for rejecting otherwise good claims. In light of these points, we might describe the moral philosophy we are considering as qualified deontology.[211]

If this analysis is broadly correct, we have grounds for thinking that the norm of 'consilience' is relevant to negligence law's operations. On the account offered by Jules Coleman, '[t]he value expressed in the norm of consilience is that, other things being equal, it is good when a theory can bring a diversity of phenomena under a single explanatory scheme – and the greater the range of phenomena thus explained, the better'.[212] Moreover, Coleman points up the relevance of consilence to tort law. For he identifies corrective justice as a means by which to bring a wide range of considerations (including 'wrongdoing', 'repair', and (personal) 'responsibility') under a single explanatory scheme.[213] However, he adds that his 'corrective justice account [of tort as a whole] is embedded in a broader explanatory scheme that points to the *fundamental unity* of distributive and corrective justice'.[214] On the question as to how this 'fundamental unity' arises, Coleman argues that a commitment to 'fairness as reciprocity among free and equal persons' informs both ideals of justice.[215] Coleman thus presents us with an egalitarian bridging notion of the sort that we encountered earlier, in our examination of the general duty of care test in *Caparo*.[216]

---

211 For more detailed discussion of qualified deontology, see R. Mullender, 'Tort Law, Human Rights, and Common Law Culture' (2003) 23 *OJLS* 301, 308-309. (Among the features of qualified deontology that give expression to its egalitarianism is a notion of reasonableness that extends beyond the parties to a negligence claim. On reasonableness in this (wide) Rawlsian sense, see M. Siu, 'Conflict in Canengus: the Battle of Deontology and Consequentialism' (2010) 7 *The Journal Jurisprudence* section 4. See also J. Rawls, n 152, above, on the Hegelian theme that 'society is held together … by a sense of reasonable order').)

212 J. Coleman, *The Practice of Principle: In Defence of a Pragmatist Approach to Legal Theory* (Oxford: Oxford University Press 2001), 41.

213 *Ibid*, 43 and 53.

214 *Ibid*, 53 (emphasis added).

215 *Ibid.*

216 See ns 208-210, above, and associated text.

While we can bring corrective justice and distributive justice into the coherent relationship contemplated here, there is, however, a difficulty with this analysis. Corrective justice resists reduction to a component in a scheme of distributive justice. Thus we encounter tension of the sort highlighted by Hutchinson and Morgan. However, it remains the case that we can show negligence law to have a high degree of coherence. For a commitment to egalitarianism yields a basis on which to explain and defend the law's operations. Moreover, the egalitarianism we have detected in the discourse of negligence law provides a basis on which to explain its close relationship with the other forms of talk we have surveyed. When we seek to discover 'the place' from which 'all these diverse statements ... come', we find that they have a common source.[217] They are the 'witness and external deposit' of our moral life.[218] And they tell us that we are the denizens of a social context in which a commitment to an egalitarian philosophy of government exerts a powerful hold over our imagination.[219] This is a body of practical thought concerned with fashioning institutions that secure the interests of all relevant people adequately.[220]

Conclusions

The analysis of negligence law in 'The Canengusian Connection' provides a basis on which to explain why those seeking to make sense of this branch of tort run the risk of disorientation. Hutchinson and Morgan drive home the point that the discourse of negligence law is highly pluralistic and, as a result, the facts at stake in the case they describe prompt widely divergent responses. In this respect, their fictive account of negligence law captures important realities. This becomes plain when we examine cases such as *Lamb v Camden LBC*, where three English Appeal Court judges base their (concurring) judgments respectively on doctrine relating to the acts of third parties, a congeries of remoteness and 'instinctive feelings', and the

[217] The source of the quotations in the text is M. Foucault, n 1, above. (See also J. Faubion, ed, *The Essential Works of Michel Foucault 1954-1988*, vol 2, *Aesthetics: Method and Epistemology* (New York: New York Press, 1998), 261 (where Foucault describes his critical-historical method of 'archaeology' as concerned with 'a certain implicit knowledge [*savoir*]' 'that 'makes possible, at a given moment, the appearance of a theory, an opinion, a practice'). See also L. Downing, n 54, above, 39, above, (noting that (in his archaeological investigations) 'Foucault begins from the observation that in order for something to be thought or institutionalized as knowledge (*connaissances*), certain conditions for that type of thought must already be in place at a more fundamental level (*savoir*)'.)

[218] On law as 'the witness and external deposit of our moral life', see O.W. Holmes, 'The Path of the Law' (1897) 10 *Harvard LR* 457, 459.

[219] On the egalitarian philosophy of government' as a feature of Western practical life, R. Mullender, 'Law, Morality, and the Egalitarian Philosophy of Government' (2009) 29 *OJLS* 389.

[220] *Ibid*, 407-410.

availability of first-party (loss) insurance. We can, however, press our analysis of 'The Canegusian Connection' and the body of law it concerns further by drawing on Laurence Sterne's *Tristram Shandy*. For Sterne, as we have noted, wrote on the topic of a scampering discourse. By this he meant a discourse that was apt to move rapidly in a wide variety of (sometimes unpredictable) directions. Moreover, Sterne offered an (anthropological-cum-psychological) explanation for the sort of discourse he described that has relevance to negligence law. He identified those who participate in debate as apt to ride 'Hobby-Horses'. He also argued that people who advance their views in a 'hobby-horsical' fashion typically exhibit a reluctance to pay close attention to the views of others. These are points to which Hutchinson and Morgan lend support in 'The Canengusian Connection'. They present us with judgments in which judges ride hobby horses. Likewise, they indicate that those astride these hobby-horses often fail to find in the views of their colleagues reasons to dismount.

While Sterne's account of a scampering discourse is richly suggestive, the writings of Mikhail Bakhtin and Michel Foucault enable us to develop it in ways that throw light on the discourse of negligence law (see Appendix 1, below). Bakhtin's account of a heteroglossia has relevance not only to the novel as a literary genre but also to tort and law more generally. As Hutchinson and Morgan make clear, the discourse we have been examining is one in which a wide range of voices clamour for our attention. Moreover, Bakhtin's account of the centrifugal and centripetal forces at work in a heteroglossia has obvious relevance to negligence law. Some judges seek, as in *Chester v Afshar*, to pull the law in a new direction by talking the language of 'rights' and 'respect' rather than 'wrongfully inflicted harm'.[221] Others, to take another example (*Gordon v Aztec Brewing Co*), place emphasis on harm while losing sight of wrongfulness as a salient concern. These arguments exert a centrifugal force. For they undermine settled assumptions about the core of negligence law. But we must set arguments such as these alongside others that exert a centripetal force. Among these arguments, we may number those where judges stick to what Sterne called 'the common track' by, for example, engaging in the incremental elaboration of existing heads of liability.[222]

While Bakhtin's concept of heteroglossia affords a means by which to gain analytic purchase on the discourse we are examining, Foucault's notion of heterotopia throws light on a threat to it. The assumptions made by some of those who take a particular view of negligence law may be so firm as to

[221] See also *Lachambre v Nair* [1989] 2 WWR 749 (Sask QB), 763 (on so-called infringement of autonomy).
[222] L. Sterne, n 66, above, 38.

render them incapable of seriously entertaining analyses that differ from their own. We might thus describe them as inhabiting a world of ideas that cuts (or that threatens to cut) them off from those around them. If this is the case, it is a state of affairs that bears some similarity to the (much more extreme) situation described by Foucault in his account of heterotopia. Certainly, the American Law Institute's growing enthusiasm for an economic analysis of negligence doctrine provides a basis on which to suggest that it has taken up (or is on the way towards taking up) residence in a narrow world of ideas.[223]

While using Sterne, Bakhtin, and Foucault to gain analytic purchase on the body of law surveyed by Hutchinson and Morgan, it became clear that we were dealing with not one but, rather, three discourses (see Appendix 2, below). The narrowest of these discourses has to do with negligence law. Those who adopt the point of view internal to this branch of tort identify themselves (more or less self-consciously) as having a highly specific central concern. This is providing redress for harm wrongfully (carelessly) inflicted by one person on another while the two stood in a proximate relationship. But while those who embrace negligence law's internal point of view share this central concern, they are nonetheless able to advance a wide range of arguments. Among them, we may number arguments for the incremental development of existing doctrine and counter-arguments that have to do with the value of certainty (which elaboration of existing doctrine by judges threatens to compromise).

But negligence law is not simply a space or field of interpretative possibility within which a range of arguments may unfold.[224] On occasion, it provides a springboard for developments that carry those responsible for them into a new discourse. Hutchinson and Morgan alert us to this possibility when Lefft J sees in the doctrine of informed consent the outlines of a new and democratic system of risk-management and accident compensation. While Lefft J's 'vision' would, if implemented, mark a dramatic departure from the *status quo*, we have examined examples of judges bending negligence law in new directions. We saw this when Traynor J criticised his colleagues in *Gordon v Aztec Brewing.*[225] On his analysis, they were, through their use of the *res ipsa loquitur* doctrine, bending negligence law in the direction of strict liability. To embark on a journey of this sort is to leave negligence law's

[223] The position staked out by the American Law Institute in its third *Restatement* (1999) provides an example of the association between enthusiasm and 'monologism in action' examined in P. O'Callaghan, n 200, above, section 6.

[224] The point made in the text might be developed by reference to Coleridge's idea of 'multeity in unity', on which see *ibid*, sections 2 and 7.

[225] See ns 178-1-180, above, and associated text.

internal point of view behind and to take up residence in a different world of ideas (sustained by a distinct discourse). This point also applies to *Chester v Afshar* (where the development we scrutinized was inchoate in character). For the majority of their Lordships exhibited a concern with ideas ('autonomy', 'dignity', etc) that are the stuff of a tort strongly oriented towards the protection of human dignity and human rights law.[226] Thus the decisions in *Gordon* and *Chester* are vulnerable to the appeal to the paradigm case (according to which negligence law is centrally concerned with the wrongful infliction of harm).[227]

Alongside the types of argument we have so far considered – those rooted in the discourse of negligence law and those that grow out of this discourse and head in a new direction – we must set a third group. Arguments in this group are critical of tort. But even here we find a point of intersection with the discourses of negligence law and tort more generally. For it is often the case that those who cleave to, say, negligence law's internal point of view nonetheless have critical things to say about, *inter alia*, existing doctrine. But criticism of this sort does not call for a departure from existing liability regimes. Rather, it calls for them to be more adequately operationalized. Matters are quite different when we turn to arguments in the third group. For they urge the adoption of new institutional means by which to address the problems tackled by judges in negligence law and tort more generally (*e.g.*, the various proposals for reform made by Patrick Atiyah). Those who call for reform on the model contemplated here do not find in the points of view internal to tort law authoritative reasons for action. Instead, they find in this body of law clues as to how we might do distributive justice more adequately.

While distinct from one another, the discourses we have examined share a commitment to egalitarianism (see Appendix 3, below). At the most general level, this commitment finds expression in the proposition that all those affected by the law's operations occupy a plateau of equality.[228] In light of this point, we have a basis on which to conclude that the discourses we have examined share a commitment to the same philosophy of government. This is the egalitarian philosophy of government. But this is (as Hutchinson and Morgan make clear) a philosophy that we can seek to operationalize in a variety of ways. While we cannot pursue the matter in detail here, this is a

---

226 See *Lachambre v Nair*, n 221, above, and associated text.

227 See n 138, above, and associated text.

228 On the commitment to equality mentioned in the text (and its relation to law and contemporary political philosophy), see R. Dworkin, *Law's Empire* (London: Fontana, 1996), 222 and 296, and W. Kymlicka, *Contemporary Political Philosophy: An Introduction* (Oxford: Oxford University Press, 2002, 2nd edn), 3-4.

point to which the political philosophy of Michael Oakeshott has relevance. According to Oakeshott, we can seek to underwrite our commitment to egalitarianism in two very different models of human association. The first of these models is 'civil association'. This is a modest-rule governed framework within which people may 'pursue the activities of their own choice with the minimum of frustration'.[229] The second model is enterprise association. Enterprise associations focus on the pursuit of a desired goal (*e.g.*, the pursuit of a distributively just end-state).[230] The first of Oakeshott's two models has affinities with negligence law while the second finds expression in the practical proposals made by Prudential and Lefft JJ (and, likewise, in Man Chun Siu's contribution to this collection). Moreover, strict liability on the model argued for by Wright J has about it the look a *tertium quid*. For it is as much a species of social insurance as it is a means by which to do corrective justice.

Just as 'The Canengusian Connection' draws attention to the association between particular types of argument and distinct models of human association, so too it prompts reflection on three theoretical matters. They are the normativity (or oughtness) of law, the spaces (or fields of interpretative possibility) within which legal arguments resonate, and what we might call 'movement' (the ways in which participants in legal disputes may shift, in the course of argument, from one discourse to another). While none of the judges in 'The Canengusian Connection' declare the law to be the (more or less adequate) 'witness and external deposit of our moral life', they nonetheless assume this to be the case. In this way, Hutchinson and Morgan lend support to the view that tort seeks to reflect and refine moral impulses in the societies that it regulates. Likewise, they convey a sense of the limited 'space' (or field of interpretative possibility) within which arguments for fault-based liability have force. This becomes clear when Wright J identifies himself as a proponent of strict rather than fault-based liability. This, he explains, is because negligence law uses the criterion of fault to limit (in ways that he considers unjust) the rights-based protection enjoyed by individuals. If we agree with him, then the idea of movement from fault-based to strict liability has obvious attractions. While Hutchinson and Morgan do not present us with examples of judges engaging in such movement, they nonetheless provide us with tools with which to make sense of such a change of direction. For example, just as Wright J grasps the limitations of negligence doctrine (as a body of law concerned with the careless infliction of harm), so too do the majority in *Chester v Afshar*. Thus

229 M. Oakeshott, 'On Being a Conservative', in *Rationalism and Politics and Other Essays* (London: Methuen, 1977) 183.

230 M. Oakeshott, *On History and Other Essays* (Oxford: Basil Blackwell, 1983) 153, and M. Oakeshott, *On Human Conduct* (Oxford: Clarendon Press 1975), 289 and 315.

when Lord Steyn, for example, scampers off in a new direction, we are in a position to understand what is going on. And if Sterne's account of discourse and its deficiencies is accurate, we should consider ourselves fortunate to have read an essay that continues to throw light on the forms of legal argument we have surveyed.

While talk of normativity, space, and movement enables us to gain analytic purchase on the dramas that unfold in 'The Canengusian Connection' and in cases like *Chester*, there is much that remains to be said. Among other things, Hutchinson and Morgan present us with a form of life that accommodates diversity and the disputes that come in train with it. In this, their fiction intersects with that of Sterne. This is because there is something of the spirit of Shandeism in the way Doctrin CJ and her colleagues go about their business.[231] But, if we wanted to press the analysis further, we could do no better than to drawn on an Australian philosopher, John Anderson. For he urges us 'not to ask of a social institution: "What end or purpose does it serve?" but rather, "Of what conflicts is it the scene?"'.[232]

[231] On the spirit of Shandeism, see n 86, above, and associated text.

[232] A. MacIntyre, *After Virtue: A Study in Moral Theory* (London: Duckworth, 1985, 2nd edn), 163.

Appendix 1: Negligence Law as a Discourse

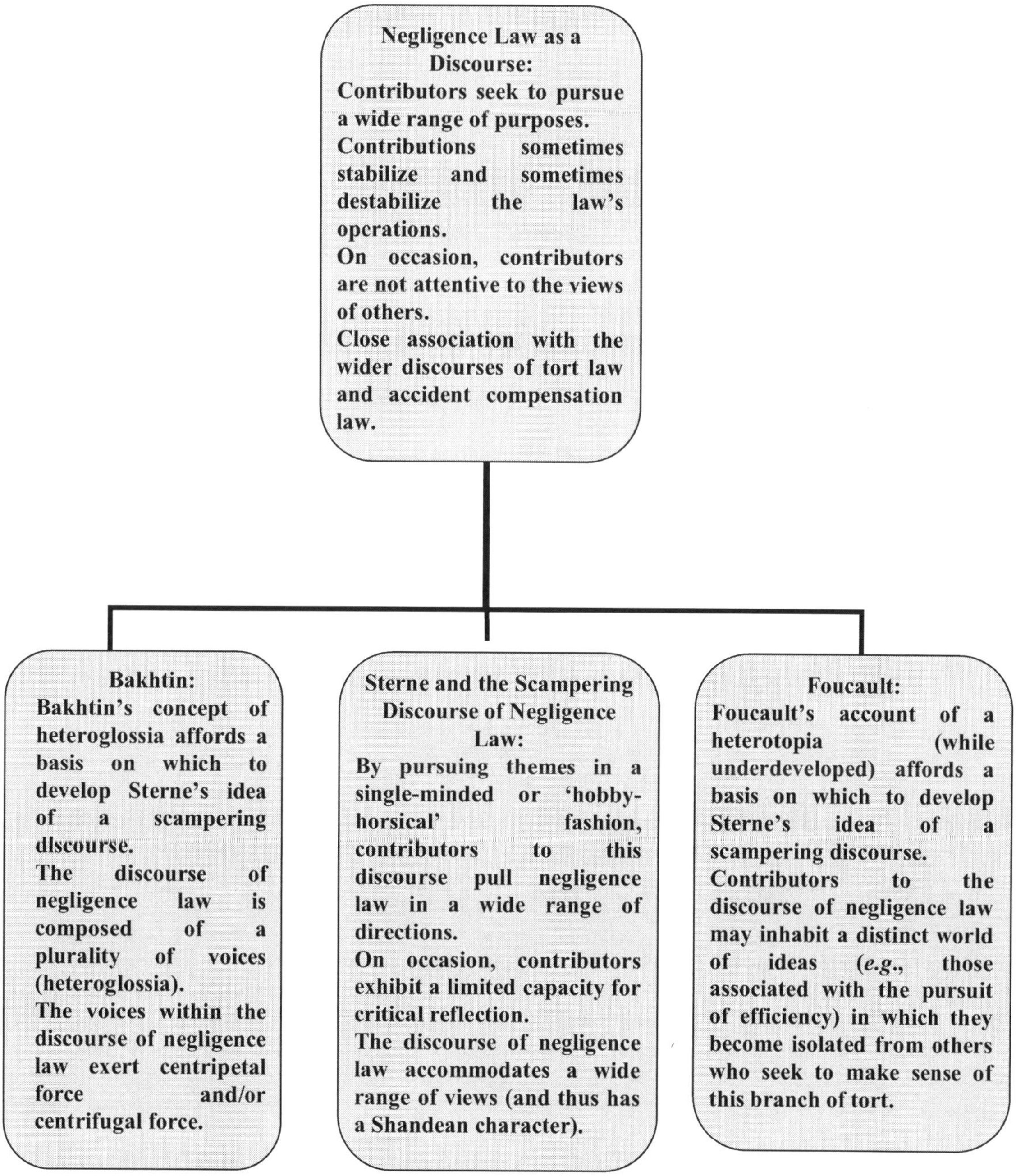

Appendix 2: Discursive Diversity

Three Discourses:
While the judges in 'The Canegusian Connection' respond to a claim in negligence, we can see them as participating in distinct but closely related discourses.
(We find in each of these discourses a shared commitment to egalitarianism and shared terminology (*e.g.*, 'risk' and 'harm').

The Discourse of Negligence Law:
Doctrin CJ: applies existing doctrine in conformity with, *inter alia*, the doctrine of the separation of powers.
Wright J: emphasises the ideal of corrective justice.
Mill J: emphasises the consequentilaist impulses in the law.

Discourses that Grow out of Negligence Law's Internal Point of View:
Wright CJ: strict liability.
See also Traynor J's critique of the Californian Supreme Court and *Chester v Afshar* (House of Lords majority): their concern with 'autonomy' and 'dignity' carries negligence law in the direction of battery and human rights law.

The Discourse of Accident Compensation Law:
Prudential J's arguments for a (New Zealand-style) accident compensation scheme.
Lefft J's arguments for society-wide risk-regulation on a democratic model.
Patrick Atiyah on, *inter alia*, no fault compensation and first-party insurance.

Appendix 3: Three Discourses in Egalitarian Context

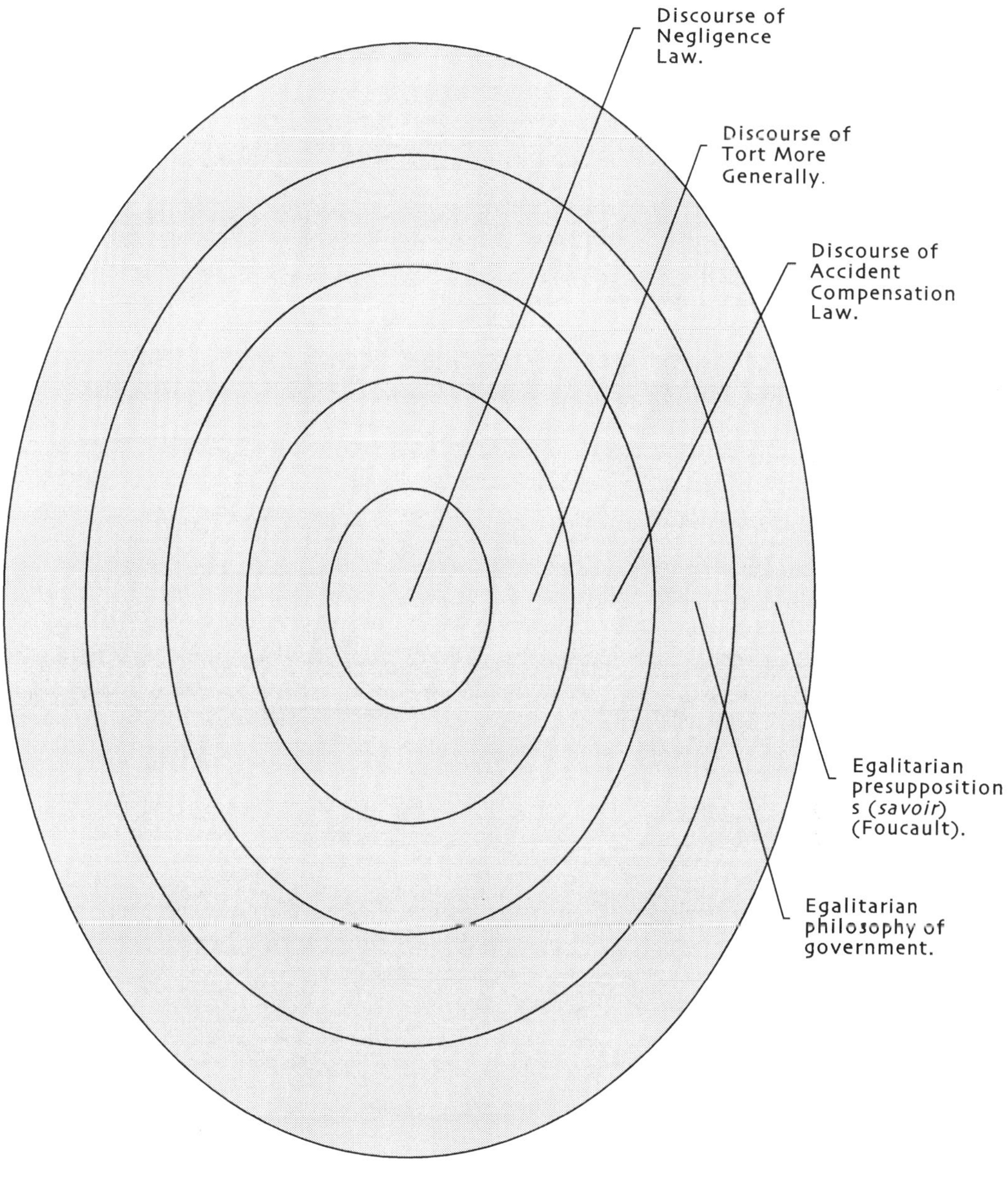

The reader should not draw from Appendix 3 the conclusion that negligence law necessarily occupies a central place in the practical life of Canengus. The diagram's purpose is to relate the discourse of negligence law to more general bodies of legal and political thought and ultimately to the presuppositions that they share with one another.

Made in the USA
Monee, IL
05 November 2026

67813125R00210